THE SCIENTIFIC ASPECTS
OF
SPORTS TRAINING

This publication is sponsored and approved by
The Canadian Association of Sports Sciences.

THE SCIENTIFIC ASPECTS
OF SPORTS TRAINING

Compiled and Edited by

A. W. TAYLOR, Ph.D.

Surgical-Medical Research Institute
and Faculty of Physical Education
University of Alberta
Edmonton, Canada

With a Foreword by

Fernand Landry, Ph.D.

President of The Canadian Association of
Sports Sciences and
Director, Départment D' Education Physique,
Université Laval, Quebec City, Canada

CHARLES C THOMAS · PUBLISHER
Springfield · Illinois · USA

Published and Distributed Throughout the World by
CHARLES C THOMAS · PUBLISHER
Bannerstone House
301-327 East Lawrence Avenue, Springfield, Illinois, U.S.A.

*With THOMAS BOOKS careful attention is given to all details of
manufacturing and design. It is the Publisher's desire to present books
that are satisfactory as to their physical qualities and artistic possibilities
and appropriate for their particular use. THOMAS BOOKS will be true
to those laws of quality that assure a good name and good will.*

Library of Congress Cataloging in Publication Data

Taylor, Albert W
   The scientific aspects of sports training.

   1. Physical education and training.
I. Title. [DNLM: 1. Sport medicine. 2. Sports.
QT260 S414 1974]
GV711.T39   613.7   73-19669
ISBN 0-398-03028-6

Printed in the United States of America

K-8

Dedicated to Mary-Jill and Scott,
inspiration personified.

CONTRIBUTORS

Allen, M.: Cross Country Coach, Ottawa Ski Club, Ottawa.

Cameron, B.: Cross Country Coach, Ottawa Ski Club, Ottawa.

Cooke, F.: Cross Country Coach, Ottawa Ski Club, Ottawa.

Cumming, G. R., M.D.: The Children's Hospital of Winnipeg and Department of Pediatrics and Medicine, University of Manitoba, Winnipeg.

Eynon, R., M.Sc.: Faculty of Physical Education, University of Western Ontario, London.

Ferguson, R. J., Ph.D.: Department of Physical Education, University of Montreal, Montreal and Department of Research, Institute of Cardiology of Montreal.

Fracas, G., M.A.: Faculty of Physical Education, University of Windsor, Windsor.

Fried, T. S., M.D.: The Workmen's Compensation Board, Downsview.

Gowan, G., Ph.D.: School of Physical Education, McMaster University, Hamilton.

Hermiston, R., Ph.D.: Faculty of Physical Education, University of Windsor, Windsor.

Hetherington, R., M.Sc.: Laurentian University, Sudbury.

Jetté, M., Ph.D.: Department of Kinanthropology, University of Ottawa, Ottawa.

Kelly, R., A.T.: Faculty of Physical Education, University of Alberta, Edmonton.

Leyshon, G., Ph.D.: Faculty of Physical Education, University of Western Ontario, London.

Marcotte, G., Ph.D.: School of Physical Education, Laval University, Quebec City.

Mendryk, S. W., Ph.D.: Faculty of Physical Education, University of Alberta, Edmonton.

Peronnet, F., M.Sc.: School of Physical Education, University of Montreal, Montreal.

Radford, P., Ph.D.: School of Physical Education, McMaster University, Hamilton.

Rao, S., M.D.: Division of Respiratory Diseases, University of Alberta, Edmonton.

Reid, G., Ph.D.: School of Physical Education, Queen's University, Kingston.

Reid, D. C., M.C.S.P.: Dip.T.P., School of Rehabilitation Medicine, University of Alberta, Edmonton.

Sawula, L., M.Sc.: Faculty of Physical Education, University of Alberta, Edmonton.

Sproule, B. J., M.D., M.Sc.: Division of Respiratory Diseases, University of Alberta, Edmonton.

Sturrock, D., M.Sc.: Vancouver School Board, Vancouver.

Talibi, T., M.D.: Edmonton Cardiac Fitness Institute and Royal Alexandra Hospital, Edmonton.

Taylor, A. W., Ph.D.: Faculty of Physical Education and Surgical-Medical Research Institute, University of Alberta, Edmonton.

Thoden, J., Ph.D.: Department of Kinanthropology, University of Ottawa, Ottawa.

Wallingford, R., Ed.D.: Physical Education Division, Laurentian University, Sudbury.

Wenger, H. A., Ph.D.: Department of Kinanthropology, University of Ottawa, Ottawa.

Wilberg, R. B., Ph.D.: Faculty of Physical Education, University of Alberta, Edmonton.

Yarr, A. D., Ph.D.: School of Physical Education, Dalhousie University, Halifax.

FOREWORD

THE PROMOTION, advancement, exchange and diffusion of contemporary scientific knowledge in the field of sport and physical activity has been the focus of the collective efforts of the membership of the *Canadian Association of Sports Sciences* since the foundation meeting of Winnipeg, in 1967.

In the pursuit of the objectives set forth by its founding members representing both the *Canadian Medical Association* and the *Canadian Association for Health, Physical Education and Recreation*, CASS/ACSS has known six (6) very busy and productive years.

Annual scientific sessions have been held in Winnipeg (1967), Toronto (1968), Calgary (1969), Quebec (1970), Toronto (1971) and Vancouver (1972). In that period, distinguished members of the Association have written and/or edited considerable material relative to sport and training: *Frontiers of Fitness* (Shephard), *Training: Scientific Basis and Application* (Taylor), *Environmental Effects on Work Performance* (Cumming, Snidal and Taylor), *Sources of Equipment for Sport Sciences Laboratories* (Walker).

This new book edited by Dr. Taylor, *The Scientific Aspects of Sports Training*, stands out as another very significant contribution to the domain of sports sciences. Endurance training is discussed in the light of recent findings: a section on rehabilitative training deals with such pertinent, delicate and controversial topics as the rehabilitation of athletes following injury, and the use of physical activity in the evaluation of coronary proneness and in the treatment of chronic lung disease; lastly, the theme of training is presented and discussed in as many as seventeen (17) different sports activities.

The list of contributors who have answered the call of Dr. Taylor is made up of individuals whose knowledge and professional competence have long been recognized in this country. This is again ample evidence of the fact that across this nation, sports scientists and members of CASS/ACSS characteristically remain available to assist athletes, coaches, sports associations and other individuals or groups, in their efforts to improve sports performances and to develop, preserve or recover physical fitness.

Performances on the sports fields are improving in an asymptotic but ever constant fashion; likewise the body of knowledge pertaining to physical activity and sport is expanding at an ever increasing tempo. It is consequently not surprising to observe that too often there is considerable distance between the levels of preoccupation, the perspectives of services and even the professional and technical language of athletes, coaches and scientists as they relate to one and the same object: training and performance. On a second thought, I personally do not believe that we are dealing here with two solitudes ignoring each other, but with two curves that are simply long in merging together. Significant advances have been made in that aspect in the last decade. The dialogue is very much engaged and sustained in many countries of the world. Dr. Taylor's book will undoubtedly serve to intensify the dialogue between special groups, athletes, coaches and sports scientists. All have so much to gain by becoming better partners and associates in the enterprise.

FERNAND LANDRY

PREFACE

A GREAT NUMBER of research papers attempt to scientifically explain the effects of prolonged exercise and training upon various physiological, psychological and sociological variables. To this date no book has been compiled which attempts to translate much of the scientific data and to relate it to training for specific sports. The purpose of this book is to attempt to set down much of the scientific data in layman's terms in such a manner that objective facts and figures can be helpful and useful to the athlete, coach and scientist in their interpretation and application for practical purposes. The authors are drawn from many Canadian schools and are considered to be experts not only in Canada but at an international level of coaching, research, and competition.

A.W.T.

CONTENTS

THE SCIENTIFIC ASPECTS
OF
SPORTS TRAINING

PART A

ENDURANCE
TRAINING

CHAPTER I

ENDURANCE TRAINING— SCIENTIFIC APPLICATION

A. W. Taylor

Endurance training can be defined as progressive, regular exercise carried out over an extended period of time with the result that certain adaptations, both physiological and functional, occur. Åstrand and Rodahl [4] have stated that "an adaptation takes place to a given load; in order to achieve further improvement the training intensity has to be increased." Endurance training, therefore, is a relative function of the work intensity and duration, during a regular exercise session, and throughout the total training regimen. There is, however, no direct linear relationship between amount of training and the training effect. As well, there are psychological and physiological limits of the effects of training, and these vary from individual to individual. For an excellent tabular review of training effects the readers are referred to reference 4. Shephard [70] calls interval training "continuous training" which is described as a form of work whereby the subject exercises at a moderate and relatively steady intensity of exercise for long periods of time ranging from fifteen minutes to several hours. This type of training is designed mainly to stress the oxygen transport system. Research has demonstrated that tolerance for prolonged exercise develops best in those individuals participating in continuous training, thus demonstrating a definite specificity effect.

Since the response to the training regimen at any given time depends largely upon the current level of fitness of the subjects, then a relatively more vigorous activity will have to be initiated if the course of training is to be maintained. [72]

CIRCULATORY SYSTEM AND BLOOD ADAPTATIONS

Shephard [70] has stated that "training is associated, not only with an increase in the overall maximum oxygen intake, but also with the development of individual links in the oxygen conductance chain. The most noticeable response is an increase of the stroke volume of the heart, both at rest and in exercise. The pulse rate at rest and in submaximum work is thus decreased, and the maximum output of the heart per minute is increased in direct proportion to the increase of maximum oxygen intake. Hemoglobin content of unit volume of blood and the total blood volume are also increased." It is well established that physical conditioning increases the maximal cardiac output, but conflicting opinions have been expressed concerning the possible effects on cardiac output at submaximal work loads.[11] Wyndham *et al.*[97] found no change in submaximal cardiac output in Bantu miners after three months of training and heat acclimatization. Ekblom *et al.*[16] on the other hand, have observed increases from 22.7 to 24.2 1/min in exercising subjects. Similar results have been found in animal studies.[61] A lower cardiac output for a given level of oxygen uptake has been observed in athletes and untrained subjects after a training program.[2,16] This decreased cardiac output has been attributed to a redistribution of blood flow from the organs and non-working muscles to the muscles being exercised. Rowell *et al.*[67] and Castenfors [10] have found that the decreased splanchnic and renal blood flow during exercise is less pronounced in trained than in untrained subjects. Resting splanchnic and renal blood flow is apparently unchanged by training. Myocardial blood flow can be expected to be reduced at a given work load after training because the heart rate and often the peripheral resistance is reduced.[11] Working muscle blood flow is also, therefore, reduced.[33]

Sweat constituents remain relatively constant after training. Sweating, however, starts at a lower body temperature following training. There is also a greater sweat production for a given level of exercise. The skin temperature thus tends to be lower, and the same quantity of heat can be lost from the body with a smaller flow of blood to the skin. The deep body tissues become more tolerant of an increase of temperature, and this further reduces the blood flow required for heat dissipation.[70]

It is well substantiated in the literature [6,16,46,66,89,97] that resting heart rate is decreased after training. Heart rate is also decreased for a given work load [6,35,97] although maximal heart rate appears to be relatively constant.[4,16] The decreased heart rate and decreased cardiac output for a given work load observed after training have led to conflicting data for stroke volume [6,16,97] primarily due to the indirect methods of measurement. It is generally accepted that stroke volume does increase during submaximal exercise to account for a good proportion of the increased cardiac output with exercise.[6,16,97] Training also results in a more rapid return to pre-exercise resting values for heart rate, cardiac output, stroke volume and circulatory flow.

Endurance training has been demonstrated to increase circulatory hemoglobin [6,46] and blood volume [6,46] although no change has been seen.[29] The increases are dependent upon the initial level of fitness of the subjects.[21] Experiments with rats trained by endurance swimming, resulted in no effect upon total leucocyte count, total erythrocyte count, sedimentation rate, hematocrit, erythrocyte osmotic resistance, and haemoglobin per unit volume of blood.[55] Red blood cells were less resistant to osmotic pressure after training.[29]

The number of capillaries per mm² has been shown to be the same for trained and untrained muscle. However, the average size of the muscle cell in well trained muscle was larger than the untrained muscle cell. Endurance training, thus, brought about, increases in the number of capillaries per muscle fiber.[40] Carrow *et al.*[9] did demonstrate increased capillary density and capillary to fiber rations in skeletal muscles of trained rats.

The literature indicates that there is an increased oxygen extraction from the blood by the trained working muscle. The PO_2 in muscular venous blood after training is decreased.[14] Increased $A-VO_2$ differences have been observed in swimmers, runners and skiers,[6,16] athletes utilizing endurance-type training methods.

Endurance training has also resulted in higher mean blood pressure during[16] and after exercise,[77] a phenomenon primarily brought about by an increased exercise systolic pressure and a decreased exercise diastolic blood pressure. Training has also been shown to produce decreased systolic and diastolic blood pressure at rest,[75] higher left ventricular pressure and increased maximal rate of pressure (dp/dt) in rats.[61]

Although the heart plays a significant role in both the circulatory and respiratory system and is primarily important in the oxygen-transporting system, certain training adaptations will be discussed under the heading of the circulatory system for the sake of convenience. Heart volume has been observed to increase with endurance training[4,19] although it is most important to review the literature most carefully as the pitfall of relative weights must be considered—an excellent discussion of this often-used error is found in references 23 and 28. The ECG recording of the trained heart at rest has been observed to demonstrate longer PQ, QRS and QT_c intervals, higher T waves in lead II, left axis deviation of the T waves, higher R waves in the right and deeper S waves in the left precordial leads, and deeper S waves in the right and higher R waves in the left precordial leads.[92]

BLOOD AND TISSUE METABOLITE ADAPTATIONS

Lactic acid has been thoroughly studied for several years. It is a well known fact that although resting lactate levels remain relatively unchanged after a prolonged exercise regimen, training does result in lower absolute lactate levels under submaximal working conditions,[3,16,68,82] increased tolerance for excessive lactate levels with maximal exercise,[16] increased work capacity and time to fatigue and decreased recovery time.[82] A similar tolerance effect has as well been found for skeletal muscle tissue with an accompanying decrease in tissue lactate after training for a similar work load.[73,78] Holloszy [42] in his classical article has stated this:

> A two-fold increase in the capacity to oxidize *pyruvate* occurred in the muscles of rats subjected to a program of strenuous exercise. Concomitantly, the activities of the enzymes of the mitochondrial electron transport chain approximately doubled in the muscles of the exercised rats. The concentration of cytochrome c also increased two-fold, providing evidence that the rise in respiratory enzyme activity is due to a net increase in enzyme protein. This is suggested by the finding of a general increase in mitochondrial protein. The finding that mitochondria obtained from the muscles of the exercised animals exhibited a high level or respiratory control and tightly coupled oxidative phosphorylation indicates that the increase in mitochondrial electron transport capacity is associated with a rise in the capacity to produce ATP. . . .
>
> It is well known that physically trained individuals, as compared to untrained, are characterized by the ability to obtain a higher maximum rate of O_2 consumption during strenuous exercise and to maintain lower levels of blood lactate during moderate exercise. It has been suggested that cardiovascular adaptations resulting in the delivery of more blood and O_2 to the working muscles, are responsible for these effects of training. However, it is not possible to explain on this basis the finding that trained individuals have lower blood lactate concentrations than untrained even when the exercise load is light, as it has been shown recently that cardiac output and, therefore, also peripheral blood flow, is actually lower at a given level of submaximal exercise in the trained than in the untrained state. Trained muscle appears to compensate for this decrease in blood flow and meet their O_2 requirements during work by increased extraction of O_2 from the blood, as evidenced by a greater A-VO_2 difference. It appears likely, therefore, that during moderate exercise the rate of aerobic metabolism of pyruvate in the muscles of sedentary individuals is limited not by the supply of oxygen but by the capacity of mitochondria for pyruvate oxidation. The increase in respiratory activity induced in the muscle by physical training could play a major role in decreasing lactate production during submaximal exercise.

Although resting glucose levels are not affected by training, postexercise values are found to be higher in trained subjects suggesting preferential use of fats and tissue glycogen for exercise purposes. Plasma immunoreactive insulin falls during exercise of 50 to 70 percent MVO_2, more in the trained than the untrained state.[64] Serum iron increases after exercise in the trained state.[1] Training has been demonstrated to produce smaller increases in plasma corticosterone after exercise [18] although resting values remain unchanged or slightly elevated [17]; postexercise decreased thyroxine levels due to increased peripheral deiodination of thyroxine [51]; decreased liver and increased fecal cholesterol [30] although no changes have been observed in resting plasma cholesterol levels [30,48]; decreased resting plasma lipids and phospholipid concentration in lipoprotein classes [8]; increased mobilization of free fatty acids after stress and exercise [84,86] and at the point of fatigue [12,27]; and an increased sensitivity of fat cells to norepinephrine after training.[31] Increased mobilization of catecholamines has as well been observed after training for submaximal exercise.[85] Fatty acid oxidation provides a major portion of the energy for muscle metabolism during prolonged submaximal exercise. A progressively greater proportion of the energy is derived from carbohydrate as the intensity of the exercise increases.[86] The relative amounts of carbohydrate and fat utilized at different work loads depends upon the level of physical fitness, with fatty oxidation serving as a more important source of energy for submaximal work in physically trained than in untrained men and animals.[45]

Training also has been observed to produce decreased ascorbic acid levels in brain, spleen and adrenals.[48] Numerous blood and plasma enzymes have been measured during exercise and after training. The results of several studies will be listed in this article for the sake of simplicity and refer only to trained subjects: (a) decreased after exercise—aldolase,[20] lactic dehydrogenase,[20] glutamic oxalacetic transaminase,[20,49] glutamic pyruvic transaminase [20]; (b) increased after exercise—glutathione,[76] glutamic oxalacetic transaminase,[1] creative phosphokinase [49]; (c) increased with training—succinyldehydrogenase,[33] lactic dehydrogenase,[49] creative phosphokinase [49]; (d) no change or a return to resting, pretraining values after a short period of time—hexokinase,[71] phosphofructokinase.[71]

MUSCLE SYSTEM AND INTRACELLULAR INCLUSION ADAPTATIONS

Muscular strength and hypertrophy are directly related to the constituent components previously mentioned. It would be appropriate at this time to mention some studies on muscular strength and endurance which were the forerunners of much of the physiological and biochemical research being investigated today. Müller [58] defined trainability as the increase in strength resulting from training, i.e. the disposition of a muscle to respond to repeated contraction of a certain strength, duration, and frequency with an increase in strength. This disposition is apparently not influenced by age, sex or muscle group, but by the trainability of the muscle. The increase in strength is slower when the muscle is trained isotonically perhaps due to the necessity to learn a more complex pattern of activity.[65] Endurance and muscular strength increase in practically the same proportion with muscular training. With the same muscle tension the greatest holding time remains unchanged throughout the training.[41] Eccentric training of muscles, in particular forearm extensors, is accompanied by an increase in the strength of the antagonists.[74] During submaximal contractions the force developed per unit of muscle is reduced. Due to the ability of the muscle to recruit individual muscle fibers, increases in strength can occur without increased size.[71] Strength is retained after training for extended periods of time although muscular endurance does not seem to decrease in a similarly proportioned manner.[75] Endurance training appears to increase strength to a greater extent than strength training increases muscular endurance.[77] If a contraction surpasses a certain strength and duration, the contraction is the cause of a lasting excitation in the muscle, which does not diminish before 24 hours. This causes a gradual increase of the cross section and the maximum strength of the muscle.[58]

Holloszy *et al.*[42] have stated that the skeletal muscle that has adapted to strenuous exercise contains approximately twice as many cristae per gram as untrained muscle. Therefore, the functional steady state in which oxygen consumption balances ATP hydrolysis during submaximal exercise must be attained at lower concentrations of Pi and ADP in the working muscle cells of trained muscle. This must be so because oxygen consumption is the same in the untrained as in the trained state for a given submaximal work load.

The muscular system has been found to increase in size,[75] both skeletal and cardiac muscle, only when the work intensity exceeds that normally experienced by the muscle.[47,71] The diameter increases but not the fiber number, therefore, an increase in the size of the muscle cells occurs.[57] A 15 percent increase in the myofilamental protein in the gastrocnemius muscle of guinea pigs[39] and a two-fold increase in the myofibrillar count accompaning hypertrophy in the soleus muscle of cats[13] have been reported.

Investigations with skeletal muscle have revealed that there is a rapid synthesis of protein during the process of hypertrophy. The synthesis appears to be evenly distributed among all of the muscle fractions such as the sacroplasm, myofilaments and mitochrondria, although a decrease in myofibriller protein has been seen.[32] This newly formed muscle has the same functional capacity of the preexisting muscle.[22] Similar results have been found for cardiac unit and total protein.[24] The oxidative capacity of both heart and skeletal muscle can, therefore, be increased by training.[71]

The gastrocnemius muscle of endurance trained rats have been found to contain more than two times as many mitochrondria per unit area as sedentary controls. The mitochrondria are more numerous and appear to be larger with more densely packed cristae.[25,26] In recent years a great deal of research has been carried out on intracellular components such as glycogen, phosphocreatine minerals, and myoglobin. The Scandinavian team of Bergström, Hultman and Saltin, utilizing the muscle biopsy technique, have initiated investigations with human subjects. Endurance training increases the liver and muscle glycogen content.[15,27,63] The high initial resting values after training assist the muscle to carry out prolonged exercise for extended periods of time.[27,69,81] Similarly increased glycogen values are found in cardiac muscle after training and trained hearts are capable of greater glycogenesis during a fast.[62] The increased glycogen content has been observed to be accompanied by increased phosphorylase activity,[15,80] and increased glycogen synthetase activities.[52,87]

The literature also indicates that endurance training increases skeletal muscle myoglobin content,[54,60,95] brings about a higher percentage of water and increased absolute dry weight,[75] results in less intramuscular fat[75] and increased glutathione content,[76] increased phosphocreatine,[59] increased calcium,[59] increased magnesium,[59] elevated heart lactic dehydrogenase activity after exercise,[24,28] greater oxidation of palmitate in gastrocnemius homogenates,[56] increased aldolase,[38] increased absolute cytochrome oxidase activity,[43] increased absolute cytochrome C concentration,[43] elevated hexokinase initially and then transiently returns to pretraining levels,[5] two-fold increases in citrate synthase, DPN—specific isocitrate dehydrogenase, and succinate dehydrogenase activities[44] and 35 to 50 percent increases in glutamate dehydrogenase and α ketoglutarate dehydrogenase and mitochondrial malate dehydrogenase activities.[44]

No changes were observed in skeletal muscle lactic dehydrogenase after exercise[24,28] nor adenosinetriphosphatase[46] cytochrome oxidase per mg of muscle or cytochrome c per mg of muscle.[43] Cardiac muscle increased in adenosinetriphosphatase[46] and aldolase.[38] Holloszy *et al.*[44] have stated that the enzymatic findings provide evidence that, unlike the constituents of the respiratory chain, the mitochondrial citric acid cycle and citric acid cycle related enzymes do not increase in parallel during the adaptive response of skeletal muscle to exercise, resulting in a change in mitochondrial composition.

RESPIRATORY SYSTEM ADAPTATIONS

The adaptations that occur in response to a vigorous program of prolonged exercise, such as long distance skiing, swimming and running, manifest themselves in functional terms as an increase in endurance. The most obvious effect of physical conditioning is the increased capacity to carry out work.[21,46] The foremost indicator is increased oxygen uptake for the same absolute work load[16,96,97] and increased maximal oxygen uptake.[93] This increased maximal oxygen uptake with training is primarily due to neither increased arterial O_2 content nor increased A-VO$_2$ difference, but to the increased amount of oxygen transported by the larger cardiac output, which in turn was due to a larger stroke volume, since maximal heart rate is relatively constant.[36,53] Resting oxygen consumption does not significantly differ between trained and nontrained subjects or in the same subjects after training.[88] Saltin *et al.*[68] found that training with even middle aged and older men, produced a considerable improvement in aerobic power after ten weeks. The mean values for maximal oxygen uptake increased approximately 20 percent and no differences were found between the age groups tested. The major benefit of this improved aerobic power is that a certain submaximal effort can be performed with a lower heart rate.

Byrne-Quinn *et al.*[7] found the hypoxic ventilatory drive of athletes to be only 35 percent of that of nontrained subjects. Reuschlein *et al.*[66] observed no changes after training in D_2 or pulmonary capillary blood values at rest or during exercise. Increased vital capacity, and respiratory recovery after exercise have previously been observed.[75] The relationship of lung diffusing capacity to oxygen uptake is unchanged by training, but since the maximum oxygen uptake is increased a corresponding small increase in the maximum diffusing capacity may be presumed.[70]

NERVOUS SYSTEM ADAPTATIONS

The improvements in mechanical efficiency which come with practice or training are really a measure of the effect of training on the central nervous system and not essentially a measure of improved metabolism in the sense of more economical intracellular activity.[75] An indirect assessment of the mechanism behind the improved mechanical efficiency after endurance training may be due to the increased vascularity of the motor cortex as demonstrated in growing guinea pigs, with the progressive development of motor activity.[76]

Clausen[11] has noted in his fine review article that differences in muscular endurance can be attributed or related to the pattern of activity imposed upon the muscle fibers by their motor neurons. Neurons of small size have a lower threshold and, therefore, discharge more frequently than larger neurones. Consequently, muscle fibers innervated by small neurons are used most often, and this is undoubtedly the reason for their high degree of endurance. In accordance with this concept, it has been shown that red muscle fibers are innervated by small motor neurons, while white muscle fibers are innervated by large neurons, and furthermore the crossing of the innervation by transplantation causes transformation of white fibers to red and vice versa.

Thus, the composition of a muscle seems to depend on the average stimulus to which its motor pool is subjected. Training represents an increase in this average stimulus and it is reasonable to expect that the observed increase in mitochondrial content takes place in the rarely used fibers that have an anaerobic enzymatic profile, rather than in the continually active red fiber. In other words training renders white or intermediate fibers more 'red.'[94] Tweit *et al.*[91] noted that some physical component was involved in the improvement in total body reaction time and this was related to improvements observed in an agility run and the Sargent jump. Total body reaction time was improved by training.

ORGAN WEIGHTS, CONNECTIVE TISSUE BIOSYNTHESIS AND CONSTITUENT ADAPTATIONS

Permanent changes in an organism ascribed to exercise, that is adaptations which facilitate the performance of more exercise, equal the trained state.[75] Training has been found to result in increased adrenal weight [24,29,55] and heart ventricle weights whereas decreased liver and spleen weights were observed [24,29] although training has also been observed to have no effect on spleen weights.[90]

Endurance training has also been observed to result in increased lung to body weight ratio,[75] decreased fat pad weight and cellularization,[79,83] decreased kidney weight,[24] and increased heart weights.[89,95] Training causes an hypertrophy of the intercellular substance of connective tissue, increasing the volume of tendons and ligaments,[50] and hypertrophy of the diaphragm of rabbits and dogs.[76] Glutathione content of rat liver and kidney have been noted after training, as well as decreased liver cholesterol [30,48] and increased fecal cholesterol.[30]

REFERENCES

1. Ahlborg, B., Brohult, J.: Immediate and delayed metabolic reactions in well-trained subjects after prolonged physical exercise. *Acta Med Scand, 182:*41–53, 1967.
2. Andrew, G. M., Guzman, C. A., Becklake, M. R.: Effect of athletic training on exercise cardiac output. *J Appl Physiol, 21:*603–608, 1666.
3. Åstrand, P. O., Hällback, I., Hedman, R., Saltin, B.: Blood lactates after prolonged severe exercise. *J Appl Physiol, 18:*619–622, 1963.
4. Åstrand, P. O., Rodahl, K.: *Textbook of Work Physiology.* McGraw-Hill, New York, 1970.
5. Barnard, R. J., Peter, J. B.: Effect of training and exhaustion on rexokinase activity of skeletal muscle. *J Appl Physiol, 27:*691–695, 1969.
6. Bevegård, S., Holmgren, A., Jonsson, B.: Circulatory studies in well trained athletes at rest and during heavy exercise, with special reference to stroke volume and the influenc of body position. *Acta Physiol Scand, 57:*26–10, 1963.
7. Byrne-Quinn, E., Wek, J. V., Sodal, I. E., Filley, G. F., Grover, R. F.: Ventilatory control in the athlete. *J Appl Physiol, 30:*91–98, 1971.
8. Carlson, L. A., Mossfeldt, F.: Acute affects of prolonged, heavy exercise on the concentration of plasma lipids and lipoproteins in man. *Acta Physiol Scand, 62:*51–59, 1964.

9. Carrow, R. E., Brown, R. E., Van Huss, W. D.: Fiber sizes and capillary to fiber ratios in skeletal muscles of exercise rats. *Anat Rec, 159*:33–38, 1967.

10. Castenfors, J.: Renal function during exercise. *Acta Physiol Scand, 70:* Supp. 293, 1967.

11. Clausen, J. P.: Effects of physical conditioning—A hypothesis concerning circulatory adjustment to exercise. *Scand J Clin Lab Invest, 24*:305–313, 1969.

12. Cobb, L. A., Johnson, W. P.: Hemodynamic relationships of anaerobic metabolism and plasma free fatty acids during prolonged, strenuous exercise in trained and untrained subjects. *J Clin Invest, 42*:800–810, 1963.

13. Denny-Brown, D.: Experimental Studies Pertaining to Hypertrophy Regeneration and Degeneration. In Adams, R. P., Eaton, L. M., Sky, A. M. (Eds.): *Neuromuscular Disorder: Proceedings of Association for Research in Nervous and Mental Disorders.* Williams and Wilkins, Baltimore, 1964, pp. 147–196.

14. Doll, E., Keul, J., Maiwald, C.: Oxygen tension and acid-base equilibria in venous blood of working muscle. *Am J Physiol, 215*:23–29, 1968.

15. Edgerton, V. R., Barnard, R. J., Peter, J. B., Simpson, D. R., C. A. Gillespie: Response of muscle glycogen and phosphoryease to electrical stimulation in trained and nontrained guinea pigs. *Exp Neurol, 27*:46–56, 1970.

16. Ekblom, B., Åstrand, P. O., Saltin, B., Stenberg, J., Wallström, B.: Effect of training on circulatory response to exercise. *J Appl Physiol, 24*:518–528, 1968.

17. Frenkl, R., Csalay, L.: On the endocrine adaptation to regular muscular activity. *J Sp Med Phys Fit, 10*:151–156, 1970.

18. Frenkl, R., Csalay, L., Csákváry, G., Zelles, T.: Effect of muscular exertion on the reaction of the pituitary—Adrenocortical axis in trained and untrained rats. *Acta Physiol Acad Sci Hung, 33*:435–438, 1968.

19. Frick, M. H., Konttinen, A., Sarajas, H. S. S.: Effects of physical training on circulation at rest and during exercise. *Am J Cardiol, 12*:142–147, 1963.

20. Garbus, J., Highman, B., Altland, P. D.: Serum enzymes and lactic dehydrogenase isoenzymes after exercise and training in rats. *Am J Physiol, 207*:467–472, 1964.

21. Glass, H. I., Edwards R. H. T. DeGareta A. C., Clank, J. C.: Co red cells labeling for blood volume and total hemoglobin in athletes: Effect of training. *J Appl Physiol, 26*:131–134, 1969.

22. Goldberg, A. C.: Protein synthesis during work-induced growth of skeletal muscle. *J Cell Biol, 36*:653–658, 1968.

23. Gollnick, P. D.: Cellular adaptations to exercise. In Shephard, R. J. (Ed.): *Frontiers of Fitness.* Thomas, Springfield, 1971.

24. Gollnick, P. D., Hearn, G. R.: Lactic dehydrogenase activities of heart and skeletal muscle of exercised rats. *Am J Physiol, 201*:694–696, 1961.

25. Gollnick, P. D., King, D. W.: Effect of exercise and training on mitochondria of rat skeletal muscle. *Am J Physiol, 216*:1502–1509, 1969.

26. ———: The immediate and chronic effect of exercise on the number and structure of skeletal muscle mitochondria. *Med Sport, 3*:239–244, 1969.

27. Gollnick, P. D., Soule, R. G., Taylor, A. W., Williams, C., Ianuzzo, C. D.: Exercise-induced glycogenolysis and lipolysis in the rat: Hormonal influence. *Am J Physiol, 219*:729–733, 1970.

28. Gollnick, P. D., Struck, P. J., Bogyo, T. P.: Lactic dehydrogenase activities of rat heart and skeletal muscle after exercise and training. *J Appl Physiol, 22*:623–627, 1967.

29. Gollnick, P. D., Struck, P. J., Soule, R. G., Heinrick, J. R.: Effect of exercise and training on the blood of normal and splenectomized rats. *Int Z Angew Physiol, 21*:169–178, 1965.

30. Gollnick, P. D., Taylor, A. W.: Effect of exercise on hepatic cholesterol of rats fed diets high in saturated or unsaturated fats. *Int Z Angew Physiol,* 27:144–153, 1967.

31. Gollnick, P. D., Williams, C.: Effects of training on the lipolytic response of isolated fat cells to norepinephrine. *Physiologist* 12:00–00, 1969.

32. Gordon, E. E., Kowalski, K., Fritts, M.: Protein changes in quadriceps muscle of rat with repetitive exercises. *Arch Phys Med Rehabil,* 48:296–303, 1966.

33. Grimby, G., Häggendal, E., Saltin, B.: Local Xeron [133] clearance from the quadriceps muscle during exercise in man. *J. Appl Physiol,* 22:305–310, 1967.

34. Guth, L.: Trophic influences of nerve on muscle. *Physiol Rev,* 48:645–687, 1968.

35. Hall, V. E.: The relation of heart rate to exercise fitness: An attempt at physiological interpretation of the bradycardia of training. *Pediatrics,* 32:723–729, 1963.

36. Hartley, L. H., Grimby, G., Kilbom, Å., Nilsson, N. J., Åstrand, I., Ekblom, J., Saltin, B.: Cardiac output and gas exchange at submaximal and maximal exercise. *Scand J Clin Lab Invest* 24:335–344, 1969.

37. Hearn, G. R., Gollnick, P. D.: Effects of exercise on the adonosine tripnosphatase activity n skeletal and heart muscle of rats. *Int Z Angew Physiol,* 19:23–26, 1961.

38. Hearn, G. R., Wainio, W. W.: Aldolase activity of the heart and skeletal muscle of exercised rats. *Am J Physiol,* 190:206–208, 1957.

39. Helander, E. A. S.: Influence of exercise and restricted activity on the protein composition of skeletal muscle. *Biochem J,* 78:478–482, 1964.

40. Hermansen, L., Wachtlova, M.: Capillary density of skeletal muscle in well-trained and untrained men. *J Appl Physiol,* 30:860–863, 1971.

41. Hettinger, T., Müller, E. A.: Muscular performance and training. (Unpublished data).

42. Holloszy, J. O.: Biochemical adaptations to muscle. *J Biol Chem,* 242:2278–2282, 1967.

43. Holloszy, J. O., Oscai, L. B.: Effect of exercise on α-glycerophosphate dehydrogenase activity in skeletal muscle. *Arch Biochem Biophys,* 103:653–656, 1969.

44. Holloszy, J. O., Oscai, L. B., Don, I. J., Molé, P. A.: Mitochondriae citric acid cycle and related enzymes: Adaptive response to exercise. *Biochem Biophys Res Comm,* 40:1368–1373, 1970.

45. ———: Biochemical adaptations to endurance exercise in skeletal muscle. In Pernow, B. and Saltin, B. (Eds.): *Muscle Metabolism During Exercise.* New York, Plenum Press, 1971.

46. Holmgren, A., Mossfeldt, F., Sjöstrand, T., Ström, G.: Effect of training on work capacity, total hemoglobin, blood volume, heart volume and pulse rate in recumbent and upright positions. *Acta Physiol Scand,* 50:72–83, 1960.

47. Howell, M. L.: Brief Notes on Certain Training Methods For Sport. Paper Presented at 1967 CAHPER Convention.

48. Hughes, R. E., Jones, P. R., Williams, R. S., Wright, P. F.: Effect of prolonged swimming on the distribution of ascorbic acid and cholesterol in the tissues of the guinea pig. *Life Sci,* 10:661–668, 1971.

49. Hunter, J. B., Critz, J. B.: Effect of training on plasma enzyme levels in man. *J Appl Physiol,* 31:20–23, 1971.

50. Ingelmark, B. E.: Der Bau der Sehnen wä hrend Verschiedener Altersperioden und unter wechselnden funktionellen Bedingungen 1. *Acta Anat,* 6:113–118, 1948.

51. Irvine, C. H. G.: Effect of exercise on thyroxine degradation in athletes and non-athletes. *J Clin Endocrinol Metab, 28*:942–948, 1968.
52. Jeffress, R. N., Peter, J. B., Lamb, D. R.: Effects of exercise on glycogen synthetase in red and white skeletal muscle. *Life Sci, 7*:957–960, 1968.
53. Knehr, C. A., Dill, D. B., Neufeld, W.: Training and its effects on man at rest and at work. *Am J Physiol, 136*:148–156, 1942.
54. Lawrie, R. A.: Effect of enforced exercise on myoglobin concentration in muscle. *Nature, 171*:1069–1070, 1955.
55. McAtee, B. M., Grollman, S.: The effects of exercise and training on the hematology of the famale albino rat. *J Sports Med Phys Fit, 17*:205–213, 1967.
56. Molé, P. A., Holloszy, J. D.: Exercise-induced increase in the capacity of skeletal muscle to oxidize palmitate. *Proc Soc Exp Biol Med, 134*:789–792, 1970.
57. Morpurgo, B.: Ueber Activitats-Hypertrophie der Willkurlichen Muskeln. *Virchow Arch Path Anat, 150*:522–554, 1897.
58. Müller, E. A.: Physiology of muscle training. *Rev Can Biol, 21*:303–313, 1962.
59. Palladin, A. V.: The biochemistry of muscle training. *Science, 102*:576–578, 1945.
60. Pattengale, P. K., Holloszy, J. O.: Augmentation of skeletal muscle myoglobin by a program of treadmill running. *Am J Physiol, 213*:783–785, 1967.
61. Penpargkul, S., Scheuer, J.: The effect of physical training upon the mechanical and metabolic performance of the rat heart. *J Clin Invest, 49*:1859–1868, 1970.
62. Poland, J. L., Blount, D. H.: The effects of training on myocardial metabolism. *Proc Exp Biol Med, 129*:171–174, 1968.
63. Procter, H. A., Best, C. M.: Changes in muscle glycogen accompanying physical training. *Am J Physiol, 100*:506–510, 1932.
64. Pruett, E. D. R.: Glucose and insulin during prolonged work stress in men living on different diets. *J Appl Physiol, 28*:199–208, 1970.
65. Rasch, P. J.: Isometric exercise and gains of muscle strength. In Shephard, R. J. (Ed.): *Frontiers of Fitness.* Thomas, Springfield, 1971, pp. 98–111.
66. Reuschlein, P. S., Reddan, W. G., Burpee, J., Gee, J. B. L., Rankin, J.: Effect of physical training on the pulmonary diffusing capacity during submaximal work. *J Appl Physiol, 24*:152–158, 1968.
67. Rowell, L. B., Blackmon, J. R., Bruce, R. A.: Indocyanine green clearance and estimated hepatic blood flow during mild to maximal exercise in upright man. *J Clin Invest, 43*:1677–1690, 1964.
68. Saltin, B., Hartley, L. H., Kilbom, Å., Åstrand, I.: Oxygen uptake, heart rate, and blood lactate concentration at submaximal and maximal exercise. *Scand J Clin Lab Invest, 24*:323–334, 1969.
69. Saltin, B., Hermansen, L.: Glycogen stores and prolonged severe exercise. *Symposia of the Swedish Nutrition Foundation, 5*:1–33, 1967.
70. Shephard, R. J.: *Endurance Fitness.* Toronto, University of Toronto Press, 1969.
71. ———— (Ed.): *Frontiers of Fitness,* Springfield, C. C. Thomas, 1971.
72. ————: Intensity, duration and frequency of exercise as determinants of the response to a training regimen. *Int Z Angew Physiol, 26*:272–278, 1968.
73. Short, F. A., Cobb, L. A., Kawabori, I., Goodner, C. J.: Influence of exercise training on red and white rat skeletal muscle. *Am J Physiol, 217*:327–331, 1969.
74. Singh, M., Karpovich, P. V.: Effect of eccentric training of agonists on antagonistic muscles. *J Appl Physiol, 23*:742–745, 1967.
75. Steinhaus, A. H.: Chronic effects of exercise. *Physiol Rev, 13*:103–147, 1933.
76. ————: *Toward an Understanding of Health and Physical Education.* Dubuque, W. C. Brown, 1963.

77. Taylor, A. W.: A physiological analysis of the effects of two training programs. *J Sports Med Phys Fitness,* 11:252–256, 1971.
78. ————: Skeletal muscle lactate and pyruvate levels after exercise. *Can J Physiol Pharm,* (in press).
79. Taylor, A. W., Booth, M., McBean-Hopkins, K.: Lipid regeneration in the rat after exercise. In Taylor (Ed.): *Training-Scintific Basis and Applications.* Springfield, Thomas, 1972.
80. Taylor, A. W., Booth, M., Rao, S.: Skeletal muscle phosphorylase activities after maximal and submaximal exercise in trained subjects. *Can J Physiol Pharm,* 50:1038–1046, 1972.
81. Taylor, A. W., Lappage, R., Rao, S.: Skeletal muscle glycogen stores after submaximal and maximal work. *Med Sci Sports,* 3:75–78, 1971.
82. Taylor, A. W., Lovlin, R.: Produzione Di Lattato E Di Piruvato Con Carichi Di Lavoro A Livello Massimale E Submassimale *Med Dello Sport,* 24:89–96, 1971.
83. Taylor, A. W., McBean-Hopkins, K.: DNA content of regenerating epididymal fat pads. *Growth,* 35:341–348, 1971.
84. Taylor, A. W., McPhee, M.: Carotid occlusion, dehydration, catecholamine release, and FFA mobilization in dogs. *Experientia,* 27:1251–1253, 1971.
85. Taylor, A. W., Schoeman, H. J., Esfandiary, A. R., Russell, J. C.: Effect of exercise on urinary catecholanine excretion in active and sedentary subjects. *Rev Can Biol,* 30:97–105, 1971.
86. Taylor, A. W., Schoeman, D. S., Lovlin, R., Lee, S. K.: Plasma free fatty acid mobilization with graded exercise. *J Sports Med Phys Fitness,* 11:234–240, 1971.
87. Taylor, A. W., Thayer, R., Rao, S. R.: Skeletal muscle glycogen synthetase activities after maximal and submaximal exercise in trained subjects. *Can J Physiol Pharm,* 50:411–415, 1972.
88. Terjung, R. L., Tipton, C. M.: Exercise training and resting oxygen consumption. *Int Z Angew Physiol,* 28:269–272, 1970.
89. Tipton, C. M.: Training and bradycardia in rats. *Am J Physiol,* 209:1089–1094, 1965.
90. Tipton, C. M., Tharp, G. D., Schild, R. J.: Exercise, hypophysectomy, and spleen weight. *Am J Physiol,* 21:1163–1167, 1966.
91. Tweit, A. H., Gollnick, P. D., Hearn, G. R.: Effect of training program on total body reaction time of individuals of low fitness. *Res Q,* 34:508–513, 1963.
92. Van Ganse, W., Versee, L., Eylenbusch, W., Vuylsteek, K.: The electrocardiogram of athletes, comparison with untrained subjects. *Br Heart J,* 32:160–164, 1970.
93. Varnauskas, E., Björntorp, P., Fahlén, M., Přerovský, I., Stenberg, J.: Effects of physical training of exercise blood flow and enzymatic activity in skeletal muscle. *Cardiovasc Res,* 4:418–422, 1970.
94. Von Linge, B.: The response of muscle to strenuous exercise. An experimental study in the rat. *J Bone Joint Surg,* 44:711–728, 1962.
95. Whipple, G. H.: The hemoglobin of striated muscle. *Am J Physiol,* 76:693–707, 1926.
96. Williams, C. G., Wyndham, C. M., Kok, R., Von Rahden, M. J. E.: Effect of training on maximum oxygen intake and on anaerobic metabolism in man. *Int Z Angew Physiol,* 24:18–23, 1967.
97. Wyndham, C. M., Benade, A. J. A., Williams, C. G., Strydom, N. B., Goldin, A., Heyns, A. J. A.: Changes in central circulation and body fluid spaces during acclimatization to heat. *J Appl Physiol,* 25:586–593, 1968.

CHAPTER II

THE PHYSIOLOGY OF ENDURANCE TRAINING

H. A. WENGER

THE PURPOSE OF this chapter is to present the different patterns of endurance training programs and to discuss the physiological adaptations brought about in response to chronic exercise. The emphasis will be mainly on the functional and structural changes as well as certain metabolic changes which occur in the cardiovascular, respiratory, and muscular systems as a result of endurance training. This discussion will involve training programs which utilize continuous rather than interval work since interval training and its ramifications is presented in another chapter of this book.

The interrelationship of the cardiovascular, respiratory, and muscular systems in the intake, transport, and utilization of oxygen has led many to refer to them collectively as the oxygen transport system. The primary objective of endurance training is to increase the efficiency of this oxygen transport system so that more work can be performed with the same stress to the body or the same amount of work can be accomplished with less strain imposed upon the individual. In the field of athletics, endurance training seeks to maximize a person's ability to do prolonged work and hence improve performance in a specific event or sport.

Before we attempt to delineate the quality and quantity of training necessary to achieve the above objectives, the general and specific effects of chronic, continuous exercise will be examined.

Åstrand and Rodahl[1] state that there is no linear relationship between the amount of training and the training effect which can be achieved. That is, if the amount of training is doubled, the magnitude of the physiological improvements will be less than two-fold. They also emphasize that a physiological adaptation will take place to a given workload and in order to achieve further improvements, the intensity of the training program must be increased.

The results of some research [14,38] also points to a so-called ceiling effect in maximum aerobic capacity. A cross country skier with an mVO_2 of 5.48 litres/min trained daily with an intensive program over an eight-year period. In that time, he won two Olympic gold medals and then was found to have increased his mVO_2 by only 12 ml/min to 5.60 litres/minute. A number of other examples of this ceiling effect are reported by Ekblom.[14] There is also very little difference in measured mVO_2 of distance runners tested by Dill[13] 20 to 25 years ago and the maximum values which are reported today. Lash had a mVO_2 of 81/ml/kg/min and a time of 4.07.4 minutes for the mile while Jim Ryun had a mVO_2 of 80 ml/kg/min in 1967 and a time for the mile of 3.51.3 minutes. Faulkner[17] comments that "apparently, modern training programs are not training the aerobic capacity of athletes any better than did the training programs of the 1930's and the 1940's. World class athletes of the past 30 years may well have reached man's capacity for aerobic work. Improvement must . . . be attributed to an improved efficiency of running or to an increased anaerobic capacity."

The similar values in aerobic capacity of both Lash and Ryun even though they were from different eras with different training programs, does lend credence to the theory that a ceiling for aerobic capacity does exist. This ceiling would, however, vary depending upon the functional and structural capabilities of the individual.

Both the gross and metabolic functions of the cardiovascular, respiratory and muscular systems have been shown to change as a result of chronic exercise. In particular, those functions which are vital to an improved ability to do prolonged work alter in a positive direction as a result of training.

By supplying sufficient amounts of oxygen to the working muscle during exercise, the most efficient metabolic pathways (aerobiosis) can be incorporated for energy production. In order to supply sufficient oxygen, one must increase the cardiac output or increase the oxygen carrying capacity (hemoglobin) of the blood, or increase the rate of removal of oxygen by the working muscle, or a combination of these factors. The hemoglobin concentration has not been shown[37] to vary with training under normal environmental conditions. Endurance training, however, does ellicit an increase in maximal cardiac output by increasing the stroke volume of the heart.[37] The stroke volume of the heart is also increased at submaximal work loads as a result of training[14,15,37] although the cardiac output at the submaximal workloads remains unchanged or may even decrease. This results in a substantial decrease in heart rate.[39,46] Clausen[10] has proposed that a decreased cardiac output at submaximal workloads as a result of training is brought about by a decreased shunting of blood (from the periphery and gut) to the working muscle. He (Clausen) maintains that because of the increased ability of the metabolic machinery in the muscle cells to utilize oxygen that less blood must perfuse the musculature to provide the oxygen requirement. An increased rate of oxygen utilization by the muscle cells would thus increase the A-VO_2 difference across the working muscle and hence decrease the amount of blood which would have to be shunted away from the periphery and gut. The oxygen required to perform the submaximal workload could be supplied, then, by an increased removal of oxygen and a concomitant decrease in muscle blood flow. Certain studies have in fact shown that renal blood flow [8] and splanchnic blood flow [35] are higher in trained versus untrained subjects indicating that, as a result of training, less blood is directed away from the gut area to the working muscle.

An increased rate of oxygen utilization by muscle fibers due to endurance training would have wide implications in the performance of both maximal and submaximal exercises. It would mean that less blood would have to be directed to the working muscle in submaximal exercise thus putting less stress upon the cardiovascular system and it would provide a legitimate means to increasing the maximal oxygen consumption, which would enhance a person's ability to perform prolonged work. This increase in rate of oxygen utilization could be attained by an increase in the concentration of and/or an increase in the activity of the oxidative enzymes in the mitochondria. An increase in the number of mitochondria could also achieve the same end. Holloszy [23] did show that the mitochondrial fraction taken from the gastrocnemius muscle of trained rats displayed a two-fold increase in the ability to oxidize pyruvate. He also reported that a corresponding two-fold increase in activity of certain oxidative enzymes also occurred. Two recent reviews [18,27] enumerate a number of studies which have shown that chronic, endurance type exercise will increase the concentration and activity of many oxidative enzymes in the mitochondria of skeletal muscle. Gollnick and King [20] have also shown that the number and size of mitochondria in skeletal muscle can be increased by endurance training. These increases in the enzymes of the citric acid cycle, the cytochromes and the mitochondria themselves would seem to indicate that at least the capacity of the skeletal muscle to utilize oxygen at an increased rate is improved by chronic exercise. If, in fact, this increased capacity is utilized to its fullest extent during *in vivo* performance of the whole musculature, it would play a major contribution in improving the maximal oxygen uptake of the whole body. Since the performance capacity of an individual "is related to the maximal oxygen uptake in exercises with large muscle groups vigorously involved for one minute or longer," [1] the training effect on the metabolic efficiency at the cellular level should be vital to the improved performance of prolonged work.

The work of Barnard *et al.*[2] indicates that endurance training can affect the oxygen debt—particularly the lactic acid portion of this debt. Their study involved dogs and revealed that the peak lactic acid levels following training were much lower than in the pretrained state. They also report that the lactate removal following exercise was much more rapid in the trained state. They suggest that an increased efficiency in aerobic metabolism could bring about the lower peak lactic acid levels. It is also possible that an increased capacity of the myocardium, skeletal muscle, kidney, and liver to remove the lactic acid and use it as a metabolic substrate could lower the peak values as well as assist in removing the lactate during recovery. The possibility that these tissues could increase their capacity to utilize lactate for energy production during work would also mean that stored glycogen would not have to be catabolized as early and hence could be available in the later stages of prolonged work, permitting a trained individual to work at the same load for a longer period of time. It would also mean that recovery for a trained individual would be enhanced.

Biochemical and histochemical research has shown that the capability of the musculature to utilize oxygen is improved by training. However, Barnard and Peter[5] found a poor correlation between cytochrome concentration and the running time to exhaustion in guinea pigs. This would suggest that the maximum performance of the whole animal is not limited by the muscle cytochrome concentrations. Since maximum performance is highly related to maximum oxygen consumption it would also suggest that maximum oxygen consumption is not limited by the concentration of the cytochromes in the skeletal muscle. Although the limiting factor for maximum aerobic capacity has not been definitely established, the above results[5] might indicate that the cardiovascular system is the limiting factor, since an increased capacity for oxidative phosphorylation did not correlate well with corresponding improvements in prolonged performance. Saltin[36] compared two months of intensive training with several years of training and found that there was very little difference in the maximum heart rates and maximum A-VO_2 difference. However, the maximum oxygen consumption was significantly higher in the group which trained for several years. This would point to stroke volume as the cardiovascular parameter which contributes to an increased mVO_2 with prolonged training. Saltin[36] proposes that stroke volume is, most likely, the factor which distinguishes the champion athlete from the well-trained individual.

One of the factors which could lead to an increased stroke volume is an increase in heart volume. Sjostrand[45] in a cross-sectional study showed a positive relationship between heart volume and stroke volume. Saltin *et al.*[37] demonstrated that an 11 percent increase in heart volume was associated with a 17 percent increase in the stroke volume as a result of two months of endurance training. Since heart size could limit the stroke volume, an increase in heart volume would seem to be a legitimate mechanism by which endurance training could improve the aerobic capacity.

As previously mentioned, increased concentrations and/or increased activity of oxidative enzymes or increased number of mitochondria could contribute to an increased maximum oxygen consumption. Another factor which could also play a role in improving the aerobic capacity is an increase in the effective blood flow in the muscle tissue. Carrow, Brown, and

Van Huss [7] have shown a marked increase in the number of capillaries per fiber in red and white muscle as a result of endurance training. The greatest increase occurred in white fiber as opposed to red. Hyman [26] explains that post exercise hyperemia, or blood buildup, is less evident in the trained muscle than the untrained. Elsner and Carlsen [16] found that immediate postexercise hyperemia was greater in untrained subjects than in a trained group. They suggested that flow may be greater during exercise in the trained subjects due to an increased capillarization. When the exercise ceased, local vasodilator influences were eliminated more quickly and hence the postexercise hyperemia was decreased in the trained group. Thus, it would seem that endurance training can increase the effective blood flow to a muscle during exercise by an increased capillarization or by an increased dilation of existing vessels. This would serve to not only increase the aerobic capacity of the muscle, but would also assist in removing metabolites to enhance performance and recovery times. Saltin *et al.*[37] failed to demonstrate an increase in the number of capillaries in biopsy samples prior to and following a training program of approximately two months. This might indicate that an increased capillarization would occur in response to chronic exercise over a much longer period of time or might indicate that the dyes used in the histochemical examinations [7] indicated an increased dilation of existing vessels rather than the formation of new ones. Whether the increases in capillary density reported by Carrow *et al.* were due to generation of new vessels or the opening of existing vessels seems to be a moot point since in either case it would result in an increase of the effective muscle blood flow.

The aerobic and anaerobic metabolic pathways cannot provide vital energy to perform work if there is no fuel substrate present. Carbohydrate, in the form of glucose or glycogen, and fat in the form of triglycerides, serve as the fuel for energy production. The percentage participation of fat and carbohydrate in the energy production depends upon a number of factors including the severity and the duration of the work in relation to the subject maximal aerobic power and his diet. Christensen and Hansen [9] found that in exercise of an aerobic nature, fat metabolism contributed 50 to 60 percent of the energy. The role of fat as an energy source increased to providing 70 percent of the energy when the aerobic work was prolonged for up to three hours. However, when the work was of sufficient intensity to necessitate engaging the anaerobic metabolic processes, they reported [9] that carbohydrate was the energy source. This might lead one to believe that fat stores and fat metabolism would be more vital to prolonged performance than carbohydrate. However, Christensen and Hansen showed that subjects fed a diet high (90%) in carbohydrate for several days could perform at a standard workload for up to three hours whereas subjects fed a diet high in fat content could perform that same workload for only an hour. At the end of the exercise when both groups were exhausted, it was found that the blood sugar levels were reduced below normal. Ingestion of 200 gms of glucose at the time of exhaustion served to raise the blood sugar level and also enabled the subject to continue work for another hour. Rodahl et al.[32] have also shown evidence that decreased blood sugar levels can serve to limit the performance of prolonged work. The mechanism is probably associated with a decreased efficiency of the CNS which requires optimum blood sugar levels in order to function properly. However, if glycogen is available in the muscle, it will be the preferred form of carbohydrate for the muscle to catabolize. Thus, in the presence of muscle glycogen, the blood sugar levels would not be lowered to a level which would impede the functioning of the CNS and hence limit performance. The mechanism by which stored glycogen is used in preference to blood glucose is probably the lowered levels of circulating insulin [25] in response to heavy exercise. This would serve to lower the amount of glucose which is transported from the blood into the muscle cells. As well, the hexokinase enzyme responsible for phosphorylating glucose to facilitate its passage into the muscle cells is inhibited by the products associated with glycogen catabolism.[24] Thus, if a training regimen could be designed to increase the muscle glycogen stores, it would effectively serve to increase the endurance capacity of the individual. Bergstrom *et al.*[6] observed that there is glycogen overcompensation in response to depleting the glycogen stores by prolonged heavy exercise. They reported that by first depleting the glycogen stores by heavy, prolonged exercise; then maintaining these low levels with a low carbohydrate diet for three days; followed by a few days of a high carbohydrate diet, the concentration of glycogen in the muscle could be almost tripled. Along with this large increase in glycogen stores, the work time at 75 percent of maximum aerobic capacity was extended to approximately three hours whereas it was only 115 minutes at normal glycogen levels. However, a word of caution should be given at this point. Each gram of glycogen is stored together with 2.7 gms of water. In events where weight is a prime factor in performance (or a prerequisite as in wrestling), the overcompensation of glycogen could be deleterious to performance. Although both carbohydrate and fat are used as sources of energy for muscular work, high levels of blood sugar and blood lactage tend to inhibit fat mobilization.[19] Thus, if the work is of a high enough intensity to produce blood lactate, the use of fat as an energy source is decreased. This means that carbohydrates which are stored in limited quantities will supply the majority of the fuel for the work. Thus the duration of the work will be determined by the amount of stored glycogen when the lactate levels are high because the role of fat as an energy source will be limited. The greater the proportion of fat which can be used as fuel during the work, the longer will the stores of glycogen last, and the longer will be the time over which the work can be performed. It has been shown [47,48] that a trained individual can work at a relatively high oxygen uptake in relation to his maximum (60–65%) without any elevation of blood lactate, whereas in an untrained individual, blood lactate levels increase at workloads which are 40 to 50 percent of the person's maximum. Thus by endurance training not only can the maximum aerobic capacity of an individual be increased but the percentage of his maximum at which lactic acid is produced is also increased. This means that a trained person can perform more work per unit of time (i.e. perform a task at a greater intensity) for a longer period of time. This is brought about because even at the higher workloads, less lactic acid will be produced and hence fat mobilization will be inhibited to a lesser extent. Thus, more of the energy for the work can be obtained from the abundant fat stores and, correspondingly, the glycogen stores will be depleted at a slower rate.

Although we know much about the physiological responses to training programs in general, we are not as fortunate in knowing much about the training programs per se. Many researchers [11,12,14,15,22,37] have reported that general exercise programs of running, jogging, walking, and sports participation will increase the ability of a person to perform prolonged work as measured by mVO_2, blood lactate, and physical work capacity. However, the precise quality and quantity of the training stimulus necessary to achieve optimal improvements has generally been neglected although recent investigations [33,40,41,43,46] have attempted to shed some light on the problem. The qualitative and quantitative aspects of a training program can be altered or controlled by varying such factors as the intensity of, duration of, frequency of, or total work performed in each training session. In an attempt to determine which factors are the primary stimuli for improved endurance fitness, two studies [41,43] found that intensity of effort was the most important. However, in these studies the increased intensity given to a particular group contributed to a greater amount of work performed by that group and this greater amount of work (not necessarily the increased intensity) could have accounted for the measured improvements in aerobic capacity. Sharkey [40] equated the total absolute work performed by three training groups, working at different intensities, and reported no significant difference between the groups. However, the failure to equate groups on initial fitness level or giving the same absolute workload rather than the same relative workload to each subject could have led to the non-significant results.

A recent investigation [46] equated groups on initial fitness levels and total work performed and then varied the relative intensities and the duration of the work in the training program. The group which trained at 100 percent of their mVO_2 showed a significantly greater improvement in mVO_2 and physical work capacity than a group which trained a 60 percent of mVO_2 even though the work performed by the two groups was identical. However the responses at submaximal workloads between the two groups were not different. Roskamm [33] has substantiated the important role that the intensity of work in each training session plays in achieving optimal improvements in endurance fitness. He also equated groups on total work performed and then found that high intensity, interval type training elicited better improvement than low intensity, continuous work. Although the interval versus continuous format tends to confound the comparison of high and low intensity groups, the importance of intensity as a training stimulus was shown.

Åstrand and Rodahl [1] emphasize the importance of the overload principle in achieving maximal improvements in the oxygen transport system. The work of Karlsson *et al.*[28] illustrates how critical the intensity of effort is in overloading this oxygen transport system. While running at a speed of 22.75 Km/hr for 20 seconds then ten seconds' rest followed by running etc., the oxygen consumption became maximal whereas when running in an identical pattern at 22.0 km/hr the oxygen consumption was decreased to 90 percent of maximal. Thus with a very minor decrease in intensity of work the extent to which the oxygen transport system was taxed decreased by 10 percent.

Although a few researchers [21] did not find an increase in the level of aerobic enzyme activity with a particular training program, Holloszy [23] found this to be due to insufficient intensity in the training program. He increased the intensity of work and observed a two-fold increase in the capacity of certain mitochondrial (aerobic) enzymes to oxidize pyruvate. This further illustrates the importance of a sufficient level of intensity within a training program in order to increase the ability of the body to perform prolonged work.

Many researchers [15,22,31,39] have reported increases in mVO_2 of the magnitude of 10 to 20 percent with training, however there are examples of increases in aerobic capacity in excess of 30 percent.[11,29,30,46] It is very difficult to compare these variations in improvement because the training programs were, in most cases, not quantified. It would seem legitimate to assume that either discrepancies in the initial capacities of subjects or discrepancies in the intensity of the training stimulus could account for the differences.

The consensus at this time would seem to be that the intensity of work in each training session is the most important factor in achieving maximal improvements in endurance fitness. However, as Shephard [43] points out, the training program with the highest intensity of work, longest duration, and greatest frequency would be the ideal program for maximal gains. The relative importance of frequency, duration, total work and their relationship to initial fitness level still require further investigation. The necessity for further research is also apparent in the lack of information regarding the precise quantity of exercise necessary to produce a predetermined increase in endurance fitness. In order to obtain a training effect in the oxygen transport system, the system must be subjected to an overload. The rate of doing work (i.e. intensity) would seem to be the most productive method in overloading the system. If a reduction in stress to this system when performing submaximal workloads is the objective of the training program then long, slow, distance training is sufficient. If maximum performance of prolonged work is the objective, however, the intensity of work must be increased so that the anaerobic metabolic processes are overloaded as well. This would mean that it is necessary to train the anaerobic system in order to obtain maximal performance in endurance events.

REFERENCES

1. Åstrand, P. O., and Rodahl, K.: *Textbook of Work Physiology*, Toronto, McGraw-Hill, 1970.
2. Barnard, R. J., Foss, M. L., and Tipton, C. M.: The effect of training and various workloads on the lactacid-alactacid oxygen debt response of exercising dogs. *Int Z Angew Physiol*, 28:120–130, 1970.
3. Barnard, R. J., Edgerton, V. R., Peter, J. B.: Effect of exercise on skeletal muscle. I. Biochemical and histochemical properties. *J Appl Physiol*, 28:762–766, 1970.
4. ————: Effect of exercise on skeletal muscle. II. Contractile properties. *J Appl Physiol*, 28:767–770, 1970.
5. Barnard, R. J., and Peter, J. B.: Effect of exercise on skeletal muscle. III. Cytochrome changes. *J Appl Physiol*, 31:904–908, 1971.
6. Bergström, J., Hermansen, L., Hultman, E., and Saltin, B.: Diet, muscle glycogen and physical performance, *Acta Physiol Scand*, 71:140, 1967.
7. Carrow, R. E., Brown, R. E., and Van Huss, W. D.: Fiber sizes and capillary to fiber ratios in skeletal muscle of exercised rats. *Anat Rec*, 159:33, 1967.
8. Castenfors, J.: Renal function during exercise. *Acta Physiol Scand*, 70: Suppl. 1967.
9. Christensen, E. H., Hansen, O.: Arbeitsfähigkeit und Ehrnährung, *Scand Arch Physiol*, 81, 160, 1939.
10. Clausen, J. P.: Effects of physical conditioning: a review, *Scand J Clin Lab Invest*, 24:305–312, 1969.
11. Cureton, T. K., and Phillips, E. E.: Physical fitness changes in middle-aged men attributable to eight week periods of training, nontraining, and retraining. *J Sports Med Phys Fitness*, 4:1–7, 1964.
12. Davies, C. T., Tuxworth, W., and Young, J. M.: Physiological effects of repeated exercise. *Clin Sci*, 39:247–258, 1970.
13. Dill, D. B.: A longitudinal study of 16 champion runners. *J Sports Med*, 7:4–27, 1967.
14. Ekblom, B.: Effect of physical training on the oxygen transport system in man. *Acta Physiol Scand*, suppl. 328, 1969.
15. Ekblom, B., Åstrand, P. O., Saltin, B., Stenberg, J., and Wallstrom, B.: Effect of training on the circulatory response to exercise. *J Appl Physiol*, 24:518–528, 1968.

16. Elsner, R. W., and Carlson, L. D.: Postexercise hyperemia in trained and untrained subjects, *J Appl Physiol*, 17:436–440, 1962.

17. Faulkner, J. A.: New perspectives in training for maximum performance. *JAMA*, 205:741–746, 1968.

18. Gollnick, P. D.: Cellular adaptations to exercise. In Shepherd, R. J. (Ed.): *Frontiers of Fitness*. Springfield, Thomas, 1971.

19. Gollnick, P. D., and King, D. W.: Energy release in the muscle cell. *J Med Sci Sports*, 1:23–31, 1969.

20. ————: Effect of exercise and training on mitochondria of rat skeletal muscle. *Am J Physiol*, 216:1502–1509, 1969.

21. Gould, M. K., and Rawlinson, W. A.: Biochemical adaptation as a response to exercise. *Biochem J*, 73:41–44, 1959.

22. Hartley, L. H., Grimby, G., Kilborn, A., Nilsson, N., Åstrand, I., Bjure, J., Ekblom, B., and Saltin, B.: Physical training in sedentary middle-aged and older man. III. Cardiac output and gas exchange at submaximal and maximal exercise. *Scand J Clin Lab Invest*, 24:335–344, 1969.

23. Holloszy, J. O.: Effects of exercise on mitochondrial oxygen uptake and respiratory enzyme activity in skeletal muscle. *J Biol Chem*, 242:2278–2282, 1967.

24. Hultman, E.: Studies on muscle metabolism of glycogen and active phosphate in man with special reference to exercise and diet. *Scand J Clin Lab Invest*, Suppl. 94, 1967.

25. Hunter, W. M., and Sukkar, Y. Y.: Changes in plasma insulin levels during muscular exercise. *J Physiol*, 196:110, 1968.

26. Human, C.: The circulation of blood through skeletal muscle. *Pediatrics*, 32:671–676, 1963.

27. Jeffress, R. N., and Peter, J. B.: Adaptation of skeletal muscle to overloading, a review. *Bull Los Angeles Neurol Soc*, 35:134–144, 1970.

28. Karlsson, J., Astrand, P. O., and Ekblom, B.: Training the oxygen transport system in man. *J Appl Physiol*, 22:1061, 1967.

29. Naughton, J., and Balke, B.: Physical work capacity in medical personnel and the response of serum cholesterol to acute exercise and training. *Am J Med Sci*, 247:286–292, 1964.

30. Pollock, N. L., Cureton, T. K., and Greninger, M. S.: Effects of frequency of training on working capacity, cardiovascular function and body composition of adult men. *J Med Sci Sports*, 1:70–74, 1969.

31. Ribisl, P. M.: Effects of training upon the maximal oxygen uptake of middle aged men. *Int Z Angew Physiol*, 27:154–160, 1969.

32. Rodahl, K., Birkhead, N. C., Blizzard, J. J., Issekutz, B., Jr., and Pruett, E. D. R.: Physiological changes during prolonged bed rest. In: *Nutrition and Physical Activity*. Stockholm, Almquist and Wiksell, 1967.

33. Roskamm, H.: Optimum patterns of exercise for healthy adults. *Can Med Assoc J*, 96:895–898, 1967.

34. Roskamm, H., Reidell, H., and König, K.: *Körperliche Aktivitat und herzund Kreislaufer krankungen*. Munich, Johann Ambrosius Barth, 1966.

35. Rowell, L. B., Blackmon, J. R., and Bruce, P. A.: Indocyanine green clearance and estimated hepatic blood flow during mild to maximal exercise in upright man. *J Clin Invest*, 43:1677, 1964.

36. Saltin, B.: Physiological effects of physical conditioning. *J Med Sci Sports*, 1 (I): 50–56, 1969.

37. Saltin, B., Blomquist, G., Mitchell, J., Johnson, R., Wildenthal, K., and Chapman, C.: Response to exercise after bed rest and after training—a longitudinal study. *Circulation*, 38: suppl. VII, VII–I–78, 1968.

38. Saltin, B., and Åstrand, P. O.: Maximal oxygen uptake in athletes. *J Appl Physiol,* 23:353, 1967.
39. Saltin, B., Hartley, L. H., Kilborn, A., and Åstrand, I.: Physical training in sedentary middle-aged and older men, II. Oxygen uptake, heart rate, and blood lactate concentration at submaximal and maximal exercise. *Scand J Clin Lab Invest,* 24:323–334, 1969.
40. Sharkey, B. T.: Intensity and duration of training and the development of cardio respiratory endurance, *J Med Sci Sports,* 2 (4): 197–202, 1970.
41. Sharkey, B. T., and Holleman, J. P.: Cardio respiratory adaptations to training at specified intensities. *Res Q,* 38:698–704, 1967.
42. Shephard, R. J.: The development of cardio respiratory fitness. *Med Serv J Can,* 21:533–544, 1965.
43. ————: Intensity, duration and frequency of exercise as determinants of the response to a training regimen. *Int Z Angew Physiol,* 26:272–278, 1968.
44. ————: *Endurance Fitness.* Toronto: University of Toronto Press, 1969.
45. Sjostrand, T.: Functional capacity and exercise tolerance in patients with impaired cardiovascular function. In *Clinical Cardiopulmonary Physiology.* New York, Grane and Shattar, Inc., 1960.
46. Wenger, H. A.: Total work, intensity, and duration of a training program as determinants of endurance fitness. Unpublished Ph.D. thesis, Department of Physical Education, University of Alberta, Edmonton, 1971.
47. Williams, C. G., Wyndham, C. H., Kok, R., and von Rahden, M. J. E.: Effect of training on maximum oxygen uptake and on anaerobic metabolism in man. *Int Z Angew Physiol,* 24:18–23, 1967.
48. Wyndham, C. H.: Circulatory mechanism of anaerobic metabolism in working muscle. *S Afr Med J,* 39:1008–1014, 1965.

PART B

INTERVAL
TRAINING

CHAPTER III

INTERVAL TRAINING

FRANÇOIS PERONNET and RONALD J. FERGUSON

THE PURPOSE OF this chapter is to describe the physiological basis of intermittent work and to subsequently explain its practical utilization in the form of interval training. The mechanisms by which interval training might effect physiological adaptations are related to the acute and chronic stimulus of intermittent work. A knowledge of the energy sources for muscle cell contraction is a prerequisite for the understanding of intermittent work.

ENERGY SOURCES IN EXERCISE

Functional, Temporal and Quantitative Relationships

The immediate source of energy for the initiation and maintenance of muscular contraction is the hydrolysis of adenosine triphosphate (ATP) with a concomitant transfer of inorganic phosphate groups to the myofybrils.[8] The processes involved in supplying ATP for contraction are presented in schematic form in Figure III–1 and include adenosine diphosphate (ADP), creatine phosphate (CP), glycolysis, and the oxidation of pyruvate and free fatty acids in the mitochondria.

These processes are described in detail and by order of solicitation as functions of time (Fig. III–2a) from the onset of tension development to the maximum rate of the oxidation reactions.[17] The corresponding critical work rates (CWR),* defined as the maximum power able to be maintained

---

* According to Samson, Scherrer and Paleologue, in a given time period T, the quantity of energy (E) available for work can be expressed by the equation ($E = A + Bt$) where A represents the energy reserve capable of being mobilized in that period and B the quantity of energy delivered by the circulation per unit time t. With an efficiency R, the amount of work W performed in time T is $W = R (A + Bt)$ and power developed $P = \dfrac{a + bt}{T}$ ($a = RA$, $b = RB$). The total work performed is the limiting work (W lim) and the duration is the limiting time period (t lim). Therefore the critical work rate is given by the relation $CWR = \dfrac{W\ lim}{T\ lim}$ and is an hyperbolic function of time (Fig. III–2b).

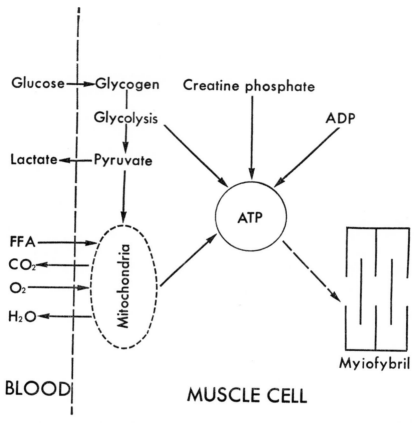

Figure III–1. Schematic diagram representing the cellular processes involved in the production of ATP for muscle contraction.

for a given time period leading to exhaustion, are shown in Figure III–2b. A verticle section at 15 sec indicates that creatine phosphate and anaerobic glycolysis are contributing equally to the total energy requirement and to a much greater extent than the oxidative reactions which are dependent on myoglobin and to the as yet insufficient supply of extra-muscular oxygen. Although the muscle ATP concentration is small (6 mM/kg muscle) and only represents an energy reserve of approximately 1.2 kcal, it is available within two seconds [17] and serves the energy required for short-term contractions (Fig. III–2b). ATP can be rapidly resynthetized in from one to five seconds by the hydrolysis of ADP (2 ADP → 1 ATP + 1 AMP) (17) and from the creatine phosphate (CP) stores (17 mM/kg muscle) [4] which constitute a reserve approximating 3.6 kcal. The former is of negligible importance. The latter (CP + ADP → ATP + C) is progressively utilized with time and becomes the principal energy supply for work of five to ten seconds duration.[17] With longer work times glucose or glycogen is degraded

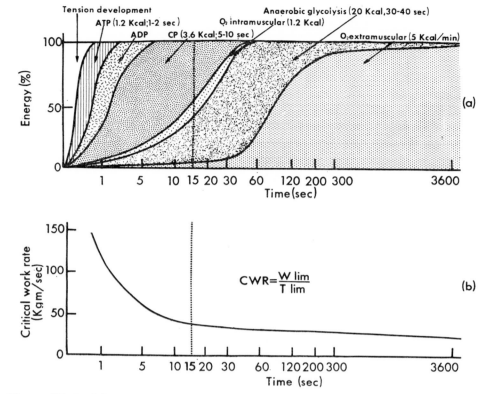

Figure III–2. (a) Estimated quantitative and temporal relationships among energy processes during muscular exercise as adapted from Keul.[17] For example, creatine phosphate (CP) is equivalent to 3.6 kcal and attains a maximum rate of utilization in 5 to 10 sec. (b) For a critical work rate (CWR) of 40 kgm/sec leading to exhaustion in 15 sec (vertical section) CP and anaerobic glycolysis are the major contributors to the total energy requirement.

to pyruvic acid via the glycolytic pathway with a respective generation of two or three molecules of ATP per six-carbon unit. Pyruvate is oxidized in the mitochondria with a further production of 36 molecules of ATP via the Krebs cycle and the electron transport system.[4] Utilizing oxygen dissolved in muscle tissue (50 ml) and linked to myoglobin (240 ml) (1,17) and considering oxygen supplied by the circulation to be negligible, this source would be equivalent to 1.5 kcal and be exhausted in about 30 seconds.

In heavy work, the production of pyruvic acid continues and reaches a peak around 30 to 40 seconds.[17] The rate of glycolysis surpasses the oxidative capacity of the mitochondria and the excess is reduced to lactic acid (LA). From 1 to 1.5 gm LA per kg body weight can be formed.[21,4] This could represent an additional 16.5 to 30 kcal available for muscular work, apart from the formation of ATP, brought about from a continuous supply of oxygen to the mitochondria via respiration and circulation. Normally aerobic and anaerobic glycolysis are taking place simultaneously. The highest rate of oxygen consumption (maximal aerobic power or $\dot{V}O_2$ max) can be reached within two to three minutes at critical work rates which can be maintained for a few minutes at the most. An individual with a $\dot{V}O_2$ max of 3.5 litres/min (17.5 kcal/min) can furnish energy at the rate of about 12 kcal/min for 1.5 to 2 hours if the work intensity is reduced to 70 percent of the maximum aerobic power.[25]

CONTINUOUS AND INTERMITTENT WORK

Mosso [10] in the late 19th century noted that the time to fatigue and total work done in index finger flexion varied with the contraction cadence and rhythm (i.e. where relaxation and contraction times varied). He con-

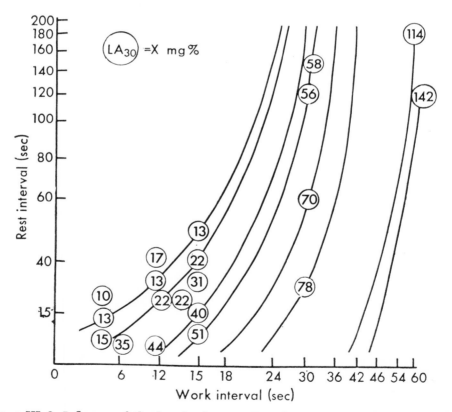

Figure III–3. Influence of the length of rest and work intervals on blood lactic acid values after 30 min intermittent work (LA₃₀). Values are taken from Christensen *et al.*[6] Astrand *et al.*[3]

cluded that better results were obtained with short periods of contraction and relaxation than when longer contraction periods were compensated for by increasing the duration of the rest pauses.

The effect of various combinations of work and rest intervals ranging from five to 180 seconds have been studied by Christensen *et al.*,[5,6] Astrand *et al.*,[2,3] Margaria *et al.*[22] and Fox *et al.*[12] They found that running and cycling with repeated extremely high work rates for short time periods, alternated with rest pauses, allows an individual to accomplish a considerable quantity of work for a prolonged period without fatigue.

Longer work intervals or continuous work of high intensity results in the accumulation of a high blood lactate concentration which is related to early fatigue and cessation of work.[1,2,3,6,22] Some results of Christensen *et al.*[6] and Åstrand *et al.*[3] are summarized in Figure III–3. Lactic acid values at the end of 30 minutes' intermittent work (LA_{30}) are indicated for various combinations of work (abscissa) and rest (ordinate) intervals. LA_{30} for comparable work rates and for several work to rest combinations are illustrated by the hypothetical "isolactacid" curves. For given rest intervals (e.g. 15 sec) LA_{30} increases with the length of the work interval. Con-

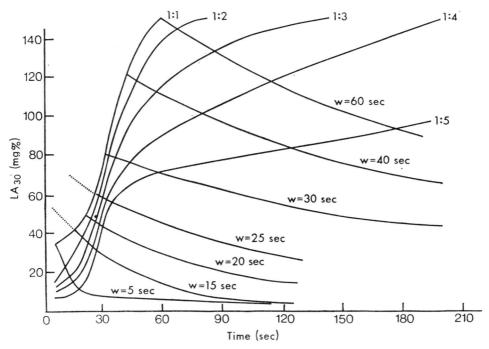

Figure III–4. Theoretical curves of lactic acid after 30 min intermittent work (LA_{30}). Ascending curves represent work to rest ratios of 1:1 to 1:5 (work interval read from abscissa). Descending curves illustrate the influence of the length of the rest intervals (read from abscissa) on LA_{30} for work intervals ranging from 5 to 60 sec.

versely for a given work interval (e.g. 15 sec) LA_{30} decreases with longer rest intervals.

The independent effects of the length of the work and the rest interval on LA_{30} are shown in Figure III–4 (curves constructed from Fig. III–3). The ascending curves of LA_{30} shift to the right as the ratio of work/rest intervals varies from 1:1 to 1:5 for any work interval read from the abscissa. On the other hand, LA_{30} values at any rest interval, read from the abscissa, are illustrated by the descending curves representing work intervals ranging from 5 to 60 seconds. The duration of the work interval is the more important determinant of LA_{30}. When it is less than 20 sec LA_{30} remains low. Work intervals of 60 sec result in high LA_{30} (e.g. 150 mg%) unless the rest interval is four to five times as long. LA_{30} rises steeply as the work interval increases from 20 to 60 seconds and appears to be maximum at about 30 seconds. If the work interval does not exceed 30 seconds LA_{30} would remain less than 80 mg% as long as the rest interval is at least as long as the work interval.

TRAINING

It is evident that continuous exercise can only be performed at a relatively low CWR (15 to 30 kgm/sec) the energy of which is assured by oxidative processes. Continuous prolonged work would specifically train the oxygen transport system. Muscular strength and speed are related, among other things, to ATP, CP and their related enzyme systems. Strength and speed would tend to respond to high intensity (90 to 100 kgm/sec) exercises of short duration (1 to 10 sec). Anaerobic endurance is related to the ability to produce and tolerate high levels of lactic acid during somewhat lower work rates (30 to 50 kgm/sec) lasting about one minute.

Whichever physiologic processes involved, the adaptation to training is also related to the intensity, frequency and total work accomplished. In spite of the high CWR developed during each exhaustive exercise of strength, speed and anaerobic endurance, the quantity of work performed is not large. In order for the total work to be an adequate training stimulus, the exercise must be repeated several times at each session. However, this is not intermittent work or interval training in the true physiologic sense, since each effort is performed to exhaustion or by definition cannot be prolonged at that intensity (e.g. maximum weight lift). Therefore, it is work which is *necessarily* intermittent since the work time (t_{lim}) depends uniquely on the CWR or the interruptions are inevitable, or the exercise cannot be repeated until the subject has recuperated. On the other hand, in *voluntary* intermittent work, such as interval training, the work time is not completely dependent on the work rate.

Short Interval Training

Short duration intermittent work ($\leqslant$ 30 sec) is probably accomplished by the alternate utilization and restoration of the muscle's reserves of creatine phosphate, ATP and oxygen. This reconstitution of energy reserves was noted by Margaria [20] as the rapidly decreasing portion of the recovery oxygen curve, and was termed the "alactacid oxygen debt." Early studies of intermittent work by Christensen *et al.*[5,6] and Åstrand *et al.*[2,3] showed that high work rates of short duration could be repeated with relatively low LA values. They attributed their findings to the alternate depletion and reconstitution of the muscle's oxygen store (myoglobin) and calculated oxygen reserves equivalent to 430 ml. However, data of Bjork [3] as well as more recent evidence [1] indicate that muscle myoglobin would account for a maximum of 240 ml of oxygen. From the rate of decline of the first portion of the recovery oxygen curve, Margaria [22] estimated that 25 sec would be the half repayment time of the "alactacid debt." He concluded that rest periods of 25 sec would be sufficient to resynthesize the reserves of ATP and CP after short (e.g. 10 sec) bouts of supramaximal work. However, this hypothesis was not supported by the data of Saltin and Essen.[26] Fox *et al.*,[12] using the basic assumptions of Margaria, compared supramaximal short intermittent work to continuous work with respect to the relative contribution of the various energy sources. In addition to low LA values, there is also little change in the arterial glucose level [18] during short intermittent work. These data indicate the major role of the energy reserves immediately available and the minor importance of anaerobic glycolysis in this type of work. Besides being a stimulus to the training of speed and strength, it appears that the avoidance of high LA levels, when repetitively performing very high work rates, may also be a stimulus to the oxygen transport system. As previously mentioned, the work rate in short intermittent work can be considerably higher than in continuous work.

The mechanisms for an improved aerobic capacity with training include increases in cardiac output and a widening of the arteriovenous oxygen difference.[24] Increases in the mitochondrial protein content and oxidative enzyme activity have also been implicated.[15] It was originally hypothesized [14,23,27] that short interval training resulted in a specific stimulus to the myocardium secondary to an elevated stroke volume at the onset of each rest interval. Cumming [7] has reported elevated postexercise stroke volumes as measured by dye-dilution curves. These data support the hypothesis of Reindell *et al.*[23] that an elevated stroke volume in the rest intervals, secondary to a rapidly decreasing heart rate and temporarily sustained venous return, would be the stimulus for myocardial hypertrophy. The above mentioned data was obtained in the supine position and it is not known if the conclusions can be applied to the athlete working in the upright position.[5,7]

Reindell *et al.*[23] and Gerschler [14] several years ago recommended that runners perform repeat intervals at 100 or 200 meters and never longer than 400 meters. Knuttgen *et al.*[19] demonstrated a 15 percent increase in the aerobic capacity of young adults after two months of training using 15 sec work/15 sec rest intervals. This was compared to a 23 percent increase in a similar group performing 3 min work/3 min rest interval training. On the other hand, Fox *et al.*[13] obtained increases in aerobic capacity of nine and seven percent with students following short interval (mean 19 sec) and long interval (mean 154 sec) training respectively. Reindell *et al.* reported myocardial hypertrophy, as evidence by increases in the cardiac volumes of athletes submitted to intense short interval training. An increase in the maximum oxygen-pulse was also reported.

Long Interval Training

As previously mentioned, short intermittent work involves little anaerobic glycolysis. Track (long sprints to middle and long distance) and many team sport athletes who require relatively high aerobic capacities also require the ability to produce and tolerate high levels of LA (anaerobic glycolysis) during sprints at the end of a race or during intermittent high levels of work (e.g. hockey). This anaerobic endurance which would also allow the athlete to utilize a high aerobic capacity for longer periods would not be developed in short interval training.

As the work interval becomes longer more energy is furnished by anaerobic glycolysis and higher levels of LA are produced. With work intervals of two to four minutes duration (work rate lower than that used in Fig. III–3) oxidative reactions can be near maximum.[6] This is evidenced by the high oxygen consumption, heart rate and arterio-femoral-venous oxygen difference observed.[18] The rest pauses allow for the reconstitution of the immediate energy reserves and for partial removal of the previously produced lactic acid. Ferguson *et al.*[11] found 12 percent increases in the aerobic capacities of each of two groups submitted to eight weeks of continuous and long interval (3 min work/1 min rest) training, the total work time and average heart rates during the training sessions were equal for both groups. However, the work rate in long interval training can be higher than during continuous prolonged exercise since the anaerobic processes are also utilized in each work interval. The total work accomplished is then greater despite the elevated LA level. The utilization of this form of interval training should be a stimulus for the simultaneous improvement of aerobic (maximal oxygen consumption) and anaerobic (production and tolerance of lactic acid) endurance.

Implications for Training Programs

Despite the necessity to emphasize the training of specific energy processes, skills and movement patterns, varying the modalities within a training program is probably desirable. Although few systematic studies of interval training relating energy sources to specific sport activities are available, it is possible to relate short- and long-term interval training to these activities (Fig. III–5). Short interval and prolonged continuous exercise appear to be advisable for aerobic endurance events (e.g. cross-country skiing). Short interval and specific exercises of speed and strength would be applicable to activities such as sprinting. Long interval training

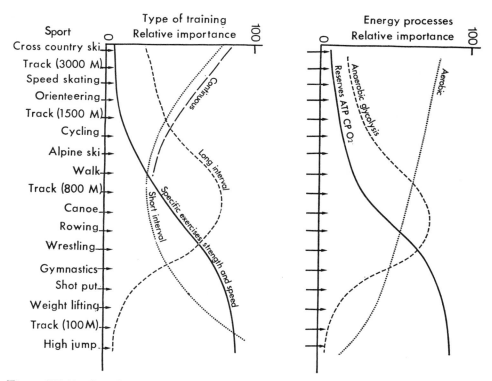

Figure III–5. The relative importance of specific energy processes and type of training with respect to various sport activities.

is most suitable to middle distance events combining the qualities of aerobic and anaerobic endurance (e.g. track, 800 m).

Interval training is therefore a process which is characterized by the use of voluntary intermittent work. The interruption of the work at a predetermined interval prior to exhaustion avoids the depletion of specific energy reserves. The rest periods allow for their reconstitution and fatigue is retarded. Under these conditions more work is accomplished for a work rate which would rapidly bring about fatigue in continuous work.

REFERENCES

1. Akeson, A., Bjork, G., and Simon, R.: On the content of myoglobin in human muscles. *Acta Med Scand, 133:*37, 1968.
2. Åstrand, I., Åstrand, P. O., Christensen, E. H., and Hedman, R.: Intermittent muscular work. *Acta Physiol Scand, 48:*448, 1959.
3. ————: Myoglobin as an oxygen-store in man. *Acta Physiol Scand, 48:*454, 1960.
4. Åstrand, P. O. and Rodahl, K.: *Textbook of Work Physiology.* New York, McGraw-Hill Book Co., 1970.
5. Christensen, E. H., Hedman, R., and Holmdahl, I.: The influence of rest pauses on mechanical efficiency. *Acta Physiol Scand, 48:*443, 1960.
6. Christensen, E. H., Hedman, R., and Saltin, B.: Intermittent and continuous running. *Acta Physiol Scand, 50:*269, 1960.
7. Cumming, G. R.: Stroke volume during recovery from supine bicycle exercise. *J Appl Physiol, 32:*575, 1972.
8. Davies, R. E.: A molecular theory of muscle contraction: calcium dependent contractions with hydrogen bond formation plus ATP-dependent extension of part of the myosin actin cross bridges. *Nature, 199:*1068, 1963.
9. Edwards, R. H. T., Melcher, A., Messer, C. M., and Wigertz, O.: Blood lactate concentrations during intermittent and continuous exercise with the same average power output. In Taylor, A. W.: *Muscle Metabolism During Exercise.* New York, Plenum Press, 1971, p. 425.
10. Fabre, R., and Rougier, G.: *Physiologie Médicale.* Paris, Maloine, 1963, p. 1016.
11. Ferguson, R. J., Montpetit, R., Dubuc, R., and Gingras, Y.: L'entraînement du système de transport d'oxygène par la course continue et par intervalles. *Kinanthropologie, 2:*171, 1970.
12. Fox, E. L., Robinson, S., and Wiegman, D. L.: Metabolic energy sources during continuous and interval running. *J Appl Physiol, 27:*174, 1969.
13. Fox, E. L., Bartels, R. L., Billings, C. E., Matthews, D. K., Bason, R., and Webb, W. M.: Intensity and distance of interval training programs and changes in aerobic power. *Med Sci Sports, 1:*18, 1973.
14. Gerschler, W.: Interval training. *Rev Edu Phys, 2:*99, 1962.
15. Gollnick, P. D., Ianuzzo, C. D., and King, D. W.: Ultrastructure and enzyme changes in muscles with exercise. In *Muscle Metabolism During Exercise.* New York, Plenum Press, 1971, p. 69.
16. Kayser, C.: Physiologie, Tome II. Système nerveux et muscle. Paris, Editions Médicales Flammarion *1963:*1017, 1963.
17. Keul, J., Doll, E., Keppler, D.: *Energy Metabolism of Human Muscle.* Basel, S. Karger AG, 1969.
18. Keul, J., and Doll, E.: Intermittent exercise: metabolites, PO_2 and acid-base equilibrium in the blood. *J Appl Physiol, 2:*220, 1973.
19. Knuttgen, H. G., Ollander, B., Nordesjo, L. O., and Saltin, B.: Interval training and physical fitness of young male adults. *Med Sci Sports, 1:*59, 1972.
20. Margaria, R., Edwards, H. T., and Dill, D. B.: The possible mechanism of contracting and paying the oxygen debt and the role of lactic acid in muscular contraction. *Am J Physiol, 106:*689, 1933.

21. Margaria, R.: Energy source for aerobic and anaerobic work. In Margaria, R. (Ed.): *Exercise at Altitude*. Amsterdam, 1967, p. 15.

22. Margaria, R., Oliva, R. D., Diprampero, P. E., and Cerretelli, P.: Energy utilization in intermittent exercise of supramaximal intensity. *J Appl Physiol, 6:*752, 1969.

23. Reindell, H., Roskamm, H., and Gerschler, W.: L'entraînement par intervalles ou interval training. No de diffusion 152, Institut National des Sports et Centre de Documentation et de Recherche de l'ENCEPS, Paris.

24. Saltin, B.: Physiological effects of physical conditioning. *Med Sci Sports, 1:*50, 1969.

25. Saltin, B., and Karlsson, J.: Muscle glycogen utilization during work of different intensities. In *Muscle Metabolism During Exercise*. New York, Plenum Press, 1971, p. 289.

26. Saltin, B., and Essen, B.: Muscle glycogen, lactate, ATP and CP in intermittent exercise. In *Muscle Metabolism During Exercise*. New York: Plenum Press, 1971, p. 419.

27. Veyssieres, A., Gastaud, M., and Ardisson, J. L.: Les effets physiologiques de l'entraînement intermittent. *Cahiers Sci l'Ed Phys, 2:*3, 1970.

PART C

REHABILITATIVE TRAINING

CHAPTER IV

THE REHABILITATION AND RECONDITIONING OF ATHLETES FOLLOWING AN INJURY OR ILLNESS

S. W. MENDRYK

THE REHABILATATIVE PROCESS and therapeutic techniques and procedures utilized in the treatment of an athlete initially following the onset of an injury does not differ significantly from those employed with nonathletes from the general population. The period of recuperation from injuries of athletes and nonathletes, provided the extent and severity of tissue, organ and systemic damage is similar, also does not differ appreciably. It is important to realize, however, that the athlete is being rehabilitated for re-entry into a particular sport or athletic activity which usually makes a much greater demand of the cardiovascular, skeletal and muscular systems than the nonathlete from a generally more sedentary population. Furthermore, the forces and stresses encountered by athletes, especially in so-called contact activities, are usually much greater than the average patient is likely to encounter at the conclusion of a successful rehabilitative program. Thus, if a totally adequate rehabilitative program is to be devised for the athlete then there is a need for cooperation and an interplay of knowledge of the role and functions of the team doctor, physical therapist and athletic trainer, and physical educator or coach.

It is essential that individuals concerned with the rehabilitation of athletes be cognizant of the need for the total rehabilitation of the individual rather than the desireable but limited objective of returning an injured segment or part of the body to the normal or preinjury status. This is particularly the case when the training program of an athlete is interrupted as even relatively short periods of inactivity can bring about undesirable changes in strength and endurance of areas or parts of the body unaffected by injury and especially in the level of cardiovascular fitness required for specific activities.

The primary purpose of a rehabilitative or reconditioning program is to restore the normal functions in the performance of a game, sport, athletic or physical activity that were attained by an athlete prior to an injury. The restoration of a previously obtained level of performance is achieved by the development of strength, and muscular endurance, flexibility, power and skill. One or more of these elements serves as the fundamental bases of a reconditioning program and can be medically prescribed either for a specific or general purpose. Kraus [5] has described a therapeutic exercise as "a movement prescribed and performed in proper form, and aimed at the development of a given muscle quality or qualities." However, even though a therapeutic exercise in a rehabilitative program can and usually is prescribed with a specific purpose in mind, exercises which are aimed at general body conditioning can also be termed therapeutic. Instruction as to form, execution and dosage of exercise is medically prescribed for either a specific or general purpose.

THE ROLE OF THE PHYSICIAN PARAMEDICAL PERSONNEL AND ATHLETIC SPECIALIST IN THE REHABILITATION AND RECONDITIONING PROCESS

It is strongly recommended that a thorough medical evaluation and assessment of injury received by an athlete be made by a qualified sports physician prior to initiating a therapy and physical reconditioning program. The sports physician will determine the nature and extent of injury from a medical observation of the amount of swelling, discoloration, temperature, localized pain, and irregular or abnormal joint or body segment alignment and contour. The prescription and supervision of therapeutic modalities and a physical therapy program is the sole responsibility of a qualified sports physician, physiatrist, or orthopedic physician. The physical reconditioning program is administered by paramedical personnel such as a physical therapist, athletic therapist, accredited athletic trainer or physical educator specially trained in corrective and adaptive physical education. The athletic specialist is responsible for implementing and conducting a specific conditioning program to prepare an athlete for reentry into active sports or athletic participation. The athletic specialist in this phase of the program attempts to redevelop strength and muscular endurance, power, flexibility, and cardiovascular endurance as utilized for a specific sport or athletic activity or event. The athlete is retrained for a particular sport, athletic activity or event. The specific training program for a particular sport or athletic event should only be initiated upon the approval of a medical practitioner. In certain instances medical practitioners may approve a specific sports training program concurrently with the physical therapy program that normally precedes the specific conditioning program. The following diagram briefly outlines the functions of medical, paramedical and athletic specialists in evaluation, treatment and rehabilitation of an injury.

PERSONNEL	FUNCTION
Medical Practitioner	
Team Physician	Diagnosis, Prescription and Supervision of Treatment and Medications
Orthopedic Surgeon	
Physiatrist	
Paramedical	
Physical Therapist	Administration and Implementation of Treatment Prescribed by Medical Practitioners
Athletic Trainer	
Specialist in Corrective Adaptive Physical Education	
Athletic Specialist	
Physical Educator	Administration and Implementation of a Training and Conditioning Program for a Particular Athletic or Sports Activity or Event.
Coach	
Athletic Trainer	

BASIC ELEMENTS OF THE REHABILITATIVE PROGRAM

Muscular Strength and Endurance

One of the commonly observable outcomes of an injury or debilitating disease is that of muscular atrophy resulting from disuse of the body or one of its segments or parts. There is a lessening in the circumference and mass of muscular tissue. Abramson and Delage [1] have stated that prolonged immobilization of the skeleton leads to bone atrophy and that weight-bearing and normal activity that involves muscular contraction with concomitant pull on the attachments to the bone prevents atrophy of the bone. Other tissues such as tendons and ligaments associated with muscular function also tend to be adversely affected as a result of inactivity. It is apparent, that the maintenance of strength in uninjured body regions or the redevelopment of strength of injured or disused areas of the body is a primary objective of the rehabilitation program.

Muscular strength from an operational point of view refers to the maximum amount of contractile force of a particular muscle group in a single contractile effort. Of equal importance in the rehabilitation program is the development of muscular endurance which can be defined as the ability of muscles to perform work over a prolonged period of time. Two forms of muscular endurance are recognized, isometric and isotonic. In the isometric form, a maximum static muscular contraction is held and the muscles maintain a fixed length. In the isotonic form, the muscles continuously move a submaximal load so that they alternately shorten and lengthen. Although muscular strength and muscular endurance are discrete and separate elements, they are usually developed concomitantly in rehabilitative programs. Nevertheless, it should be remembered that muscle groups of the same strength may possess different degrees of endurance and thus the measurement of maximal strength in an individual is not necessarily predicative of muscular endurance in the same individual. The development of muscular endurance, however, does depend upon a level of muscular strength. Muscular strength is a prerequisite to muscular endurance.

Circulatory-Respiratory Endurance

Circulatory-respiratory endurance may be defined as the ability of the circulatory-respiratory systems to function effectively in prolonged physical activity. The process of improving circulatory-respiratory endurance is commonly termed "training." Training is a complex physiological phenomena that involves the efficiency of the respiratory or breathing apparatus, the ability of the heart and circulatory system to circulate blood, degree of vascularization of musles that makes fuel and oxygen available for the muscle contraction processes and the ability to ignore the discomforts associated with fatigue. Although the exact physiological mechanisms for training are not yet fully understood, it is known that vigorous muscular activity produces marked changes in the efficiency of the body known as endurance and that endurance is highly task-specific. Therefore, it is advisable to devise circulatory-respiratory programs that duplicate or simulate as much as possible the conditions that are likely to be encountered in a particular game, sport or physical activity. Obviously, such programs devised for rehabilitating and reconditioning athletes after an illness or injury should be geared to the disability and exercise tolerance of the individual.

Flexibility

The joints of the body are held together by muscles, tendons, ligaments and connective tissue. The range of movement of the joints is termed flexibility. The term implies extension as well as flexion and also includes other movements which are normally possible. Immobilization and inactivity of a joint results in a loss of flexibility of a joint due to an adaptive shortening of connective tissue in the vicinity of the joint. One of the primary purposes of a rehabilitative program is to restore the complete range of joint motion or mobility. This purpose is achieved either by passive manipulation or by graded voluntary muscular movement that in progressive stages over a period of time stretches the muscles, tendons, ligaments and connective tissue that surrounds a joint. The degree of flexibility required for performance varies from one athletic activity to another. Similarly flexibility of a joint or body segment may vary considerably to another joint or body segment in the same individual.[8] Unless contraindicated by a medical advisor it is generally desireable to restore the range of movement normally found in a specific joint or body segment prior to injury or immobilization.

REHABILITATIVE PHYSICAL THERAPY PROGRAM

The principles of rehabilitative exercise based on sound physiological principles were espoused by Duchenne[3] more than 100 years. Physical therapy programs utilizing exercise are generally classified into four major categories: passive, active-assistive, active and resistive.

Passive exercise involves the movement of body segments or parts by the therapist with no active contraction of involved muscles by the patient. The purpose of this phase of exercise program is to maintain ranges of joint motion, to prevent the development of contractures, and to prepare the patient for the active-assistive stage that follows.

The active-assistive stage involves active contraction of muscles by the patient with the assistance of the therapist. The aim of this phase of the program is to restore nervous system function, to activate the sensory-motor system and to utilize postural-reflex mechanisms.

The third category, the active exercise phase, involves the active participation of the patient without therapist assistance. The exercises are prescribed by a physician and are aimed at simulating or duplicating movements that are necessary for daily living or for vocational preparation.

The last phase involves active participation by the patient against a resistive force which can be applied by the therapist or by specially designed resistance equipment or apparatus. One of the most frequently utilized methods for treating injured athletes has been developed by Delorme.[2] Delorme's method is a form of progressive resistive exercise that attempts to increase muscular strength, muscular endurance and power of a body part or segment. Klafs and Arnheim,[4] present a concise review of physical rehabilitative exercises for various body regions.

It is apparent that the physical rehabilitation exercise program is a continuum along which the injured athlete moves from the onset of injury until restoration of normal capacity and function. In most instances rehabilitative exercises of athletes is largely confined to the active and es-

pecially the resistive categories of treatment. The active or resistive phases
can be combined and run concurrently with a training and conditioning
program for a specific activity if prescribed by the sports physician.

RECONDITIONING AND RETRAINING FOR A SPECIFIC ACTIVITY

The program of reconditioning and preparing for a specific activity
after the completion of a successful physical therapy and training program
for a specific activity usually falls within the scope of the coach or physical
educator. It is the coach or physical educator who has knowledge and technical expertise relating to the development or reattainment of skills and
performance, and to the specific structural and physiological demands to
be encountered by the athlete in the activity. Although exercises prescribed by the medical practioner are designed to strengthen and recondi-
tion weak muscles, joints, segments or parts of the body in a general manner, an exercise program that is specific to the task, event, or activity is the
best method of preparing for performance for a particular task, event or
activity. Morehouse and Rasch [7] have stated "each athletic event makes
specific demands in terms of its pattern of load, rate, repetition and duration. The neurophysiological adjustments to these demands are also specific." Thus, it is important to remember that this phase of the program
should attempt to duplicate or simulate the neurophysiological patterns to
be encountered in the performance of a specific task, event or activity.

It is also important to remember that standardized methods and procedures used to assess general physical fitness, strength, and endurance,
although desirable in motivating athletes, do not necessarily prepare the
individual for the specific demands to be encountered in an activity. For
example, it is common knowledge that a comprehensive reconditioning
program designed to strengthen the muscle groups that result in knee
stability is only the first phase of the reconditioning program. The athlete
must also be exposed to the stresses and forces to be encountered in running in an activity such as football in gradual and a progressive manner in
regard to the load and intensity of specific game and practice exercises and
drills. Symptoms of pain, tenderness or swelling in a body part that has
recently been reconditioned signifies the need for caution and perhaps a
reevaluation of the athlete's capacity to perform. The athlete must not
exceed his capacity to perform at any time throughout the therapy or reconditioning program otherwise he is likely to be reinjured. A recent
study [6] has shown that one of approximately five players returning to football competition after a therapy and reconditioning program has reinjured
the same body area or part indicating that the therapy and reconditioning
program is either inadequate or incomplete.

Lastly, the athletic specialist should be cognizant of the fact that inactivity resulting from the curtailment of a training program due to an injury may bring about undesirable changes in skill relating to performance in an activity and as a consequence detrimentally affect the confidence of an athlete even though there has been a complete restoration of previously attained strength and physical status. The reattainment of an acceptible skill performance level after an injury contributes to a feeling of self-confidence and self-sufficiency of an athlete and assists the athlete in overcoming a fear of inadequate performance or a fear of reinjury that may exist.

In summary, there are three phases in the process of rehabilitating and reconditioning athletes following an injury or illness. Firstly, is prompt medical diagnosis and prescribed treatment of an injury or pathological condition. The second phase involves the implementation of a medically prescribed therapy program by the paramedical specialist. Generally, the longer the period of inactivity and immobilization the greater the need for rehabilitation and the more prolonged is the period of the therapy program. The third phase of the process focuses on the utilization of specific exercises and activities that closely approximate or duplicate those conditions encountered by the athlete upon reparticipation in a game, sport, athletic or physical activity. The athletic specialist alters and adjusts the load, intensity, and duration of the exercises and physical activities in a manner that does not exceed the tolerance and performance level of the athlete at any time during the specific activity reconditioning period.

REFERENCES

1. Abramson, Arthur, S., and Delagi, Edward F.: The contributions of physical activity to rehabilitation. *Res Q, 33* (2):365, 1960.
2. DeLorme, L. L.: Restoration of muscle power by heavy resistance exercises. *J Bone Joint Surg, 27*:645, 1945.
3. Duchenne, G. B.: *Physiology of Motion,* Translated and edited by E. B. Kaplan. Philadelphia, J. B. Lippincott Company, 1949.
4. Klafs, Carl E., and Arnheim, Daniel D.: *Modern Principles of Athletic Training.* St. Louis, C. V. Mosby, 1969.
5. Kraus, Hans: *Therapeutic Exercises.* Springfield, Thomas, 1949.
6. Mendryk, Stephen W., and Dufresne, Lawrence W.: Implications of the Incidence, Nature and Causes of Football Injuries for Coaches and School Administrators. Presented at the Research Section Meeting C.A.H.P.E.R. Convention, Waterloo, Ontario, June 6, 1971.
7. Morehouse, L. L., and Rasch, Philip J.: *Sports Medicine for Trainers.* Philadelphia, Saunders, 1964.
8. Sigerseth, Peter O.: Flexibility. In Larson, L. (Ed.): *Encyclopedia of Sports Sciences and Medicine.* New York, The MacMillan Company, 1971.

CHAPTER V

SELECTED PROBLEMS OF THE THIGH AND KNEE TO ILLUSTRATE SOME BASIC TECHNIQUES OF REHABILITATION

DAVID C. REID and RAYMOND KELLY

MANAGEMENT OF TRAUMA to the musculoskeletal system is too large a topic to be dealt with in a single chapter. Any attempt to do so would be a series of half truths and misleading statements. There are, however, several basic principles of treatment that can be discussed. Examining data collected over the last few years indicates that shoulder, ankle and knee problems are the major injuries occurring in most sports. Consider for a moment the latter of these three regions.

The human knee is remarkable in its ability to encompass the two seemingly incompatible properties of stability and mobility and in order to accomplish this many subtle anatomic mechanisms are necessary. Therefore, it is not surprising that knee injuries comprise a great proportion of the problems that present themselves at any athletic clinic. Furthermore, the ability to deal intelligently with knee problems is usually concomitant with the ability to treat other areas successfully. For these reasons the authors will use some selected problems of the thigh and knee to illustrate some basic principle of rehabilitation. Drug therapy and indications for surgery will not be discussed since this is the province of textbooks on medicine.

Factors Related to Stability of the Knee Joint

The stability of the knee joint is particularly dependent on the strength of the surrounding muscle groups and their fascial expansions.[22] In the past the great emphasis in any reeducation program for posttraumatic and postsurgical knees has been strengthening of the quadriceps group. Unfortunately this is often to the exclusion of hamstring work. It is the authors' firm belief that for stability of the knee and reeducation in a minimum of time, equal attention can and must be given to the hamstring group. What is more, it is becoming evident from some of the recent work that muscle imbalance may be a major contributing factor in recurrent muscle tears.[38] This applies equally for the quadriceps, hamstrings and adductor groups.

On the medial side of the knee the stabilizing action of the quadriceps is through the medial quadriceps expansion. This passes in an inferior and posterior direction and mingles with the fascia of the leg and with the tibial collateral ligament. Greenhill, through observation at surgery and on cadavers, concluded that in addition to some rotation force these expansions will exert an active stabilizing effect.[12,22] This is not only by their direct attachment to the tibia but also by adjusting the tension of the medial ligament. Stability is further enhanced by the fibrous expansions of the medial hamstrings, along with that from sartorius which form a band of tissue referred to as the pes anserinus.

On the lateral side of the knee the lateral quadriceps expansion blends with the fibers of the iliotibial tract (fascia lata). This is further reinforced by fibers from biceps femoris giving similar reinforcement to the lateral joint structure as the previously discussed contractile elements give to the medial side of the knee joint.[27]

Joint Position in Relation to Exercise

Much controversy exists over the most effective range in which to give isotonic muscle work for any particular group following trauma or surgery to the joint over which they work. Also there are many different opinions as to the best position for isometric work. Leverage principles, cross sectional area, and length-tension properties of muscle groups are responsible for the change in force throughout the range of motion. However the muscle power developed over a joint is also related to the joint stability in any particular part of the range. The knee extensors for instance usually develop their greatest power at an angle of 60° while the knee flexors peak at 10° and again at 45° of flexion. There is, of course, considerable individual variation. Soft tissue injuries do not influence these angles of greatest power. The weakest force is generated by the quadriceps at 30° of flexion and the weakest hamstring pull is at 110° of flexion.[37,16,50,51] (Fig. V–1)

The obvious conclusion would be that resistance should be applied in a midrange to coincide with the angles of greatest strength. In addition, where pain is present due to synovial effusion or intracapsular haemorrhage, the midrange represents the position of least intra-articular pressure and hence the most comfortable position.[19,41] Contrary to this, it is common practice to exercise the knee extensors through the last 30° of extension, their range of least strength. As Brewerton points out, many therapists require the patient to work his quadriceps maximally when the weight aim and load are greatest, but the extensor mechanism least efficient.[14]

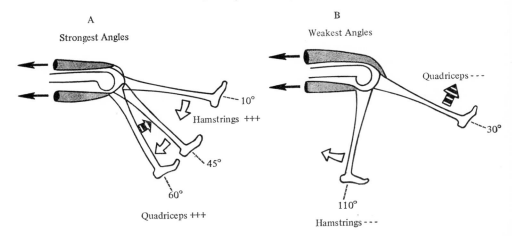

A
Strongest Angles

B
Weakest Angles

Figure V–1. A illustrates the angles at which the greatest strength may be developed by the quadriceps and the hamstring groups. B shows the angles of least strength.

In any event the cardinal rule is to exercise the limb in the least painful position. This not only gives maximal improvement in strength, but presents less danger of "flaring" up an acute synovitis. This holds true for all synovial joints. A recent experiment by Gough and Ladley on the effectiveness of different foot positions on the quadriceps contraction in both normal and post-meniscectomy patients indicated that the strength of contraction was consistently enhanced when the foot was held in the dorsiflexed position.[21] This held true for several types of quadriceps exercises. The position of inversion and eversion seems much less consistent and significant in its effect on strength of contraction.[4,5]

Reflex Inhibition

Following surgery to a joint muscle atrophy is often noticed despite prompt restitution of movement.[35] This may be further complicated by a reflex inhibition of these groups.[17] The quadriceps femoris are the most frequent examples of this phenomenon. Frank synovial effusion and joint distention gives a marked reduction of electromyographic activity in the quadriceps; however, reflex inhibition is a noncomplicated phenomenon in which pain induces voluntary as well as reflex inhibition leading to neurotrophic atrophy. Muscle atrophy is rapidly apparent and loss of strength throughout the range is accentuated by the inability to complete the last few degrees of extension or to lock the knee. In severe cases no voluntary contraction of the muscle is possible. This type of inability to complete extension is referred to as "quads lag" and has been constantly referred to in the literature as a specific inability of vastus medialis to complete the rotation component of the last few degrees.[3,23,28] However, the authors feel that the only selective function of vastus medialis over and above that of producing extension, is patella alignment, counteracting the tendency of vastus lateralis to laterally dislocate the patella.[15] Early loss and atrophy of the vastus prominence is more readily noticed in vastus medialis because of the lowness of insertion, the obliquity of fibres and the thinness of the fascial covering of that part of the leg.[34,35] As has been seen, the quadriceps as a whole exert poor leverage over the last 15° to 20° of extension and a 60 percent increase in power is required to complete the movement.[8,10,16] One must also bear in mind that in accordance to physiologic laws the power of a muscle decreases as it becomes shortened past its midrange. Isometric muscle work is usually sufficient to limit the amount of atrophy until the condition of the knee is such that more vigorous isotonic work can be begun. With severe reflex inhibition quadriceps contraction must be initiated with faradic impulses which is used concurrently with voluntary effort. There are several texts that give detailed accounts of this technique.[33,46]

Functional Strapping for Rotatory Instability

Many of the joints of the body lend themselves to a supportive type of strapping, which can vary from a light reinforcement limiting one aspect of range, to a heavy strapping which is tantamount to a plaster cast. By contrast very little restriction can be placed on the knee before performance is seriously hindered. It is therefore necessary to consider a functional type of strapping. A large number of different techniques are described in the literature which probably indicates the lack of a uniformly good method.[9,24] The procedure to be described is the authors' modification of a technique first described by Biggs [9] and is used to counteract instability of the medial compartment of the knee joint. The rationale for its use only becomes clear when one considers the underlying joint structures and the changes leading up to rotatory instability.

Rotatory instability, as it was first described by Slocum,[47] may be considered as increased lateral rotation of the tibia on the femur. Clinically the patient complains of a feeling of "giving way" on cutting and turning.[20,47] The initial injury and subsequent instability, are elicited during running when the foot is planted with the heel cleats fixed and the athlete pivots on the partially flexed knee. The authors suggest that since the foot is usually fixed the instability could be regarded as a medial rotation of the femur on the tibial condyles.

There is usually about 20° of medial rotation of the femoral condyles on the tibial condyles at the knee when the tibia is fixed and the knee is partially flexed. Tearing of the structures that normally limit this rotation will lead to rotatory instability.[40,47] These structures are (1) the deep portion of the tibial collateral ligament (middle section of the capsule), (2) the superficial fibers of the tibial collateral ligament, (3) the anterior cruciate ligament, (4) the vastus medialis through its action on the medial portion of the extensor mechanism, (5) and the medial meniscus being squeezed between the medial femoral and tibial condyles at the extremes of rotation. [2,11,13,25,47] It has been shown that as the rotational stress increases past the limit of range there is a serial tearing of first the deep fibers of the tibial collateral ligaments then the superficial fibres of the medial collateral ligament and finally the anterior cruciate ligament. All these events occur correspondingly earlier if an adduction stress is combined with rotation [47] (Fig. V–2). Frequently the degree of stress that is necessary to produce tearing of the cruciate ligaments will also damage the menisci. This combination of tibial collateral ligament tear, anterior cruciate ligament tear and medial meniscus damage is in fact the well known triad described by Abbott in 1944.[2]

The support to be described should not impede the normal function of the knee to such a degree that the athlete is placed in danger of further injury due to his lack of mobility. If he requires more than the spiral support for the medial ligament then the underlying structures are too severely

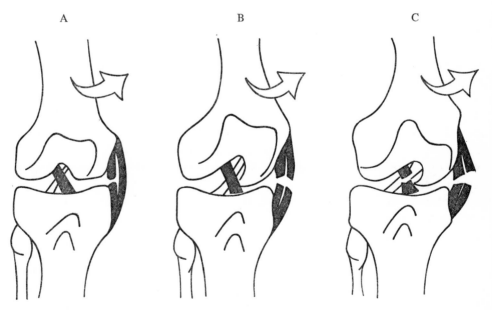

Figure V–2. As the femur is forced into medial rotation there is successive tearing of the medial joint structures as described in the text. This occurs correspondingly earlier when the rotation strain is combined with an adduction stress. A shows tearing of the deep portion of the tibial collateral ligament. In B, the superficial fibers of the tibial collateral ligament are also torn. C shows rupture of the anterior cruciate ligament along with complete tearing of the tibial collateral ligament.

damaged or the governing musculature is insufficient to allow him to participate safely. Before applying the tape, the skin is prepared in the normal fashion, being shaved clean, and some Tinc Benzoin spray applied which comes under a variety of trade names.* The patient assumes a walking position with the feet about 14 inches apart on a low table in order to make the leg more accessible. Initially both legs are in the neutral position but most of the body weight supported on the knee to be taped. Without moving the position of the foot the leg to be taped is flexed to about 20° at the knee and rotated externally at the hip as much as possible. This may be regarded as medial rotation of the tibia and if the position is correct the medial longitudinal arch will be raised. This position is held until the taping is completed. The popliteal fossa is packed with cotton batton padding, and a gauze or synthetic material wrapping applied to prevent skin irritation. It is felt that strapping procedures to the knee require more extensive proximal and distal support than has previously been advocated by other authors.[29] One or two four-inch elastic tape anchors are applied around the upper thigh and another around the inferior of the belly of gastrocnemius. Commencing at the distal anchor on the lateral aspect, two-inch elastic tape is firmly applied in a spiral manner until the proximal anchors are reached. The tape passes successively, anteromedially over the anterior border of the tibia, posterolaterally across the popliteal fossa and finally superomedially across the lateral aspect of the thigh. (Fig. V–3)

A   B   C   D

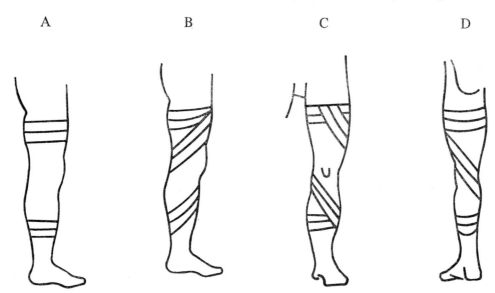

Figure V–3. The application of functional strapping to prevent rotational instability of the knee. Figure V–3A shows the position for the anchors. B, C and D illustrate the direction taken by the spiral taping technique.

---

* Tuf Skin®, Q.D.A., Cramer Products

This is repeated until five or six two-inch strips have been applied. These strips should overlap to some degree. The strapping is then secured proximally and distally with four-inch elastic tape anchors. In some cases it may be advisable to complete the procedure by applying a six-inch tensor bandage to the area.

In addition, this technique should be augmented in the case of football players by replacing the heel cleats with a heel plate. This lessens the danger of the heel being firmly planted in situations that would be likely to cause trauma to the medial aspect of the knee.

QUADRICEPS CONTUSIONS

The quadriceps themselves may be subject to direct trauma. The quadriceps contusions or as they are referred to by athletes "cork injuries" or "charlie horse" may occur during the most innocuous of noncontact sports through an unfortunate combination of circumstances. They seem to occur with uniform frequency in most contact sports despite the protective equipment. It is not being suggested that all protective padding is inadequate for the severity of injury would be far greater if this equipment did not exist. Truly one could say that nothing short of a full set of medieval armour would completely eliminate this type of injury. Often quadriceps contusions, initially minor in nature, have become increasingly acute because of mismanagement. Many athletes present themselves with these injuries one or two days after they occurred because according to them "it wasn't too bad at the time." All of these injuries should be considered serious until they have healed. It is only necessary to see one instance of massive bleeding with haemorrhage from groin to knee combined with total loss of extensor function to appreciate the hazards of each and every quadriceps contusion, no matter how minor it may appear at the outset.

There are many degrees of quadriceps injuries and in reviewing the literature there are almost as many methods of treatment as there are authors, however the following treatment has proved consistently successful. Often the helmet or knee of one player hits the anterolateral aspect of the thigh of another with sufficient impact to cause bleeding of crushed and disrupted muscle fibers. In conjunction with the tissue damage there is usually a considerable amount of muscle spasm involved. With these facts in mind it is apparent that both the bleeding and the spasm must be treated immediately. If muscle length can be maintained during the acute phase, the subsequent functional recovery is accelerated. With these thoughts in mind the quadriceps are stretched by as complete flexion as possible. (Fig. V–4)

Ideally this initial treatment is followed by a cryotherapy routine two

A   B

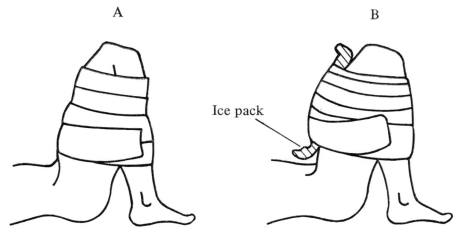

Ice pack

Figure V–4. A method of wrapping quadriceps contusions with a 6″ elastic wrap based on a method described in the Modern Principles of Athletic Training. (A) Simple wrapping (B) Wrapping incorporating icepacks.

or three times daily for the next two days. This consists of ice massage for five to seven minutes after which the athlete attempts twenty strong isometric hamstring contractions. Each contraction is held for about six to ten seconds. This entire routine may be repeated two or three times each session. Good reciprocal relaxation of the quadriceps is usually obtained. When the athlete is able to flex his knee to 90° in the test position shown in Figure V–5, the routine is modified. The patient is treated in the lying position with the legs fully extended. Now ice massage is given for five minutes followed by two minutes of flexion and extension exercises carried out in the manner to be described. The leg is flexed to its maximum extent by an unassisted isotonic contraction and at the limit of the range the athlete grasps around his ankle and attempts to produce additional flexion by gentle passive pressure. This is followed by a slow extension of the leg until 180° is achieved and then the foot is dorsiflexed and a strong isometric contraction is attempted and held for ten seconds.[45] This sequence is repeated for two minutes. As soon as full range is recovered, as compared to the sound leg, resisted exercises for both quadriceps and hamstrings may be commenced.[18,30] The decision to allow the athlete to return to light training or competition may be made by using the functional tests described in the following section. In the early stages a pressure wrap may be worn between treatments. It should be noted that the authors feel that there is no place for heat and massage in the immediate care of quadriceps contusions. The danger of increased haemorrhage and myositis ossificans precludes this. In any event, increased pain and decreased range should immediately alert the therapist to this danger and an X-ray is then indicated. Treatment is immediately stopped and is not recommended until medical clearance is

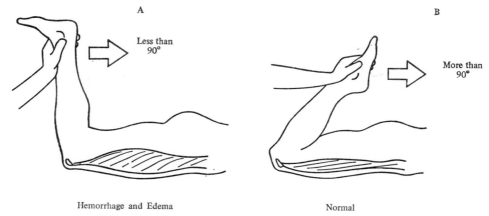

Figure V–5. A shows the limitation of range brought about by an acute quadriceps contusion or by subsequent adhesion and organization of the hematoma. B shows the normal range. (After Hirata, I.: *The Doctor and the Athlete*. Philadelphia, J. B. Lippincott, 1968.)

given by an orthopaedic surgeon. Although the initial treatment as described may be painful, it is preferred to long periods of inactivity or to subsequent chronic problems.

FUNCTIONAL TESTING

In order to assess the progress of the treatment the following test may be carried out. The athlete is placed in the prone position in order to fix the pelvis and lumbosacral spine. The heel is then passively approximated

Figure V–6. Position to test for full functional recovery. The quadriceps are on a full stretch. Notice tension is placed on rectus femoris over both the hip and the knee joint.

to the buttock by knee flexion. This angle is measured on the sound side and then compared to the injured leg. When the limb is moved into the painful or restricted range the lumbosacral spine arches and the buttock on the affected side rises. In addition the athlete should not be allowed to return to light training until he can demonstrate knee flexion to 90° full weightbearing on the injured leg. With any degree of quadriceps contusion the athlete should be provided with additional protection for a period of time. Game fitness is demonstrated by the ability to adopt the position shown in Figure V–6.

The experienced athletic therapist should have a series of functional and return-to-game fitness tests for all the major joints.[48]

PROPRIOCEPTIVE NEUROMUSCULAR FACILITATION

Basic Principles

There is a special exercise technique developed by Kabat, Voss and Knott which makes use of diagonal and spiral movement patterns which may be facilitated or reinforced by massive sensory inflow.[31,44,47] Although these techniques were initially devised to help the grossly weak or spastic neurological patient, their great versatility and sound physiological basis have enabled the therapist to adapt them for use in the treatment of the injured athlete. They are excellent for strengthening and are probably the most effective method of restoring lost range to a joint. The following outline of the rationale behind the techniques of proprioceptive neuromuscular facilitation (P. N. F.) is brief but will serve as a basis for understanding its application.

The basic aim of P. N. F. is to stimulate the anterior horn cells to a maximal degree of activity. Furthermore the knowledge of reciprocal innervation and facilitation and inhibitory reflexes are utilized. The resting anterior horn cell maintains a level of activity which is a balance of excitatory and inhibitory factors. Cell activity can therefore be increased in two ways, either a raise in the excitatory factors or a decrease in the inhibitory factors. The anterior horn cell has a critical excitatory level and each stimulus arriving in the vicinity of an anterior horn cell or its dendrites may either raise or lower the local excitatory state of the cell. When the excitatory state equals the critical excitatory level, the anterior horn cell will become active and fire. Basically there are four ways of achieving this critical excitatory level: (1) voluntary initiation from a cortical level, (2) initiation from extrapyramidal or any other subcortical level, (3) local and general reflex acts acting at a cord level, (4) sensory feedback at a cord level. To raise the excitatory level of the anterior horn cell, and hence qualify for the term "facilitation," the small individual stimuli can compound in the following three ways:

1. Spatial summation i.e., many different stimuli occurring simultaneously.
2. Temporal summation i.e., a repetition of the same stimuli over a period of time.
3. Recruitment by irradiation or use of the subliminal fringe effect.

In the case of weakness, the strength of the contraction may be augmented, and where there is difficulty in initiation of movement, the raised excitatory level of the anterior horn cell may be sufficient to allow volitional movement. Practically this facilitation is achieved by voluntary effort by the patient, which is an enteroceptive stimulus. In addition several exteroceptive stimuli are used; the patient's ears, eyes, skin. The auditory stimulus consists of clear precise commands, with the right intonation and correct timing. The patient is asked to watch and concentrate on the moving limb hence achieving visual stimulation. Tactile stimuli is used by the careful placing of the therapist's hands over the contracting muscle groups, and avoiding stimulation of the antagonists. The resistance is applied in such a way that the patient's limb is guided through the desired pattern. Lastly proprioceptive stimuli are used by giving stretch and compression at the beginning of movements to initiate reflex contraction via muscle spindle activity.[7] If pressure or stretch produce pain they should be avoided and approximation is not advisable in the presence of active inflammation of a joint.

PATTERN OF MOVEMENT. In sports activities where the demand for maximal efficiency of muscle and joint activity is at its highest and greatest, analysis of movement patterns show consistent diagonal movements. This is not simply a manifestation of the neural innervation of limb and trunk components, but a result of the basic mechanics imposed by muscle and joint structures. These patterns are carried over into the proprioceptive techniques. In particular it is the rotation components of the movement that are difficult to reproduce, but essential if maximal advantage is to be made of this system of exercise. The patterns are named according to the movement taking place in the proximal joints of the limbs, e.g. leg patterns named according to hip movement. Extra description can be added to clarify the pattern.

MAXIMAL DEMAND. Massive sensory inflow can cause excitement of adjacent anterior horn cells by an overflow of activity which is referred to as recruitment. Maximal resistance ensures the strongest possible muscle contraction and hence maximal anterior horn cell activity. This requires experience by the therapist to accurately match the capabilities of the patient in any particular part of the range of movement.

REPEATED CONTRACTIONS. As the name implies, repeated efforts are made to perform a movement. Each contraction increases the level of excitation of the anterior horn cells controlling the particular muscles. This form of activation uses the principle of temporal summation. At the same time the strong contractions will cause overflow, i.e. recruitment. Usually several isometric contractions are followed by an isotonic contraction in the desired range.

RECIPROCAL INNERVATION. A single sensory neuron has numerous connections in the spinal cord, both directly by branching and indirectly via internuncial neurons. The synapses at the end of these many connections may be excitatory or inhibitory. Hence some techniques of exercise stimulate one group of muscles while simultaneously producing relaxation of the antagonistic muscle group. Reciprocal inhibition, reciprocal innervation and reciprocal relaxation are terms often used to describe the same phenomenon. This principle has obvious application in the relaxation of a tight or spastic muscle group.

Basic Techniques

SLOW REVERSALS. This technique consists of an isotonic contraction of one group of muscles producing a full range of movement followed immediately by isotonic contraction of the antagonists to return the limb to the starting position. It is important to get a smooth change of direction without a pause between the two patterns of movement if the level of summated activity is to be utilized. This type of exercise utilizes two basic physiological principles that may be utilized for both strengthening and mobilizing work. Firstly a muscle will contract more strongly following maximal work of its antagonists and secondly, if a muscle contraction is strong the subsequent relaxation is more complete, i.e. the stronger the contraction, the more complete the relaxation.

STATIC CONTRACTION FOLLOWED BY RELAXATION. This technique may also be referred to as the hold-relax or contract-relax method and is used for gaining range where pain or spasticity is the limiting factor. All descriptive terms apply to the tight or spastic group. Using strict definitions the hold-relax technique indicates that no movement is allowed during the resistance phase while contract-relax allows some rotation. Essentially both methods utilize a maximal contraction of the muscle group with no movement through range allowed (except rotation as previously mentioned) which should be followed by maximal relaxation of that group. The followup is important since having relaxed the tight group the limb should be carried into the restricted range either by passive movement or by concentric contraction of the antagonist. It is usual to start this technique at a point in the range just short of the point of limitation.

RHYTHMIC STABILIZATION. This is a concurrent cocontraction of all the muscles around the joint. In the basic technique no movement is permissible. Any range may be chosen for the series of isometric contractions. It is a useful technique for maintaining the strength of a very painful joint, or a joint in a plaster cast.

SUMMARY

Many of these special terms, that have now come to assume such significance with the development of proprioceptive neuromuscular facilitation techniques are simply descriptive of phenomena of which the athletic therapist has long been aware. Furthermore, many of these therapists in the past have adapted these techniques intuitively to achieve excellent results.[39] However, success with intuitive treatment, like success with empirical treatments should not allow the therapist to abandon the search for the understanding of the true physiological reason behind a response. Only with full understanding of the techniques that are available can treatments be safe, efficient and new and useful methods of therapy be developed.

The term "acute injury" is often used loosely in clinical settings. However, from the data derived from an analysis of about 1500 patients with ankle and knee ligamentous injuries, only 18 percent were seen in the first three hours post-trauma and only 68 percent within the first 24 hours. Of these, many were not actively treated until some time later. Since these first few hours are critical in the treatment or maltreatment of traumatic injuries, it is not surprising that many of them go on to be chronic problems. In addition, many authors are referring to a group of patients presenting themselves over 48 hours posttrauma and hence their approach and philosophy of treatment is different. This should be held in mind when evaluating the literature.

These points have been set out to provide a sound anatomical and physiological background for exercise therapy. These principles can be used at any joint, and clinical proof is found in the improvement of the athletes.[42,43] Athletes with a long history of injuries should be assessed for muscle strength, muscle imbalance and muscle tightness. A planned preseason program can then be drawn up, which may in fact be pursued throughout the playing season.[1,6,48] The prescription of exercise to produce a desired response may be just as specific as the prescription of any other medical modality, and, as with other modalities, must be modified as the condition of the athlete changes. The cliché of ice, elevation, compression and rest still holds true for the acute injury. Active exercise should be incorporated as soon as the acute nature of the injury subsides sufficiently. This is usually 48 hours post-trauma. The use of ultrasound, short wave diathermy, diapulse and faradism are simply adjuncts to the basic active rehabilitation of the injured part.

REFERENCES

1. Abbott, H. G., and Kress, J. B.: Preconditioning in the prevention of knee injuries. *Arch Phys Med Rehab, 50*:326–333, 1969.
2. Abbott, L., Saunders, J. De C., Bost, F. C., and Anderson, C.: Injuries to ligaments of the knee. *J Bone Joint Surg, 26*:503–521, 1944.
3. Barnett, C. H.: Locking at the knee joint. *J Anat, 87*:91–95, 1953.
4. Basmajian, J. V.: Reeducation of vastus medialis: A misconception. *Arch Phys Med Rehab, 51*:245–246, 1970.
5. ———: *Muscles Alive: Their Function Revealed by Electromyography.* Baltimore, Williams and Wilkins, 1967.
6. Bender, J.; Kobes, F. J.; Kaplan, H.; and Pierson, J. K.: Strengthening muscles and preventing knee injuries with a controlled program of isometric exercise. *Res Bull J Health Phys Educ Recreat, 31*:37–42, 1964.
7. Bobath, B.: Observations on adult hemiplegias and suggestions for treatment. *J. Chart Soc Physio, 45*:279–289, 1959.
8. Bierman, W., and Ralston, H. T.: Electromyographic study during passive and active flexion of the knee of the normal human subject. *Arch Phys Med Rehab, 47*:71–75, 1965.
9. Biggs, E. R.: Adhesive strapping of the injured knee. *J Natl Athletic Trainers Assoc, 1*:3–4, 1958.
10. Bos, R. R. and Blosser, T. G.: An electromyographic study of vastus medialis and lateralis during selected isometric exercises. *Med Sci Sports, 2*:218–223, 1970.
11. Brantigan, O. C. and Voshell, A. F.: Ligaments of the knee joint. The relationship of the ligament of Humphrey to the ligament of Wrisberg. *J Bone Joint Surg, 28*:66–67.
12. ———: The tibial collateral ligament: Its function, its bursae and its relation to the medial meniscus. *J Bone Joint Surg, 25*:121–131, 1943.
13. ———: The mechanics of the ligaments and menisci of the knee joint. *J Bone Joint Surg, 23*:44–66, 1941.
14. Brewerton, D. A.: The function of vastus medialis muscle. *Ann Phys Med, 2*:164–168, 1955.
15. Bruce, J., and Warmsley, R.: Excision of the patella: Some experimental and anatomical observations. *J Bone Joint Surg, 24*:311–325, 1942.
16. Clark, H. and Baily, T.: Strength curves for fourteen joint movements. *J Phys Med Rehab, 14*:12–16, 1950.
17. DeAndrade, J. R., Grant, C., and Dixon, A.: Joint distension and reflex muscle inhibition in the knee. *J Bone Joint Surg, 47A*:313–322, 1965.
18. Donoho, C. R. and Rylander, C. R.: The football knee: A general plan for rehabilitation of a sprained knee. *Del Med J, 38*:20–22, 1966.
19. Eyring, E. and Murray, W.: The effect of joint position on the pressure of intratricular effusion. *J Bone Joint Surg, 46A*:1235–1241, 1964.
20. Galway, R.: Shift of tibia under stress. *The Medical Post 16*, July 1971.
21. Gough, J. V., and Ladley, G.: An investigation into the effectiveness of various forms of quadriceps exercises. *Physiotherapy, 47*:8, 356–361, 1971.
22. Greenhill, B. J.: The importance of the medial quadriceps expansion in medial ligament injury. *Can J Surg, 10*:312–317, 1969.
23. Hallen, L. G., and Lindahl, O.: Muscle function in knee extension. An E.M.G. study. *Acta Orthop Scand, 38*:4, 434–444, 1967.
24. Hirata, I.: *The Doctor and the Athlete.* Philadelphia, J. B. Lippincott, 1968.

25. Jack, E. A.: Experimental rupture of the medial collateral ligament of the knee. *J Bone Joint Surg,* 32-B 396–402, 1950.
26. Kaplan, E. B.: Some aspects of functional anatomy of the human knee joint. In *Clinical Orthopaedics.* Philadelphia, J. B. Lippincott, 1958.
27. ———: The iliotibial tract. *J Bone Joint Surg,* 40A, 817–832, 1958.
28. Katz, B.: Quadriceps femoris strength following patellectomy. *Phys Ther Rev,* 32:401–404, 1952.
29. Kelly, R.: Immediate Care of Quadriceps Contusions. Paper presented at Quebec Section of Canadian Physiotherapy Assoc. Symposium on Sports Medicine, Laval, 1970.
30. Klein, K. K.: The deep squat exercise and its effect on the ligaments of the knee. *J Assoc Phys Ment Rehab,* 15:6, 1961.
31. Knott, M., and Voss, D. E.: *Proprioceptive Neuromuscular Facilitation: Patterns and Techniques.* London, Harper and Row, 1968.
32. Leach, R. E., Stryker, W. S., and Zohn, D. A.: A comparative study of isometric and isotonic quadriceps exercise programs. *J Bone Joint Surg,* 7:1421–1426. 1965.
33. Licht, S.: *Electrodiagnosis and Electromyography.* Connecticut, Elizabeth Licht Publ, 1961.
34. Lieb, F. J. and Perry, J.: Quadriceps function: An anatomical and mechanical study using amputated limbs. *J Bone Joint Surg,* 50A. 8:1535–1548, 1968.
35. ———: Quadriceps function: Electromyographic study under isometric conditions. *J Bone Joint Surg,* 53A: 4, 749–758, 1971.
36. Mendler, H.: Post operative function of the knee joint. *J Am Phys Ther Assoc,* 43:435–441, 1963.
37. ———: Knee extensor and flexor force following injury. *Am J Phys Ther,* 47:35–45, 1967.
38. Merrifield, H. H.: Bilateral Force, Torque and Power Imbalance as Contributory Factors in Hip Joint Adductor Strains in Selected Hockey Players. Paper presented at C.A.S.M./A.C.S.M. joint meeting. Toronto, 1971.
39. Pinkston, D.: Analysis of traditional regiments of therapeutic exercise. *Am J Phys Med,* 46:713–731, 1967.
40. O'Donohue, D. H.: Surgical treatment of fresh injuries of the knee. *J Bone Joint Surg,* 32-A. 721–738, 1950.
41. Petersen, I., and Stener, B.: Experimental evaluation of the hypothesis ofligaments in muscular protective reflexes. III. A study in man using the medial collateral ligament. *Acta Physiol Scand,* 48:51–61, 1959.
42. Reid, D. C.: *Functional Anatomy and Joint Mobilization: A Manual of Kinesiology.* Edmonton, Univ. of Alberta Press, 1970.
43. ———: The shoulder girdle: Its function as a unit in abduction. *J Chart Soc Physio,* 55:57–59, 1969.
44. Rood, M.: *Approaches to Treatment of Patients with Neuromuscular Dysfunction.* Iowa, William C. Brown Publ, 1967.
45. Rose, D. L.: Brief maximal isotonic exercises in the treatment of knee injuries. *JAMA,* 171:1673–1675, 1959.
46. Scott, P. M.: *Electrotherapy and Actinotherapy.* London, Balliere, Tindall and Cassell, 1965.
47. Slocum, D. B.: Rotatory instability of the knee. In *A.A.O.S. Symposium on Sports Medicine.* London, C. V. Mosby Comp. 1969.
48. Sullivan, G. F.: Conditioning procedures in prevention of knee injuries. *J Natl Athletic Trainers Assoc,* 4:12, 1969.

49. Voss, D. E.: Proprioceptive neuromuscular facilitation. *Am J Phys Med,* 46:838–885, 1967.
50. Williams, M., and Stutzman, L.: Strength variation through the range of joint motion. *Phys Ther Rev,* 39:145–152, 1959.
51. Williams, M., and Lessner, H.: Biomechanical analysis of knee function. *J Am Phys Ther Assoc,* 43:93–99, 1963.

CHAPTER VI

EXERCISE TESTING OF INDIVIDUALS PRONE TO CORONARY ARTERY DISEASE

T. TALIBI

MAXIMUM STRESS EXERCISE TESTING is carried out on coronary patients in order to document the cardiovascular and pulmonary physiological responses. The main purpose, of course, is to extend the physical examination of the patient for the purpose of aiding diagnosis and also to determine the possibility of the risk at this period. Another reason is the accurate prescription of work load capacity. During this examination clinical symptomotology is also assessed and the physician, supervising the test, can observe how significant the clinical symptoms are—such as dyspnea, fatigue and chest pain. The time duration is also very important to assess the level when these symptoms occur in relation to the level of his maximum work capacity. The relation of work load to cardiac rhythm disturbances is also analyzed. During stress exercise testing ischaemic changes in the heart muscles are also documented and when an appropriate therapy has been instituted, this being medical or surgical, this test will reveal if there are any changes in the patient's clinical symptoms.

Stress exercise testing, carried out in so-called middle-aged individuals who may be susceptible to coronary artery disease in later years, can evaluate myocardial ischaemia, detected before the usual clinical manifestation of myocardial infarction or angina pectoris.

Large muscle masses must be utilized in order to increase the metabolic activity to the maximum. Two types of ergometers have been utilized in stress testing:

a) the bicycle, where the work is performed against a resistance which can be defined in physiological terms. The utilized oxygen levels are independant of the body weight.

b) the other ergometer used is the treadmill. In this test the maximum oxygen utilized is proportional to the body weight, therefore the patients could be compared with age matched normal subjects with similar mechanical abilities and body weight.

These exercise tests should be monitored, should be single tests and there should not be the necessity to repeat the procedure. These tests should produce a reappraisable value. Maximal stress exercise tests are applicable to most patients. In certain cases predicted maximum levels should be considered as an actual maximum level for that test period.

History, physical condition and appropriate laboratory data should be obtained before the actual patient testing in order to observe the predicted maximum or the actual maximum level. Some patients who suffer from neuromusculatory or musculoskeletal diseases, which make it difficult to test in this manner can be tested by arm exercises.

These tests should definitely be supervised because of the risk of arrhythmias and sudden death.

MULTISTAGE TREADMILL TEST

A multistage treadmill test is composed of seven stages. The speed changes from 1.7 mph to 6 mph and the grade is also changed from a 10 percent grade to a 22 percent grade. Calorie utilization of each stage is then known and calculated. Each stage lasts for three minutes. The test is also a realistic one because you can test all normals and also super athletes in 21 minutes. Most of us at age 40 to 50 are tested in 12 minutes. So it is quite physical and practical to be used in a clinic and hospital environment. Heart rate response, the duration of the test and oxygen consumption at each stage separates the normal from the cardiac. Most important separation is the oxygen consumption per stage and this oxygen difference is quite significant if it is also age corrected.

Prior to this test the patients are examined by a physician and also they are monitored during this procedure by a physician. The test should not be done in the absence of a physician who is experienced in cardiac emergencies. The work load should be increased progressively by raising the speed and grade every three minutes. There are no rest periods during this increased work load and the test is only stopped when there are signs of extreme clinical fatigue or there are limiting signs noticed by the physician. The maximum oxygen intake is calculated by a maximum stage with the highest speed and grade. If the duration of the last stage is short then it is very likely that the oxygen intake is already at that level. The maximum heart rate for the individual is also determined—this heart rate provides assessment of the magnitude of the stress upon the heart muscle. It is interesting to note that the increase in the pulse rate is not relative to the increase in the work load and patients, when holding the handrail, can tolerate maximum stress exercises a few minutes longer after they have reached their maximum pulse. At the maximal stages of testing these patients will present symptoms of fatigue, chest pain or exhaustion which will be manifested by cutaneous shut down of circulation, which is developed as the last sign of circulatory adaption in order to supply more blood to the vital organs.

After completion of the test the physician involved should again examine the patient to find the possibility of any new information. A few cardiac patients will develop a gallop rhythm or some will produce a pulmonary congestion. Electrocardiograms, of course, should be examined before and after the test from the point of view of rhythm production and the repolarization phase.

THE HAZARDS OF STRESS TESTING

In daily living there are problems with which cardiac patients or their families report that they have difficulties—sometimes even sudden death has occurred as a result of moderately unusual exercise (shovelling snow or dirt, pushing heavy objects, carrying loads, etc.). So this raises the question whether or not this sort of testing should be done even under supervision. With experience we can say that this test can be done if certain principles are applied.

If the patient has an acute myocardial infarction the test, of course, is not done. However, there is a condition when a patient has a myocardial infarction without clinical diagnosis (a so-called silent infarct). Therefore when a patient having a clinically undetected infarction participates in a stress test, he might experience great difficulties. To prevent these occurrences, preliminary examination is most essential, especially in patients prone to coronary disease. Arrhythmias should be expected and therefore the patient's cardiogram should definitely be monitored by an experienced physician with an oscilloscope or a direct writing recorder. The most dangerous arrhythmia is a sudden onset of ventricular tachycardia. By this we mean any extrasystole—three or more in a row—this is by definition a paroxysmal ventricular tachycardia—and the test should be terminated immediately. Situations have also been seen when cardiac output is not adequate at the stress level and the patient presents signs of cerebral ischaemia with a change in the gait or slight confusion during testing. At that moment the test should be stopped. On rare occasions one might observe sudden onset of left ventricular disfunction with pulmonary oedema and, of course, the test again has to be stopped. Ventricular fibrillation could also occur during stress testing usually following ventricular tachycardia. This arrhythmia should be respected and the DC defibrillator should be available. This also means that one should have appropriate drugs and oxygen available.

CHAPTER VII

GRADED EXERCISE IN THE TREATMENT OF CHRONIC LUNG DISEASE

B. J. Sproule and S. Rao

An improvement in exercise tolerance results when either patients with chronic obstructive lung disease [3,8,18,19,21,22] or normal subjects follow a program of training using gradually increasing increments of submaximal exercise. The mechanisms whereby these favourable changes occur are unclear. Fitness may be defined [26,29] as the ability of the exercising individual to maintain internal equilibria as closely as possible to the resting state and to rapidly restore the equilibria when exercise ceases. Individual performance can be measured in terms of "maximum aerobic power," which is the amount of oxygen consumed while working at maximal levels, generally expressed as millilitres of oxygen consumed per kilogram of body weight per minute. Its magnitude is the most generally accepted indicator of "fitness," with a value of 45 mm per Kg per minute for 25-year-old males, declining to 40 ml per Kg per minute at age 60, comparing to quantities of 85 ml per Kg per minute consumed by champion athletes.[26]

Patients with obstructive lung disease are deterred from physical activity by dyspnea, which is associated with loss of muscle tone and efficiency, ease fatigability and then increasing dyspnea resulting in a self-perpetuating vicious circle. If oxygen is breathed during the training period, hypoxic patients show more pronounced improvement, but despite fairly spectacular changes in symptomatology dramatic changes in measured cardiorespiratory parameters have not been noted.[3,19,21,30]

EXERCISE PROGRAM

It is well established that the pulmonary patient, despite limitation of performance by the capacity of the respiratory system, can carry out graded exercise safely and without undue fatigue.[3] Thus badly delibitated patients as well as those with early obstructive lung disease who, because of dyspnea, have given up certain activities which were either necessary or enjoyable, are candidates for exercise training. The execution of a physiologically oriented complete treatment program [17,27] is a prime requisite for successful rehabilitation and other ancillary aids, such as tracheobronchial toilet, treatment of heart failure and infection, are essential if a satisfactory exercise program is to be initiated.

ASSESSMENT OF PHYSICAL PERFORMANCE FOR TRAINING

A numerical estimate of the physical working capacity of a patient with respiratory disability is of great help.[1,2,7] However, the subjective tolerance of effort is of paramount importance and this, as evaluated by both observer and subject, should be the end point of each exercise period. This is less inexact and unscientific than it may appear, for even the most elaborate and sophisticated measurements fail to monitor subtle interrelationships which are reflected as "distress" by the observer as well as by the exercising subject.

The main forms of exercise in the laboratory are the treadmill, the step test, the bicycle ergometer and the hand ergometer. Factors which influence the specific choice of apparatus are cultural background, familiarity and availability. Since the object is to produce general cardiorespiratory stress, the end point should be dyspnea and general exhaustion, rather than local muscle weakness. The hand ergometer therefore is usually inappropriate. In urban and sedentary North American populations, bicycle performance is often terminated by weakness of the thigh muscles, and the treadmill and step test are therefore preferred, although the bicycle ergometer has many advantages in terms of portability and ease of carrying out ancillary measurements.

Most subjects must be taught to use either the treadmill or bicycle and a proper combination of load and speed arrived at, such that the patient will work moderately hard. If the subject is markedly incapacitated, a speed of one mile per hour at no grade is a sensible baseline for treadmill stressing. In a more fit subject, when a speed of three miles per hour for five to ten minutes is attained, the grade can then be increased by one percent increments up to five percent. The choice of an ultimate proper combination of speed and grade is a matter of judgment and is dependent upon the subjects walking habits and leg length. Arbitrary time intervals should be employed early and then the subject encouraged to push himself as long as he can.

Many studies on the influence of prescribed courses of exercise varying in duration, intensity and frequency on the "maximum aerobic power" of normal subjects have been carried out.[25] Exercise at levels above 50 percent of VO_2 max does improve maximum aerobic power, particularly in athletes. Understandably if stress is pushed to close to VO_2 max, the degree of improvement attained is enhanced, but in the subject with a depleted cardio-respiratory reserve, such a program has to be modified by considerations related to patient safety and tolerance.

In prescribing physical stress to a patient with cardiorespiratory dis-ability, ventilatory capacity has been used as a guide to a suitable level of exercise for the first attempt. Cotes[7] suggests three arbitrary levels with an FEV_1 sec of less than 500 cc calling for an initial stress of one mile per hour at zero grade, an FEV_1 sec of 750 cc indicating settings of two miles per hour at zero grade, and an FEV_1 sec of greater than one litre calling for an initial trial at two miles per hour and a ten percent grade. If the subject can work five minutes at the set load a slightly faster speed is imposed.

The MVV and the ventilatory equivalent for oxygen can also be used to estimate initial work levels. A Nomogram has been drawn up which estimates VO_2 max from measured levels of MVV and of ventilatory equivalent for oxygen.[1] Once an estimate of the VO_2 max has been made the individual can then be worked at levels which have been found to produce certain proportions of VO_2 max, determined by use of another Nomogram which relates oxygen consumption, weight and treadmill grade and speed.[2] It is customary to work disabled patients at a level of approxi-mately 50 percent of maximal oxygen uptake.

The program of exercise training must be augmented by unsupervised exercise on the hospital wards with an increase in the duration and in-tensity of this exercise each day. Patients when discharged should be en-couraged to continue the training program by regular walking up and down stairs at home and by using aids such as a stationary bicycle exerciser.

PHYSIOLOGICAL EFFECTS

General activity does not apparently affect static lung dimensions in normal subjects since it has been shown that neither bedrest nor general training results in changes in total lung capacity, vital capacity, or forced expiratory volume.[24] The same is true of patients with chronic lung dis-ease.[30] Swimming and diving, demanding as they do that a large per-centage of the vital capacity be utilized with each breath, do cause an in-crease in total lung capacity.[23] In bicycling and running, however, perhaps since the tidal volume never exceeds 50 to 55 percent of the individual's vital capacity,[7] no appreciable change in the static dimensions of the lung have been demonstrated.[19,30]

In normal subjects pulmonary ventilation at submaximal exercise and oxygen uptake at lower than maximal levels have not been influenced by training.[3,19,30] Patients with obstructive airway disease have less oxygen consumption and CO_2 production at the same submaximal level of exertion following a training program.[19] It is probable that this is related to a decreased oxygen cost of breathing as well as to more efficient and complete utilization of oxygen by working tissues.

The ventilatory equivalent (O_{2ve}) is the ratio of ventilation in litres per minute to the number of liters of oxygen consumed per minute and a smooth incremental relationship from rest to exercise is seen. The O_{2ve} is normally 20 to 25 litres of ventilation per litre of oxygen consumption and patients with obstructive airway disease demonstrate levels of about 35 litres per litre, while disability from pulmonary fibrosis is associated with ventilatory levels of from 40 to 45 litres per litre of oxygen consumed. Although the oxygen Ve is frequently used as gauge of training,[15] it serves as a very inexact criterion of developing "fitness," [30] and in obstructed patients factors such as increased dead space ventilation account for an appreciable increment in total ventilation unrelated to general conditioning.

The dyspnea which is most responsible for decreased activity is importantly related to an increased work of breathing and to an associated increase in the oxygen metabolic cost of breathing. It is of considerable interest that an increase in dynamic compliance and a decrease in the work of breathing has been documented to occur following the training of patients with chronic lung disease.[30] The improvement in compliance is not necessarily associated with a fall in nonelastic resistance and therefore seems to reflect a true change in pulmonary elasticity. The decrease in respiratory work is not always associated with a decrease in minute ventilation and thus it appears there is a true reduction in overall respiratory work. The findings suggest that intercostal muscles, when trained, are capable of operating more efficiently.

An increase in the single breath diffusing capacity of the lungs has been found to eventuate from training normal subjects and to be associated with an increased maximal cardiac output.[24] The training of patients with airway obstruction however has not resulted in any changes in steady state DCO.[19,30]

A change in measured blood gases has not been noted either in normal subjects or in patients with obstructive lung disease to result from a regime of exercise.[19,30] However a somewhat more sophisticated index of gas transport (the A-a pO_2 gradient) is narrower following the training of both normal subjects and obstructed patients, indicating an equalization of ventilation to perfusion by the exercise program.[9]

An increase in the total oxygen delivered to tissues,[19,20] which is induced by exercising young subjects, occurs because of an increase in both maximal cardiac output and in A-V oxygen difference.[24] Since the maximal heart rate achieved does not change, the cardiac flow changes are as a result of an increase in stroke volume. The successfully trained patient with chronic lung disease shows an ability to exercise at submaximal levels using a lower cardiac output and a wider A-V oxygen difference than before, indicating an enhanced capacity to extract oxygen from the blood circulating through the exercising peripheral tissues.

Despite the above indications of more efficient peripheral activity, the anaerobic metabolic cost of work expressed by measurement of oxygen debt, excess lactate and lactic acid are little affected by training.[19,30]

Although the literature on the effect of training young people and particularly athletes is voluminous, there are only a few isolated reports on the cardiorespiratory response to training middle-aged or older individuals. The effects as measured seem to be less than in younger people, probably because the stress to which the subjects are subjected is less. Patients with obstructive disease are usually middle-aged and many may also be compromised by hypoxia on exercise. It has been shown that the response to training may be accelerated when oxygen is administered during the training period and also that the developing polycythemia, which normally accompanies an exercise regime, is not seen if the exercise is carried out under hyperoxic conditions.[19] Although from a teleological sense it is, up to a point, useful to enhance oxygen carrying capacity by increasing red cell mass; this is not true if the resulting viscosity changes are sufficient to impede the circulation.[9] The hypoxic and acidotic red cell has a greater than normal internal viscosity and therefore the patient with chronic lung disease, with noncompliant red cells, can develop viscosity increases at lower levels of hematocrit than does the normal person. Oxygen training is helpful by reducing a deleterious increase in red mass under such circumstances.

The increased ability to work resulting from a program of regular exercise is specific and the improvement achieved is more pronounced while carrying out precise tasks, probably related to better coordination and economy of movement, although there may in addition be changes in particular muscles. In an electron microscopic study, the number and size of mitochondria seemed to be unaffected by either bed rest or training,[23] but it has been demonstrated that regional blood flow does increase significantly with training.[20] It appears likely, in the absence of anatomic changes in the trained human muscle, that untrained subjects do not activate all the available motor units in the working muscle even during maximal exercise.

Since an individual's capacity to perform prolonged exercise is increased by training and the ability develops slowly and by mechanisms which remain unclear, the possibility of a change in substrate composition in the exercised muscle deserves consideration and investigation.

Glucose and glycogen are broken down initially in the sarcoplasmic portion of the muscle. This process consists of an anaerobic degradation of glucose and glycogen to pyruvate. If oxygen is freely available, pyruvate is converted to acetyl COA and in turn oxidized to CO_2 and water via the

Krebs Cycle. Complete oxidation of one molecule of glucose yields 36 molecules of ATP which supplies the energy for muscle contraction. An important factor which limits the ability to perform prolonged heavy exercise is accumulation of lactate. While it has been generally held that the increase in lactate production during exercise is as a result of a relatively insufficient supply of oxygen, it has recently been postulated that this is not so.[14] The suggestion is that an increase in lactate production results from an imbalance in the muscle between the glycolytic and the oxidative mechanisms and is based on the fact that exercising femoral venous oxygen tension is sufficiently high so that it should be capable of aerobically supporting muscular activity.

Glycogen in both muscle and liver examined under an electron microscope exists in small particles. It has long been known from studies of animal tissue and inferred from the respiratory quotient measured in exercising man, that carbohydrate is utilized. It has recently become possible to obtain biopsies from exercising human muscle and to measure the quantity of glycogen contained therein.[4,16] A progressive fall in the quantity of glycogen contained in muscle occurs as exercise proceeds with virtual depletion at the time of exhaustion. The rate at which glycogen is depleted depends upon the intensity of exercise and at high metabolic rates (70 to 80% of maximal aerobic capacity), the time that a subject is capable of sustaining activity is correlated with the initial muscle glycogen content.[29]

The manner in which the carbohydrate stores of muscle and liver, which are used to provide ATP for the contractile process, are mobilized is not completely known. Glycogen degradation is mediated by the enzyme phosphorylase, resulting in glucose-1-phosphate which is further metabolized via glycolysis, the Krebs Cycle and the electron transport system to produce carbon dioxide, water and ATP. Glycogen mobilization is therefore controlled by the phosphorylase system, and is catalyzed by the adenyl cyclase system in response to adrenaline, noradrenaline and hypoxia. How the latter activates phosphorylase is unknown but it has been shown that in normal young volunteers, total phosphorylase and its active form (Phosphorylase A) is increased with training.[5]

Glycogen resynthesis from glucose-1-phosphate occurs via glycogen synthetase. Glycogen, phosphorylase and glycogen synthetase can all currently be measured but an evaluation of changes in all these substrates under conditions of training in normal and abnormal individuals has not been carried out. Some studies which indicate a difference between fit and sedentary individuals in respect to initial glycogen levels and to depletion and reconstitution of glycogen, have been done. There is, however, no information available from patients with lung disease. We have obtained some preliminary data on such patients and in Figure VII–I, values for

GLYCOGEN DEPLETION CURVES IN ATHLETIC & SEDENTARY
SUBJECTS & PATIENTS WITH CHRONIC LUNG DISEASE

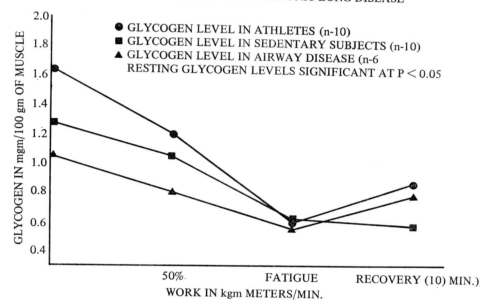

muscle glycogen in the resting state and at submaximal and maximal exercise, as well as at ten minutes of recovery are outlined. The resting glycogen levels of the chronically obstructed patients are low. They appear to deplete glycogen fairly completely with exercise and then recover much like the athlete does.

The ability of the body to compensate for severe compromise and of patients with a severe limitation of their oxygen carrying capacity to exercise up to levels approaching or suppressing maximal oxygen uptake is worthy of comment. We have found that 11 out of 15 patients with severe mitral stenosis [6] and seven out of nine severely anemic individuals [28] were able to work hard enough to reach maximal values. The levels of exercise carried out by the anemic subjects were just as high as those of the normals, while the oxygen uptakes were only about 60 percent of normal.

Therefore, despite diminished oxygen transport and increased respiratory mechanical work, the anemic subjects were able to perform with no greater subjective distress and the achieved cardiac outputs and stroke volumes were comparable with those of normal subjects.

The study suggested that there might have been some alteration of intracellular intermediary metabolism, and more recent studies measuring levels of 2,3, DPG in red cells of anemic subjects indicate that a shift of the oxygen dissociation curve related to increased 2,3, DPG might be in part responsible.[11]

Studies on patients with chronic obstructive airway disease have also indicated them to be able to operate phenomenally well at low levels of oxygen tension [26] and it may be that part of their ability to compensate is related to changes in the dissociation curve. Faulkner has done studies which would indicate that the dissociation curve may be shifted and 2,3, DPG may be increased in exercise, but this work is not universally accepted.[13]

It does, however, seem obvious that many of the major changes which occur following a period of exercise training, most particularly in the individual with chronic obstructive lung disease, are changes which occur at the level of the working muscle and further work to elucidate the details of this is proceeding.

From a practical point of view however it is heartening to note the general improvement which can be achieved by regularly and progressively exercising patients who are compromised not only by severe obstruction of the airways, but also by concomitant generalized debility.

REFERENCES

1. Armstrong, B. W., Workman, J. M., Hurt, H. H. and Roemich, W. R.: Clinico-physiologic evaluation of physical working capacity in persons with pulmonary disease. *Am Rev Resp Dis,* 93:90, 1966.
2. ———: Clinico-physiologic evaluation of physical working capacity in persons with pulmonary disease. *Am Rev Resp Dis,* 93:223, 1966.
3. Bass, H., Whitcomb, J. F. and Foreman, R.: Exercise therapy: Therapy for patients with chronic obstructive pulmonary disease. *Chest,* 57:2, 116, 1970.
4. Bergstrom, J., Hermansen, L., Hultman, E. and Saltin, B.: Diet, muscle glycogen and physical performance. *Acta Physiol Scand,* 71:140–150, 1967.
5. Booth, M.: Adaptations of muscle glycogen phosphorylase to exercise and training. Unpublished M.Sc. thesis, University of Alberta, 1970.
6. Chapman, C. B., Mitchell, J. H., Sproule, B. J., Polter, D. and Williams, B.: The maximal O_2 uptake test in patients with predominant mitral stenosis. *Circulation,* 22:4, 1960.
7. Cotes, J. E.: *Lung Function,* 2nd ed. Oxford, Blackwell, 1968.
8. Cotes, J. E. and Gilson, J. C.: Effect of oxygen and exercise ability in chronic respiratory insufficiency. *Lancet,* 270:872, 1956.
9. Dintenfass, L. D. and Read, J.: A hypothesis. *Lancet,* 1:570, 1968.
10. Donald, K. W., Wormald, P. W., Taylor, S. H. and Bishop, J. M.: Changes in the oxygen content of femoral venous blood and by blood flow during leg exercise in relation to cardiac output reponse. *Clin Sci,* 16:567–591, 1951.
11. Eaton, J. W. and Brewer, G. J.: Studies of red cell glycolysis and interaction. *Adv Exp Med Biol,* 6:95, 1970.
12. Eldridge, F.: Blood lactate and pyruvate in pulmonary insufficiency. *N Engl J Med,* 275:878, 1966.
13. Faulkner, J. A., Brewer, G. J. and Eaton, J. W.: Adaptation of red blood cells to

muscular exercise. Red cell metabolism and function. *Adv Exp Med Biol,* 6:213, 1970.

14. Gollnick, P. D. and King, P. W.: Energy release in muscle cell. *Med Sci Sports,* 1:23, 1969.

15. Kipping, H. W. and Moncrieff, A.: The ventilation equivalent for oxygen. *Q J Med,* 1:17, 1932.

16. Lappage, R.: The effects of exercise upon the skeletal muscle glycogen stores of active and sedentary subjects. Unpublished M.Sc. thesis, University of Alberta, 1970.

17. Miller, W. F.: Chronic inflammatory bronchopulmonary disease. *Arch Int Med,* 107:589, 1961.

18. Miller, W. F. and Taylor, H. F.: Exercise training in the rehabilitation of patients with severe respiratory insufficiency due to pulmonary emphysema. *South Med J,* 55:1216–1221, 1962.

19. Paez, P. N., Phillipson, E. A., Mansangkay, M. and Sproule, B. J.: The physiologic basis of training patients with emphysema. *Am Rev Resp Dis,* 9:944, 1967.

20. Petren, T., Sjostrand, T. and Sylewen, B.: Der Einfluss des trainings auf die Haufigkeit der Kapillaren in Herz and Skeletmuskulatur. *Arbeitphyshiol,* 10:376–385, 1936.

21. Pierce, A. K., Paez, P. N. and Miller, W. F.: Exercise training with the aid of a portable oxygen supply in patients with emphysema. *Am Rev Resp Dis, 91*:5, 653, 1965.

22. Pierce, A. K., Taylor, H. F., Archer, R. K. and Miller, W. F.: Response to exercise training in patients with emphysema. *Arch Int Med, 113*:78, 1964.

23. Saltin, B.: Physiologic effects of physical training. *Med Sci Sports,* 1:30, 1969.

24. Saltin, B., Blomqvist, G., Mitchell, J. H., Johnson, R. L. Jr., Wildenthal, K., and Chapman, C. B.: Response to exercise after bedrest and after training. *Circulation (Suppl)* 7, 1968.

25. Shephard, R. J.: Intensity, duration and frequency of exercise as determinants of the response to a training regime. *Int Z Angew Phys, 26*:272–278, 1968.

26. ———: Optimum patterns of exercise for healthy adults. *Can Med Assoc J, 96*:899, 1967.

27. Sproule, B. J.: Drugs for chronic bronchitis. *Can Med Assoc J,* 89:1234, 1963.

28. Sproule, B. J., Mitchell, J. H. and Miller, W. F.: The response of anemic subjects to exercise. *J Clin Invest, 39*:278, 1960.

29. Taylor, A. W., Lappage, R. S. and Rao, S.: Skeletal muscle glycogen stores after submaximal and maximal work. *Med Sci Sports, 3*:75–78, 1971.

30. Woolf, C. R. and Suero, J. T.: Alterations in lung mechanics and gas exchange following training in chronic obstructive lung disease. *Dis Chest,* 55:371, 1969.

PART D

SPECIFIC SPORTS
TRAINING

CHAPTER VIII

FIELD EVENTS

G. GOWAN

A CONSIDERABLE AMOUNT of information on track and field is available from many parts of the world.[30,31] However, examination of current knowledge on training for the field events supports the belief that the related scientific research that has been completed to date has been somewhat limited in its contribution to the advancement of training knowledge per se. Much of it confirms familiar and well-established methods; occasionally, publications complicate, rather than simplify, the theoretical background. As a consequence, the principles of training are largely built empirically. They result from an amalgam of experience and discriminate observations, appropriately systematized by logical thinking.

It is within this context that any survey of training must occur. In an attempt at simplification, in the interests of clarity, jumping events and throwing events will be discussed separately. While the two major groups contain common principles, the jumper is primarily concerned with the application of selected principles in order to project the body, whereas the thrower applies principles to better project implements.

JUMPING

Throughout this chapter, technical knowledge of the events is assumed. Those readers with little previous background, should consult texts in track and field.[3,7,45]

There is general agreement that modern day training is a year-round requirement. Additionally, there is consensus that the training year should be divided into periods of time, or seasons, wherein training activities will demonstrate a certain bias.

Analysis of event requirements is an essential first step leading to the selection of training activities. Such analysis permits the athlete to plan his yearly program in a manner which will maximize the contribution made by training.

Common Factors in Jumping Events

Approach Run

In all jumping events the approach run must be viewed as an essential preparation for an effective take-off. The athlete must, therefore, strive to achieve several objectives related to this section of the event:

1. optimum horizontal momentum at take-off;
2. optimum limb positions and relationships to permit advantageous use of muscular power and leverage at take-off;
3. consistency and precision in take-off motor patterns, which coincide with the take-off mark.

Next, must follow an examination of available activities and practices, from which selection can be made. Certain of these activities may be of a general nature, such as sprinting and progressive resistance exercises, while others may be specifically related to an individual event, and may be classified as technique training, with the primary aim of establishing and consolidating neuromotor patterns.

The percentage of time to be devoted to "general," or "conditioning" training versus "technique" training in this context is debatable. It is influenced by numerous variables amongst which are the age, athletic experience, performance level and long- and short-term goals of the performer. Caution must also be exercised in the area of "transfer" from the "conditioning" training to the "technique" training. It is probably safe to suggest that the major benefits to be gained from the former are the adaptive changes, both physiological and psychological, which increase the likelihood of the jumper effectively accommodating the neuromotor patterns required to produce optimum event performance. In other words, the "general" training better equips the athlete to master the "specific."

This does suggest, if sprint training is used as an example of the "general," that awareness must be developed concerning the difference between sprinting in a racing context and sprinting, or fast running, as an integral part of an approach run. Modifications are required in the latter which necessitate the learning of motor skills specific to the approach runs of the different events. The meeting of such requirements demands technique training over a considerable period of time. While the long jumper, for example, will not be disadvantaged by the possession of great sprinting ability, he must appreciate that it is his ability to control, and effectively utilize, his terminal horizontal momentum which is of paramount importance. To exemplify by further reference to long jumping: The conditioning work of sprinting, flexibility exercises, and progressive resistance activities will likely contribute to improved sprinting ability. To stop at this stage in the training is to remain incomplete. Specific technique training must now involve the learning of a starting pattern of movement, utilization of check marks; consistent reproduction of the acceleration phase, consistent physical preparation for take-off, coincidence of the take-off stimulus, and the resultant movement patterns with the take-off board.

This overall task requires appropriate time allotment. Experience reveals that many jumpers neglect this aspect of technique training to the detriment of performance.

While the approach run for each jumping event can be analyzed in similar fashion to the simplified example given above, motor patterns involved are sufficiently different to demand specific technique training. Queries may be raised concerning long and triple jumping in this regard, since the length of the runs, starting procedures, and the terminal horizontal momentum, are seen to be similar. However, the preparation for the execution of the take-off in triple jump is quite different from the long jump, particularly when triple jumpers utilize the "running" or "Polish" technique.[32]

Take-Off

This is a most important, if not the most important, aspect of jumping. Each take-off incorporates common principles which can be more beneficially utilized as a result of preparation via suitable conditioning activities. Each jumper is attempting to apply effective force over great range. This, in turn, demands neuromuscular preparation and flexibility activities, which will permit the athlete to achieve this aim. Complexity is added by the limited time available in which to apply force; even after achieving limb positions at take-off which permit force to be applied over great range. Ability to effectively work over great range, in limited time, increases the impulse at take-off, so markedly increasing the jumper's effectiveness.

The selected progressive resistance exercises, whether they be weight training[27] or jumping exercises, are generally assumed to have some transfer value. At worst, there is belief that such experiences instill a confidence in the jumper that he is better prepared to effectively cope with the neuromotor patterns demanded by the specific take-off.

There are very important technical differences at take-off in the four jumping events.[12] This demands specific event training which, while occurring concurrently with the conditioning work, receives increasing attention, and a disporportionate increase in time allocation, as the competitive season approaches. Naturally, individual requirements determine the percentage of training time allocated to different aspects of an athlete's preparation.

Up to this point in the analysis of the requirements of the jumping events there appears to be ample justification for insisting upon an intensive, selective conditioning program as a base from which very specific technique training in approach run and take-off can be developed. It is following the take-off phase that there appears to be equal justification for separate consideration of each event. This is due to the differing requirements of the event phase usually referred to as "form in the air." A submission is made that both the triple jump and pole vault can continue to require conditioning and technique training following take-off whereas the long jump and high jump require concentration in technique training. It is conceivable that purists would argue that both long and high jumpers require considerable flexibility, particularly in the hip region, but this apart, there appear to be reasonable grounds for a separation of the events as proposed.

The flight in the air in long jumping is a function of the approach run and take-off. Since many coaches would support Prost's [33] contention that 90 percent of long jumping success is accounted for in the first two phases of the event, there is, perhaps, a clear guideline concerning the priority to be given to different aspects of the event in training. Certainly it would be unwise to totally neglect form in the air, since a well-executed hitch-kick can enhance the landing position of the jumper.[12] Nevertheless, this would seem to be classifiable under specific skill practice in technique training. While it is true to report that form-in-the-air training, using very short approach runs at moderate speed, is to be seen on frequent occasions, the "specificity concept" of motor activity suggests the need for this type of training to be associated with total run-up and take-off movement patterns. Many track and field athletes become very adept in physical skills which are different from those they attempt in competition through lack of awareness of this concept!

Similar comments can be made for the bar clearance in the high jump. The movement patterns necessary for effective clearance can best be learned when the bar is negotiated as a function of a very precise pattern of movement associated with the run-up and take-off. The flight path of the jumper's center of gravity is determined as a result of actions at take-off; consequently, movement of body parts in the air are designed, in one sense, to enable the bar to be brought close to the high point of the jumper's center of mass. Thus, specific skill training is of considerable importance here, but because this phase of the event becomes relatively valueless if an effective approach run and take-off have not been achieved, priorities for training time are easy to establish.

Examination of the triple jump and pole vault reveals marked differences in training requirements. Because the triple-jumper has two additional landing/take-off efforts, consideration must be given to both conditioning and technique training. This event is extremely demanding physically.[23] Technical limitations are imposed upon the athlete who is inadequately conditioned to withstand the stresses which are encountered at the end of one phase and the simultaneous beginning of the next. This necessitates a most conscientious and intensive conditioning program.

Pole vault form in the air presents similar problems.[14] In order to gain maximum technical benefits from correct relationships between athlete and pole, there is need for conditioning training involving progressive resistance work and gymnastically oriented movements. Only when this adaptation has been made can technique training be maximized.

As with all events, it is impossible to indicate the percentage of total time that will be allocated to each aspect of training since weightings may be different from athlete to athlete, from time to time within a given training year or cycle, and from year to year.

Landing

The impact of modern technology has been of enormous benefit to track and field. The high-jumper is no longer faced with problems of landing, and therefore landing technique does not require special attention. While it is accepted that the pole vaulter is descending from great heights, he can now commit his concentration to successful bar clearance in the knowledge that his safe landing is assured. This is true even though the resultant of the earlier vaulting actions will produce a landing on the back and shoulders. The only hazardous landing problem to be faced by the modern vaulter results from an ineffective approach run or faulty take-off, or a broken pole. In the former case, alertness, quick reactions, and perhaps good conditioning, may reduce the severity of the situation. In the latter example avoidance tactics are less predictable, though frequently, the horizontal component in the take-off is sufficient to carry the vaulter into the landing area.

Long jump and triple jump landings are of considerable importance since they can influence the final performance. It is suggested that in both horizontal jumps, form in the air is more dependent upon technique training for successful landings, than upon conditioning training. This is to say that the movement of body parts about the common center of gravity during flight have the major effect upon the attainment of a successful "leg shoot", so enabling the athlete to place the heels as far ahead of the body as possible, while still "saving" the jump. No amount of physical conditioning will enable the athlete to achieve a good landing position if mechanical principles have been violated. If, for example, great angular momentum has resulted at take-off, appropriate limb movements during flight are required to attempt to counter this. If an inadequate take-off position has been further aggravated by a body position in flight which produces a small moment of inertia and a consequent high angular velocity, the hips will be retarded upon landing. The achievement of acceptable landing positions almost certainly implies a well-executed take-off, mechanically sound movements in the air, and the achievement of a hip position, immediately prior to landing, which permits a good "leg shoot." If the criteria above are being met consistently and landing problems continue, then there may be cause for investigation of physical conditioning components. However, it seems clear that the conditioning training demanded for the accomplishment of aspects of these events described earlier, is more than adequate to meet landing demands.

CONDITIONING TRAINING—SOME CONSIDERATIONS

Selection of appropriate conditioning training for jumpers, or throwers for that matter, has to be somewhat speculative in view of the debatable facets of progressive resistance exercise and the lack of precision in terminology. However, some encouragement must be gained from the realization that progressive resistance exercise principles are well established as important adjuncts to improved sporting performance. Valid explanations are still required—ideal combinations of repetitions, sets and weights, recovery from, and frequency of training need continued investigation with top flight performers as subjects. Isotonic and isometric merits and problems require classification.

Despite these limitations, the effects of P.R.E. on performances in a varied range of physical activities appear most significant. The empirical experiences of countless athletes and coaches cannot be ignored. These experiences must be critically examined and compared with relevant research literature in order to select activities which will enhance an athlete's performance.

The basic aim of conditioning training, in the context of this chapter, is to provide a variety of physical activities which will produce adaptation which will enable athletes to perform more effectively in their chosen events. It is because the empirical evidence suggests that the underlying assumption is being met that conditioning training is so prominent in competitive sport.

Conditioning for Jumping

Running

Since all jumping events require some form of running, this form of conditioning training would seem to be justified. With the possible exception of high jumping, sprinting ability is of great importance and therefore this form of running training is recommended. Modern high jumping approach runs, particularly since the advent of the "Fosbury Flop" technique, are becoming relatively long and fast and athletes use appropriate running training in their programs.

The precise form of sprint training within conditioning training is debatable, but in view of the fact that few runways exceed 150 feet and also because modern jumpers rarely use approach runs in excess of this distance, a training emphasis similar to that of 100 meter sprinters would appear appropriate. (See chapter on Training for Sprinting)

There does not appear to be any justification for cross country or Fartlek running, since the jumping events are entirely anaerobic. Any necessary endurance required of the jumper is likely needed to enable him to extend the volume of work done in out-of-season training sessions and is probably of a local muscular endurance type. Certainly the modern jumping competition format provides for adequate recovery time between efforts. Perusal of training programs reveals interesting variance concerning the type of running activities employed.[11,19,23]

Progressive Resistance Exercises

It is this aspect of training which has received the greatest increase in time allocation during the last two decades. As the renowned Russian coach, V. Dyachkov, states; "The process of physical training, conducted in close unity with the perfection of jumping techniques and the formation of special motor habits, has become the leading factor in the training of jumpers."[8]

Great importance is given to "all-round physical training" aimed at development of general motor skills for both speed and strength and consisting of exercises with the barbell, discus and hammer throwing, running and gymnastics. This aspect of training takes up to 50 percent of the available time and is equally applicable to experienced jumpers.

Other exercises are utilized for mobilizing and for development of resilience. In particular, those which provide for rhythmic alternation of tension and relaxation are selected. They include skiing, easy running, motor games and easy swimming. These exercises occupy approximately 25 percent of training time.

"Special physical fitness," according to Dyatchkov, is attained chiefly through exercises that are directly aimed at developing the muscle groups determining "push-off power." The assumed close relationship of "special physical fitness," exercises with the actual technique of the event is evident.

Jumping exercises (for instance, the hopping and jumping in the hop, step, and jump) which have a basically different pattern in the push-off movement than in high jumping, are excluded from the training of high jumping, since they hamper the mastery of a correct take-off technique. What is applied are such exercises in which the take-off foot is advanced by a forward motion without stressing the impact when it contacts the ground: series jumps following one another, with the roll over from the heel to the sole and single high jumps with a running start, and also such which lack the phase of placing the take-off foot before pushing off.[8]

Dyatchkov also asserts that both research and training practice support the use of barbell exercises. These exercises, in which preference is given to rapid movements such as jerks and snatches, are believed to serve the double purpose of enhancing take-off power and heightening the dermination of the jumper. The weights mainly utilized during these sessions equal 70 to 85 percent of the optimal weight that the jumper can lift. Optimal lifts occur once per week during the preparatory period and once per two weeks during the actual season. Repetitions are few.

"The number of lifts amounts to three to four in the case of the light weights, dropping to one to two lifts with the increase of the weight of the barbell."[8]

Four types of exercises are reported: squatting with a heavy weight, 242–330 pounds (110–150 kg); jumping up and squatting, with lesser weights, 176–198 pounds (80–90 kg); jumping up and down with slight bending at the knees, 220–286 pounds (100–130 kg); rising on the toes and jumping on the toes, 220–286 pounds (100–130 kg).

The springy jumping up and down with knees slightly bent receives major concentration. However, variance of performance is deliberately introduced. Weights used, speed of jumping up and down, and angle of knee bend are changed. This is done to prevent the rapid adaptation of the jumper's organism to identical and repeated conditions for fulfilling the exercises, and also the stresses involved which could deter the further development of the muscles of the jumper's balance and motor machinery.

Different weights and different activities are employed in a single training session. Jumps with the barbell, rapid jumping exercises without the barbell, stretching and loosening exercises, and sprinting are typical.

Imitative exercises designed to replicate high-jumping movements are included very frequently, presumably in the belief that such movements will assist the athlete in producing precision and automation of jumping patterns. The value placed upon these imitative exercises may account for the relatively small percentage of time allocated to actual jumping over the bar. Some 12 to 16 percent of total training time is utilized for actual high jumping; an average, 1200 to 1300 jumps per year!

Mention was made earlier in the chapter about the seeming value of concurrent conditioning and technique training. Dyatchkov reports that coaches, doctors and physiologists working jointly on problems of the most favorable sequencing of the main methods of training, have found that exercises with moderately heavy barbells appeared to act as a stimulus for subsequent muscular activities. Consequently, jumps and jumping exercises, following a day or two after weight training, were very successful. The opposite sequence produced inferior results.

The model offered by Dykatchkov [11] in a most comprehensive article would be well worthy of adoption in principle. It indicates the need for prolonged and intensive physical conditioning, even for experienced jumpers. This need is based upon the assumption that such conditioning forms the essential base upon which more specific conditioning exercises can be developed, and which, additionally, provides the framework upon which technique training can be built. Versatility is inherent in the model in an apparent attempt to account for the numerous variables associated with the jumpers' training.

Various articles dealing with the different jumping events support the importance of extensive conditioning training, though the percentage of time allocated to different aspects of preparation shows considerable variance and terminology is not common.[19,26,39,41] Hopper,[16] in an article highlighting some of the technical necessities in jumping take-offs, implies a need for conditioning activities which will permit short-lived forces of up to five times body weight to be transmitted through limbs specially braced to do so.

Predominant factors for quality performance in the jumping events appear to be speed, power, mobility and neuromuscular skill. Since motion results only when force has been applied, the ability to apply force effectively is an important quality. The change in speed of a jumper depends not only upon the force applied but also upon the time for which it operates, its impulse. The dynamic nature of jumping activities makes it very difficult for the athlete to apply force effectively. According to Dyson:

". . . to be able to accelerate his body or a throwing implement, an athlete must be capable of moving at a greater speed than the ground or the missile moving away from him. And the greater his speed, in comparison, the greater his effective force will be. Clearly, then, the ability of an athlete to apply force depends not only upon strength but also upon speed." [12]

Strength is defined as the ability of a muscle to exert force against resistance. As such, it is associated with a single muscular effort.

In jumping, an athlete must develop the ability to do work. In order to do work a force must move a body through some distance. Work = Force × Distance. More importantly for the jumper is the time taken to do this work. This rate of work is termed "power" and jumpers base much of their conditioning training on the development of this quality. Power = Work ÷ Time.

Mobility, related to the range of movement about a joint, is clearly required if the athlete is to move his limbs over optimum ranges and in certain motor patterns.

Since the qualities listed and described above are affected by training and as there is consensus that they are important components of successful performance, the best results should be obtained by emphasizing these factors in training, with the end product constantly in mind.

Technique Training

While the rigorous conditioning training appears justifiable and based upon sound principles, it is, nevertheless, a means to an end. It is therefore imperative that the athlete practices and perfects the technique of his actual event.

The specificity of the neuromuscular skill requirements should be appreciated in this aspect of training. Any modifications of the complete event, such as shorter or slower approach runs, low cross bars, weighted equipment, or imitative movements should be viewed cautiously, at least until much more evidence is available concerning their real value and in spite of their current use.[10,37,48]

The support for specificity seems plausible and while this situation remains there is good reason to insist upon strict replication of the competitive situation in technique training. If the analysis of the event reveals the possibility of appropriate technique practice of a part of the whole, the athlete should be instructed to return the part to the whole on frequent occasions.[40] It is also feasible that certain parts of an event warrant a greater concentration of time and effort. The relative importance of different phases should be reflected in training percentages, while still appreciating the totality of the event.

Dobroth is quite clear in the establishment of priorities. "Without question, training for the run-up and take-off is the most important part of learning to jump."[6]

This statement would receive widespread support, particularly since bar clearance is a function of the run-up and take-off. The words "learning to jump" could be changed to "learning to improve jumping performance" without loss of validity.

Successful technique training implies sound technical knowledge in order that appropriate neuromuscular skills can be inculcated and appropriate observations made of performance. Assuming this, certain factors must be understood if quality training is to be achieved.

To be successful, technique training demands great concentration. This inevitably results in fatigue and indicates the need for spacing this type of training session. It is suggested that the fatigue of the central nervous system, resulting from maximum jumping efforts, requires a restoration period of from two to five days.[9]

Training sessions must attempt to provide at least preparatory experiences for the athlete by the simulation of competitive demands associated with the following:

1. different durations of waiting periods between jumps;

2. different qualities of facilities, particularly track surfaces;
3. varying weather conditions.

Undoubtedly the importance of such factors are related to the experiences of the athlete. It is also true to state that, when possible, early season competition provides an excellent opportunity for the most valuable technique training. This latter technique training opportunity also provides for the experiencing of important psychological factors of performance which are often difficult to simulate in a training session.

The percentage of total training time allocated to technique training is dependent upon many variables. Examination of current practices reveals much variance. Certainly stated percentages can be misleading if left unexamined because it is possible that an athlete who allocates only 10 to 15 percent of his time to technique work may, nevertheless, be doing a great deal of jumping or throwing due to his great total training load.

COMMON FACTORS IN THROWING EVENTS

Preparatory Phase

In different throwing events the athlete utilizes preliminary movements which will enable him to arrive in the basic throwing position with the maximum number of technical advantages permitted by the rules of the event. An efficient technique permits the athlete to exert the forces of his entire body over the greatest practicable range and, therefore, for the longest time period. Preliminary movements present the athlete with better opportunities to achieve this objective. Such movements overcome the inertia of the implement and additionally produce muscular quickness into the throwing position when muscular power and leverage have enormous effect upon the implement's release velocity.

It follows that training activities must account for the demands of preliminary movements, whether they be a straight approach run, a glide across a circle, or rotational movements across a circle. Each event exhibits its technical peculiarities in this regard, but it appears reasonable to suggest that, with the exception of the hammer throw, it is the skill learning component which requires the greatest time allocation. Javelin and discus are relatively light implements which demand skillful control, rather than brute force, during the approach run and running rotation turn respectively. The 16-pound shot is certainly not the major limiting factor in the development of a more effective glide for a shot putter. Clearly an adequate muscular component is required to enable the thrower in these events to achieve the necessary movements "en route," but it is argued that the physical conditioning associated with the actual throwing phase provides a more than adequate preparation.

The hammer throw presents a different problem because the nature of the event requires complex motor patterns as the turns commence. In addition, the 16 pound hammer head is located at the end of a wire and a handle or grip, which produces a total implement almost four feet in length. This creates many additional control problems for the athlete. Sheer mass is of importance in increasing the radius of movement, so increasing the implement's speed. As the axis of the thrower's turning movement passes through his feet and the common center of gravity of athlete and hammer, the heavier athlete (providing he is adequately strong) can bring his shoulders closer to this axis than a lighter athlete. Also, as the speed of the hammer head increases during successive turns, the thrower experiences increasing difficulty with balance and control. The hammer's centrifugal pull in a sagittal plane and the equal and opposite force from the ground and thrusting against the feet increasingly tend to rotate him forward. Thus the thrower needs to be adequately conditioned to ensure attainment of maximum benefits from technique training.

Throwing Position and Delivery

This phase of throwing can be compared to the take-off in the jumping events. If the preliminary objectives have been achieved, the following are true:
1. the inertia of the implement has been overcome;
2. the implement is being accelerated;
3. the thrower is achieving "muscular quickness" as a preparation for the phase of the throw when it will be of maximum benefit;
4. the thrower is moving into a basic throwing position which permits the application of force over the greatest practicable range;
5. force is being applied to the missile, as far as practicable, in the intended direction of the throw.

The description which follows suggests the possible benefits which may result from extensive conditioning training, as a basis for the achievement of appropriate technique work. Obviously total separation of the two aspects is not warranted, though the achievement of effective technique is in many cases limited by the absence of adequate physical conditioning.

> In a summation of throwing forces therfore, the levers of the body should operate so that each can make a maximum, or very near maximum, contribution to speed. Hence the use of slower but more forceful muscles and levers first (i.e. of the trunk and thighs); while the faster but relatively weaker joints (i.e. of the arms, hands, lower legs and feet) exert their forces after the missile has developed considerable speed. While the feet and hands transmit force during the earlier movements, their own smaller forces are added only towards the end of a throw. It is important that each lever, having attained top speed, should continue at that speed in support of the movements which follow, bringing about not only a summation of forces, but a summation of rotations, too.[12]

The assumption that strength training plays a major role in contributing to effective technique provides the prime reason for the weight training programs of the great throwers of the world. However, from the description above, it is also clear that timing and coordination of the various body segments are essential. The appropriate motor patterns must be learned and perfected. If (and this word is selected deliberately) the adaptations resulting from progressive resistance training change the coordination and timing of the throw in subtle ways, it becomes important for the athlete to do a certain amount of conditioning and technique training concurrently. Intuitively, this procedure would appear to be sound, if for no other reason than the technical adaptation to accommodate changes produced by a progressive resistance program would be gradual and, therefore, easily established.

CONDITIONING FOR THROWING

Traditionally, throwers have the reputation for being determined progressive resistance exercise devotees, particularly in association with weight training. Relatively small portions of training regimes are occupied with running activities and those activities that are used generally involve short distance, maximum effort, sprints. This type of running is classified as a "power" activity and, as such, is assumed to be closely linked with throwing requirements.

The justification for conditioning activities, particularly those which may enhance a thrower's ability to apply force more effectively, receives ample support in an excellent article by Hopper[17] in which he discusses the development of maximum explosive effort.

While weight training forms a major part of a thrower's conditioning work, considerable variation in content is demonstrated. There is increasing support for year-round weight training, however, views differ regarding the advisability of attempting to increase strength during the competitive season. Those who support the maintenance, as opposed to the increase, of strength, base their views on the belief that it is more beneficial to develop qualities that influence the application of strength, namely, speed or quickness, neuromuscular coordination, flexibility, relaxation, and mental attitude.[20]

There is, additionally, the appreciation that many throwing movements occur in the horizontal plane. This factor has implications for the selection of appropriate exercises of a strengthening nature, particularly since so many weight lifting exercises involve work in a vertical plane.

Mobility is associated with range of movement and since this is clearly associated with successful throwing, some attention should be given to mobility exercises. According to Paisch,[24] mobility exercises can be done with or without resistance, working the joints carefully and gradually through an increased range. He also suggests specific event exercises, concentrating on taking the joints through movements similar to those of the throw.

A study by Sermeev [35] provides interesting information on mobility. Specially constructed testing equipment was used to determine the amount of active flexion and extension and carrying of the straightened leg. One thousand four hundred and forty sportsmen and over 3,000 children and adults, nonsportsmen, were measured for hip joint movement. It was found that mobility in the hip joints is not equal for various movements and is not developed identically in various age periods. The years 7 through 11 account for the greatest growth period, at 15 years the greatest mobility is achieved, after which there is a gradual decrease. Significant drops in mobility occur after 50 years of age.

In all investigated movements the amount of passive mobility was found to be greater than active mobility. The youngest school children were found to have the biggest difference between active and passive movement, 35 to 50 degrees; adults and older school children, 20 to 40 degrees. This decreases with age as the muscular-ligamentous apparatus becomes less elastic. In sportsmen, mobility in the hip joint changes with age. In a group of gymnasts mobility increased between the ages of ten and 16 years. After this, mobility tends to lessen, mainly as a result of their training not including mobility promoting exercises. Mobility in the hip joint changes unequally in sportsmen of different specialities. Gymnasts show greatest change and team sportmen the least. The level of sports preparation dictates the amount of mobility in the hip joint with the highly qualified sportsmen achieving the greatest mobility.

In an experiment involving young track and field athletes it was found that four specialized exercises, of 18 to 26 repetitions each, resulted in indices of mobility in the hip joint showing a mean increase of 28 percent, while a control group, training as usual, remained almost at the beginning level. When the specialized training was discontinued there was an immediate lessening in mobility.

Technique Training

Many of the statements made in connection with technique training for jumping are appropriate here and the principles involved are certainly the same. While it is true that the throws can be broken down into a preparatory phase and a delivery phase there is continued need for caution in spending too much time in practicing these segments in isolation, thereby losing movement totality.

Views on the intensity of throwing in training have been subject to change over time. Greater appreciation of the ramifications of muscular and nervous fatigue, has produced a trend towards quality rather than quantity. Easy throwing, using high repetitions, is not recommended, since this practice almost certainly means that the thrower is learning an inappropriate skill.

In order to obtain maximum returns from technique training, a qualified observer should be present on numerous occasions. In this way valuable additional feedback is made available to the athlete and faults can be detected and eradicated with minimal unlearning. The utilization of almost instant visual feedback via video tape is a splendid means of augmenting kinaesthetic and auditory feedback.

Related Literature

The additional review of literature is intended as an example of research and scholarly articles associated with training.

Sabin and Chudinov [34] investigated training methods of highly qualified sportsmen by questionnaire method. They concluded that year-round training, high quality training make-up, suitable rest, appropriate general and specialized physical preparation, rational training, and pedagogical control are required for the active growth of sports mastery. An examination of training loads from aspects of biochemistry, physiology and the theory of physical education was undertaken by Volkov and Zatsiorskil. [44] Fundamental criteria for the best choice of loads were discussed. Specificity of training loads—intensity, length of segment overcome, duration of rest intervals, character of rest, and number of repetitions—were described and discussed. The article concluded with a discussion of the systematic use of maximum loads in training and with a warning about overtraining. Kazakov and Kolosova [21] reported on the use of an arterial oscillograph during training. This instrument shows the dynamic indices of systolic and diastolic arterial pressure and the mean pressure and also more clearly distinguishes the hemodynamic changes. The authors stated that the use of the oscillogram during training and restoration periods can help the doctor and trainer to alter methods of training and individual work load dosages and is invaluable in that it can be used by any qualified trainer or teacher. It is interesting to note the reference to the close liaison between the doctor and coach in this positive, developmental role, rather than in the equally important, but somewhat negative injury treatment role of many doctors associated with sport.

A report on the training of the Soviet Gymnasts by Ukran [42] is worthy of appraisal. The gymnasts trained according to a four year plan constructed on basic annual cycles. Each year consisted of the Preparatory Period of three to six months, the Competitive Period of five to eight months, and the Transitory Period of training. Studies made of top Soviet Gymnasts during training give a clear picture of load changes. There is gradual growth, first in volume, then in intensity. This reaches a maximum about the middle of the cycle and is maintained for some time. Significant decrease in load volume follows while intensity remains high for the start of competition. The competitive cycle is composed of four phases. The maximum amount of training takes place during the third phase; less in the first; still less in the fourth; and the minimum amount in the second. Each phase consists of specific training aims and serves as a guide only. A gymnast's individuality is always taken into account as is the importance of an uninterrupted competitive cycle. Conclusions were:

1. sufficiently high loads during training are necessary for success;
2. variation of training loads is advisable;
3. during competitive periods the beginning load is not significant in total volume and intensity, the loads increase gradually and at the end of the cycle load volume is lowered, but intensity is increased;
4. the four phases of training in each competitive period are: (a) single elements and combinations of these; (b) continuation of (a) with whole routines included; (c) working out and combining elements plus whole routines; (d) strengthening the routines.

Federov [13] investigated development of speed-strength qualities in 11 to 12-year-olds and hypothesized that speed and strength developed simultaneously is more effective than speed and strength or endurance trained for individually. The aim was to determine the best training regime for 11 to 12-year-olds to enable good early development and sports success during the teens. Investigations of speed-strength development were undertaken for one school year, with two groups of fifteen boys each. One group devoted 50 percent of the time to speed-strength training and 50 percent to all-round general training. The other group devoted 75 percent of the time to speed training and 25 percent to strength training. Training sessions lasted two hours each, three times per week. Both groups started with 45 to 50 minutes of warm-up exercises and concluded with similar exercises. The balance of training time was specific for each group.

Tests used for training evaluation included broad jump, triple jump, shot (3 kg), the press, and 30 meters dash. Chest cage measurements of inspiratory capacity, dynamometer readings of left and right hands and legs, and height and weight changes, were recorded. Pre- and post-training measurements were taken.

Results showed that the group spending 50 percent of time on speed-strength training had a greater increase in weight resulting from greater muscle mass and were better in all other indices, while height and growth was constant in both groups. Youngsters wishing to specialize in sports involving throwing and jumping were recommended to spend not less than 50 percent of training time in speed-strength exercises.

While the 50 percent all-round training may have had an equally important influence upon the results of the superior group as measured, and while results with a larger N or numerous replications would be very valuable, studies of this type are encouraging for two reasons. First, the study continued for a whole school year, as opposed to the four or six weeks of so many investigations. As such, it would seem more appropriate to modern training practices. Second, the aim of the study was realistic in attempting to produce information which is applicable to best selection of training activities.

Three articles indicate the need for caution in interpreting research in the strength, power, endurance complex. Glencross [15] reviewed literature on the measurement of human power output. Human power production was classified according to the duration of the work performed, e.g. for a continuous sequence of movements, as in running or cycling, or a single explosive movement of less than one second in duration, like shot putting or jumping. Review of methods used to measure power indicated that sports-type skill methods are somewhat inadequate and invalid. Mechanical methods, based directly on the calculation of the components of force, time and distance, depend upon accurate measurement if reliability is to be assured. Physiological methods utilize measurement of the metabolic process. Energy output is assessed by calorimitory, or oxygen consumption and the respiratory quotient. In order to measure the total external power output it is essential to be able to measure all the work performed by the moving parts of the body at optimal speed and load conditions.

Adamson [1] discussed various misconceptions concerning strength and endurance by critically reviewing selected literature. In a later article, he commented upon the inappropriate use of the term "power," particularly as applied to athletic activities. ". . . . . .Power, in the strict mechanical sense, will not be a useful parameter of impulsive muscle action. The real measure of the action is the $F \times t$ impulse itself and the manner in which coordinated muscle action can generate the largest possible impulse." [2]

A review article by Pickering [28] reevaluated isometric training and provided guidance for selection of progressive resistance exercises.

Training with weighted implements or by using weighted jackets, belts or wrist and ankle weights, is not uncommon. Lewis [23] reported the development of satisfactory leg power and jumping ability over a four-week period with performers who were already at a high level of fitness. The Lewis Sports Training Belt was the resistance device utilized. While specific studies in this area, associated with track and field, appear to be lacking, Straub[38] showed that related research is both incomplete and conflicting. There is considerable need for study utilizing good research design and involving jumpers and throwers engaged in year round training.

Statistical techniques, utilizing factor analysis, may be of value in aiding the selection of both participants and training activities, following the recognition of primary event requirements. The limits of factor analysis associated with the subjective naming of the factors derived, should be understood in the examination of any work of this type. Zatziorskii and Matveev[47] conducted a study on the factorial structure of training condition in throwers. Three experiments resulted in the isolation of such factors as:

Experiment 1

a. strength factor and total body dimensions;

b. coordination;

Experiment 2

a. anthropometric measures;

b. coordination of thrower's movement;

Experiment 3

a. physical dimensions with weight having the highest factor loading;

b. level of achievement of the thrower's motor movements;

c. static strength of the muscular groups.

Simon[36] performed a factor analysis of the Olympic Decathlon and isolated six factors which he named: cardiorespiratory endurance, throwing strength, running speed, spring, javelin, and pole vault. Zacheorskii and Godek[46] factor analyzed the results of 54 Olympic decathletes. Their results showed that special training should be given for great strength, sprint preparation, and running endurance. Strength and sprinting ability were considered to have the greatest meaning for good results. They indicated that more meaningful analysis would be possible with additional information on anthropometrical measurements, physiological data, medical examination and exercise results.

The selection of a take-off leg for jumpers receives little consideration. Ilin[18] considered that choice is usually made in view of asymmetrical development of motor qualities or asymmetrical development of coordination of one side or the other. Results from his large study are interesting for those concerned with the teaching and training of young jumpers. He concluded:

1. there is no innate predisposition in man to asymmetrical legs in motor qualities as there is no relation to asymmetry in the arms;

2. only in those people who mainly used one leg was functional asymmetry of the motor qualities observed;

3. the choice of take-off leg has no bearing on the strength of the leg.

Further study is suggested to determine if the presence of arm asymmetry could influence the choice of take-off leg.

Behnke and Royce[4] described body size, shape and composition of several types of athletes. Various anthropological measurement techniques are available which have potential value for the selection of athletes for various sports disciplines. Knowledge of body composition can be useful in definitive evaluation of physical potential. Examination of height and weight statistics of both men and women throwers in the 1968 Olympic Games reveals a predisposition of tall, heavy, athletes into the events. Such information can be valuable as part of the selection process of potential top class performers.

The psychological aspects of training cannot be ignored and more time and effort is being devoted to the fuller understanding of psychological parameters. Platzbecker[29] discussed the psychological make-up of top performance athletes. He considered that the capacity of a human being to bring his maximum achievement to fulfillment is dependent upon his degree of sensitivity. Athletes appeared to strive for security, recognition and power. Psychological dangers associated with intensive training were also discussed.

While there is increasing concern over drug abuse in modern sport, this topic is worthy of separate treatment and only passing mention will be made here. Keul, Reindell and Roskamm[22] considered the pharmaceutical possibilities of increase in bodily efficiency. The ramifications of doping are considered in the article and objections to drugs are listed. Drugs exist which can bring an individual to a state of fitness that he cannot achieve himself through a systematic program of training, proper nutrition, adequate amount of sleep and a natural easing of tension.

Carlile[5] offered sound advice by listing ten principles of training. Coaches and athletes should have this knowledge as a basis for the employment of modern training methods.

It is perhaps appropriate to conclude this review by supporting a plea by Pelton[25] for the need for replication of research in an attempt to avoid administrative errors, sampling errors, computational errors and population errors, and also to strengthen the generalizations and interpretations which can be understood by the practitioner.

As stated at the outset, much work remains to be done if fuller understanding of the best training methods is to be achieved. Much progress has been made, however, in terms of improved performances despite conflicting evidence by athletes following different training routines. Perhaps it is important to remember that there are, "many ways to skin a cat." Until such time as final proof is available in answer to the many questions on the training for field events, programs must proceed on the knowledge currently available. The concerned coach should always remember he is using training as a means of assisting a performer to improve.

> For one thing that no two people are born exactly alike. There are innate differences which fit them for different occupations. So the conclusion is that more things will be produced and the work will be more easily and better done, when every man is set free from all other occupations to do, at the right time, the one thing for which he is naturally fitted. . . . You remember that no one man can practise many trades or arts satisfactorily. They will need the most complete freedom from other occupations and the greatest amount of skill and practice, and also a native aptitude for their calling.
>
> Plato, *The Republic,*
> Chapters 6 and 7.

The advisor may additionally gain assistance in activity selection from the prayer of the philosopher-theologian, Reinhold Neibuhr.

> Grant me serenity to accept the things I cannot change; courage to change the things I can; and wisdom to know the difference.

REFERENCES

1. Adamson, G.: "Some misconceptions concerning strength and endurance, *Roy Can Legion's Coach Rev, 12:*3–4, 1966.
2. Adamson, G. T. and Whitney, R. J.: The fallacy of athletic power *Roy Can Legion's Coach Rev, 15:*1–2, 1969.
3. Amateur Athletic Association: Specific Event Booklets, 26 Park Crescent, London.
4. Behnke, A. R. and Royce, J.: Body size, shape, and composition of several types of athletes. *J Sports Med Phys Fitness, 6:*75–88, 1966.
5. Carlile, F.: Ten principles of training. *Track Technique, 1:*23–29–30, 1960.
6. Dobroth, J.: The high jump. In Wilt, F. and Ecker, T. (Eds.): *International Track and Field Coaching Encyclopedia.* New York, Parker Publishing, 1970.
7. Doherty, J. K.: *Modern Track and Field.* Englewood Cliffs, N.J., Prentice-Hall, 1963.
8. Dyatchkov, V. M.: Problems involved in the training of Soviet high jumpers. *Track Technique, 5:*138, 1961.
9. ———: Do not copy but create. *Sports Life Russia, 3:*10, 1963.
10. ———: High jumping exercises. *Track Technique, 25:*779–781, 1966.
11. ———: High jumping. *Track Technique, 36:*1123–1155, 1969.
12. Dyson, G. H. G.: *The Mechanics of Athletics.* London, University of London Press Ltd. 1962.
13. Federov, O. V.: Development of speed-strength qualities in youngsters. *Theory Practice Phys Culture, 3:*72–74, 1963.
14. Ganslen, R. V.: *The Mechanics of the Pole Vault.* St. Louis, J. S. Swift, 1965.
15. Glencross, D. J.: A review of relevant literature on the measurement of human power output. *Phys Educ, 57:*67–74, 1965.
16. Hopper, B. J.: Rotation—A vital factor in athletic technique. *Track Technique, 15:*468–471, 1964.
17. ———: Development of maximum explosive effort. *Track Technique, 27:*850–853, 1967.

18. Ilin, E. P.: Function asymmetry of the legs. *Theory Practice Phys. Culture*, 1:22–25, 1963.
19. Jarver, J.: The long jump. In Wilt, F. and Ecker, T. (Eds.): *International Track and Field Coaching Encyclopedia*. New York, Parker Publishing, 1970.
20. Jesse, J. P.: Explosive power for the shot put. *Track Technique*, 14:424–427, 1964.
21. Kazakov, M. B., Kolosova, T. B. and Hodakov, N. M.: Oscillographic Observations of Field Athletes. *Theory Practice Phys Culture*, 3:26–28, 1963.
22. Keul, J., Reindell, H., Roskamm, H., and Weidemann, H.: Pharmaceutical possibilities of increase in bodily efficiency. *Sportarzt und Sportmedizin*, 2:48–49, 1966.
23. McNab, T.: *Triple Jump*. London, Amateur Athletic Association, 1968.
23a. Lewis, A. D.: The improvement in jumping ability through use of the Lewis Sports Training Belt. *N Z J Health, Phys Educ Rec*, 3:17–23, 1968.
24. Paisch, W.: The Javelin Throw. In Wilt, F. and Ecker, T. (Eds.): *International Track and Field Coaching Encyclopedia*. New York, Parker Publishing, 1970.
25. Pelton, B.: A need for replication in research in health, physical education and recreation. *Res Q*, 613–615, 1970.
26. Perrin, W.: The pole vault. In Wilt, F. and Ecker, T. (Eds.): *International Track and Field Coaching Encyclopedia*. New York, Parker Publishing, 1970.
27. Pickering, R. J.: Strength Training for Athletics. London, Amateur Athletic Association, 1965.
28. ————: Reevaluation of isometric training. *Track Technique* 27:835–836, 1967.
29. Platzbecker, P.: The psychological make-up of the top performance athlete. *Sportarzt und Sportmedizin*, 3:99–102, 1966.
30. Powell, J. T.: A compilation and analysis of classified indexed and/or completed research in track and field athletics 1900–1963 inclusive. *Roy Can Legion's Coach Rev*, 7–12, 1967.
31. ————: A compilation and analysis of classified indexed and/or completed research in track and field athletics 1960–1968 inclusive. Park II. *Roy Can Legion's Coach Rev*, 8–11, 1970.
32. Prihoda, L.: The olympic triple jump. *Roy Can Legion's Coach Rev*, 6–8, 1966.
33. Prost, R.: The training of the long jumper. *Amicale des Entraineurs Francais d'Athletisme*, 19:9–15, 1968.
34. Sabin, S. A., and Chudinov, P. E.: Generalizations and analyzations of the training of qualified sportsmen. *Theory Practice Phys Culture*, 7:21–24, 1963.
35. Sermeev, B. C.: Development of mobility in the hip joint in sportsmen. *Theory Practice Phys Culture*, 12:25–26, 1966.
36. Simon, J.: Factor analysis of olympic decathlon. *Hermes T. Inst., Lien Opvoed, Univ. Kath Levven*, 2:159–171, 1968.
37. Starzynski, T.: Triple jump exercises. *Track Technique*, 15:473–476, 1964.
38. Straub, W. F.: Effect of overload training procedures upon velocity and accuracy of the overarm throw. *Res Q*, 370–379, 1968.
39. Tang Eng Yoon, P.: The Triple Jump. In Wilt, F. and Ecker, T. (Eds.): *International Track and Field Coaching Encyclopedia*. New York, Parker Publishing, 1970.
40. Tev-Ovanesyan, I.: Tev-Ovanesyan on the long jump. *Track Technique* 27:858–860, 1967.
41. Toomsalu, R.: Training and technique of Soviet hop-step-jumpers. *Track Technique*, 1:26–29, 1960.
42. Ukran, M. L.: Training load dynamics of the strongest Soviet gymnasts. *Theory Practice Phys Culture*, 10:24–27, 1964.

43. Volkov, N. I., and Zatsiorskii, V. M.: Several questions on the theory of training loads. *Theory Practice Phys Culture, 6:*20–24, 1964.
44. Wilt, F., Ecker, T., (Eds.): *International Track and Field Coaching Encyclopedia.* New York, Parker Publishing, 1970.
45. Zacheorskii, V. M. and Godek, M. A.: Basic training factors with decathlon athletes. *Theory Practice of Phys Culture, 8:*27–30, 1963.
46. Zatziorskii, V. M. and Matveev, E. N.: Study of the factorial structure of training condition in throwers. *Theory Practice of Phys Culture, 32:*9–11, 1969.
47. Zivkovic, M.: How I train Yugoslavian high jumpers. *Track Technique, 14:*420–424, 1964.

CHAPTER IX

SPRINTING

P. Radford

. . . The star sprinter is born and not made and no one without natural fleetness of foot can ever become a champion.[5]

DEAN CROMWELL

SUCH GREAT DIFFERENCES exist between the task of running a 50 metres sprint indoors and running 400 meters outdoors that to discuss "sprinting" or "sprinters" as one generic group could be misleading. It is far more useful to distinguish between the different types of sprint events, and so for the purposes of this chapter four categories will be discussed:

Acceleration sprints—(Indoor dashes; distances up to 60 meters approximately)

Pure sprints	—100 yds/100 metres
Extended sprints	—200 meters/220 yds
Modified sprints	—400 meters/440 yds

Events in each of these categories have their own set of unique problems to overcome. Athletes who are successful in one category may not be successful in another, and training and racing principles that are developed by athletes, coaches and theorists often apply to only one or two categories of sprint events and rarely to all four.[15] The opening quotation, for example, may apply to sprinters in all sprint events, but it most obviously applies to the Acceleration sprinter or Pure sprinter, and indeed the "natural" qualities that the most successful of these athletes typically bring to their events are so considerable that many authorities in the past have seriously wondered whether training of any kind would improve their performances. It is certainly true that no training that we know of today can make great Acceleration sprinters or great Pure sprinters out of those who do not already have ample talents of their own. At the other end of the sprint scale, the athletes competing in the Modified sprints are much less confined by their "natural" sprinting ability, and wise and systematic training can transform performances in these events. There is probably no single approach which could legitimately be labelled "sprint training" and the demands of events from each category must be assessed separately.

Athletic performances are often difficult to understand because they are

105

the result of a complex interplay of many factors. A sprinter's performance in a 100 metres race involves the use of anaerobic mechanisms to produce work, but the efficiency of that work is also affected by the body structures of the athlete (body type, limb length, etc.),[36] neuromuscular mechanisms, skill, experience, anxiety levels, motivation, level of expectancy, and many other factors. From race to race some of these factors will change and the total performance will be modified.

Training programs produced for athletes should never be rigid, but should be the result of several processes working together:
   a. understanding of the event,
   b. understanding of the athlete (personal peculiarities, strengths and weaknesses),
   c. understanding of the effects of training.

Failure to observe important information from any one of these areas would result in the reduced efficiency of a training program.

Although this chapter is primarily concerned with the first of these three areas of understanding, the reader must always base decision on information from all three categories.

THE DEMANDS MADE BY THE SPRINT EVENTS

Success in the Acceleration, Pure and Extended sprints rests upon the efficiency of the anaerobic mechanisms of the athlete, whereas the sprinter competing in the Modified sprints has an additional aerobic component which will contribute to the final performance.[26]

Although athletes and coaches must be aware of the differences between aerobic and anaerobic metabolism, training principles cannot be created from this alone. Aerobic and anaerobic components do not exist as dichotomous units of total metabolism, but work together and overlap each other in various ways dependent upon the nature of the task and the nature of the individual performing the task. Even under the broad banner of "anaerobic metabolism" there are several distinct mechanisms which tend to play a greater or a lesser role in any given short-term, high-quality performance.[18,26] Individual events, therefore, tend to make specific demands upon the athlete, and although athletes have always had their own individual ways of exploiting their talents, a closer look at the different sprint events will help in more specifically understanding the qualities that athletes need if they are to be successful.

In the Acceleration sprints athletes produce the fastest limb speeds of all sprinters—in some cases over five strides per second for males.[11,19,22] The most challenging task facing these athletes is the rapid production of immense amounts of work in extremely short periods of time, hence the muscular power of the athlete is of very great importance. (In this chapter the word "power" is used in the way that has become accepted in popular athletic parlance.) Athletes are said to be "powerful" if they can produce high levels of work in extremely short periods of time. Their power increases if they produce the same work in less time, or if they produce greater work in the same time. Although "power" may have several components [14] it is popularly thought of as being explosive or dynamic in nature. The meanings of the word "power" are, of course, much more precise when associated with the principles of mechanical work [1,4] or physiological work,[2,9,25] its use in this chapter refers to the ability of the athlete to perform dynamic work, and involves the whole neuromuscular process which results in work performed.[28]

A greater proportion of the Acceleration sprint than any other sprint race is taken up with the start, and so success in the start is of obvious importance. The time taken to reach top running speed will vary from athlete to athlete, but for the good sprinter it will tend to take the total distance run, for very little top-speed running is done in the indoor dashes; as soon as acceleration is complete the race is over.[16,17,24,38] Forces exerted by athletes tend to differ from individual to individual and from one starting technique to another, but we may expect the athlete to exert resultant forces of between two and one-half and three times body weight,[30] with the average sprinter producing work at the rate of approximately 13.0 horse-power.[12]

Production of work at these rates requires great strength and great speed of movement, and the way in which athletes optimize the resources that they have depends in no small measure on neuromuscular skill, and it would be misleading to suggest that development of strength alone will produce improvements in starting performance; one must also look at the athlete's ability to make subtle changes in the neuromuscular timing to produce the most desirable movement patterns. One writer refers to the "skill in matching the speed of the foot with the speed of the ground as it approaches"; this seems to be a much neglected idea. There is considerable variation with the first few strides of a sprint race and changes occur in the ratios of time spent on driving, support and airborn phases of the stride,[23] and although this is also affected by strength and limb structure, the element of neuromuscular skill must not be underestimated. Studies that analysed the running stride cycle have shown that sprinters are likely to be in contact with the ground for 40 percent of the time,[21,22] but the variability of this figure should always be remembered. Rigidity of motor pattern may well be a liability to the sprinter, for it seems that for each stage of the race, almost indeed, each stride, the pattern of the stride undergoes some change.

The subtle change in striding rate are probably not deliberate, even though the sprinter often does consciously decide whether to take long strides or short. The problem does not necessarily resolve itself into the old dilemma of limb speed vs. stride length [19,22,32] there are many possible ways of achieving any given stride length. That mysterious element, natural ability, for these events probably resides in the neuromuscular organizations which enables these slight changes to take place whilst working close to maximum work output. It has been suggested that it is limb-speed itself which is responsible, this, however, seems unlikely, for the sprinter could always produce greater limb speeds if he were allowed to reduce the total work output.[35]

Although it is extremely unwise to consider the start as a separate and distinct part of the sprint race, the ways in which the athlete's start initiates the entire acceleration pattern are outside the scope of this chapter. It must be appreciated, nevertheless, that the sprinter is initiating a series of skilled movements by means of which great limb speed is combined with great application of force. Early in the race, when acceleration is greatest, the sprinter has the power of choice in resolving the perpetual stride length/ stride rate dilemma. As speed increases and the acceleration component of the total velocity dwindles to nothing, the ability of the athlete to manipulate stride length and stride rate becomes much less. In this regard the event can "take over" the athlete who steadily loses control over the whole task. So, although the sprinter may be able to run on the spot with over ten "strides" per second, in a race four and one-half to five strides per second are more likely. The problem of control over leg speed and stride length is greater for the Pure sprinter than the sprinter in the Acceleration sprints, for the developing momentum up to top speed running increasingly carries the athlete over the foot which is in contact with the ground and produces a certain range of movement and length of stride so that the athlete's ability to control leg speed/stride length rapidly diminishes.

For the sprinters in Acceleration sprints there must be sufficient strength and power, and sufficiently rapid mobilization of energy to succeed, sufficient neuromuscular skill to channel the power adequately, and a disposition which enables them to perform at peak efficiency whilst under extreme stress. The ability to do this seems to depend in no small measure on developing a familiarity with the specific tasks.

One of the greatest problems facing the Pure sprinter is in developing any familiarity with top speed running. Attempts to learn from the experience received from running at less than maximum speeds seems to be of little use in perfecting the skills of top-speed running, but the sensations associated with top-speed running are particularly elusive and difficult to recreate in training. The ritual of the routine training session is unlikely to provide the motivation for absolute top-speed running, and few Pure sprinters can approach their competitive bests in their daily training. No distance run in training that is less than 50 to 55 metres can give the good sprinter the sensations and the experience he needs because of the time that is necessary to reach top-speeds, and so most starting practices fail to provide top-speed sensations. Training sessions in which sprinters must run many repetitions or run over-distances tends to deplete the athlete's anaerobic resources and so make the production of top-speed running extremely unlikely. The desire to run at top-speed in training poses unique problems: what are the Pure sprinters to do? If they run over very short distances in training (25–35 metres) they can perform many repetitions and are therefore able to train the anaerobic mechanisms without getting into the limiting problems of lactate build-up, but they do not experience top-speed running nor do they develop the ability to link the early and the later stages of the ultimate race into one developing and cohesive whole as they eventually must. On the other hand running 70 to 80 metres or more at top effort helps solve the problem of linking, and may give them the necessary experience of top-speed running but the supply of high energy phosphates within the muscle are greatly depleted which makes repeated performances unlikely.

It is assumed, of course, that the sprinter has the prerequisite ability to move limbs quickly and an advantageous power to body-weight ratio; if these are assured it seems that the Pure sprinters' particular problems center around the skill aspects of their performance, with learning how to exploit their power, and with attempts to experience the sensations of speed often enough to maintain an internal "model" of their performance which they rely on in the heat of competition. Thus quality of performance should concern them more than volume of training and the specific nature of the Pure sprint must never be forgotten. If one was to claim that the problems were primarily neuromuscular rather than the concerns of conditioning and those of work physiology, it would be easy to be criticized for oversimplification, nevertheless such a statement may help highlight important and necessary differences between the Acceleration and Pure Sprinters' training and the training of runners in longer events.

It may seem that I am advocating a complete abandonment of traditional training procedures for the Acceleration and Pure sprinter in favor of the experience of high-quality running which is a kind of regular rehearsal of competition: such a position would be absurd and not a little naive. Developing the strength and muscular endurance of the athletes has obvious advantages and the young, developing sprinter may need a great deal of work along fairly conventional lines. The chances of optimum improvement in sprinting performance would seem to be much enhanced if strength and power are developed while careful attention is also given to skill and the appropriate sensations of speed. Few sprinters have ever improved without running fast during their training or preparation phase (some sprinters deliberately *race* themselves into better performances). Some have survived, and indeed, flourished on very little high-quality running in training, or on very little training of any sort, whilst others have used rigorous programs of repetition running and/or heavy weight training and found success. Using an athlete's training as evidence to support any theory is dangerous for many reasons; attitudes toward training are often confused with both athletes and coaches, on occasions, falling into the trap of viewing training as intrinsically valuable. Some suffer from feelings of guilt at achieving success if they have not done the amount of training that they believed should be done to reach that level of performance, and so they train harder in order to approach closer to their belief of what is necessary. For others, training becomes a weapon with which to intimidate their opponents or to convince themselves. We must try not to be confused by those sprinters who attribute their success to Divine intervention, patent drinks or cross-country running, or who appear to do virtually no training at all, for the surprising thing is not that training practices are so different, but rather that they are so similar!

The sprinter in the Extended sprints differs very little from the Pure sprinter. Perhaps a slight loss in leg speed can be tolerated and perhaps excessive tensions within the body have to be more deliberately checked, but the greatest difference is that the top-speed section is considerably extended. For many sprinters this section never reaches top-speed but becomes a long optimum-speed section which is slightly below absolute top-speed. Although empirical evidence suggests that this is true even for the great performers much less information is available for the Extended sprints than the Pure sprint events.

The sprinter in the longer, Modified sprint events has quite different problems, here the sprinters must learn to work their anaerobic resources to their very limit. This is usually a physically unpleasant experience, but a tolerance of this must be developed for the events also have a larger aerobic component than any other sprint events. The prolonged nature of the task requires far greater economy of effort; any wastage of resources has to be eliminated. Therefore, limb speeds are not as fast, the acceleration phase is less extreme, the importance of power and strength is probably not so great, and the skills required are related more to smooth economical running patterns that allow the athletes to run relatively close to their own top-speeds but with a minimum of energy expenditure.

TRAINING FOR SPRINTING

General Introduction

There are probably very few absolutes in sprint training, and perhaps there is no Right Way to success, for not only do athletes differ considerably in their strengths and weaknesses, but their tolerance for different types of work differs greatly. Furthermore, these strengths, weaknesses and tolerances change during an athlete's career and an appropriate training program followed at the age of eighteen, for example, may be quite inappropriate for the same athlete at, say, twenty-four. Athletes who diligently follow the published training work-outs of other athletes seldom achieve comparable results, and although this "cook-book" approach to training is tempting, particularly to the new coach, its impersonal nature and its rigidity are crippling factors. I am told that the secret of producing good tea is in the blending—so it is with training. It is not enough to know what the ingredients are and what should be left out; one has to know how much of something is desirable, and when it should be included. This is likely to be slightly different for each athlete which makes the problem facing the coach horrifyingly complex, but if he is aware of the multidimensional aspects of his task he is more likely to be of use to the athlete.

Although I am assuming some general structure which attempts to hold the year's training together in a cohesive, logical and constructive manner,[34] many of the decisions made by the coach will be on-the-spot responses to unplanned situations. Below, are some of the factors that the coach must consider before deciding on a training program.

All sprint training will have a strong *anaerobic* bias, but there must also be a *strength* and *power* emphasis. The sprinter must be efficient in accelerating his own body weight, and if his strength and power improve, so must his potential for success.

The *specificity* of the event is also of importance, and the athlete must neither forget the specific applications of his training nor the skills that he must employ, and one of my main departures from the traditional schools of thought on sprint training is that the *skill* of sprinting is more important than is often realised.

Closely related to this consideration of skill is the need for experiencing the *sensations* and the *intensity* of competition, and the value of *event rehearsal*.

Training must also contain enough *variety* to keep the boredom which often accompanies the repetition of identical work over long periods of time. Consideration must also be given to the quantities of training and rest. These may be thought of in relative terms also in achieving the balance between highly intensive and less intensive work.

Seasonality of training is also important, for in this one sees the development month by month to the eventual competitive season. Although some coaches and athletes believe that sprint training should be a year-round occupation, many sprinters seem to need only two or three months preparation before racing, and some even less than this. There is one important consideration regarding out-of-season training for sprinters, and that is that if changes are to be made in power and strength, or if changes are to be made to the athlete's skill or technique, a lot of time is necessary and these modifications cannot be made hurriedly at the same time that the athlete is preparing directly for competition. Many of the most significant modifications to an athlete's performance are made in the out-of-season period of training.

Now let us look more specifically at each of the four sprint categories.

The Acceleration Sprints

Athletes who specialize in these events typically spend less time on their precompetition training than other athletes. Their concerns are centered around the rapid mobilizing of their energy resources, strength, power and the skills of starting and acceleration. Most of their work must be at high intensity.

The suggested ingredients of their training are:

STRENGTH AND POWER. Resistance activities. There are many excellent texts which give a good background in resistance training and the activities that can be used.[20,31] Traditional weight training activities are not generally popular with these athletes, and it must be admitted that neither weight training with relatively heavy loads, nor fast, dynamic lifting with lighter loads always produces the results that athletes are looking for. It may be that not enough thought has been given to the specificity of the work required by the sprinter.[13] Most traditional weight training activities for sprinting tend to be based on antigravity principles (e.g. squats, cleans, bench stepping, etc.) and although there is some antigravity work in sprinting,[20,21] the application of forces includes a considerable horizontal component.[11,21,22,30] The application of forces in a sprint stride tend to follow quite a different pattern from that experienced in normal istonic or isometric exercises,[4] and the more specific work-loads produced by isokinetic resistances may help to solve these problems.[27] Many sprinters tend to sing the praises of weight training much more enthusiastically than they actually follow their own advice, choosing instead to rely on such activities as short, explosive hill-running and fast sprint-starts as their resistance work. Activities such as harness-running and running with weighted belts, jackets and cuffs, should be treated with caution, for although they have the apparent virtue of specificity, the neuromuscular coordinations involved in the running stride may possibly be interfered with by these techniques. Repeated practice of the sprint-start still remains one of the most useful sources of resistance work for the sprinter, and one whose importance in this connection is often overlooked.

SENSATION OF SPEED. During the last ten years or so I have come to view this aspect of training as being probably the most important of all. How to get sprinters to experience in training what they will experience in competition has always been a problem. Competitive training and the use of time-trials are obvious ways of attempting to overcome this problem, but they do not always work. Other techniques have been used such as running against mechanical rabbits, pulling the athlete behind a car or motorcycle traveling at or above racing speed, running downhill, running on fast-moving treadmills. All systems have their problems, mechanical rabbits are difficult to find unless you live near a dog track and then the running surface is likely to be unsuitable, being pulled behind a car or motorcycle produces an obvious safety hazard and the sensations of speed that the athlete has may be quite unlike those experienced when he has to produce his own forces by himself. Downhill running often produces the illusion of speed only, and the mechanics of the stride are modified so that he checks forward momentum each time a foot strikes the ground, which is the reverse of what the athlete must do when racing. Fast-moving treadmills have fewer drawbacks and many advantages, but are not available to the average sprinter. Nevertheless, provided that the sprinter and coach are aware of the great importance of this sort of sprint work, some situation can usually be devised whereby the athletes can run on a good running surface with light-weight shoes and the help of whatever wind is about, and so strive for maximum quality of performance and the feeling of speed.[7,8,29]

SKILL. The athlete must be skilled in his response to the gun and in his total acceleration. Thus his start and acceleration must be practiced and at a speed as close as possible to that of competition. Indeed, all skill work, such as improving the use of the arms, should be practiced at racing speeds or as close to it as possible. Some purists who insist that the start and acceleration are inseparably connected and that each part of the acceleration phase is linked to every other part, would see no advantage in practicing part of the start or acceleration separately. For them all starting practice must be at top speed and for at least 50 metres. However, for the athlete who wants to work on a specific point of technique at the start, short starts over 15 to 30 metres may be mixed in without harm.

INTENSITY AND FREQUENCY. Almost all of the useful work done by the Acceleration sprinter is of a very high intensity, and the better the sprinter, the greater the intensity at which he can work.[3,10,24] This inevitably means that the good sprinter will not be able to produce great quantities of training. This has been a problem in track and field, for coaches have often been unhappy with the small amounts of work done by this type of athlete and mistakenly prescribed additional work, as if believing that more training is better training. A skilled acceleration sprinter may only be able to benefit from high-intensity workouts twice a week, or three times at the most. Within certain limits it seems that the better the athlete is, the greater are the demands and the less is the volume that can be tolerated. This is almost certainly because the skilled sprinter has learned to mobilize and coordinate his energy resources much more effectively than the novice, thus the energy cost of running at top speed is very much more for the great sprinter than for the poor sprinter.[37]

The Pure Sprints

Training for the Pure Sprints will not differ very much from the training for the Acceleration Sprints. In fact, most athletes who specialize in the Pure sprints also run Acceleration sprints during the indoor season, although it is by no means true that those who excel at the Acceleration sprints will also excel at the Pure sprints. In this category of sprint running there is a section of top-speed running to consider, as well as the characteristic loss of speed at the end of the race.[24,34]

It seems that for the great sprinter, the loss of speed at the end of the race can be held to a minimum if limb speed is carefully controlled in the middle section of the race, and if the athlete is as familiar as possible with top-speed running. Many striving sprinters put their trust in a running program of starts up to 50 meters in length, acceleration sprints, plus several repeats at slightly longer than racing distance, which are inevitably slower than racing speed. These sprinters never experience top-speed running except in competition, and it is little wonder that they so often suffer from extreme tension and loss of form in the final stages of the race.

In training the sprinter in the Pure sprints must follow the advice given under the preceding headings, but must additionally include sprints of 20, 30 and 40 meters at *top running speed*. These runs usually follow a longer and less intensive acceleration (as much as 100 meters) than that of competition, and so the entire distance run may range from 110 to 170 meters approximately, with all the emphasis on the top-speed section at the end.

The Extended Sprints

As the sprints become longer, so the concern for economy becomes greater. The lavish wastage of energy in the Acceleration sprints, which is tolerated so long as it is accompanied with great energy production and mobilization, would be disastrous in these longer events. Limb speeds tend to be less and the control of tension becomes even more important. Although average speeds tend to be higher in a 200 meters than in a 100 meters race (when the effect of the turn has been allowed for), the top-speed reached in a Pure sprint is probably never reached in an Extended sprint, and the sensation of speed at the end of 100 meters is seldom experienced in a 200 meters. The acceleration is less severe and the general intensity is lacking, but the top-speed section has to be considerably extended. The bias of training for the extended sprints should be to combine the intensive work discussed under previous headings with controlled sprints over distances up to 300 meters.

Additionally the athlete must acquire specific skills such as accelerating on a turn, running in as smooth and controlled a way as possible around a turn, and running out of a turn; all of these should be practiced at racing speed.

All of these points should be considered in addition to heeding the advice given about the Acceleration and Pure sprints.

The Modified Sprints

Unlike other sprinters, the 400 meters runners have to work beyond the limit of their anaerobic capacity, and so aerobic factors have to be considered. Examination of the sprint times of 400 meters races shows that the successful sprinters in these events fully exploit their anaerobic abilities [33] thus making the Modified sprints still *primarily* anaerobic events.

In these events, therefore, the sprinter must be much more concerned with the volume of his training and he must develop a tolerance for work by doing great amounts of extended sprinting and high-intensity aerobic work. Thus, distances between 150 meters and 600 meters are amongst the most often used. Producing the sensations of competition is relatively simple, and a coach with a fertile imagination can produce an almost endless variety of running tasks of appropriate intensity, load and duration: fast, steady running, acceleration runs, pace-fluctuation runs, slow-fast runs, etc., etc. If this sort of extended sprinting and running is done over distances ranging from about 10 secs up to about 80 secs, and if it is combined with strength and power training, and if the economy of running is stressed, the athlete has many of the essential ingredients for success. However, the event also demands a considerable apprenticeship, and modifications made through training do not come quickly, so the athlete must work, be patient, and continue to work.

REFERENCES

1. Adamson, G. T., and Whitney, R. J.: The fallacy of athletic power. *Coach Rev,* 6:4, 1–2, 1969.
2. Astrand, Per-Olof, and Rodahl, Kaare: *Textbook of Work Physiology.* New York, McGraw-Hill, 1970.
3. Blochin, I. P., Gandelsman, A. B. and Popova, G. M.: Oxygen consumption in running 100 m. *Teor Prakt fiz Kult,* 32:9, 454–49, 1969.
4. Cavagnor, G. A., Komarek, L. and Mazzaleni, S.: The mechanics of sprint running. *J Physiol,* 217:709–721, 1971.
5. Cromwell, Dean B.: *Championship Technique in Track and Field.* New York, McGraw-Hill, 1941, p. 29.
6. deVries, H. A.: *Physiology of Exercise for Physical Education and Athletics.* Dubuque, Iowa, Wm. C. Brown Co., 1966.

7. Dintman, G. B.: *Sprinting Speed: Its Improvement for Major Sports Competition.* Springfield, Illinois, Charles C. Thomas, 1971.

8. ———: Techniques and methods of developing speed in athletic performance. *Proceedings of the International Symposium on the Art and Science of Coaching,* vol. 1. Toronto, October 1971.

9. Di Prampero, Limas, F. Pinera and Sassi, G.: Maximal muscular power, aerobic and anaerobic, in 116 athletes performing at the XIXth Olympic games in Mexico. *Ergonomics, 13*:6, 665–674, 1970.

10. Djyachov, B.: Do not copy but create. *Sports Life Russia, 3*:10, 1963.

11. Dyson, G. H. G.: *The Mechanics of Athletics,* 4th ed., London, University of London Press, Ltd., 1967.

12. Eggleton, M. G.: *Muscular Exercise.* Kegan Paul, Trench, Trubner, and Company, 1936.

13. Fiddus, K., Stache, H. J. and Schille, D.: The significance of electromyographic examination of muscles for strength. *Wychowanie Fizyczne, Sport, 10*:1, 67–87, 1966.

14. Glencross, D. J.: A review of relevant literature on the measurement of human power output. *Phys Educ, 57*:67–74, 1965.

15. Gorojanin, V. S.: Correlations between results in races of 30 to 300 m and training exercises. *Teor Prakt fiz Kult, 30*:7, 20–23, 1967.

16. Henry, F. M.: Force-time characteristics of the sprint start. *Res Q, 23*:3, 301–318, 1952.

17. ——— and Trafton, I. R.: The velocity curve of sprint running with some observations on the muscle viscosity factor. *Res Q, 22*:409–422, 1951.

18. Hermansen, Lars: Anaerobic energy release. *Med Sci Sports, 1*:32–38, 1969.

19. Hoffman, Karel: Stature, leg length, and stride frequency. *Track Technique, 46*:1463–1469, 1971.

20. Hopper, B. J.: Film analysis and how it works. *Coach Rev, 3*:3, 9–10, 1965.

21. ———: Characteristics of the running stride: 2, Speed of the driving foot. *Coach Rev, 7*:3, 3–4, 1969.

22. ———: Characteristics of the running stride: 1, Fundamental relations. *Coach Rev, 7*:2, 4–5, 1969.

23. Housden, F.: Mechanical analysis of the running movement. In Wilt, Fred (Ed.): *Run, Run, Run.* Los Angeles, *Track and Field News Inc.,* 1964, pp. 240–242.

24. Ikai, M.: Dynamics of Sprint Running with Respect to the Speed Curve. Paper presented at the *First International Seminar on Biomechanics,* Zurich, 1967.

25. Karpovich, P. V.: *Physiology of Muscular Activity,* 6th ed. Philadelphia, W. B. Saunders Company, 1966.

26. Keul, Joseph and Nett, Toni: 'Oxygen debt' and anaerobic energy formation. *Track Technique, 44*:1408–1410, 1971.

27. Lay, P. A.: Isokinetic contractions. *Track Technique, 43*:1373–1375, 1971.

28. Margaria, R.: Capacity and power of the energy processes in muscle activity: their practical relevance in athletics. *Int Z Angew Physiol Einschl Arbeitsphysiol, 24*:4, 352–360, 1968.

29. Ozolin, N.: How to improve speed. *Track Technique, 44*:1400–1401, 1971.

30. Payne, A. H., Slater, W. J. and Telford, T.: The use of a force platform in the study of athletic activities—A preliminary investigation. *Ergonomics, 11*:2, 123–143, 1968.

31. Pickering, R. J.: *Strength Training for Athletics,* 2nd. ed. London, Amateur Athletic Association, 1968.

32. Rachev, K.: Dynamics of the age and methods of developing speed in running. *Bull Com Olymp*, Bulgare, *14*:9, 9–15, 1969.

33. Rompatti, K.: Racing tactics. In Wilt, F. and Ecker, T. (Eds.): *International Track and Field Coaching Encyclopedia*. New York, Parker Publishing, 1970.

34. Sabin, S. A. and Chudinov, P. I.: Generalizations and analyzations of the training of qualified sportsmen. *Theory Practice Phys Culture*, 7:21–24, 1963.

35. Slater-Hammel, A.: Possible neuromuscular mechanisms as limiting factors for leg movement in sprinting. *Res Q, 12*:745–757, 1941.

36. Tanner, J. M.: *The Physique of the Olympic Athlete*. London, George Allen and Unwin, 1964.

37. Trancioveanu: Myotonametric investigations in sprinters. *Studii de sociologie, psihologie, biologie si metodica a educatiei fizice si sportului*. Bucuresti, pp. 213–227, 1970.

38. Zatziorskii, V. M. and Primakov, I. N.: The dynamics of starting acceleration in running and its factors, their determination. *Kinanthropologie, 2*:1, 69–81, 1970.

CHAPTER X

LONG DISTANCE RUNNING

R. WALLINGFORD

AN ATTEMPT is made in this chapter to synthesize the most salient research findings related to distance running. An account of how this research may be appropriately applied to the practical situation is given and a discussion of current training trends is presented. Topics considered include: the physical and physiological make-up of the distance runner; the factors which may influence his performance capacity, particularly those dealing with the environment and nutrition; and the difficulties inherent in adjusting the appropriate training routines to individuals for optimum improvement.

THEORETICAL ASPECTS OF LONG DISTANCE RUNNING

Physical Characteristics

Since a great deal of misinformation is current in the minds of many coaches as to what a champion distance runner "looks like" it would undoubtedly be useful to briefly describe some physical parameters which constitute a typical successful distance runner. Contrary to many popular beliefs the champion distance runners have been relatively short in stature. The Boston Marathon winners [9] from 1897 to 1965 have averaged 5′7″ (170.1cm). Marathon runners competing in the Olympic Games [34] of 1960 were 5′7½″ (171.1cm) while 5,000 meter and 10,000 meter runners averaged 5′8½″ (174.4cm) in the same Games. A study [8] of six female champion distance runners in the United States showed an everage height of 5′5″ (164 cm).

Using a system developed for classifying body builds which rates each individual from one to seven on each of the three common body classifications of endomorphy, mesomorphy and ectomorphy, Tanner [34] noted the marathon runners as averaging readings of 2.6, 4.4 and 3.6 and the 5,000 to 10,000 meter runners as being 2.2, 4.2 and 4.3. These readings indicate that distance runners are, as most expect, low in endomorphy or fat, moderately high in muscle, and also moderately high in apparent thinness or ectomorphy. Tanner also points out from his measurements that the body build of the distance runner varies little from that of the typical 400 meter runner other than the fact that the 400 meter runners were much taller. The body proportions appeared to be quite similar. The distance runners were on the average the shortest of the track and field athletes. However, the best long distance runners today are significantly taller than their predecessors of 40 years ago.[17] Costill[9] adds that when superior and inferior groups of distance runners were compared, no difference was found between the average height of the groups. However, the superior runners were found to be significantly lighter which was essentially due to less body fat. Brown[8] has made the interesting observation in studying the relative body fat of female distance running champions that the fat measures were inversely related to the athletes' duration of training. Data collected by the author on Canadian Pan American Games endurance athletes in Cali, Colombia indicated that in many instances the fat measures of the Canadians were higher than the average fat measures recorded by Tanner in his sample of Olympic athletes. The measurements compared with Tanner's were from fat folds on the biceps, triceps and subscapular

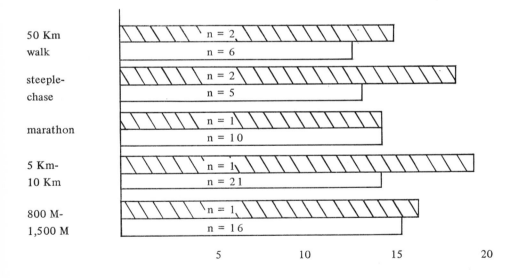

mm fat totalled from biceps, triceps
and subscapular sites

⟨⟨⟨⟩ Canadian Pan Am athletes (1971)
⬜ Olympic athletes (Tanner)

Figure X–1. Comparative Fat Fold Measures.

sites. Fat measurements are taken with a fat caliper which measures the thickness in mm of the skin and subcutaneous fat. Fat caliper measurements are necessary for accurate determinations as appearances are deceiving. Some heavily muscled runners may have less measured fat than thinner looking ones.

As has been noted the most significant observation we can make about the physical nature of the successful distance runner is that he basically has little fat. Changes in fat measures give a crude indication of the superficial transformations which occur with training. However, the most significant identifiable changes occur in the cardiorespiratory make-up of the distance runner.

Relevant Physiological Changes

In order to sustain repetitive contractions, as is necessary in endurance running, there must be a particularly efficient supply line to the active muscles. The evaluation which provides the most information on the endurance capacity of the athlete is the maximum oxygen uptake, abbreviated MVO_2. This assessment measures the amount of oxygen which can be absorbed from the air brought to the lungs in a given unit of time. Several factors are involved in the achievement of a high reading, mainly the ability to inspire considerable quantities of air, have an efficient diffusion of oxygen from the lungs to the capillaries, have a large cardiac output and also a large consumption of oxygen at the working muscles so as to assist the diffusion of oxygen into the muscles. With the above information it is not surprising that research workers have found a high correlation between oxygen uptake and the ability to perform endurance events. The maximum oxygen uptake is commonly expressed in the number of litres of oxygen absorbed per minute. In order to compare individuals on a more equitable basis, as a larger person quite naturally will absorb more oxygen than a smaller one, the oxygen uptake is frequently expressed in number of ml per kg of body weight per time unit (ml/kg/min).

Good as this test may be as the single best predictor of endurance running ability there still are certain limitations in its interpretation and in its application of results. The astute coach should inquire as to the form of exercise used in the test. Was the athlete exercising on the treadmill or the bicycle ergometer when the evaluation was made. Treadmill running has been found to give superior results for runners. Shephard [31] has suggested that the lack of sufficient quadriceps strength in runners may necessitate the maintenance of widespread sustained muscular contractions while riding which partially occlude the blood supply to the working muscles and thus interfere (lower) with the expected oxygen utilization by the legs. Another problem with the use of the bicycle with North American runners is that many of them may not be familiar with riding and thus may not be skilled enough to work effectively at heavy loads. Brown [8] has noted a particularly high discrepancy, 25 percent, between the treadmill and the bicycle tests with female athletes. The coach should therefore be cautious about placing too much credence on oxygen uptake readings which are low and have not been done on the treadmill. The last major study done on Canadian endurance runners, in connection with the 1967 Pan American Games, employed the bicycle ergometer.[11]

Another confusing factor which the unsuspecting coach may fall victim to is the too literal interpretation of statements from research experts. Griffith Pugh [25] of Great Britain when talking about MVO_2 of athletes states "International athletes require at least 78 ml/kg/min." Pugh on the other hand has published results from his own study [24] of six international three milers whose average oxygen uptake at sea level was 65 ml/kg/min. Other notable exceptions include Peter Snell whose MVO_2 was measured at 72.3 ml/kg/min [19] and Derek Clayton, at present, the world's fastest marathon runner (2hrs:08min:33sec) whose recorded MVO_2 was 69.7 ml/kg/min.[10] One must be particularly cautious about over generalizations as these major exceptions point out.

Once the coach is aware of the aforementioned limitations he can employ the oxygen uptake test as a means of gaining more knowledge of the athlete. Improvements in oxygen uptake can be reassurance that the training is progressing well. It may also indicate physiological development before improvement is apparent in the competitive situation.

If equipment required to assess the maximum oxygen uptake is not available at the nearest university physical education centre other avenues of testing may be employed. An easy measure to take and one that has been used as an indicant of cardiovascular endurance is the resting heart rate. In time through training the resting heart rate will gradually lower from its initial rate. Arthur Lydiard [20] purportedly placed a great deal of faith in this measure as an assessment of the basic endurance fitness. Resting heart rate has been used as a moderate indication of performance capacity as low resting rates correlated 0.52 with running performance in the American Collegiate Cross-Country Championships.[21] Changes in the resting heart rate provide useful information. Merely a slow heart rate does not necessarily indicate optimal levels of fitness. A person may naturally have a slow rate.

The Harvard Step Test [18] which measures the heart rate drop after exercise is even more highly correlated with endurance running ability than the resting pulse measures.[16] From the practical point of view the coach could administer the Harvard Step Test fairly easily or teach athletes to do the test on their own. This test does induce a certain amount of stiffness so should not be administered a few days before regular competition.

Pulse rates during activity have been used to convey useful information.

DeVries [12] mentions Karvonen's work on the pulse rates required to improve exercise tolerance of the heart. At certain intensities of work the heart will actually undergo a training effect and improve its stroke volume and thus lower its resting rate. The level of running required is approximately 150 beats per minute, which is obtained by subtracting resting heart rate from the maximal heart rate, multiplying this by 60 percent and then adding the result to the resting heart rate.

A system used by coaches as a rule of thumb for interval training was to raise the heart rate to 180 beats per minute during the run then jog until mentally recovered or until the heart rate dropped down to an assumed 120 beats per minute before recommencing the run. These generally used figures have come under criticism by Nett [22] who claims the recovery rates more often read 150 to 160 beats per minute rather than the 120 as previously supposed in the typical interval training session.

An area of legitimate concern for distance running coaches might be the hemoglobin concentrations of the blood. Rare though it may be there have been cases of runners training with light shoes on hard surfaces who through the shear trauma of pounding feet on the firm surfaces destroy great numbers of red blood cells.[33] Rompotti [28] has suggested a blood test for athletes may be useful as a guide to the amount of training which should be undertaken. He proposes: that with 14 gm per 100 cc of blood or above athletes may train with maximum intensity, athletes between 13 and 14 gm may train with caution and those below 12.5 gm should do only very little training or rest.

The maximum oxygen uptake test used wisely can convey useful information to the coach and athlete. Although important, this test should not be considered infallible; it must be interpreted along with the individuals' actual performance. Hopefully, the MVO_2 test will become more widely used in Canada so as to assist the coach and athlete in evaluating the training that is most conducive to physiological improvement. It is premature, however at the present time, to use this test as anything but a secondary source of appraisal for the selection of athletes for teams.

Environmental Factors

Discussion has taken place on certain physiological changes which take place with distance running. Superimposed on these particular adjustments the runner frequently must also contend with alterations in altitude temperature and humidity all of which can detract from optimum performance. With knowledge of how certain factors impair performance, steps may be taken to provide specific training in order to minimize these deleterious effects.

There have been several studies carried out on the effects of altitude on the performance capacity of long distance runners. Perhaps Pugh's study [24] is most definitive in noting the decrement in performance for international three milers. The increase of time taken at an altitude of 2270 meters for four subjects as compared with sea level was 8.5 percent or times slowed approximately 69 seconds on the average in running three miles, on going from London to Mexico City. On the termination of the study, 29 days at altitude, the decrement in sea level times was 5.7 percent. The acclimitization effect was an improvement of 2.7 percent or equivalent to 20 sec in average times taken. It is interesting to note that running times for three miles were still basically improving when the study was terminated.

Balke[6] in studying the effects of altitude on runners maximum oxygen uptakes noted that the athletes who were taken to altitude for a period of a few weeks then brought to sea level for a period of time and then returned to altitude again seemed to have remarkable improvements in their measured MVO_2's both at sea level and altitude. Furthermore the high MVO_2's were accompanied by fast races. Astrand on the other hand doubts the effectiveness of training at altitude to improve sea level performances.[5] There is a high probability that even if the yo-yo or up and down from altitude procedure were effective physiologically the disruptions to the person's mode of living could be such as to nullify the other possible gains.

Inordinate environmental heat during competition can cause a devastating impairment in performance. Although a three percent lowering of body weight through sweating is not particularly disruptive to body functioning,[37] as the body temperature remains in the 101 to 102 degree Fahrenheit range, with further water losses rectal temperatures will rise proportional to the deficit. When deficits reach four to eight percent of body weight, body temperatures in the 105 degree F range are found. These are not uncommon temperatures for athletes competing in the heat of the day. Trained athletes appear to be able to gauge the effort expended with the inability to lose heat and thus do not incur any particular danger. Problems could occur if the body's natural protective mechanism was interferred with by use of artificial stimulants, or through illness the body's fluid reserves were depleted before the competition. Sohar[32] cites the case of a runner who had diarrhea for a few days and cut out fluids in his diet to check the intestinal problem. Without restoring these fluids he competed in an endurance race and was a near victim of heatstroke.

The author is reminded of the British 6-mile A.A.A. championship race in 1955 which was run in severe heat. Gordon Pirie, who purportedly had cut down his fluid intake the day of the race, experienced sufficient cerebral confusion to stop in the race one lap short of the official finish.

A study conducted by Robson[27] on the athletes at the 1958 Commonwealth Games revealed that 20 percent of the distance runners and 27 percent of the marathon runners restricted their fluid intake (unwisely) on the date of competition. Hopefully, the importance of never restricting the natural urge to drink fluids before competition is appreciated by all at the present time.

Coaches may be helpful in reminding athletes to constantly consume a lot of fluids when they train and race in the heat. Adolf [1] suggests that although tradition is against it, loading the stomach with water before exercise is not harmful, and could be very helpful if a serious water shortage is imminent due to heat. A word of caution here is that athletes should practice ingesting quantities of water gradually before exercising in training runs, before attempting it in a major race.

A particular environmental problem Canadian distance runners face is in preparing themselves for competition in warm climates during the severe Canadian winters. This problem was attacked by Wallingford and Quinney in an attempt to prepare a runner living in Sudbury Ontario for competition in warm and fairly humid Puerto Rico in February. The attempted acclimatization involved the subject running 30 minutes per day for thirteen days on a treadmill which was moving at 10.5 MPH for ⅔ of the running time. The treadmill was situated in a room with a temperature of 85 degrees F and 75 percent relative humidity. The heart rate showed a significant lowering ($p \leqslant 0.05$) under the same conditions by the termination of the acclimatization period.

Training in cold sub-zero weather although uncomfortable should not be looked upon as being injurious to health. Distance runners can take comfort from the fact that cross-country skiiers train and race for literally hours in sub-zero weather without ill effects. The danger of freezing lung tissue appears to be nonexistent as studies done on animals and referred to by Gillon [15] claim that dogs required to breathe air at −100 degrees C had the air warmed to body temperature by the time it reached the alveoli.

Wet cold conditions, on the other hand, could present problems of excessive lowering of body temperature or hypothermia. Pugh [23] has noted problems which certain competitors in the Four Ends Walk in Great Britain had encountered when they were exposed to such conditions. Some competitors who had been soaked through by the rain and unable to generate too much heat from their physical activity perished due to what was believed to be excessive loss of body temperature. Pugh verified that subjects with wet clothing and working in a cold room at work rates of 800 Kg/M/min and lower, had higher oxygen consumptions than control subjects working in comfortable rooms. However, when the work rate exceeded 800 Kg/M/min the extra work seemed to generate enough heat so that experimental subjects had no higher oxygen uptakes than their controls. This experiment would infer that competitors not able to generate sufficient heat through normal muscle metabolism under wet and cold conditions would require part of their oxygen uptake for shivering purposes. This would further impede their progress and could lead to further lowering of total body temperature. The better trained athlete can generate more heat through his activity and thus minimize the probability of this occurrence. Caution, on the other hand, must be exerted in not using completely waterproof materials which would impair normal ventilation processes of the body.

Distance running performances are unquestionably impaired by altitude and or excessive heat. Whether training at altitude assists competitors at sea level is still a disputed issue. Certainly for most athletes training at altitude diminishes the impairment at altitude. Running may be carried out in extremes of both heat and cold, but during competitions in the heat every precaution should be used to insure optimal fluid intakes. In wet and cold conditions special attention should be given to competitors who are untrained enough to generate high levels of heat through their activity.

In spite of research indicating the extreme physiological stress on runners competing in the heat,[26,37] major international distance races continue to be held at times when there is a good probability that the temperatures will be excessive. Due to the impairment of performances at altitudes and in excessive heat, track and field administrators should be aware of the unfairness of having long distance races scheduled at cities high above sea level or at times of the day when high heat is probable, when times from such races are used for selection purposes.

NUTRITIONAL FACTORS

Although it is basically agreed that a distance runner who has a balanced diet cannot gain any particular advantage by taking food supplements [3] it is possible for a runner by altering his diet somewhat to increase the stores of glycogen in the exercising muscles. Since it is accepted that the ability to continue high quality physical effort is related to the amount of glycogen remaining in the muscles,[7] any increase in glucose storage offers great theoretical advantages for those engaged in running for more than one hour.

If a carbohydrate rich diet is administered to a runner without previous exercise, only a moderate increase in muscle glycogen will take place. A carbohydrate rich diet administered for three days after exhaustive work would raise the muscle glycogen level far above normal. The highest levels, however, would be recorded when exhaustive physical work was followed by high fat and protein diets for three days and then by three days' diet of exclusive carbohydrates.[4] Perhaps the major detraction to this diet is the added stress of adjusting to restricted types of foods placed on the athlete the week before he is to compete. It is suggested that an athlete not attempt this routine before a major race for the first time. The athlete may find when he is on the high protein and fat diet that training is particularly difficult and this could have an adverse psychological effect. The distance runner may also find this diet particularly hard to adhere to if he is not eating meals in his own home or in a cafeteria type situation.

There is some evidence [29] that magnesium levels in the body may be lowered through particularly heavy sweating. For this reason it might be helpful for the distance runner when training heavily in the warm weather to insure eating some foods containing large concentrations of magnesium.

Runners who must cram training sessions in soon after taking nourishment may take comfort from the fact that Fordtran and Saltin [13] have found experimentally that one hour of exercise which loads the oxygen transporting system to 71 percent of maximum oxygen uptake will not affect gastric emptying of a solution containing 13.3% glucose and 0.3% NaCl. Gastric emptying of a test solution consisting of pure water was very slightly inhibited by exercise. There was also no difference in the amount of acid recovered from the stomach during rest and exercise.

In summary, it appears that distance runners can store more glycogen in the exercising muscles if they follow strict diets for the days before competition. How much the availability of extra glycogen actually helps marathon runners to improve their times has not been established. Distance runners in the past have been guilty of restricting their fluid intake and thus jeopardizing their ability to cope with the heat. There is evidence that distance runners should pay attention to replenishing magnesium stores of the body through the consumption of magnesium rich foods after heavy perspiring.

PRACTICAL ASPECTS OF LONG DISTANCE RUNNING

General Factors

In the theoretical aspects of long distance running it has been noted that the maximum oxygen uptake must be increased as high as possible for optimum performance. It has also been pointed out that the top distance runners as a group are characterized by having slow heart rates and very little body fat. Informative as these tests may be in depicting a distance runner, successful racing requires more than the possession of these qualities. There must be an ability to reproduce high speeds for the duration of races. Achievement of this ability to race fast is a complicated problem. Part of the complication is contingent on the fact that runners react as individuals. They have great differences in their present physical and psychological states. Their training and racing is influenced by their current levels of fitness, their abilities to adapt to stresses of training and racing as well as their personal responsibilities which are superimposed on all the athletic ones. Keeping these facts in mind helps us explain the phenomenon of two athletes for a certain period of time doing the same training and yet racing at different levels. It is also possible for two runners to race at the same level and have vastly different approaches to their training.

Research to date has not been able to clearly differentiate one approach to training as being particularly better than any other for top level performances. The better runners use, to a greater or less degree, these techniques: steady running, interval training and resistance training. This training is usually coupled with extensive competition. Stating hard and fast training programs therefore is somewhat pointless. What all programs tend to have, however, is a considerable quantity of mileage actually covered per week, 80 to 150 miles, for runners aspiring for international success. Those who cover closer to 80 miles per week must basically include much more quality running than those who cover 150 miles. Even those doing 150 miles per week usually include from 10 to 20 percent of their training at speeds at which they plan to race. The common ingredients of all successful training regimes seem to include considerable mileage, daily or as is more common twice daily training, and maintenance of this training seven days a week throughout the year. It frequently takes several years for an athlete to achieve his best performance. In fact a study [36] carried out in Great Britain indicated that of the elite British distance runners studied, it took them on the average nine to ten years of active competition before achieving their best performances. Many achieved their all time best performances even later than this.

Beginning Training

The key to training is in the application of gradual and consistent effort. In order to select the appropriate level of exertion, the beginner must develop a sensitivity to his reactions from training. If he can "digest" each session as it comes along and look forward to the next he is coping well. If, however, he has negative and unenthusiastic feelings about his training he probably is doing too much.

It is usually best for a beginning runner to start off with steady running. Once this is achieved for thirty minutes daily without undue stress, the runner may consider blending accelerations of from 400 to 800 meters into the run. He may also consider doing some interval training on a track or other suitable location whereby he runs a set distance at approximately the pace he hopes to achieve in a race, takes a rest jog, and then repeats. The faster sections should only consist of a fraction of the total distance the athlete is preparing for. An example may be a three miler doing repeat

400 or repeat 800 meters with recovery jogs of approximately half the running distance. It is important that the athlete gradually accustom himself to this type of training otherwise a reversal of form and motivation is imminent.

Most runners also attempt to build up one long run a week of about two hours' duration. The beginner may find one hour sufficient but in time he can gradually up the distance.

Many runners prevent excessive drains on their physical reserves at one time by breaking their training down to at least two training sessions a day. Research conducted in Russia [14] indicated that better results were achieved by a group of runners doing twice a day training with the same amount of total running as compared with other groups doing the running in one session.

It is common for runners to get a certain amount of stiffness after increases in the training load. Stretching exercises may help alleviate some of this stiffness but caution should constantly be exerted in doing the stretching slowly and gently. Running on snowy or slippery surfaces frequently adds to the usual stiffness.

As far as equipment is concerned some considerations might be given to wearing nylon jackets with hoods in the winter time as they are quite light and somewhat wind proof and alternating the training shoes in workouts which helps prevent blisters as different pairs of shoes seldom rub in the same place. Chaffing in between the legs on long runs may be diminished by wearing nylon bikini briefs under the shorts.

Racing

As races approach the runner should devote special effort to similating in training what he is going to be doing in races. A person preparing for a three mile or 5,000 meter race should practice running the distance at as close to race conditions as possible the week before the actual race. This race practice will assist the athlete in expending high quality effort for the approximate time of the race. It is usually wise not to bother timing the athlete for this effort as without the stimulus of competition, the time would not be very fast. This could cause a very undesirable psychological reaction. As race time approaches the athlete will have to experiment as to how much time he should ease down his training before racing. Some athletes only ease down before particularly important races; others ease down regularly the day or two before. Most runners continue some form of running even the day before races but this is usually an easy run. Distance runners accustomed to heavy training sometimes "feel" more familiar going through the routine of training the day before racing than of completely resting. The same variability is present in warm-ups. A very fit athlete can take a fairly arduous warm-up and profit from it. On the other hand, an unfit runner may dissipate what little reserves he has in the warm-up. It should be understood that once a race starts, the runner must produce a high quality effort and if his body is not adequately prepared for this by warming up properly, the athlete may spend part of valuable race time getting his body in optimum functioning order. Warm-ups are of lesser significance in marathon running but some form of adjustment to running should take place here as well.

Success in racing is ultimately contingent upon how patient the person is in adhering to a gradually escalating training routine over a considerable length of time. It is not so much dependent upon the "God"-given attributes of natural endowment although some physiologists [2,38] would argue this point. Clearly the athlete must select priorities in his life. How much time and energy is he willing to devote to running? What activities does he do in living life that give him minimal return? Can any of these low satisfaction return activities be cut out in preference for more training?

Perhaps by continually reevaluating everything a runner does in a day, the athlete can lead a life that more closely maximizes the twenty-four hours.

Running need not detract from the important aspects of an athlete's life, indeed, it may even force an organizational plan that enables him to be more selective in how he spends his time in terms of doing things that give high levels of satisfaction.

REFERENCES

1. Adolf, E. F.: *Physiology of Man in the Desert*. New York, Hafner, 1969, p. 152.
2. Astrand, P. O.: Physical performance as a function of age. *JAMA*, 205:729, 1963.
3. Astrand, P. O., and Rodahl, K.: *Textbook of Work Physiology*. New York, McGraw-Hill, 1970, p. 456.
4. ———: *Textbook of Work Physiology*. New York, McGraw-Hill, 1970, p. 468.
5. ———: *Textbook of Work Physiology*. New York, McGraw-Hill, 1970, p. 585.
6. Balke, B.: An address given at the Pan-American Congress on Sports Medicine, Winnipeg, 1967.
7. Bergstrom, J., Hermansen, L., Hultman, E., and Saltin, B.: Diet, muscle glycogen and physical performance. *Acta Physiol Scand*, 71:129, 1967.
8. Brown, C. H. and Wilmore, J. H.: Physical and physiological profiles of champion women long distance runners. Abstracts of A.C.S.M. & C.A.S.S. Joint Meeting, Toronto, 1971.
9. Costill, David L.: *What Research Tells The Coach About Distance Running*. Washington, AAHPER, 1968, p. 2.
10. Costill, D., and Branham, G.: How Clayton measures up. *Runner's World*, 6:21, 1971.
11. Cumming, G. R.: Fitness investigation at Pan Am Games-67. (Mimeographed), Winnipeg.

12. DeVries, H. A.: *Physiology of Exercise.* Dubuque, Brown, 1966, p. 78.
13. Fordtran, J. S. and Saltin, B.: Gastric emptying and intestinal absorption during prolonged severe exercise. *J Appl Physiol,* 23:331, 1967.
14. Formichev, A. and Fruktov, A.: Effectiveness of twice-a-day training. *Track Technique,* 4:98, 1961.
15. Gillon, R.: Two winter killers. *World Health,* 20: 1969.
16. Ishiko, T.: Aerobic capacity and external criteria of performance. *JCMA,* 96:746, 1967.
17. Jokl, E. and Jokl, P.: *Physiological Basis of Athletic Records.* Springfield, Thomas, 1968, p. 73.
18. Karpovich, P. V. and Sinning, W. E.: *Physiology of Muscular Activity.* Philadelphia, 1971, p. 289.
19. Lindsay, J. E.: Structural and functional assessments on a champion runner. *Res Q Am Assoc Health Phys Educ,* 38:355, 1967.
20. Lydiard, A.: Distance training by Arthur Lydiard. *Track Technique,* 2:35, 1960.
21. Montoye, H. J., Mack, W. and Cook, J.: Brachial pulse wave as a measure of x-country running performance. *Rs Q Am Assoc Health Phys Educ,* 31:174, 1960.
22. Nett, T.: New views on pulse rates. *Coaching Rev,* 6:11, 1969.
23. Pugh, L. G. C.: An address given to the 5th Pan-American Congress on Sports Medicine, Winnipeg, 1967.
24. ———: Athletes at altitude. *J Physiol,* 192:619, 1967.
25. ———: Physiological factors in marathon running. *Road Runners Club Newsletter,* 75:31, 1971.
26. Pugh, L. G. C. E., Corbett, J. L. and Johnson, R. H.: Rectal temperatures, weight losses and sweat rates in marathon running. *J Appl Physiol,* 23:347, 1967.
27. Robson, H. E.: What our leading athletes eat and drink. Fitness and Recreation Consultant Services Department of National Health and Welfare, 2426:12:59.
28. Rompotti, K.: Blood test as a guide to training. In *Run Run Run.* Los Altos, California, Track and Field News, 1964, p. 186.
29. Rose, L. I.: Serum electrolyte changes after marthon running. *J Appl Physiol,* 29:4:449, 1970.
30. Saltin, B. and Astrand, P. O.: Maximal oxygen uptake in athletes. *J Appl Physiol,* 23:353, 1967.
31. Shephard, Roy J.: Valves and limitations of strength in achieving endurance fitness for sports. International Symposium on the Art & Science of Coaching, Toronto, 1971.
32. Sohar, E., Michaeli, D., Waks, U. and Shibolet, S.: Heatstroke caused by dehydration and physical effort. *Arch Intern Med,* 122:159, 1968.
33. Streeton, J. A.: March haemoglobinuria. *Brit Med J,* 1:567, 1970.
34. Tanner, J. M.: *Physique of the Olympic Athlete.* London, George Allen and Unwin, 1964.
35. Ward, A. P.: *Middle Distance Running.* London, King & Jarrett, 1967, p. 30.
36. Wyndham, C. H., and Strydon, N. B.: The danger of an inadequate water intake during marathon running. *S Afr Med J,* 43:893, 69.
37. Wyndham, C. H., Strydom, A. J., Van Rensburg, A. J. and Benade, A. J. S.: Physiological requirements for world-class performances in endurance running. *S Afr Med J,* 43:996, 1969.

CHAPTER XI

SOCCER

T. S. FRIED, M.D.

ELEVEN PLAYERS constitute a soccer team according to the rules of the F.I.F.A. However, to form a winning team, these eleven athletes have to be both skilled and fit.

In the 1930's, a team was built on individual players. A few talented athletes could win the game. Gradually, however, systems were introduced. The accent was placed on teamwork and the talent of a few individuals was no longer enough to decide the result of a game.

During the 1940's, the team with the most modern system of play advanced to the top. From the 1950's, more and more research effort was directed towards exercise physiology. Furthermore, apparently fundamental science began to be applied to the task of coaching athletes. The better conditioned team was now able to win against opposition that might include famous stars and very modern systems of play.

Nowadays, a professional soccer team is scientifically selected from genetically superior players. It is trained scientifically to develop maximum endurance, strength and speed, and it is coached to improve the neuromuscular coordination of individual players.

Technical aspects of coaching are described in another section of this book but in the present article only the physiological approach to training of the soccer player will be discussed.

The game of soccer involves continuous quick movements, running and jumping interspersed with brief periods of jogging; the work load is submaximal or maximal for most of the time. Reflexes have to be quick, as the acceleration is rapid; quick reflexes are also needed for dribbling. The strain on both the cardiorespiratory and the neuromuscular systems is very high.

With traditional patterns of play, physiological requirements differed among team members. The defence lines required stronger players with a greater endurance than in the offensive lines where speed and quick reflexes were more important. However, this difference has faded away in modern soccer. The defensive player has to be able to drive the ball to the front line and also on occasion to attack the opposition's defense. Sim-

131

ilarly, the forward line has to be able to come back for the ball and help the defense when the opposition is pressing hard. Each player has to be able to change his post as the need arises, but also to return as quickly as possible to his original position on the field.

With the exception of the goalkeeper, each member of the team should undergo very vigorous endurance training in order to be fit for the ninety-minute playing time. The goalkeeper, unlike the rest of the team, is involved only in short bursts of running with adequate recovery intervals. He needs very quick reflexes and maximum development of neuromuscular coordination.

Selection of Players

Heredity is very important in determining the ability of an athlete to participate in a demanding sport, since many physiological variables such as transport capacity of the cardiorespiratory system have a large inherited component. The physical constitution and the physiological characteristics of a prospective soccer player should thus be assessed before he is selected for a soccer team. Assessment should include not only simple physiological tests, but careful observation during participation in recreational activities and endurance athletic events. Before exposure to vigorous training, the prospective player should undergo a medical examination of his general health with special emphasis on the exclusion of either congenital or acquired abnormalities of the cardiorespiratory system. Special attention should be paid to any abnormality of the joints. Instability of the ligaments or joint deformity would be clear contraindications to selection for the team. The knee joint is perhaps the most important joint for the field player, while the shoulder joint of the goalkeeper is the most vulnerable.

With regard to simple laboratory tests, the hemoglobin content of the blood should always be checked before final selection. There is a normal range of variation, but in a young and athletic man, a reading of 14 to 16g/100 bil should be obtained. If the soccer player does not have a top-level hemoglobin content, he will be unable to transport needed oxygen without deficit under the stressful oxygen demands of increased muscular performance and cardiorespiratory response. Physiologically lower hemoglobin level can often be corrected by suitable attention to diet and provision of iron supplements; however, the latter are not necessary if serum iron levels fall in the normal range.

Development of Strength

The development of local muscular strength could be accomplished by a combination of isometric and isotonic exercises. Unfortunately, there is little improvement of cardiorespiratory performance as muscular strength is developed by isometric exercise and this is thus not recommended as a routine training procedure. The lack of cardiorespiratory response is not surprising in view of the low oxygen cost of isometric exercise. Although straining itself may increase pulse rate, the immediate post-effort rate does not usually exceed 100 to 105 beats per minute, and this is insufficient to produce cardiorespiratory training. Isometric exercise should be reserved for specific needs, such as rehabilitating injured athletes, when muscle building and maintenance must be accomplished without putting irritating and unnecessary strain on the injured joint.

Local muscle development can also be achieved by isotonic exercise, and this has the advantage of producing beneficial effects upon cardiorespiratory function. This type of program is thus recommended for most purposes.

Although most of the body muscle mass is activated in a soccer game, the heaviest work load falls on specific muscle groups, particularly the quadriceps, hamstrings, gastrocnemius and the anterior and lateral compartments of the leg muscles.

At one time, coaches commonly believed that the symmetrical development of the body was a necessary step in order to achieve maximum athletic performance. Recent research, particularly by the cardiorespiratory physiologists has suggested that excessive weight, whether fat or muscle tissue, decreases the relative aerobic power and thus performance. Maximum oxygen intake can be improved by losing an excessive bulk of passive muscles just as well as by reducing the amount of fat tissue in the body.

Obviously, isotonic muscle contraction should be restricted to the development of local strength, with the emphasis on the muscles of the lower extremities, intentionally neglecting the upper limbs and the shoulder girdle.

Development of Endurance Fitness

A variety of different training methods are used to develop cardiorespiratory fitness, including continuous training, brief interval training, prolonged interval training and circuit training. (The last also is used to develop local muscle strength.)

Continuous training, involving moderate, but steady exercise over long periods puts the heart and circulation under a progressive stress. Brief interval training, with short bursts of maximum activity, alternating with recovery periods of light activity over equal times stimulates the heart. Depending upon the duration of the active phase, lactate may also be produced locally in the active muscles, but it is oxidized quickly during the recovery periods. With more prolonged interval training, the bursts of activity are extended to two and one-half to three minutes, and the recovery periods are also extended correspondingly. The maximum oxygen intake is developed during the active phases, and lactate floods into the general circulation after saturating the active muscle groups. This training method thus helps to develop an aerobic power. There is currently controversy as to whether any of the above-mentioned training methods give an increase of heart volume; however, it is generally agreed that endurance athletes have large hearts. The most substantial improvement of maximum oxygen intake is obtained by effective interval training; however, many coaches allow too long a recovery interval, and for this reason, continuous training can be more effective in practice.

The main merit of interval training is its similarity to soccer; the player undertakes short bursts of maximum activity, alternating with recovery periods of light activity. A typical regime would comprise sprints of a few hundred meters for 30 or 40 seconds alternating with slow jogging for a similar time. If the intervals are suitably short, brief interval training can be a very useful form of preparation for football.

Circuit training is effective in improving not only maximum oxygen intake, but also muscle strength. Unfortunately, the gains of maximum oxygen intake are usually not as great as with interval or continuous training, although much depends upon the endurance content of the circuit.

If properly arranged, a training circuit can be very effective not only to develop local muscle strength, but also to boost cardiorespiratory fitness. Circuit training may be recommended to give variety to a training program, but it is wise to supplement it by the isotonic development of local muscle strength and by brief interval or continuous training.

Development of strength in the muscles of the lower extremities is very important for such specific activities as kicking, running and jumping. If properly managed, it also plays a major role in preventing injuries, but unfortunately, improper training can contribute to injuries. When developing muscles, they should be exercised as a group, including both synergist and antagonists. The cause of hamstring strains has been investigated in football players and track athletes and it has been found that if there is a marked difference of strength between the knee flexor and extensor muscles, then the weaker muscle group was liable to sprain. Naturally, other factors often contribute to the sprain, but the imbalance is an important predisposing factor.

Nutrition

The diet of the athlete is discussed in the general section of this book. However, certain points should be discussed with specific reference to this sport.

A soccer player needs a well-balanced diet of at least 4000 to 5000 calories, depending on his physique and the amount of training that he undertakes. Simple daily measurement of body weight under standardized conditions will indicate whether he is overfed or underfed. The diet should be reduced if he gains weight, particularly if there is an associated increase of skin fold thickness, and should be increased if he is losing weight. No specific vitamin supplements are necessary, since the normal daily requirement appropriate to his increased calorie intake, is included in the normal mixed diet.

Electrolytes lost through increased sweating (sodium and potassium chloride) should be replaced. Ordinary table salt contains sodium and chloride and fruit juices and fruit are adequate sources for replacement of the lost potassium. If the loss is heavy, as may be the case in hot and humid weather, extra salt is needed. Salt tablets may pass through the body unabsorbed, and the salt is best taken in solution.

There is some controversy about provision of meals prior to a game. Some coaches feed their players with large amounts of steak and others give their players only small portions of sugars spiced with different vitamins.

A substantial meal should be finished at least three hours before the game, as the circulating blood should be distributed to the working muscles and brain rather than taking part in the processes of digestion. A light meal means in physiological terms a meal that is eliminated rapidly from the stomach. Concentrated liquids, fat and protein stay in the stomach for a long period while carbohydrates such as sucrose and glucose are quickly absorbed and metabolized.

Normal glycogen stores of the muscles are not exhausted and depletion is slower during running than in some laboratory exercises such as cycling, with less than 60 to 90 minutes of vigorous exercise, while the glycogen stores should be filled to their maximum before the game, they should supply energy for most of the players throughout the period of activity.

To boost the glycogen content of the muscles to their maximum potential, an athlete should be kept on a diet rich in fat and protein for the first three or four days of the week previous to a contest and should be on a carbohydrate rich diet during the last two days of preparation.

At halftime, strong coffee containing a dilute solution of sugar should be served. Caffeine has a direct stimulating action on the central nervous system, shortening the reaction time and relieving sensations of physical and mental fatigue. The muscle strength is also apparently increased. The circulating blood may be redistributed from the small vessels of the skin towards the active muscles and the heart, with an increase of both coronary blood flow and cardiac stroke volume. The weak sugar solution is absorbed quickly from the stomach, and may be a helpful source of energy for some players whose glycogen reserves are falling.

Part of the lost sodium and chloride could be replaced by mixing with the coffee and sugar some salt; however, except in extreme conditions, replenishment of mineralization can wait until the game has been completed.

There is controversy about the value of using oxygen prior to the game and at halftime, especially when the event takes place at high altitude. The body has little capacity to store oxygen and the major part of any inhaled oxygen is eliminated within one or two breaths. In a game such as soccer, which lasts for 90 minutes and has but one break between the two halves, the increased oxygen content of the lungs and blood can thus have little influence on the outcome of a game. Oxygen inhalation would be beneficial only if it could be carried with the athlete during a contest, but of course, this is impractical.

Oxygen inhalation in soccer is not recommended; it will not boost performance, and if it is not available for some reason, morale may be adversely affected.

The training plan for a soccer team should be prepared in some detail, taking account of the dates of games, so that the amount and quality of training, nutrition and other factors may be suitably regulated at different stages. In the preparatory phases, the abilities of the athletes should be developed to their fullest potential. During the period of competitive games, the aim should be to maintain and refine this development, and when the season is over, deterioration should be prevented.

Maximum performance can be achieved only by studying and applying the results of scientific research and development in the fields of exercise physiology and sportsmedicine. The development of the athlete's potential is the responsibility of his supervisory team; this includes the coach, trainer, the physician and the athlete, himself, with due provision for consultation with exercise physiologists, physical education specialists and psychologists as may be necessary. A joint team effort of this type will mold able players into a team capable of winning gold medals.

REFERENCES

1. American College of Sport Medicine: *Encyclopedia on Sport Sciences and Medicine.* New York, Macmillan, 1971.
2. Burkett, L. N.: Causative factors in hamstring strains. *Med Sci Sports, 2*(1):00–00, 1970.
3. Fried, T. and Shephard, R. J.: A team approach to sport medicine. *JAMA, 216*:00–00, 1971.
4. Novich, H., and Taylor, T. R.: *Training and Conditioning of Athletes.* Philadelphia, Lea & Febiger, 1970.
5. Shephard, R. J.: *Endurance Fitness.* Toronto, University of Toronto Press, 1969.

CHAPTER XII

FOOTBALL

G. FRACAS

ODERN DAY FOOTBALL is a composite of highly specialized and complex
M skills. The demands that are placed on the body both physically and
physiologically are indeed severe, and it is a difficult task to achieve the
necessary readiness to participate in this activity in a short period of time.
Consequently, numerous authorities in the field are recommending conditioning programs that spread out throughout the entire year in varying
durations and intensities. In contemporary jargon, prospective candidates
for this hard contact sport have to pay the price in time and effort in order
to meet the necessary stress and demands that will be placed on the body
during performance. Nelson[23] indicates that a player must experience a
great feeling to know that he is going into a particular game to hit harder
and longer, and to run faster and further than an opponent he will be
facing that particular day. Top conditioning in all the necessary areas that
are required to play the game is conducive to confidence on the part of a
participant especially in the latter stages of a football game when it counts
the most and fatigue settles in to drain a performer of his strength and
threaten to bend his will at this most crucial time.

In recent years, a vast array of programs for conditioning the athlete
for football have been proposed by numerous recognized experts in the
sport. In reviewing the suggested approaches, it was readily noted that
many generally accepted physical conditioning methods were in evidence
but that some of the programs were more a matter of limited opinion
predicated on practical experience rather than on scientific evidence. In
fact, one could surmise that the players were being conditioned "by ear"
and "by guess." Since conditioning programs are becoming more prevalent,
it appears essential, in order to reach effective productivity, that they be
more scientifically and intelligently designed than in the past with special
consideration to developing the entire physical and psychological structure
of the potential player. After attempting a review of the literature concerning this particular area, it can be readily concluded that more pertinent
research is a vital necessity in achieving meaningful programs. Nelson[23]
postulates that it is a great challenge to organize appropriate conditioning

programs for football since the game produces positions requiring different body builds, speed differences, and endurance limits mixed in with the different types of techniques. Similarly, the various levels of competition produce yet another obstacle to setting up adequate programs. There is a tendency for professionals to specialize producing either an offensive or defensive player. The college ranks have only a few players performing both ways, while in high school and at lower levels, many toil both ways. Hence, this does pose a definite difficulty in producing a meaningful all-purpose program for certain of these levels.

Those involved in the sport usually observe that there is no one program that will fit the needs of all the players and of all the positions. Individuals vary greatly in their needs and in their responses to training. Each player, because of individual differences, and according to the demands of the position he will be playing, will have to condition a little differently. Isolating a single player and devising a program to suit the needs of his particular position is certainly an interesting challenge requiring ingenuity and essential knowledges by the coach. Needless to say, this method would be very time-consuming, but yet, very effective, and deserving of the time. The question then is how to specifically condition the players to perform at each position. For the sake of expediency, it is not uncommon to observe groups conditioning together rather than working individually in an attempt to satisfy their own particular needs. There appears to be some similarity in executing certain basic exercises and sprints, but playing specific positions calls for different exercises, strength demands and types of running. Spackman [28] reiterates that running one hundred-yard sprints straight ahead will not prepare the offensive guards to pull out of the line and sprint laterally leading a wide sweep play which will finally culminate in moving upfield and blocking a potential tackler. He also states that running a mile pre-seasonally will not ready the backs or ends to run effective fakes and feints on pass patterns or produce the necessary change-of-pace running required for game situations. Realistically looking at football, how many movements are performed with a completely straight back against the resistance of an opponent who is not stationary or in a set position? There should be a focus on the possible solutions to these crucial obstacles when organizing a productive, total conditioning program for football.

When attempting to produce a functional program over the year, a coach has to come to grips with such important questions as selection of essential items, the design of the program, and administration of said program.[3] Originally, he has to settle on the purpose of each phase of the program and then he has to decide whether the planned program will in fact satisfy the outlined purposes. A key consideration dictates that the executuion of the agreed upon items are not in direct conflict or violate good mechanical principles. As mentioned previously, tradition rather than sound knowledge has dictated the use of certain programs. There has been minimal insight on behalf of the organizer concerning the involvement of joints and muscle groups in the attempted exercises. Individual differences are not accounted for, and, perhaps, in some cases the suggested program was either too intense or too difficult thereby precipitating a lack of the necessary motivation to persist in such an endeavour. In addition, the possibility of injury or strain could lead to a loss of interest or desire to engage in the program thus delaying the necessary preparation on the part of individuals. Therefore, it is felt that the trend today should accentuate a knowledgeable, scientific approach to the setting up of all phases of the complete conditioning program for football.

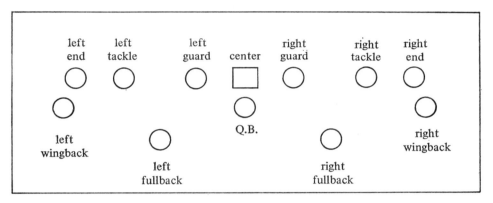

Figure XII–1. Double Fullback Offensive Formation. Offensive Personnel—Potential Specific Acts by Positions.

Center

1. Blocks lineman over him one yard away, or linebacker over him two yards away.
2. Cuts off linebacker to the right or left about two yards away anticipating his movement.
3. Cross blocks with the guard on the man over the guard either way.
4. Pass protects and covers possible interception either way (also draw and screen action).
5. Long snap for punt, protects, and covers downfield.

Guard

1. Blocks lineman over him one yard away, or linebacker over him two yards away.
2. Cross blocks on man over the tackle, or on the linebacker over the middle (odd or even defense).

3. Executes a short trap block on the defensive end (Off-tackle play).
4. Pulls out of the line and is the lead or rear blocker on the wide sweep play.
5. Pass protects and covers possible interception either way (also draw and screen action).
6. Pulls out of the line on roll-out pass protection blocking either way, and covers possible interception.
7. Punt protects and covers downfield.

Tackle

1. Blocks lineman over him one yard away, or linebacker over him two yards away.
2. Uses a down block on the man over the guard on wide sweep plays to his side (even defense).
3. Cross blocks on the man over the offensive end (off-tackle play).
4. Cross blocks on the linebacker over the guard, or over the middle (counter play).
5. Pulls out of the line to lead the blocking on quick pitch play to his side.
6. Pass protects and covers possible interception either way (also draw and screen action).
7. Punt protects, and covers downfield.

End

1. Blocks lineman over or outside of him one yard away.
2. Down block on lineman on his inside gap on off-tackle and wide plays his way.
3. Cross blocks on man over the offensive tackle (off-tackle play).
4. Double team blocks with the tackle on the man over the tackle (off-tackle play).
5. Double team blocks with wingback on the man over the end (wide plays).
6. Pass protects and covers possible interception.
7. Runs varied pass routes utilizing effective faking and feinting techniques to free himself from a possible defender.
8. Sprints upfield after receiving a pass with change-of-pace, pivoting, and other meaningful ways of avoiding possible tacklers.
9. Punt protects and covers downfield.

NOTE: When the Center, Guard, Tackle, or End are on the offside and away from the point of attack, they come across the field five to ten yards deep in an attempt to block any of the defensive personnel (backs, linebackers, etc.) in the vicinity of the attacking point (offside comes across and blocks).

DEFENSIVE PERSONNEL — POTENTIAL SPECIFIC ACTS BY POSITIONS

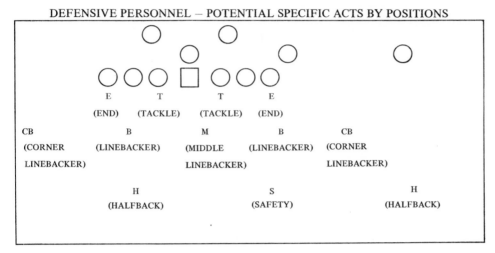

Figure XII–2. The 4–5–3 Defensive Formation.

Wingback

1. Influence block on the defensive end and blocks out on corner linebacker (off-tackle play).
2. A running drive block (seal) on closest linebacker inside (off-tackle and wide plays).
3. Double team block with the end on the defensive end over the end (wide plays).
4. Comes around on play action pass and blocks the defensive end.
5. Blocks downfield across the point of attack.
6. Runs with the ball over the middle, off-tackle, or wide using productive techniques of running with the ball (feinting, change-of-pace, spinning, etc.).
7. Streaks downfield deceiving the defender with feinting tactics in running various pass routes.

Fullback

1. Effects a trap block on the defensive man over the offensive end (off-tackle play).
2. Comes over and blocks man over the guard or tackle on pitch plays away from him (fill block).
3. Runs pertinent backfield routes with a minimum of footwork.
4. Carries the ball up the middle and off-tackle with power using effective techniques to avoid potential tacklers (feinting, spinning, etc.).
5. Picks up early on the roll-out pass and blocks the defensive end or corner linebacker.

6. Pass protects on the drop-back action and covers the possible interception either way.
7. Delays momentarily and runs either the draw or screen plays.
8. Executes certain pass routes deceptively.

Defensive End

1. Hits the offensive end, meets and wards off any inside blockers.
2. Fights to the outside on wide plays or roll-out action by the quarterback.
3. Pursues on plays away from them at the appropriate angle.
4. Rushes the passer maintaining outside leverage with varying charges (feints).
5. Attempts to block punts and comes around to block on the return.
6. Spins out of a solid angle block to get back into the play.

Defensive Tackle

1. Meets and sheds the blocker over him.
2. Attempts to split or break the potential double team block on him.
3. Takes on and wards off the trap blocker to the inside.
4. Pursues on the pull of the player in front of him either way expecting a quick down block on him to the side of the pull.
5. Rushes the passer using different charges (feints)
6. Comes in hard on a punt attempt by the other team, and then comes around to block on the return.
7. Pivots out of a solid down block to get back into the play.

Middle Linebacker

1. Wards off the blocker over him (usually the center).
2. Aggressively takes on the difficult cross blocker (either a guard or a tackle depending on the defense).
3. Pursues to either side on off-tackle and wide plays under control.
4. Slow drop on drop-back pass action and reacts to draw, screen, or man out of other team's backfield.
5. Covers the short hook zones to the side of the roll-out action by the quarterback.
6. Performs sound blitzing technique protecting himself and going directly to the ball.
7. Pivots out of solid angle blocks to get back into the play.

Inside Linebacker

1. Fights and sheds the blocker over him.
2. Aggressively takes on the down block either way and spins out, if blocked well, to get back into the play.
3. Makes an effort to split or break the double team block on him.

4. Angles back quickly to the short hook zone on drop-back pass, squares up, and is ready to move directly either way on the throw by the quarterback.
5. Drops to cover the short hook zone to the side of the roll-out action by the quarterback (over the end or over the middle).
6. Pursues to either side on wide plays.
7. Protects himself as he blitzes and goes directly to the ball.

Corner Linebacker

1. Comes across the line, meets and wards off blockers on wide plays to his side.
2. On drop-back or roll-out pass his way, he angles back to the short flat hook zone, squares away, and is ready to move either way on a throw by the quarterback.
3. A slow drop straight back on a roll action away from him covering the deep outside zone and reacting to reverse or screen plays his way.
4. Perfects man-to-man coverage techniques with good balance.

Defensive Halfback

1. Meets to shed and uses finesse (quick feint) to handle downfield blockers.
2. Comes up quickly to support and try to tackle the ball carrier as he moves across the line of scrimmage.
3. On drop-back or roll-out pass his way, he angles back to deep outside coverage, squaring away, and going directly to the ball after it is thrown by the quarterback (also done from adjusted position on strong offensive sets).
4. The angle of drop is towards deep middle when the quarterback rolls away from him, squares away, and reacts directly to the ball.
5. Emphasis on man-to-man coverage techniques.
6. Pursues a receiver on a completed pass in front of him, to either side of him (under control) or behind him.

Safety

1. Sheds downfield blockers, and uses finesse (faking) to avoid blockers.
2. Covers the deep middle zone on a drop-back action after the appropriate drop (from adjusted position also).
3. Comes up quickly to tackle when the ball carrier is moving across the line of scrimmage.
4. On roll-out pass either way, he angles back towards the side of the roll, squares away, and moves directly to the ball on the throw (also from adjusted position).

5. Utilizes man-to-man coverage techniques.
6. Pursues the receiver on a completed pass in any direction under control.

NOTE: The defensive personnel initiate the appropriate reaction in their primary area of responsibility and then pursue the ball carrier by taking the best possible angle to cut him off or catch him downfield. Many rotational movements and changes in direction are necessitated due to the nature of defensive football.

TANGIBLE COMPONENTS OF A FOOTBALL PLAYER

Numerous sources [17,20,22,28] arrive at some commonality in agreeing that the following attributes are very important for effective performance in the game of football:

1. Strength
2. Explosive Power
3. Endurance
4. Speed
5. Agility
6. Flexibility
7. Size

It would appear from the review of literature that all these desirable traits can be developed and improved upon in a well-designed program of conditioning.

Strength

In viewing a football game situation, many plays vividly portray a stronger player convincingly overcoming a weaker opponent, and there are even cases where strength triumphs over size. It is difficult to refute the premise that the entire body is used in the game. A performer meets with stiff resistance as his body drives into an opponent necessitating drive and power to move heavier opponents. Certainly, this is also evident in tackling a ball carrier who is sprinting at top speed, or when one drives into a heavy blocking shed. Needless to say, many actions accentuate the need and importance of strength.

Thus a key objective for the coach is to develop total overall body strength which will provide the player with the opportunity to express explosive muscular power in movement. This aggressive sport requires strong arms, legs, shoulders in addition to a sturdy neck since adjustments in blocking and tackling subject the head to severe and sharp contact. Jesse [17] also stresses the need for developing the midsection and lower back to adequately prepare the body for the explosive type movements requiring hyperextension of the lower back. Generally, the lower back and sides are overlooked in conditioning programs. Blocking and tackling movements exhibit hyperextension of the lower back and thus the latter area should be incorporated into the strength program. Rarely will one see a player applying his strength in a fixed position in a game. Rather, players are seen to explode with great power in lateral and violent rotational body movements. This, then, has important implications for a specific strength program.

Experts appear to agree that muscular strength is the easiest of all physical characteristics to develop and that weight training is the most effective way. This process builds functional muscle and bulk quicker and better than any other method. The overload principle allows for continuity of strength gains in the desired body areas required for execution in football allowing the muscles to become firmer and stronger with repeated resistance exercises. Developing strength in the specific muscles used to play the game of football is of major import. Thus, exercises should be performed through the full range of movement required by the specific needs of the various positions to be played in the game, especially in the preseason program. To be effective, the program should be adapted to the specific needs of the player concerning his particular stress areas and movements, rather than just on his overall body strength. Allsen and Newberry [2] conducted a study to determine the best progressive-resistance exercises for interior linemen based on their most important movements—horizontal and vertical shoulder flexion, back extension, hip extension, and plantar flexion. Results of their study indicated that strength gains were produced in all of those movements as a result of the following exercises: military press, knee extension, straight-legged dead lift, hip extension, upright rowing, biceps curl, parallel squat, sit-ups, bench press and toe raise.

Heavy resistance with low repetitions is superior for the development of muscular strength while lower resistance with higher repetitions is more advantageous in increasing muscular endurance when involved in a weight training program. Most research appears to indicate that strength training does not reduce flexibility, speed of movement, or coordination. McCormick [21] reported in his work that an increase in strength did produce an increase in the speed of movement. It would appear that the greatest strength increases result in programs involving two to ten repetitions of a particular movement. Others suggest, however, that six to eight repetitions are the most effective and then to increase the weight (intensity) rather than the repetitions (duration) to achieve increased strength gains. It is worthy to note at this point that it has been found that added weight had the tendency in certain cases to slow down a player who is either short in height or who does not have the leg base to carry the added weight.

Others favor the isometric program as an approach to strength training since it is a quick and expedient method. Expensive equipment also is not required for the program. Dyer [8] suggests that exercises have a counterpart in the weight-lifting exercises and that the players should perform these exercises at what would be the point of greatest effort in the corresponding weight lifting exercise. Yet, Jesse [17] is very adamant in his feeling that isometrics contribute little to the specific training required by any given sport. The implication here is that if strength is developed in general, it is still not a guarantee that it will be correctly applied in any given sport such as football—it has to be specific to the act of the game. However, there is sufficient support in the literature [9] signifying that isometric contraction programs are effective in producing strength gains and as such should be considered for off-season and in-season programs. Jarver [16] noted that the intensity of contractions appeared to be of greater importance in strength maintenance than the frequency at which training sessions were held, and he concluded that a single isometric contraction of greater than 50 percent intensity must be performed at least once every two weeks to maintain newly developed strength. An interesting method which involved the aspect of specificity to some degree was worked on by Biggs [4] and he suggested that the position of application for the particular isometric contraction be at the initiation of the function of the muscle, at an intermediary position, and at the termination position in the function, with three repetitions used in each position holding the contractions from six to eight seconds each. This was consistent with McCormick's [21] work on improving a place kicker's distance using isometrics. His emphasis was on the speed of the hip flexor and knee extensor muscle groups—the chief muscles used in place kicking. The conclusions indicated that the isometric group using the three most important lower leg positions in place kicking for knee extension and the proper positions of extension of the leg for hip flexion, did increase leg speed. It was thus inferred that increased leg speed could produce a longer kick provided that the force was properly applied. Of interest is the fact that this program took place from five to eight weeks before the start of pre-season practice and that each exercise involved a six-second maximum contraction. Results of this work appear to have implications, as well, for punters and passers.

Partner exercises utilizing isometric and isotomic principles are gaining in popularity also. A partner produces the necessary resistance when weights are not readily available. The body weight of the partner is wholly or partly used to provide either the necessary resistance or the load. In these dual resistance exercises, contractions are maintained for about six seconds against a resistance set up by a partner. However, in most exercises, as implied by Jarver,[16] the part of the body used is moving slowly through the whole action. The advantage of this method is that there is no limit to inventing a series of dual resistance exercises specific to the acts involved in the game of football. The challenge is to imitate the actions of a particular sport such as football and then set up resistance to the particular movements involved in the acts.

Circuit training is now becoming more prevalent in conditioning programs because of its complete adaptability and its potential for providing beneficial effects simultaneously on strength, muscular endurance, circulorespiratory endurance, and flexibility. The program incorporates intensity (load), repetitions, and time (duration) with progression being achieved by decreasing the time of the performance and by increasing loads and repetitions. A well-constructed program can provide a strenuous work-out geared to the individual's specific needs in football. Provision of a series of progressive goals that can be achieved step by step promotes added incentive. The inclusion of any number or type of exercises related to football with the inclusion of motivation makes this a most challenging program for any coach in football.

Explosive Power

Blocking and tackling requires quick bursts of explosive power—strength in action. This component involves force times velocity where force is generally or entirely derived from muscular strength resulting in explosive contact with an opponent. This principle assists in knocking over heavier opponents, since they are applying maximum force in the shortest possible time. Power combines speed and strength culminating in fast explosive movements against resistance—a most necessary and advantageous item in productive performance. Gains in the area of explosive power can be produced through thoughtful programs of weight training utilizing progressive resistance with specificity in mind—simulation of the actual acts where this trait is used in the game.

Endurance

Football is a game of many short sprints, a few long ones, with short rest periods in between bouts of work, and thus requires top cardiovascular conditioning from the players. Cardiorespiratory improvement is enhanced when oxygen debt occurs due to excessive hard running. Maximum quantities of oxygen unites with the red blood cells to be delivered to the cells for oxidation. Authorities have agreed that cardiovascular endurance depends upon the combined efficiency of the blood vessels, the heart, and the lungs in supplying oxygen to the working tissues and removing carbon dioxide, lactic acid and other metabolites from these areas. The effectiveness of these systems determines a player's capacity to continue the strenuous activity of football for lengthy periods.

Jesse [17] reveals that in a football game or practice, a player engages in about one hundred to one hundred and fifty all-out efforts against some type of resistance lasting from five to fifteen seconds for each attempt with a twenty to twenty-five second break between each effort. Bursts of speed of short duration alternate with short and long interruptions. The expenditure of energy is great thus requiring the body to deliver a much greater supply of oxygen to meet the needed demand. A series of oxygen debt bouts can occur at certain positions due to incomplete rest periods resulting gradually in general body fatigue. Therefore, this has a most detrimental effect on the skill, explosive effort, and stamina of a player towards the waning moments of a game. In addition conditioning programs have often bypassed the psychological factors of an all-out burst against resistance when the body is in the state of fatigue. One has to be psychologically conditioned to render a maximum effort at this particular time—when it really counts. Along with the physiological adaptation of the body there is a psychological tolerance to the agony and pain related to hard physical effort while short of breath. An excellent time to cater to these needs is in-season towards the end of a regular practice when the players are already fatigued utilizing specific sprints and competition. It is imperative that the players be totally informed of the physiological benefits of these activities, which will be carried on when they are so fatigued, in order to acquire their cooperation, or a lack of effort at this time will be in evidence. Understanding leads to cooperation and the much-needed motivation for these all-out bursts.

In a comprehensive study by Jackson [15] it was concluded that there was a direct relationship between improvement in cardiovascular fitness and heart rate training intensity. It was necessary to train at an intensity of 145 beats per minute or higher in order to improve cardiovascular fitness. It appears from this and other investigations that the heart rates of those being conditioned should be kept high for at least five minutes so that the necessary benefits could be derived from this training. Players should be encouraged to take and record their own maximum heart rate every time they have a strenuous running type workout to ensure their reaching these high levels. Spackman,[28] in his work, also evidenced improvement in cardiovascular endurance as verified by a lowered resting pulse rate and by a quick recovery to a resting pulse rate upon termination of a five-minute exercise bout. It would appear, then, that interval training poses an acceptable approach to developing endurance in a football player. Players would run specific distances in a specified time followed by rest intervals, and this could be repeated five to ten times. Another modification would be to have players running up and down the field utilizing the specific running required for their particular positions comparable to a game situation, with short rest intervals accounting for the huddle, as in a game. Investigators have demonstrated that intense interval runs have shown an improvement in heart function involving the heart rate, stroke volume, and cardiac output. This, once again, is consistent with the position which states that the greatest improvement in heart function results with runs that elicit maximum heart rate and cardiac output. The interval training program imposes more stress on the cardiovascular system and as such, attempts should be made by coaches, to use this approach in a most specific way to assist players in endurance training for football. Due to its common occurrence in the postrun behavior of participants it is interesting at this time to note that after hard repetitious runs it is better to jog or walk rather than to sit, stand, or lie down. The rationale for this preferred reaction by players is to dissipate lactic acid and the other metabolites as well as increasing venous return from the lower extremities, thereby recovering faster.

Speed

Football involves many sprints of a short distance, and thus quickness or the ability to get moving instantly takes precedence, initially, over speed alone. Many coaches prefer the quick or fast explosive start over a straight one hundred-yard dash when assessing the speed of their players. Martin[20] substantiates this outlook in his selection procedure for players when he requests that they sprint a distance of five to fifteen yards. The object is to pick players who have a fast start with productive final action, even though there is a lack in sustained speed. This is especially important in certain key positions such as at center, guard, or tackle. Needless to say, a rapid start followed by a quick burst of speed would be of great advantage to any aspiring player.

Dayton[7] maintains that speed can be developed and increased by continuing practice. The player must run harder and with correct running style on each attempt. Others state that speed can be improved by developing and increasing the muscular strength in the legs along with more efficiency in running involving straight fast alignment, correct body lean, and coordinated arm movements. Of importance also is the player undergoing many trials.

Agility

The body goes through a variety of complex movements in an actual game or practice in football. This attribute of moving quickly in any direction with the body under control holds a place of high esteem in the eyes of a coach. Hammer[10] suggested that agility would improve during a period of football training and playing while Hilsendager and others [12] indicated that agility could best be developed in programs designed specifically for that purpose. Their conclusions revealed that a unique factor of agility does exist in contrast to the effect of specifically designed exercises for the purposes of developing strength and speed and their effect on agility. Still the relationship of agility to speed and strength remains a debatable topic. Ramage [26] through experimentation came up with an agility program that allowed him to measure an athlete's speed, coordination, and agility, and then, to incorporate these important assets into a program for both linemen and backs. The latter program was of great assistance in evaluating the personnel and fitting them into their appropriate football positions.

However, few agility drills have been validated through objective research. Yet Brynteson,[6] in his work, showed that agility could be significantly developed through specifically designed training programs for improving agility, and that certain agility drills were better than others. The bench jump, rope skipping, quarter-eagle, forward and backward sprint, and carioca contributed significantly to agility development, whereas, the upright and four-point variation of the wave drill did little for agility. In view of the relatively small amount of research in this area it is felt that agility, perhaps, can best be improved through specific drills and exercises related to the various positions in football.

Flexibility

This particular quality refers to the range of motion through which the body parts can move in the various situations involved a game. Players will be twisting, bending, and reaching in the performance of their particular duties—blocking, tackling, and recovering from blockers. It would be most worthy to initiate stretching type exercises simulating these specific movements during any conditioning program. This usually fits in well as a prelude to the progressive resistance exercise program on strength in the off- and pre-season programs, while in-season, it works in well at the start of practice.

Size

Depending on the level of football, there are certain positions on a team that require large size. However, there are small players who possess quickness and great speed and who can be successful if used in the appropriate position despite their lack in size. Speed and quickness can counterbalance size in game situations. This component can be developed through the use of a resistive exercise program geared to building bulk in the functional muscles by utilizing a very heavy workload and minimal repetitions.

INTANGIBLE COMPONENTS OF A FOOTBALL PLAYER

When a coach attempts to screen and select prospective candidates for his team, he should be mindful of the basic requirements for each offensive and defensive position. An earnest effort should be made to locate the aspirants in positions which will produce the most beneficial performance.

Current thought [13,20,31] cite the following intangibles as worthy of consideration by a coach—courage, desire, determination, aggressiveness, football "savvy" and a dedication to the task. Walker [31] denotes courage through the medium of developing a superior pain threshold. Here a player conditions his mind and body to accept pain and to absorb and withstand this discomfiture throughout the season with determination and dedicated effort. An apparent love of contact signifies the type of individual. Determination manifests itself during the various occurrences in the practice or game by the intense efforts of the player to accomplish his goals. A player persisting in initiating the attack and thriving on physical contact best exemplifies aggressiveness. Making quick and correct decisions under severe duress in the competitive situations of football displays football "savvy." The various drills which a coach can devise to create different game situations which the players will face are an invaluable aid to determining the degree to which each candidate possesses these important intangibles. Conditioning programs could be also manipulated to arrive at these objectives.

Realistically, there is no clear-cut pattern or series of tests that can be administered to a potential candidate for football as an infallible method of concluding where or whether he should play on a team. Great insights into their ability and potential to play can be discovered in actual game-like scrimmages involving the different aspects of the game. Drills are structured for the various positions that simulate the game, and potential answers to the many questions commence to unravel in the specificity of live action. Examples of this approach can be found in the following: one-on-one drill with ball carriers, the pulling guard drill, and the defensive key drill. Offense and defense are both stressed and valuable inputs are derived by the coaching personnel as a result of the efforts of the players.

OFF-SEASON PROGRAM

This is a period that extends from the end of a competitive season until six to eight weeks before the start of the next football season. Reducing the intensity of the training just after the season is over and involving oneself in other recreational activities such as handball, squash, paddleball is a recommended procedure. The emphasis for this phase of the conditioning program is on the improvement of general body condition and muscle tone. A basic program of exercises is prescribed for this purpose involving calisthenics, stretching activities, general weight training and endurance type activities along with certain reaction drills. To break up the monotony, recreational favorites should be included on alternate days.

Brynteson [5] discovered in his study that there was a progressive deterioration in the ability to respond to exercises following a football season if inactivity was prevalent on the part of the performer. He also emphasized that the active group in his investigation that participated in a conditioning program maintained but did not improve their physical condition. Another challenging question during this particular period concerning involvement in such a program would be motivation. Very few studies have dealt with this problem in football, but Johnson [18] provided evidence signifying that motivated training did promote significant strength gains. Special motivating situations resembling the football contest were shown to significantly increase the strength scores of training groups. These results implied that a player's performance in the area of strength showed some relationship to the level of motivation present during the training period. Perhaps, when organizing this particular program, it would be beneficial to utilize motivational techniques related to the game of football such as game films, football music and position competitions among team members.

It requires time and effort to accumulate good gains in strength. Weight training devices should emphasize exercises that develop general all-round strength involving several lifts that require a full body movement, or static contractions that affect the main muscle groups used in football. After training for a month, it would be advisable to go to heavy lifts with minimal repetitions to acquire increased gains in strength and to build bulk. Cardiorespiratory work in the off-season incorporates long distance running and this type of jogging is helpful but does not prepare a player for the short sprint type of running needed in the game. Better still would be the interval training approach at this time. Running all-out for 220 yards and then jogging for 220 yards and gradually repeating this from eight to sixteen times will increase cardiovascular efficiency, and improvement in times will be in evidence. Flexibility work on the back, legs, chest, shoulders are suggested, and, as Spackman [28] recommends, the hamstrings and back should be stretched daily, the rationale being that a player can lose running speed quickly when the hamstrings and lower back are tight. Alternate day programs could involve speed and agility drills for

EMPHASIS: the improvement of general body condition and muscle tone.

STRENGTH:

a) *General* i) program should cover the development of the arms, shoulders, chest, legs, back, neck and abdomen.

ii) at least one exercise for each of the major muscle groups used in football should be in evidence.

iii) varied programs including the above could be utilized—isotonics, isometrics, partner exercises (recommended procedure would be a circuit training program employing these approaches).

iv) suggestion—one to three sets, eight to twelve repetitions, three times a week.

b) *Isotonics*

Bench Press	Half Squats	Straight Legged Dead Lift
Shoulder Shrug	Toe Lifts	Quadriceps Strengthener
Power Clean	Leg Raises	Neck Exerciser
Two Arm Curl	Bent Legged Dead Lift	Hamstring Strengthener
Bent Rowing	Sit Ups	Military Press

Isometrics (with fixed bar)		*Partner Exercises*	
Dead Lift	Bench Press	Groin Exercise	Sit Ups
Leg Squats	Leg Driver	Bridging	Pass Action
Leg Press	Punter's Exercise		
Reverse Curl	Quadriceps Press		
Straight Arm Pull			
Hamstring Press			

ENDURANCE:

a) long distance and cross-country running

b) all-out sprints of 100 yards, 220 yards using interval training approach

i) on a track, run the sides all-out, walk or jog the ends and repeat eight to sixteen times.

c) step tapping, jumping over a box at different heights as part of a circuit

d) running stairs

e) alternate day program of handball, squash, paddleball, conducive to hard all-out work-out.

FLEXIBILITY:

a) a variety of stretching type exercises as part of the warm-up.

AGILITY:

a) Rope Skipping   d) Forward and Backward Sprint
b) Bench Jump   e) Carioca
c) Quarter Eagle   f) Agility Drills Specific to Positions in Football

Figure XII–3. Sample Off-Season Program.

all the players in addition to other pertinent activities such as handball, squash, paddleball, etc. Figure XII–3 is a sample of an off-season program.

PRE-SEASON PROGRAM

This is a period from six to eight weeks before the start of pre-season practice in the fall. The intensity of training increases in this preparation phase. If possible, this program should be performed seven days a week subject to modifications based on an individual's circumstances. The focus of conditioning shifts from the general approach of the off-season to a more direct preparation for the up-coming season. The requirements of a player for his particular position dictates his program. Weight training is of a more explosive nature. The stress is on specific conditioning involving a simulation of the moves that are in evidence in the game at the various positions. Weight training devices are used such as the Universal Trainer, and lifts are adapted on this machine which resemble the moves in foot-ball in order that the range of movement required in actual performance of the specific acts are initiated against progressive resistance. This in-creases the strength of the specific muscles involved in those acts. Jarver [16] agrees with this concept by claiming that pre-season weight training should concentrate on muscle group(s) that are either exceptionally weak or that need added attention for specific participation in the various skills of the game.

Endurance work is also specific to the various positions in the game as outlined earlier in the chapter on the specific acts of offensive and defen-sive personnel. The players should start from their offensive and/or defen-sive position as in a game situation and perform the necessary sprints or running required of that position with very little rest between the runs. These are game condition type sprints with appropriate moves to the right and left, forwards, backwards, and laterally as demanded by the position, and not just straight ahead runs. Each position sprints differently, and one should condition at game situation pace. The interval training method could be utilized with the player going up and down the field gradually working from eight to sixteen times with specific running at his positions(s) in addition to short rest intervals simulating a huddle delay between each effort.

The condition level should be equal to that of playing an actual game. Real tangible goals are set so that when the players report for practice they are prepared to operate at game pace. Agility and flexibility work coincide with this specificity work and the ingenuity of a coach should devise work that is applicable for each position such as rolling, getting up, pursuing, and getting under control before potential contact with a ball

EMPHASIS: SPECIFIC CONDITIONING based on the position to be played by the individual.

STRENGTH:
a) weight training is of a more explosive nature at least six times a week.
b) use of the circuit approach and devices should be adopted to simulate the various movements required of the various positions against progressive resistance. Examples are: a hack lift instrument which provides for the drive block movement over the full range of motion required for that specific block; a leg drive set-up for backfielders; sled work for defensive techniques.
c) imperative that neck and knee exercises be in the program.
d) stress should be on specificity.

ENDURANCE:
a) interval training—all-out run of 220 yards with walk or jog of 220 yards and this is repeated eight to sixteen times.
b) specific running according to positions up and down a football field with short rest intervals between each run to account for huddle time and this is done eight to sixteen times (refer to the potential specific acts by the offensive and defensive personnel earlier in the chapter for examples of the type of running needed).

FLEXIBILITY:
a) stretching type exercises such as shoulder, groin, trunk, and lower back work as part of the warm-up.
b) addition of weight progressively in rotational positions simulating the twisting and bending movements of the game situation.

AGILITY:
a) wave drills according to the positional tasks required in the game.
   Example: pass defense — running backwards, on an angle, forward and laterally as in a game.
b) grass drills for defensive linemen and linebackers such as rolling on the ground, getting up quickly to a hitting position.

STRESS: simulate game situations at the different positions.

Figure XII–4. Sample Pre-Season Program.

carrier. The offensive and defensive systems of a coach should elicit exercises and drills to accomodate all facets of specific conditioning during the pre-season. Figure XII–4 illustrates a sample Pre-Season Program.

IN-SEASON PROGRAM

The game of football contributes little to the development of, or to the maintaining of strength. A challenging situation for a coach is to preserve strength at the desired level which has been usually gained with hard effort previous to this period without utilizing a great deal of time. The complexities of the various facets of the game allow little time for conditioning during practices. Findings have indicated that many players are weakest at the end of the season rather than at the start. Griese[9] indicates that usually little attention was given to the application of training methods for the purposes of maintaining the level of increased strength throughout a competitive season in football. Few in-season strength training programs were in evidence and he demonstrated that after 30 weeks, strength decreased 100 percent if no specific training followed a strength training period. He concludes from his scientifically controlled investigations that strength does decline rapidly after the cessation of a progressive resistance training period if there is no follow-up training.

Generally, coaches feel that a strength program is too time-consuming and many are convinced that the drills involved in practices serve to maintain an adequate level of strength. However, work in this area indicates that the physical activities involved in a regular football practice would not maintain the level of strength developed during the off-season program. Griese[9] found that players who participated in regular football practice but who did no heavy resistance work did experience statistically significant losses in strength on each of four strength tests. He thus concludes that an in-season program of heavy resistance exercises conducted once weekly in addition to the regular practice would maintain the level of strength acquired during the off-season program. Of importance here is that the strength program at this time would not produce significant gains in the level of strength gained in the off-season and pre-season programs but would maintain it. Lyne's[9] work also demonstrated that training once weekly with static contraction exercises for six seconds per muscle group did increase a newly acquired strength level achieved during eight weeks of weight training.

Based on the findings, time should be set aside in the weekly routines to maintain strength gains. Differences of opinion exist on when to conduct such a program. Spackman[28] believes that players usually will not work on their own during the season on a strength program and suggests that

EMPHASIS: To PRESERVE and MAINTAIN the GAINS made in the previous programs in all areas.

STRENGTH:
a) strength work at least once a week for forty minutes.
b) stress should be on specificity—simulation of game movements against progressive resistence.
c) could be a combination of isotonics, isometrics, partner work, and sled drills, as dictated by each individual situation—circuit approach.
d) stress on knee and neck exercises.

ENDURANCE:
a) the last fifteen minutes of each heavy practice when fatigue is in evidence in order to simulate game conditions as follows:
   i) sprint-jog across field by positions
   ii) use of parlauf
   iii) competitive relays by positions
   iv) race forty yards according to positions
   v) running up a hill and hitting hand dummies
b) ingenuity of the coach is important in this part of the program to structure meaningful all-out bursts which incorporate the following essentials:
   VARIETY, EQUAL TYPE COMPETITION, AND FUN.

FLEXIBILITY:
a) stretching type exercise in the warm-up.
b) partner exercises for the groin, trunk, etc.

AGILITY:
a) drills devised on the basis of the movements of the various positions.
   Example: pass defensive reactions; spinning out of blocks, falling, getting up, and adopting a hitting position.

Figure XII–5. Sample In-Season Program.

ten to fifteen minutes of strength work be inserted into the daily practice. Still others feel that forty minutes once a week, preferably early in the week, on pertinent strength items specific to the positions, would suffice to keep the gains. Biggs [4] recommends that strength programs twice a week is sufficient with the best work days being Monday and Thursday if the team is playing on Saturday.

In order to achieve beneficial results in endurance, it is recommended that a well-organized ten- to fifteen-minute period be incorporated towards the end of a practice session. This could involve challenging all-out running activities such as the parlauf which would equate groups on the basis of speed, along with competitions and relays by positions. The ingenuity of a coach should manufacture specific type all-out running activities which would produce a significant effect on cardiovascular conditioning especially at this time in the practice when the majority of the players are experiencing fatigue similar to a game situation. Agility and flexibilty work would be involved in each practice to round out a satisfactory inseason conditioning program. Figure XII–5 demonstrates a sample inseason program.

FOOTBALL INJURIES—CONDITIONING IMPLICATIONS

Surveys have indicated that in football there is a high incidence of injuries to the musculoskeleto system. The most vulnerable areas of the body are the knees, ankles, shoulders, and neck. Jesse[17] attributes the cause of injuries in these areas to the lack of strength in the muscles and ligaments surrounding these parts, the low level of muscular endurance, an unbalanced muscular development and the lack of flexibility. Adams[1] hints at the potential threat of football movements when he reveals that the rapid movement of a player with quick changes of direction endangers a joint structure that holds the two bones together by stretching the ligaments and tendons beyond the limits of safety. Also, the impact of a fast moving body weight could possibly tear certain joint structures. Partial or complete rupture of ligaments results because of excessive strains being placed on the muscles and ligaments surrounding certain joints. In football, the knee and ankle are the most susceptible to such injury. This substantiates the need to strengthen the ligaments and tendons surrounding the joints, and contributing to their stability. Jesse[17] found that ligaments themselves could be directly strengthened through progressive strain being placed on them, along with the muscles.

Many[1,7,27] express the feeling that it is negligence if a coach does not provide a program of exercises for the knee in all phases of the total conditioning program. To assist in preventing the occurrence and recurrence of knee injuries, it is essential to strengthen the quadricep and hamstring groups that support and protect the knee joint. This is a must for an inseason program especially for those not playing too much. Adams[1] in his work with rats found that systematic exercise of the knee joint by forced running assisted in increasing the strength of the medial collateral ligaments of their knee joints. Systematic running on an uneven surface rather than on a smooth surface also promoted a greater **increase** in ligament strength. His implications stressed that it **might be desirable** for football players to anticipate the stress of quick changes in direction and the strain of heavy body contact by preparing the ligaments of the more vulnerable joints. He recommends the mild traumatic effect of acute joint flexion under imposed weight, especially for knee joints where the ligaments are unable to resist a sudden application of force, and running on rough or uneven surfaces as well as taking part in exercises that serve to stretch the medial collateral ligaments rather than to immobilize them.

A study at Michigan State University by Thompson [29] demonstrated that knee injuries were responsible for the most missed practice time with the average knee injury causing a loss of 8.8 days, while the shoulder injury averaged 6.9 days, and the ankle injury cost 5.9 days. The lay-off produced a decided effect on the physical readiness of the player resulting in a detrimental effect on his performance. It became imperative, that during the convalescent period, the fitness of the uninjured conditionable parts of the body had to be maintained. Thus was organized an injury team for general conditioning with the program being geared specifically to the injury of the player to offset the detraining phenomenon. On-the-field conditioning programs concerned themselves with maintaining of improving cardiovascular respiratory endurance along with the muscle strength and endurance of the uninjured parts so that the injured player could return to action with as high a degree of strength and endurance as possible. The prescribed workload varied with the person's psychological and physiological make-up. Generally, a work bout of about one minute intense enough to raise the pulse rate to at least 180 beats per minute followed by a rest period of one to two minutes during which the pulse rate falls to no lower than 120 beats per minute, stimulated the desired processes. He conducted his rehabilitation program under four basic categories—Upper Body Program for those suffering from injuries to the lower extremities; Lower Body Program for those suffering from injuries to the upper extremities; Total Body Program; and Flexibility Program.

SUMMARY

In attempting to formulate a meaningful conditioning program for football, one must seriously consider the potential specific acts by the offensive and defensive personnel for his particular system of football. Due to the variety of philosophies, variances will occur especially in the pre-season and in-season programs. Generally speaking offensively a team will jog onto the field, engage in a huddle, break from the huddle to a position over the ball, and at the snap of the ball, there is a short quick blast by the line with the backs involved in more sprint-like action of a longer duration. The success or failure of the play determines the amount of running, effort and time expended on each action. Upon completion of the play, the personnel jog back to the huddle. Linemen are limited in the amount of all-out running they do, whereas, the backfielders are called upon for more sustained hard sprinting in the performance of their task. To be productive, a player in any position must be able to execute the movements and essential fundamentals for his particular position so that there is an explosive start mixed in with great body control and the ability to move well in any direction finally culminating in a solid hitting position at the instant of contact with the opponent delivering a vigorous blow and following through aggressively after the impact. All of this has important implications for conditioning.

Defensively, the team jogs onto the field to form a huddle. After breaking the huddle they walk or jog to their position and react to the developing play from a slow to fast pace. Once again, the defensive linemen are limited in their running while the linebackers, defensive backs and safety are involved in more extensive all-out running in the execution of their duties highlighting traits such as speed, mobility, reaction, and agility.

In glancing at the total picture, and readily identifiable on the part of the coach are such characteristics as strength, explosive power, speed, agility, flexibility, endurance, balance and coordination. Thus, in order to acquire appropriate preparation for each individual player, it seems worthy to consider setting up conditioning programs with specificity in mind based in the needs of each position. Programs consisting of weights only or isometrics are not enough to promote a balanced type of conditioning. There must be a variety of activities covering the characteristics cited above in order to develop a functional, productive football player.

In conclusion, it is a wise procedure to set certain objectives for each phase of conditioning in the yearly schedule realizing that conditioning and skill training are interrelated and are often carried on at the same time. The off-season program should be geared to general conditioning, while the pre-season program stresses specific conditioning relevant to the various positions on a football team based on the individual philosophies of the coaches. The main focus of the in-season program is the maintenance of all the gains made in the various areas in conditioning of the off-season program without utilizing too much time. More pertinent research is required in the area of football conditioning in order to arrive at scientifically designed programs that will produce sound and productive outcomes.

REFERENCES

1. Adams, Adran: Effect of exercise on ligament strength. Doctoral Dissertation, University of Southern California, 1965.

2. Allsen, P. E. and Newberry, M.: Weight training program for interior linemen. *Scholastic Coach,* 39:56–58, 99, 1970.

3. Annarino, Anthony: Scientific foundations for conditioning programs. *Scholastic Coach,* 38:62–63, 71–72, 1968.

4. Biggs, Ernest R. Jr.: *Conditioning for Football.* Dubuque, Wm. C. Brown Company, 1968.

5. Brynteson, Paul: Changes in selected bodily responses of college football players following their competitive season. Master's thesis, Springfield College, 1968.

6. Brynteson, Paul and Smith, Richard: Effect of selected football drills upon agility. *Scholastic Coach,* 41:84, 1971.

7. Dayton, O. W.: *Athletic Training and Conditioning.* New York, Ronald Press Co., 1965.

8. Dyer, P.: Isometrics for the high school player. *Coaching Clinic,* 2–4, June, 1964.

9. Griese, L. C.: A comparison of two training programs for maintaining increased muscular strength developed during an off-season conditioning program. Master's Thesis, University of Texas, 1967.

10. Hammer, W. M.: Physiological and performance changes during periods of football training and detraining. *J Sports Med Phys Fitness,* 5:72–75, 1965.

11. Harper, Donald D., Billings, Charles E., and Mathews, Donald K.: Comparative effects of two physical conditioning programs on cardiovascular fitness in man. *Res Q, 40:*293–298, 1969.

12. Hilsendager, Donald R., Strow, Malcolm H. and Ackerman, Kenneth J.: Comparison of speed, strength, and agility exercises in development of agility. *Res Q, 40:*71–75, 1969.

13. Hooks, Gene: *Application of Weight Training to Athletics.* Englewood Cliffs, N.J., Prentice-Hall, Inc., 1962.

14. Howell, M. and Morford, W. R.: Circuit training for a college fitness program. *J Can Assoc Health Phys Educ Recreation,* 35:30–31, 71, February, 1964.

15. Jackson, G. R.: The effect of training at three different heart rate levels upon cardiovascular fitness. Master's thesis, Temple University, 1967.

16. Jarver, J. L.: *The How and Why of Physical Conditioning for Sport.* Hong Kong, Dai Nippon Printing Co., 1970.

17. Jesse, John: *Explosive Muscular Power for Championship Football.* Pasadena, Calif., Athletic Press, 1968.

18. Johnson, B. L.: Effects of applying different motivational techniques during training and in testing upon strength performance. Doctoral dissertation, Louisiana State University, 1965.

19. Jones, Gomer: *Offensive and Defensive Line Play.* Englewood Cliffs, N.J., Prentice-Hall Inc., 1961.

20. Martin, Ben: *Ben Martin's Flexible T Offense.* Englewood Cliffs, N.J., Prentice-Hall Inc., 1961.

21. McCormick, J.: Isometrics for the place kicker. *Scholastic Coach,* 37:50–52, 66, 1968.

22. McKay, John H.: *Football Coaching.* New York, Ronald Press Co., 1966.

23. Nelson, David M.: *Football—Principles and Play.* New York, Ronald Press Co., 1962.

24. Nicolau, A.: Comparison of an experimental and a traditional program of preseason football conditioning. Doctoral Dissertation, Springfield College, 1965.

25. Pickford, Bruce: Ten station exercise circuit. *Coaching Clinic,* 18–21, December, 1964.

26. Ramage, Tom: Off-season football agility program. *Scholastic Coach, 40*:50–52, 1970.
27. Riskas, M.: The effects of weight training on hitting power in the football charge. Master's thesis, University of California, Los Angeles, 1967.
28. Spackman, Robert R. Jr.: *Conditioning for Football.* Springfield, Thomas, 1968.
29. Thompson, C.: On the field conditioning program for injured football players. *Scholastic Coach, 39*:52–54, 1970.
30. Undlin, Malvin G.: A comparison of four methods of circuit training. Master's thesis, Washington State University, 1965.
31. Walker, R.: *The Complete Book of Backfield Play.* Englewood Cliffs, N.J., Prentice-Hall Inc., 1962.
32. Ward, Paul: Strength conditioning for football. *Athletic Journal, 51*:56, 82–84, 1971.

CHAPTER XIII

WRESTLING

G. Leyshon

IF ONE WERE TO ASK a lay person what single physical attribute he as-
ciated with wrestling, the response would most likely be "strength." If
the same question were asked of an experienced coach, the answer would
be highly variable, but in all probability, it would not be "strength." The
opinion of experienced coaches is substantiated by research. Kroll [31,32]
found that wrestlers were below average in strength compared to college
freshman. Taylor [58] studying varsity wrestlers found no significant improvement in strength after an eight-week period of wrestling training. Yet
strength is not to be dismissed completely. Many coaches and trainers [19,28,29]
feel that a program of weight training to improve strength should be undertaken by wrestlers especially at the beginner level. Too great a reliance
on strength, however, may lead to a less complete mastery of technique.

In a poll taken of wrestlers, Lynes [38] found that the physical attribute
most often listed as number one in priority for wrestling success was speed.
Speed, of course, is really reaction time and as such cannot be improved. It
is entirely a matter of the type of nervous system one was blessed with at
birth. If a wrestler does not have great speed, is he to resign himself to
mediocrity? Not a bit! For one thing, research by Henry and Rogers,[43]
Clarke and Glines,[14] and Lotter and others,[37] indicates that reaction time
is highly specific. In other words, a person may have fast hands and slow
feet or vice versa. In any case, seldom is a person shortchanged completely. He need only find his area of greatest speed, and exploit it. Besides,
it is oversimplifying to state that successful wrestling depends on speed
only. There are many factors both physical and mental intermixed and
while speed is important, it is not the only contribution to wrestling success.

Let us look at a few factors which can be developed by coaching and
practicing and which make a positive contribution to success, perhaps
even offsetting a certain lack of speed. Strength, while its contribution is
not paramount, must play some part in wrestling success. Campbell [13]
found that weight training produces significantly greater increase in fitness
than does a normal conditioning program alone. Strength, fortunately, is

163

easy to develop via any number of different weight training programs most of which are recommended for the off-season. Such programs are described elsewhere in this book.

Another factor which is a requisite to wrestling success is cardio-vascular endurance. This certainly can be brought to a high level by the coach. Wrestling is an endurance activity. Brown and Ober [10] and Keen et al.[28] state that the best conditioning for wrestling is wrestling itself. This feeling is echoed by most coaches. Akgun [2] in comparing measures of maximum breathing capacities and peak expiratory flow rates in wrestlers and nonathletes, found that these measures were significantly higher in wrestlers. Tomaras [59] and Tuttle [61] recorded resting systolic and diastolic blood pressures of wrestlers after a competitive season and found them significantly lower in wrestlers as compared to "normal," indicating a high level of cardiovascular fitness. Tomaras also found that wrestlers had the highest Schneider index (a measure of cardiovascular efficiency) of all athletic groups measured. Taylor [58] found that varsity wrestlers after eight weeks of training had significant improvement in cardiovascular condition as compared to students in the service program training twice per week who showed no improvement. Rasch and Brant [48] testing U.S. Olympic free style wrestlers, found wrestling training reduced respiratory rate and increased the respiratory depth. Bachman and Horvath,[4] on the other hand, found on testing varsity swimmers and wrestlers that the swimmers improved in pulmonary function measurements while wrestlers did not. Roskamm et al.[51] in a study of German wrestlers found no increase in heart volume compared with normal subjects of the same age. Bird and Beaulieu [7] also found that the heart rates of college wrestlers during practice did not reach a high enough level to produce a training effect.

The types of drills best suited to improving cardiovascular endurance are those that adopt the Fartlek or interval training methods. Coaches ascribe various names such as "Killer Drill," "Shark Bait," or "Murder Drill," * to these drills, but they are very similar. They involve pitting one man against a series of fresh opponents. At one-minute or two-minute intervals a fresh man wrestles with one who is left in the center of a circle. This continues until the man in the center has wrestled everyone and then a new man takes his turn. Such an exercise, by constantly pitting a fresh man against a tired one forces the tired one to wrestle at a higher level of work output than would be the case if he merely wrestled the same opponent for ten minutes. Other conditioning programs such as cross-country running conditions wrestlers as they condition any other athlete and need

---

* See Gianakaris, G.: *Action Drilling in Wrestling*, Yuhasz, M., Leyshon, G., Salter, W.: *Basic Wrestling for High School Instruction* and Carson, R.: Interval-circuit wrestling, *Scholastic Coach*, 40:37, 1971.

no special mention here. There is, however, often a problem in winter months of finding a suitable area for running, in that weather conditions prevent outdoor running, and gymnasiums are usually busy with basketball teams. Shuttle runs across the mat and back for periods of time simulating a period of wrestling are an excellent substitute. Not only is the stop-start action similar to that of wrestling whereas straight running is not, but all athletes are under the eye of the coach who can encourage a maximum output more readily. In addition, an element of competition can be introduced to relieve the tedium. Another activity favored by coaches is skipping. Baker[5] found that skipping ten minutes daily at a speed of 170 skips per minute was the equivalent of thirty minutes of jogging.

Balance has long been rated highly among the assets of a successful wrestler. According to Umbach and Johnson[62] a wrestler develops balance by learning holds correctly and fighting to maintain a given position. Mumby[43] found a high correlation between wrestling ability as subjectively rated by coaches, and the ability to maintain balance under varied pressure. Panagapka and Lynes[46] compared varsity wrestlers to normal college men and found the wrestlers to have significantly better static and dynamic balance than normal college males. One should be aware here, however, that a selection factor may be at work. In other words successful wrestling requires balance so that those who have good balance may stay with the sport while those who do not may leave it.

Leyshon[34,35] reported using drills to try to develop kinesthesis in wrestlers. By blindfolding his wrestlers for the performance of various drills, he hoped to improve their kinesthetic sensibilities of which balance is a part. Giankaris[21] also describes the blindfold method of drilling. For proof that there may indeed be a positive contribution to successful wrestling by drilling blindfolded, one need only refer to newspaper reports of the success of blind wrestlers against sighted opponents. Buell[11] reported that twenty-two blind wrestlers placed in ten state wrestling meets in the U.S., several of them winning their weight class. In Ontario in 1971 a blind wrestler finished second in the all-Ontario high school tournament for the highest finish yet recorded for a blind wrestler in Canada.

Little scientific study has been done on other physical factors that are undoubtedly involved in wrestling success such as agility, flexibility and power. Per se observation would indicate that agility and flexibility are more markedly developed in wrestlers than in most other groups; however, objective data to support this premise is not available.

Body type may play some small part in wrestling success, but it is difficult from the available evidence to ascertain how much effect body type has. Umbach and Johnson[62] reported that virtually all champions are of medium build. Kroll [31] in an anthropometrical study of collegiate wrestlers found them to be "agility-type" athletes; in other words, they were not large or heavily muscled.

More recently Medved [41] found the average height of wrestlers to be slightly less than that of the average nonathlete. Hirata [24] measured all athletes at the 1964 Olympics and he found wrestlers to be in the "lean-stout" category, somewhere between weightlifters and boxers. His interesting conclusion being that when training has achieved a maximum level of fitness, the most adequate physique will decide the champion.

In comparing the physiques or body types of wrestlers one must keep in mind that in the range of ten weight classes (under present International rules, from 105.5 pounds to superheavyweights of more than 220 pounds) the concentration is greater in the first five weight classes (five classes spanning forty-five pounds). Also, unlike most other athletes, the natural weight of a wrestler is seldom that at which he wrestles. The combination of the two influences combines to create an "average" wrestler who would naturally be somewhat shorter and certainly leaner than average. Tanner [57] concluded that the exceptional ability of athletes lies less in their physique than in extraordinary physiological reserves produced by training and this is born out by observation. The range of types of physiques as measured on a modified Sheldon scale is wide indeed for wrestlers.

Without question, the biggest problem faced by wrestling as a whole is that of athletes losing weight to gain a lower weight classification. Amateur rule books and associations abound in regulations and restrictions regarding the matter and several articles have been published by such august bodies as the American Medical Association condemning the practice for high school athletes. One Iowa county medical society recommended high school wrestling be dropped from the program because of harmful crash diets.[20] Yet, the scientific evidence does not give much support to these criticisms. Tuttle [61], Byram [12], Schuster [53], James [25], Nichols [44], Boch [8], Bowers [9] all found that there were no appreciable adverse effects on wrestlers who reduced up to ten percent of their body weight by exercise and/or dehydration. In a study conducted by Singer and Weiss [54] it was found that a seven percent loss in body weight may be made without adversely affecting those factors apparently related to wrestling success. The investigators found, in fact, that response time (doing a sit-out on command) improved significantly in wrestlers who had lost their maximum of seven percent body weight. Also in this study, it was found that despite a decreasing girth in muscle there was no significant decrease in strength. Ahlman and Karvonen [1] also found that wrestlers losing up to 2.3 kg in a period of three to four hours did not show a decrease in strength.

What many lay people fail to realize is that there are differences between the responses of untrained and trained bodies to the demands of weight loss. Strydom *et al.*[55] studied the effects of humid heat on work capacity and reported that even moderate work rates caused losses of 200 to 300 ml per hour of perspiration when the room temperature was only slightly above normal room temperature. They also noted that it took men ten days to become acclimatized to the hot humid environment (97°F.) and when they did, they lost up to one liter of water in the course of five hours' work and did not require its replacement to maintain work efficiency. They performed their work after acclimatization with ease even though their rectal temperatures and heart rates were higher than normal for their rate of work under cool conditions. This study would seem to substantiate what many coaches have observed, namely, that after approximately two weeks of conditioning, most wrestlers can tolerate heavy work loads in wrestling rooms where the temperature is higher than normal, and where heavy clothing is worn.

An interesting sidelight of interest to wrestlers and coaches alike was the finding by Strydom *et al.*[55] that in 50 percent of the cases, the maximum activity of the sweat glands was *delayed* until after the first hour of work.

Yet another fact which the lay person fails to appreciate, is that in most cases, the wrestler's weight loss is temporary. In Singer's study, for example, the wrestlers were measured in midseason, yet the weight loss was seven percent of body weight spread over the week, culminating in a somewhat larger loss on the last day or so. Immediately after the weigh-in, the regaining of the lost weight begins. Palmer[45] studied wrestlers to see if the five-hour delay between weigh-in and match time was sufficient to recover. For every 2.25 pounds the individual had to regain, one liter of sugar-sweetened water was administered every thirty minutes. Salt tablets were also given. Palmer found the wrestlers regained their physiological efficiency completely in five hours under this regimen. He felt though that using a sweat box as a sole means of losing weight (illegal under NCAA Scholastic Rules) deters the working physiological performance. Kral *et al.*[30] found that wrestlers using dehydration to lose up to seven percent of body weight in a sauna had impaired performances immediately after, but later, their performances were up to par. These researchers identified two types of perspiration: a thermal sweat and an effort sweat. Effort sweat characterized the *trained* athlete and it was poor in sodium chloride, indicating the body was protecting itself against the loss of electrolytes. Kral and his associates found that trained athletes performed well with up to seven percent loss of body weight by dehydration whereas untrained men could not perform well with only a two percent loss. This latter fact is that which guides most coaches to put their charges into good physical condition before any weight loss is attempted.

Robinson[49] reported a greater sensitivity among trained athletes (in this case, runners) to thermal stimuli, and a more effective cooling of the body as a result. He concluded that well-trained men have a higher heat tolerance especially if the training was of the interval type. This, of course, is exactly what many wrestling drills are—interval training drills. The evidence seems to indicate that the best method of losing weight is by wrestling or running. Not only is the weight lost, via a combination of dehydration and the burning of fat reserves, but the conditioning which accompanies the effort is important. Then, too, one must consider the reduction of fat as a more permanent type of reduction even though training itself has been described by Kral *et al.* as a state of chronic dehydration.

One could say that losing weight to satisfy the requirements of a weight classification for wrestling while uncomfortable, is not harmful or dangerous providing that the following rules are kept in mind:

1) weight loss should not exceed seven percent of the body weight after a state of fitness is attained;

2) no attempt at weight loss should be made without a minimum of two weeks' conditioning;

3) weight loss is best handled if it is spread over a period of time, e.g. during midseason, at least a week of gradual loss of the seven percent;

4) the best way to lose temporary weight is through a combination of effort-sweat loss and thermal sweat loss;

5) recovery from dehydration is best accomplished by ingesting sugar-sweetened water and salt tablets.

DIET

The diet of a wrestler is important from two aspects. He must, like any athlete, eat a sufficient and well-balanced diet to insure his optimum physical efficiency. A wrestler, however, must take extra care in selecting his food since generally during weight losing, his intake is lower. Unlike other athletes whose margin of error is greater, a wrestler must consider the food value of every calorie he consumes. He should know that there are five basic categories of food: protein, carbohydrate, fat, mineral and vitamin. To these must be added water which is noncaloric. The primary sources of fuel for energy are carbohydrate and fat with protein acting as a secondary source. Minerals and vitamins provide no fuel, but permit the body to function properly. Protein is necessary for the repair and replacement of muscle tissue.

There are studies to indicate that the food requirements of athletes in training vary from those of the normal untrained person. Cureton [17] feels that it is doubtful that free selection of foods will provide the nutrients

THE ELEMENTS OF FOOD

Element	Use	Best Sources	Calories	Daily Minimum Amount
Protein	Building muscle tissue, Secondary fuel source	lean meat, eggs, fish, nuts	4 cal/gm	70–90 grams
Carbohydrate	Fuel	wheat products, sugars	4 cal/gm	varies as to body size and effort expended minimum is
Fat	Fuel, Padding, Insulation	fat meat, dairy products	9 cal/gm	approximately 1200–1500 cal
Minerals	Chemical balance in the body	fresh fruit, vegetables, liver	—	—daily amounts of several— may vary with the amount of activity
Vitamins	Proper body functioning	fresh fruit, vegetables, dairy products	—	—daily amounts of several— may vary with the amount of activity

necessary for anything above light or moderate work. When one considers that a wrestler cannot even practice "free selection" of foods, it becomes increasingly evident that his choice of food must be guided very carefully for he must make every portion contribute its utmost.

A sample reducing diet for wrestlers might be as follows: (It was prepared for high school wrestlers.) [6]

Breakfast: fruit (half grapefruit or an orange)
toast—2 slices (no butter or jam)
1 glass milk (skim)

Lunch: 1 bowl of soup or 1 glass of milk (skim)
1 sandwich (2 slices of bread) of meat, or fish, or peanut butter
fruit—an orange or apple

Dinner: 1 serving of meat (small hamburger, steak or chop) or 2 eggs
1 serving of salad
1 small serving of vegetable, e.g. one small potato
1 glass milk (skim)
1 serving of ice cream or fruit

A diet such as the above provides adequate amounts of protein, vitamins and minerals while reducing the number of calories, especially those obtained from fat.

The use of vitamin pills to supplement the diet has long been a point of dispute among nutritionists, doctors, coaches and others. Nutritionists maintain that with a proper diet, there are more than enough vitamins and minerals in food and taking extra vitamins does not help. Vitamins cannot be stored for the most part and the body excretes them as waste if they are not utilized. Nutritionists, however, deal largely with average people, and not with athletes in a highly trained state. There is evidence that rigorous training increases the body's requirements of certain substances in addition to carbohydrates. Cureton,[16] for example, showed wheat germ oil (which contains Vitamin E) increased the performances of endurance athletes through its effect on such things as oxygen uptake and brachial pulse wave when the wheat germ was given to the athletes as a dietary supplement. Poiletman and Miller [47] on the other hand, failed to find a significant increase in performance capacity as measured by T wave amplitudes in athletes fed wheat germ oil supplements. They hypothesized the existence of individual hyperactivity to wheat germ oil and recommended wheat germ oil supplementation in association with a training program. Turner [60] theorized that the loss of red blood cells by astronauts was a result of oxidation of the cell wall brought on by breathing a 100 percent oxygen atmosphere and by a reduced Vitamin E intake (an antioxidant). One can extrapolate from this that an endurance type athlete would oxidize his red blood cells more rapidly (evidence exists that he does) and he, therefore, would require more antioxidant in the form of Vitamin E to offset this condition.

One can safely assume that wrestling is a vigorous activity. Cureton [17] quotes a Russian study showing wrestling as having an energy cost of 12 to 16 calories per kilogram of body weight per hour. Thus a wrestler of 150 pounds expends between 1860 and 2400 calories per hour of intensive practice. This being the case, it is safe to include wrestling among those activities classed as rigorous. The fact that wrestlers restrict their diets in addition to working very hard gives added reason for employing dietary supplements such as vitamin pills, wheat germ oil and others.

For anyone concerned about the effects of limited nutrition on the growth of young wrestlers, Tanner [56] offers the advice that children have a "target" for their growth. If through substandard nutrition the growth trajectory is changed, a restoring force develops as soon as the diet is acceptable again. At this point growth speeds up until the child reaches his original trajectory and then growth proceeds at the "normal" pace once again. Such is probably the case with wrestlers.

A partial list of common foods and their caloric values are given at the end of the chapter to offer some guidelines. As a rough rule of thumb, however, one can say that if the proteins, vitamins and minerals are taken in proper quantity and carbohydrates and fats are reduced, then the amount of fat on the body will be lessened. In most cases one can eat meat, and fresh fruit (vegetables are cheaper, but sometimes less palatable), and some skim milk, and providing the quantities are not too great, lose weight. The meat provides protein, the fruit provides many vitamins and minerals as well as roughage necessary to keep the bowels open, and the milk provides minerals and some additional vitamins and protein. There are also quantities of carbohydrate and fat in such a diet, but they are considerably less than in other diets.

A glance at the table of foods and their values will show why some, like soft drinks, are labelled "empty calories." They have no nutrient value beyond their calories. Beer, too, is relatively poor as a food containing many calories, but almost no vitamins or minerals. On the other hand, liver would seem to be close to being an ideal food. Nutritionists recommend that it be eaten at least once per week. Skim milk also provides an abundance of essential elements without a great deal of calories. The wise wrestler would make himself familiar with such a table of foods in order that his selection of diet bring him the most benefit.

For those who find the emotional upset of competition prevents them from holding food down prior to a meet, Rose, Schneider and Sullivan[50] suggest the following precontest meal: 474 cc of liquid sustagen (68% CHO, 24% protein, 8% fat) with a side dish of sliced peaches, toast and honey for bulk. This meal passed through the system in two hours and eliminated precontest vomiting and muscular cramps in football players. The traditional precontest meal of steak, if it is preferred, should be eaten at least four hours before competition, for it takes that length of time to leave the stomach completely, and there should be no food in the stomach during competition.

THE PSYCHOLOGICAL ASPECTS OF WRESTLING

The psychological aspects of wrestling reflect both the wrestler and the coach. Counsilman[15] disavows the old concept of a coach as a stern disciplinarian and favors instead the idea of a coach as an educated director of young people whose interest in athletes extends beyond their athletic success. He feels that in this way he is better able to motivate the athletes. Such is the importance of motivation that it might be said to be the most important of any aspect of a wrestler to be developed. Motivation may, in fact, be accountable for the fact that so many apparently different body types can be successful in wrestling. Kroll[32] in a study of over 1,000 matches found that successful wrestlers secured the initial takedown 70 percent of the time and lost it only seven percent of the time—but that initial takedown performance was unrelated to measures of strength and speed. This suggests, that wrestling success demands something more than speed and strength. That something could conceivably be the motivation to secure the takedown and/or the sophisticated techniques necessary to accomplish the takedown. Leyshon [36] reported on methods to help motivate wrestlers. His contention being that motivation in wrestling is manifested as aggression and that aggression can be fostered by such things as special drills. One such drill involved simply adding to the expected load. If, for example, the wrestlers in practice were told they would have one more minute of any particular they would set their expectations accordingly. The coach at the end of the "last" minute would then announce that the match had gone into overtime and everyone would be required to work for another minute or two minutes, etc. This, applied infrequently, was felt to contribute to the psychological readiness of the athletes and enhance their aggressiveness.

Proper motivation can increase work output beyond what the wrestler believes to be his limit of endurance. Johnson [27] in a summary of studies of hypnosis reported that sufficiently well-motivated subjects were able to perform endurance work tasks longer than hypnotized subjects. One could, in a sense, characterize strong motivation as a type of hypnosis, and its use should be encouraged by a coach. "Wanting to be good and the will to win are vital for success." [39]

At what point can emotional excitement in anticipation of a match interfere? Johnson [26] in a comparison of wrestlers and football players found the wrestlers had a much higher emotional build-up prior to a contest than did football players. Measurements were taken of blood pressure, blood sugar and heart rate and they were all significantly higher in wrestlers. Johnson found that those wrestlers exhibiting excessive excitement rarely performed well. He suggested that coaches be aware of emotional excitement reaching detrimental levels in wrestlers and attempt to ease their tensions. Ryan [52] in a laboratory experiment corroborated Johnson's finding that intense emotional build-up interferes with the performance of difficult motor tasks.

Hammer [22] found that a high level of anxiety is not a determining factor in whether or not an individual chooses to participate in intercollegiate wrestling; however, a high level of anxiety was beneficial to those individuals participating in wrestling, for the most successful wrestlers had the highest anxiety ratings. Hammer hypothesized that in an individual sport such as wrestling a highly anxious person would be more likely to succeed than is probable in a team sport such as football. Morgan [42] indicated that world caliber wrestlers were classified as "stable" during "weight making" and during competition (between matches) and showed no tendency toward neuroticism. In other studies Morgan found that the practice of "making weight" caused a decrement in anxiety levels in wrestlers rather than the opposite. There was also a tendency to be less aggressive against society and more aggressive in socially acceptable ways under the stress of making weight in midseason. This aggressiveness is that most sought by the coach and can and should be polished and encouraged so that the best possible

COMPOSITION OF FOODS, COMMON HOUSEHOLD UNITS [40]

Food, Description, and Approximate Measure	Food Energy	Protein	Fat	Total Carbohydrate	Calcium	Phosphorus	Iron	Vitamin A Value	Thiamine	Riboflavin	Niacin	Ascorbic Acid
	Cal	Gm	Gm	Gm	Mg	Mg	Mg	I.U.	Mg	Mg	Mg	Mg
Apples, raw, 1 medium	76	.4	.5	19.7	8	13	.4	120	.05	.04	.2	6
Bananas, raw, 1 medium	88	1.2	.2	23.	8	28	.6	430	.04	.05	.7	10
Beef—Hamburger, 3 oz	316	19.	26.	0.	8	134	2.4	(0)	.07	.16	4.1	0
Porterhouse, 3 oz (without bone)	293	20.	23.	0.	9	145	2.6	(0)	.05	.15	4.0	0
Beef and Vegetable Stew, 1 cup	252	12.9	19.3	16.7	31	176	2.6	2,520	.12	.15	3.4	15
Beer—1 cup	114	1.4	.0	10.6	10	62	.0	(0)	Trace	.06	.4	(0)
Beverages (carbonated) Other than ginger ale, 8 fluid oz	107	—	—	28.	—	—	—	—	—	—	—	—
White Bread, enriched, 1 slice	64	1.9	.8	12.0	15	19	.4	0	.06	.04	.5	(0)
Whole Wheat Bread, enriched, 1 slice	55	2.1	.6	11.3	22	60	.5	0	.07	.03	.7	(0)
Butter—1 pat or square	50	.0	5.7	.0	1	1	.0	230	Trace	Trace	Trace	(0)
Cakes—Angel food (2 in sector)	108	3.4	.1	23.5	2	10	.1	0	Trace	.05	.1	(0)
Carrots Raw—1 carrot	21	.6	.2	4.6	20	18	.4	6,000	.03	.03	.3	3
Celery, Raw, 3 stalks	9	.6	.1	1.8	25	20	.2	0	.03	.02	.2	4
Cheese, Cheddar, 1 oz	113	7.1	9.1	.6	206	140	.3	400	.01	.12	Trace	(0)
Chicken, Fried, 1 breast (8 oz bone out)	210	47.0	1.0	0.	28	428	2.2	(0)	.13	.18	21.1	(0)
Chocolate beverage, made with milk, 1 cup	239	8.2	12.5	26.2	260	230	.5	350	.08	.40	.3	2
Coleslaw, 1 cup	102	1.6	7.3	9.2	47	32	.5	80	.06	.05	.3	50
Corn flakes, 1 cup	96	2.0	0.1	21.2	3	14	0.3	(0)	0.01	0.02	0.4	(0)
Eggs Hard-cooked, 1 in shell	77	6.1	5.5	.3	26	101	1.3	550	.04	.13	Trace	0
Poached	77	6.1	5.5	.3	26	101	1.3	540	.04	.12	Trace	0
Fruit cocktail, canned solids and liquids, 1 cup	179	1.0	.5	47.6	23	31	1.0	410	.03	.03	.9	5
Gelatin, dessert, ready-to-serve, 1 cup plain	155	3.8	.0	36.3	(0)	(0)	(0)	(0)	(0)	(0)	(0)	(0)
Grapefruit, raw, ½ large	104	1.3	.5	26.4	57	47	.5	20	.10	.05	.5	105
Haddock, Cooked, broiled 1 steak (4 x 3 x ½ in)	158	18.7	5.5	7.0	18	182	.6	—	.04	.09	2.6	—
Honey, 1 tablespoon	62	.1	0.	16.7	1	3	.2	(0)	Trace	.01	Trace	1
Ice Cream, plain, 1 slice	167	3.2	10.1	16.7	100	80	.1	420	.03	.15	.1	1
Lamb, Rib Chop, 3 oz without bone	356	20.	30.	0.	9	170	2.6	(0)	.12	.22	4.8	0

COMPOSITION OF FOODS, COMMON HOUSEHOLD UNITS [40]

Food, Description, and Approximate Measure	Food Energy	Protein	Fat	Total Carbohydrate	Calcium	Phosphorus	Iron	Vitamin A Value	Thiamine	Riboflavin	Niacin	Ascorbic Acid
	Cal	Gm	Gm	Gm	Mg	Mg	Mg	I.U.	Mg	Mg	Mg	Mg
Liver—Beef, 2 oz	118	13.4	4.4	5.5	5	276	4.4	30,330	.15	2.25	8.4	18
Margarine, 1 pat	50	.0	5.7	.0	1	1	.0	230	(0)	(0)	(0)	(0)
Milk, nonfat, 1 cup	87	8.6	.2	12.5	303	239	.2	(10)	.09	.44	.3	3
Oranges—1 medium	70	1.4	.3	17.4	51	36	.6	(290)	.12	.04	.4	77
Peaches—Raw, 1 medium	46	.5	.1	12.0	8	22	.6	880	.02	.05	.9	8
Water Pack, 1 cup	66	1.2	.2	16.6	12	34	1.0	1,110	.02	.05	1.7	10
Peanut Butter—1 tablespoon	92	4.2	7.6	3.4	12	63	.3	0	.02	.02	2.6	(0)
Peas—green, cooked, 1 cup	111	7.8	.6	19.4	35	195	3.0	1,150	.40	.22	3.7	24
Pies—Apple, 4 in sector	331	2.8	12.8	53.3	9	32	.5	220	.04	.02	.3	1
Pork—Ham smoked, cooked, 3 oz without bone	339	20.	28.	(.3)	9	141	2.5	(0)	.46	.18	3.5	0
Luncheon meat, canned, spiced, 2 oz	164	8.4	13.8	.9	5	91	1.2	(0)	.18	.12	1.6	0
Potatoes—Baked, 1 medium	97	2.4	.1	22.3	13	65	.8	20	.11	.05	1.4	17
French-fried, 8 pieces	157	2.2	7.6	20.8	12	61	.8	20	.07	.04	1.3	11
Raisins—dried, 1 tablespoon	26	.2	.0	7.1	8	13	.3	Trace	.02	.01	Trace	Trace
Salad Dressings—French, 1 tablespoon	59	.1	5.3	3.0	(0)	(0)	(0)	(0)	(0)	(0)	(0)	(0)
Sausage—Frankfurter, cooked, 1 only	124	7.	10.	1.	3	25	.6	(0)	.08	.09	1.3	0
Soups, canned, ready-to-serve Beef, 1 cup	100	6.0	3.5	11.0	15	62	.5	—	—	—	—	—
Spaghetti—cooked, 1 cup	218	7.4	.9	44.1	13	95	.9	(0)	.03	.02	.7	(0)
Spinach—cooked, 1 cup	46	5.6	1.1	6.5	223	59	3.6	21,200	.14	.36	1.1	54
Sweet Potatoes—1, baked	183	2.6	1.1	41.3	44	72	1.1	11,410	.12	.08	.9	28
Tomatoes—Raw, 1 medium	30	1.5	.4	6.0	16	40	.9	1,640	.08	.06	.8	35

performance can be elicited from the wrestler. The manner of achieving this flowering of aggression, unfortunately, is difficult. Each personality on a team will react somewhat differently to the coach's efforts as Arthur[3] suggests in his articulate assessment of coaching. Lawther[33] states that the type of motivational stimulus that will have the desired effect, and the degree to which it should be used are problems of individual diagnosis and prescription. The amount of motivation which is effective varies with the individual, his background, his experience, level of learning etc. Lawther also points out that the scientific evidence available indicates that emotional arousal before important contests unless it reaches an extreme degree tends to aid the performance of an experienced athlete. Leyshon[35] suggests that the coach may even use defeat to build motivation and aggression. The defeated wrestler may be "brainwashed" so that he is motivated to work harder and view the defeat as a mere stumble up the ladder of success. Arthur supports this viewpoint by pointing out that many athletes who achieved success too early or too easily never seem to achieve the heights they were capable of.

Leyshon lists the following points in developing what he terms an "attack" philosophy.

1. Have the wrestlers think offense rather than defence. The wrestler should not be a counter wrestler, but one who actively seeks the takedown, pin, escape, etc.
2. Continuous attack is a must. Each wrestler must learn that a single attempt is rarely successful, but a barrage of tries brings him slightly closer on consecutive attacks and ultimately he is successful.
3. Defeat is a temporary setback. It is important to develop an attitude of "I-did-not-lose,—I-ran-out-of-time."
4. Attack to strength. Meet the enemy at his strongest and beat him and his entire attack is gone because he will be beaten mentally.

REFERENCES

1. Ahlman, K., Karvonen, M.: Weight reduction by sweating in wrestlers and its effect on physical fitness. *J Sports Med*, 1:58–62, 1961.
2. Akgun, H.: Measurements of pulmonary function in wrestlers. *Res Q*, 39:771–772, 1968.
3. Arthur, R.: Psychological and psychotherapeutic aspects of swim coaching. *J Sports Med*, 7(4):185, 1967.
4. Bachman, J., Horvath S.: Pulmonary function changes which accompany athletic conditioning programs. *Res Q*, 39:235–239, 1968.
5. Baker, J.: Comparison of rope skipping and jogging as methods of improving cardiovascular efficiency in college men. *Res Q*, 39:240–243, 1968.
6. Bentley, F.: *Northern Wrestling. A Manual of Guidance.* 1964.

7. Bird, L., Beaulieu, G.: A Study of the cardiac cost of wrestling practice. Unpublished Study U.W.O., 1970.
8. Bock, W.: The effects of acute dehydration upon cardiorespiratory endurance. Unpublished doctoral dissertation, Ohio State University, 1965.
9. Bowers, J.: Effects of rapid weight reduction on physiologic responses of high school wrestlers. Unpublished master's thesis, Illinois State University, 1963.
10. Brown, R., Ober, D.: *Complete Book of High School Wrestling.* Englewood Cliffs, Prentice-Hall Inc., 1962, pp. 22, 23.
11. Buell, C.: *1CRH Newsletter,* Vol. 4, #8, Aug. 1970.
12. Byram, H.: Effects of weight reduction on strength and on muscular endurance. Unpublished master's thesis, State University of Iowa, 1953.
13. Campbell, R.: Effects of supplemental weight training on the physical fitness of athletic squads. *Res Q, 33:*343–348, 1962.
14. Clark, H. H., Glines, D.: Relationship of reaction movement and completion times to motor strength, anthropometric and maturity measures of 13-year-old boys. *Res Q, 33:*194–201, 1962.
15. Counsilman, J. E.: *The Science of Swimming.* Englewood Cliffs, Prentice-Hall, 1968.
16. Cureton, T.: The effect of wheat germ oil and vitamin E on normal human subjects in physical training programs. *Am J Physiol, 179:*628, 1954.
17. ———: Diet related to athletics and physical fitness. Reprinted from *J Phys Educ, 57*(2,3,4,5):1959–1960.
18. ———: Unpublished Data quoted in Diet in athletics, conditioning and training. *Nadbitka Autorska.* IV, 1964.
19. Dratz, J., Johnson, M., McCann, T.: *Winning Wrestling.* Englewood Cliffs, Prentice-Hall Inc., 1966, p. 179.
20. Gage, R.: Leyshon miffed by reports of mat injuries, crash diets. *London Free Press,* Feb. 22, 1968.
21. Giankaris, G.: *Action Drilling in Wrestling.* 1966, p. 65.
22. Hammer, W.: A comparison of differences in manifest anxiety in university athletes and nonathletes. *J Sport Med,* 7:31, 1967.
23. Henry, F., Rogers, D.: Increased response latency for complicated movements and a "Memory Drum" theory of neuromotor reaction. *Res Q, 31:*448–458, 1960.
24. Hirata, K.: Physique and age of Tokyo Olympic champions. *J Sports Med,* 6:207–222, 1966.
25. James, B.: The effects of weight reduction on the physical condition of high school wrestlers. Unpublished marter's thesis, State University of Iowa, 1950.
26. Johnson, W.: A study of emotion revealed in two types of athletic contests. *Res Q, 20:*72–79, 1949.
27. ———: Hypnosis and muscular performance. *J Sport Med,* 1:71, 1961.
28. Keen, C., Speidel, C., Swartz, R.: *Championship Wrestling,* 4th ed. Annapolis, U.S. Naval Institute, 1964, pp. 17, 201.
29. Klafs, C., and Arnheim, D.: *Modern Principles of Athletic Training.* St. Louis, C. V. Mosby Co., 1963, pp. 76, 77.
30. Kral, J. I., Zenisek, A., Hais, I. M.: Sweat and exercise. *J Sports Med,* 3:105–111, 1963.
31. Kroll, W.: Anthropometrical study of some Big Ten wrestlers. Unpublished Master's Thesis, University of Illinois, 1954.
32. ———: Selected factors associated with wrestling success. *Res Q,* 29:396–406, 1958.

33. Lawther, J. D.: *The Learning of Physical Skills.* Toronto, Prentice-Hall, Ltd., 1968, pp. 120–121.
34. Leyshon, G.: Handicapped wrestling. *Scholastic Coach, 27:*78, 1968.
35. ———: Handicap wrestling to develop kinesthesis. *Can Coach, 2:*23, 1970.
36. ———: The attack philosophy in wrestling. *Scholastic Coach, 40:*69, 1971.
37. Lotter, W.: Interrelationships among reaction times and speeds of movement in different limbs. *Res Q, 31:*147–155, 1960.
38. Lynes, W.: Qualities of a good wrestler. Unpublished Study University of Western Ontario, 1968.
39. Manfredi, D.: What makes a great athlete. *J Sport Med, 7:*165, 1967.
40. McHenry, B.: *Basic Nutrition.* Montreal, Lippincott Co., 1963, revised edition.
41. Medved, R.: Body height and predisposition for certain sports. *J Sports Med, 6:*89–91, 1966.
42. Morgan, W.: Psychological concomitants of "making weight" in the college wrestler. Paper read 12th National Conference on Medical Aspects of Sports, Boston, Nov. 29, 1970.
43. Mumby, H.: Kinesthetic acuity and balance related to wrestling ability. *Res Q, 12:*284, 1953.
44. Nichols, H.: The effects of rapid weight loss on selected physiologic responses of wrestler. Unpublished doctoral dissertation, University of Michigan, 1957.
45. Palmer, W.: Selected physiological responses of normal young men following dehydration and rehydration. *Res Q, 39:*1054–1059, 1968.
46. Panagapka, D., Lynes, W.: A comparison of balance between college normals and varsity wrestlers. Unpublished study, University of Western Ontario, 1968.
47. Poiletman, R., Miller, H.: The influence of wheat germ oil on the electrocardiographic T waves of the highly trained athlete. *J Sports Med, 8:*26, 1968.
48. Rasch, P., Brant, J.: Measurement of pulmonary function in U.S. Olympic free style wrestlers. *Res Q, 28:*279–287, 1957.
49. Robinson, S.: Training, acclimatization and heat tolerance. *Can Med Assoc J, 96:*795–799, 1967.
50. Rose, K., Schneider, P., Sullivan, G.: A liquid pregame meal for athletics. *JAMA, 178:*30, 1961.
51. Roskamm, H., Reindell, H., Konig, K.: The heart of the trained athlete. *Documenta Geigy.* 1968.
52. Ryan, E.: The effects of stress on motor performance and learning. *Res Q, 33:*118–119, 1962.
53. Schuster, A.: The effects of rapid weight reduction on the endurance and performance of wrestlers. Unpublished Master's thesis, Pennsylvania State University, 1954.
54. Singer, R., Weiss, S.: Effects of weight reduction on selected anthropometric, physical, and performance measures of wrestlers. *Res Q, 39:*361–369, 1968.
55. Strydom, L., Wydham, C., Williams, C., Morrison, J., Budell, G., Benade, A., Vonrahden, M.: Acclimatization to humid heat and the role of physical conditioning. *J Appl Physiol 21:*636, 1966.
56. Tanner, J.: Relationship of differential bodily tissues during growth and in the adult. In Wolstenholme, G. and O'Connor, M. (Eds.): *Diet and Bodily Constitution.* London: CIBA, 1964.
57. ———: Limits of human performance. *Documenta Geigy.* 1968.
58. Taylor, A. W.: The effects of training for competitive college wrestling. Unpublished Study, University of Western Ontario, 1963.

59. Tomaras, W.: The effect of wrestling upon physical fitness. Unpublished Master's Thesis, University of Illinois, 1948.

60. Turner, D.: Toronto scientist's discovery means vitamins for astronauts. *The Globe and Mail,* July 2, 1969.

61. Tuttle, W. W.: The effect of weight loss by dehydration and the withholding of food on the physiologic response of wrestlers. *Res Q, 14:*158–166, 1943.

62. Umbach, A., Johnson, W.: *Successful Wrestling.* St. Louis, C. V. Mosby Co., 1953, p. 35.

63. Yuhasz, M., Leyshon, G., Salter, W.: *Basic Wrestling for High School Instruction.* Ottawa Canadian Association for Health, Physical Education and Recreation. 1964.

CHAPTER XIV

CROSS-COUNTRY SKIING

M. Jetté, B. Cameron, F. Cooke, and M. Allen

THE CONTENT OF this chapter is the result of a review of the current literature pertaining to training and conditioning for cross-country skiing, as well as many hours of discussion with experienced coaches and athletes. The purpose of the chapter is to outline a training program adapted to the Canadian environment which is felt advisable in order that the serious competitor may achieve a high degree of success.

In formulating the program, the fundamental theories of overload, specificity, transfer of training and reversibility, which form the basis of current training practices, were considered. The program, therefore, attempts to outline the necessary stimuli required for the development of those "qualities" inherent to the successful cross-country skier. As for any general presentation of this nature, the recommended program must be adapted to the individual and to his desired level of competition.

It is a well-known fact that cross-country skiing is a most demanding sport. The major muscle groups of the body are vigorously involved in competitions that last from thirty minutes up to three to four hours. Consequently, the demands of the sport tax the cardiovascular and respiratory systems to their ultimate capacity. The calorie expenditure for a mere five km race can run as high as 1200 net calories per hour.[26] Only the most superbly conditioned athlete can endure and sustain such exertion for such long periods of time. Some of the highest maximum oxygen intakes have been demonstrated by cross-country skiers. One can therefore readily envisage the genetic endowment and amount of training required to produce such a high degree of working capacity.

Successful achievement in cross-country skiing can only come after years of continuous and arduous training coupled with relentless devotion to the sport. These attributes, we firmly believe, are possessed by many of our young Canadians.

The Coach

The quality of a sport is directly related to the level of coaching. The role of a coach is most demanding and particularly so when national and international competition is involved. In cross-country skiing, his major task is to ensure that the athlete arrives at the important competition in the most optimal state of physical and mental fitness. In order to achieve this, he must provide his athlete with the best training and techniques of instructions available coupled with a deep understanding of the skier's emotional behavior. He must be able to judge when to "push," when to "relax," when to "praise," when to "criticize." Mutual respect between athlete and coach is sacred.

The most scientifically devised program can easily be undermined by improper monitoring or even by a few careless remarks. The athlete depends on his coach for all aspects of his training and conditioning as well as for his understanding and support. Unless there exists complete confidence between the two, the success of both is doubtful.

The Athlete

Although training may be organized so that it can be enjoyable, there are certain hardships which the successful cross-country skier must be prepared to endure. The extremely arduous training and the deprivation of social life that may arise due to training may be a greater sacrifice than the potential athlete may be willing to make.

Consequently, the future international athlete should possess, in varying degrees, those personality characteristics which have been shown necessary for high level competition, such as emotional stability, independence and aggressiveness, confidence and tough mindedness.[19,25] Notwithstanding, the satisfaction and the educational experience that participation in cross-country skiing brings to the young competitor cannot be found in the classroom or in many other sports for that matter. The companionship of fellow skiers, the travel opportunities and the sense of sportsmanship, cooperation, determination and the will to succeed, so apparent to the authors of this chapter, easily eradicate the hardships that may be encountered along the path of a sound training program.

The skier who decides to start training for competition must take a complete inventory of his abilities. First, he should start by having a complete medical examination. A detailed laboratory appraisal of his individual aerobic and anaerobic capacity, his strength, flexibility and power, as well as a detailed psychological inventory should be undertaken. The information derived from these tests will enable the coach and athlete to determine possible weaknesses. Remedial action can thus be prescribed and included in the overall training program. These tests can also assist in evaluating the "potential" of the athlete for the sport. There is now sufficient information compiled on cross-country skiers to enable the coach to know which aspirant will be able to successfully maintain the training program.

Once this information has been evaluated, a training program in light of the goals of the athlete can be outlined. The setting of short- and long-term goals is adamant to successful training. Unless these goals are properly delineated, motivation, so necessary in this sport, will undoubtedly wane and performance will suffer accordingly.

PHYSIOLOGICAL AND MOTOR ABILITIES REQUIRED OF THE CROSS-COUNTRY SKIER

The requirements of the cross-country skier are very similar to those of other long distance and cross-country foot events with the exception of special motor and technique abilities.

Cross-country skiing requires, in particular, the following abilities:

1. Aerobic power
2. Anaerobic power
3. Strength and muscular endurance
4. Flexibility and balance

Aerobic Power

Aerobic power is the capacity to perform a generalized and prolonged muscular effort where the oxygen requirement is less than the maximal oxygen intake of the athlete. Aerobic power, or cardiorespiratory endurance, is related to the individual's ability to diffuse more oxygen at the level of the lungs and the cells, and to efficiently transport the greatest amount of oxygen per unit of time to the appropriate muscles, thus ensuring the minimum of lactic acid accumulation in the blood.[3] Cardiocirculorespiratory efficiency will, of necessity, be particularly dependent upon the strength, volume and functional capacity of the heart and the general diffusion capacity of the athlete.[18]

Anaerobic Power

Anaerobic power is the capacity to perform a generalized muscular effort where the oxygen requirement is greater than the maximal oxygen intake of the athlete. Anaerobic power, or stamina, is related to the individual's ability to accumulate a high oxygen debt, and therefore the capacity to tolerate the pain caused by the increased concentration of lactic acid in the blood.[3] The individual's capacity for anaerobic power is therefore both a function of his aerobic power and his physiological and psychological ability to withstand oxygen debt and pain.

Strength

Strength is the capacity which enables the athlete to develop tension during maximum contraction. Strength is a function of volume (structural elements) and of the voluntary control that one can exercise on a muscle or group of muscles.[3] Strength can be produced isotonically, i.e. when the segments involved move toward each other (concentric) or move away from each other (eccentric). It can also be produced isometrically, i.e. when muscular contraction is exerted without segment movement.

Muscular Endurance

Muscular endurance is the capacity which enables the athlete to continuously maintain a localized muscular effort during anaerobic conditions. During local muscular anaerobic capacity, the strength of contraction reduces blood flow to the muscles involved so that toxic substances cannot be adequately eliminated. This ability is a function of both the basic strength of the muscle or muscle group and the psychological ability to tolerate the localized muscular pain.[3]

Flexibility

Flexibility is the ability which permits maximum range of the involved segments and is a function of the mobility of the articulation and the extensibility of the muscles involved.[3] This ability is particularly essential to the development of the proper and powerful stride of the cross-country skier.

Power

Power is the ability which permits a muscle or muscle group to produce explosive power,[3] an essential requirement of the cross-country skier. Power calls for dynamic strength and neuromuscular speed of transmission and contraction.

DEVELOPMENT OF THE TRAINING PROGRAM

In order to ensure that the physiological and motor abilities that contribute to successful cross-country skiing are developed, we will now consider the training stimuli most apt to achieve the desired effects for each of these abilities. The reader is referred to the chapters pertaining to the physiological and biochemical aspects of training underlying the basis of the following recommended program of training.

Aerobic Power (Endurance)

Aerobic power is best developed by short interval (intermittent, distance and tempo) training.[3,14] These stimuli will result in increases in muscle mitochondria, in energy liberating enzymes in the sarcoplasm, and in the electron transport capacity, by overloading the large muscle groups and the transport systems of respiration and circulation.[6,15,16,20]

Short interval training

Short interval training exerts its effects on the volume and functional capacity of the heart. It consists of short, high intensity sprints on foot or skis lasting from thirty to sixty seconds with heart rates reaching 170 beats/min. The effort is followed by a 60 to 90-second rest period or until the heart rate has dropped to 120 beats/min. Both the work and rest period must be geared to the individual's level of conditioning. For maximum benefits, uphill running is recommended. Soccer, water polo and circuit training are also excellent methods for developing this ability.

Distance training

Distance training exerts its effects on the ventilation capacity, gas transport and diffusing capacity at the level of the lungs and muscles of the athlete.[3] It consists of running or skiing long distances lasting from 45 minutes to three hours. At the onset, the distance can be interspersed with walking or ski-striding periods. As training improves, the speed and the difficulty of the terrain can be increased. Distance training should be maintained at over 50 percent of the individual's maximum aerobic capacity with heart rates in the 130 to 140 beats/min range.

Tempo training

Tempo training, like distance training, exerts its effect on the ventilation capacity, gas transport and diffusion capacity of the athlete. It is particularly designed to enable a runner to maintain the speed and psychological stress required in competition. It consists of running or skiing at speeds equal to or greater than competition speeds, for periods changing from 10 percent to 20 percent of the duration of the competition, followed by rest periods of shorter duration.

Anaerobic Capacity

Anaerobic capacity, or oxygen debt capacity, is best developed by the "long interval" type of training.[3,21]

It consists of sprints of maximal intensity lasting for periods of one to four minutes. The intensity of the sprints should exceed the athlete's maximal aerobic capacity and should elicit heart rates of 180 beats/min or more. The stress is followed by a five to ten minutes' rest period or at least until the heart rate has returned to approximately 100 beats/min. Here again, the effective running time will be adapted to the individual's ability.

It should be noted that the optimum stimulus for speed training should be movements which are carried out at the highest speed without being detrimental to correct technique. Incorrect technique may cause the recruitment of inappropriate motor units.[15]

Strength

Strength is developed by overloading the muscle groups involved in cross-country skiing through both static (isometric) and dynamic (isotonic) training. It results in a thickening and an increase in the number of myofibrils, particularly in white fibers, leading to the hypertrophy of the fibers.

To develop strength isometrically, the intensity of effort should be maximal wit ha duration of five to ten seconds and with 10 to 15 repetitions daily. Contractions should be applied at all the angles which are of particular use to the cross-country skier since static contractions result in an increased strength only at the specific angle or angles at which the static contraction was held.[12]

Isotonic strength training using weights requires a work intensity of 80 to 100 percent of the maximal strength using one to six repetitions (high load—low repetition). Training should be carried out throughout the full range of motion required. Isotonic training of this type is reported to be the most effective method of producing muscle hypertrophy and of increasing muscle strength.[12]

Strength training programs are varied and can be accomplished by many diverse methods. Isometrics are very popular with some athletes while others prefer concentrating on combinations of weight, pulleys, gymnastics, and such practical training as ski striding.

Although the skier must possess overall strength, he should concentrate on those muscle groups required to achieve the power and explosive efforts characteristic of the cross-country athlete. He should therefore emphasize the development of those muscles involved in the pushing of the arms and of the legs.

Muscular Endurance

Muscular endurance can also be developed isometrically (static) or isotonically (dynamic).

Isometric muscular endurance is best developed by contracting two thirds of the maximal strength of the muscles involved for as long as the individual can tolerate the stimuli.

Isotonic muscular endurance, on the other hand, entails using two-thirds of the maximal strength of the involved muscles during 15 to 25 continuous repetitions.

Muscular endurance can, therefore, be developed through a multitude of programs. These include:

1. Calisthenics: sit-ups (with and without weights), pull-ups, dips, push-ups, back arches, and gymnastics (rings, parallel bars, horse)
2. Weight training: knee bends, hops, forward bends, standing presses, pull-ups

Muscular endurance is most important to cross-country skiing where rapid, explosive movements are required.

Flexibility

Flexibility is developed by ensuring a full range of movement.[3] A general program of calisthenics (stretching), along with isotonic weight training programs, will ensure proper development. Flexibility exercises should always form a part of the daily training program to eliminate stiffness.

Power

Power is the result of strength and speed of movement. Therefore, power is developed by the voluntary explosive effort of an overloaded muscle. The intensity of work should be between ⅓ to ¾ maximal and the period of effort must be produced within the minimum amount of time.

Programs such as circuit training, power training, tumbling and weight training will produce the desired effects; also useful is quick uphill running (approximately 30% gradient), rope skipping, and pole pushing on roller skates.

PRACTICAL TRAINING

A popular form of exercise which develops stamina, muscular endurance and power is the "ski stride." Ski striding is a modified walk, trot or run which imitates the cross-country skiing stride. It can be practiced with or without poles to simulate the movement which resembles the diagonal stride used in skiing. Ski striding is an excellent aid to practice the correct movement patterns and rhythm of the actual stride. The stride is generally practiced uphill to provide the necessary resistance. When striding without poles, the skier simply makes a complete extension or bounding jump from one leg to the other. The kick should be short and explosive and the runner, for an instant, should be completely in the air before he lands spring-like on his heel. Special attention must be given to the strong push provided by the articulation of the foot and toes. With poles, the movement should duplicate the actual skiing movement. The heel should land first and the movement of the extended arm and leg should be in a perfect synchrony.

DESIGN OF THE TRAINING PROGRAM

It is most important to emphasize that the athlete cannot be programmed as we program a computer. An athlete has his idiosyncracies, his moods, his ups and downs. Consequently, the competent coach is sensitive to these uncontrollable variables and must modify his program and his attitudes to meet these situations.

In outlining a training program, both conditioning and technique must be considered since they are to a certain extent interrelated. This chapter, however, is directed to the conditioning aspects of competition. There are already excellent publications dealing with techniques such as those of Brady[5] and Caldwell.[9]

Normally, the successful competitor is one who has been skiing since he was quite young. Although there may be exceptions, the chances of achieving success in international competition are limited if training was not initiated prior to the ages of 17 or 18. Therefore, the complete training program of a young skier must be planned in consideration of the goals that have been set forth.

The competent coach, in conjunction with the athlete, will design a program which he feels will achieve the specific goals that have been set for that year: i.e. increase in anaerobic capacity, strength, race times, etc. Each year, the ability of the athlete must be reevaluated and his training program redesigned accordingly. In addition, the intensity of the program must be increased each year at a level compatible with the capability of the athlete and the long-term goals that have been set. The setting of such goals makes the outlining of the program directly related to the competition aspiration of the athlete. Furthermore, it is probably the most important motivation factor in adhering to a strict training schedule. As for any training program, it must be progressive, specifically related to the individual, to his likes and dislikes. Most important, it must be year-round. One cannot afford to wait until the snow appears to begin training or to train haphazardly without any preset plan. Training is a science; if an athlete wants to compete, he must pattern his training in a systematic and scientific manner to obtain every benefit from it.

Recommended Training Program

The training program outlined in this chapter is one that has been devised to take into account the development of the characteristics fundamental to cross-country skiers in Canada. It is proposed for the élite skiers; if followed by members in lower levels of competition, it should be scaled proportionately, i.e. for a junior, the program should be approximately half of the work recommended. The program should also be adapted to the individual's capability, bearing in mind the age, sex, goals, previous training, and occupation of the athlete. The judgment of the coach and the athlete, in addition to the results of his fitness testing, are the best guides to the formulation of the program.

Phases of Training

Although it is difficult to categorically divide the program, the following phases of training of the total program are described for ease of discussion:

Phase 1   May
          Transition from skiing to dry land training
Phase 2   June to first snow
          Dry land training
Phase 3   First snow to December
          Transition period to skiing and training for competition—
          getting used to skis, and technique training (2 to 3 weeks)
          Tuning-up period (2 to 3 weeks)
Phase 4   January to April
          Competitive period
Phase 5   April
          Post racing

Phase 1   May Transition from Skiing to Dry Land Training

The purpose of this phase of the program is to gradually develop and enhance the aerobic capacity of the athlete while making the transition from snow to dry land training. The phase involves, primarily, distance running at an average speed of 7 to 8 mph or at a heart rate of approximately 140 beats/min. It should also involve some short interval training as described earlier.

A terrain similar to that employed in cross-country skiing should be selected, i.e. one that involves flats, short and long uphills and downhills.

This phase should also provide time for strength training, both isometric and isotonic, as well as for flexibility training. A recommended time allotment for the phase of the training program is as follows:

Endurance   60%
Strength   20–30%
Flexibility   10–20%

There should be three or four training sessions per week, each lasting from one to one and one-half hours each. A typical session could be as follows:

10–15 min: Warm-up (calisthenics—jogging)
30–60 min: Distance and short interval training
10–15 min: Strength training—gymnastics, circuit, power, etc.
10   min: Recovery—cooling off (walk and stretch)

Once a week, a whole day should be set aside for a 10 to 15-mile hike. This will help to develop ankle resiliency and strength.

During this month and throughout the summer, participation in such sports as rowing, track and field, cycling, swimming, tennis, soccer, and orienteering is strongly recommended.

Phase 2   June to First Snow High Intensity—Dry Land Training

The purpose of this first phase is to further increase aerobic and anaerobic capacity as well as strength. The program is similar to that of Phase 1 but with an increase in the duration and intensity of the training sessions. The program includes a five-day training week with sessions of approximately 90 minutes. Most of the time in this phase is devoted to distance training and short and long interval training.

A typical session could be as follows:

10–15 min: Warm-up (calisthenics)
60–70 min: Running—distance and/or interval
10–15 min: Recovery—cooling off (walk and stretch)
10   min: Weight training—if required

Also recommended are one or two hikes a week, either in the form of a short but fast five miles, or a longer trek, some 10 to 20 miles, in both instances carrying a heavy pack.

Some athletes prefer to devote some days wholly to distance running and other specific days to interval training. Other athletes, however, prefer to spend some of the sessions engaging in various types of running. In any event, the equivalent of three sessions should be devoted to distance and the equivalent of two sessions devoted to both types of interval training. Training is intensified as the phase progresses. Suitable relaxation and rest periods should be included in the program.

Phase 3   First Snow to December Transition Period to Skiing and Training for Competition

This is an extremely important phase and both the coach and athlete must be aware of the problems that can plague the skier. Many different groups of muscles came into use during transition from dry land to snow skiing; therefore, the training schedule must be so organized as to minimize any possible injuries such as pulled muscles and torn ligaments.

The purpose of this phase is, primarily, to get "used" to the skis again and to improve technique. Once the athlete is fully adapted to his skis, the intensity of his training can be resumed. Most of the training from now on, however, should be carried out on skis.

LOW INTENSITY TRAINING (1 WEEK)

During this stage, the athlete should ski some two hours per day on a good track and on gentle terrain where he can concentrate on his style. He should also include some strenuous running to ensure the maintenance of his fitness. The amount of time which will be devoted to technique during this period will depend on the ability and caliber of the skier.

HIGH INTENSITY TRAINING (3 WEEKS)

During these weeks, the skier should concentrate on intensive uphill training; two days of the week should be devoted to distance skiing. He should "charge" up the hills as fast as possible; on flat ground, he should ski strong sprints of 200 to 400 meters using diagonal striding and poling.

Phase 4   January to April Competitive Period

The main objective of the training program is to prepare the athlete for a national or international competition. The program should be so designed as to ensure that the athlete reaches his peak period to coincide with his planned objectives. His previous competitions should be considered as guides to evaluate the extent of his fitness and techniques. Each race should be closely scrutinized so as to provide information to enhance his performance. Notwithstanding, the athlete must ensure that periods of staleness do not interfere with his preset goals. He must remember that each race exerts a tremendous strain on his body. Consequently, he must be given the opportunity to recuperate after each race even though he may not feel it necessary.

A possible weekly competition program could be as follows:

Sunday	Competition event—later to be a short run-stretching exercise—good rest
Monday	Warm-up (Stretching exercises) Jogging interval—ski training—walking (1 to 1½ hours)
Tuesday	On skis 10 to 15 km—alternating between slow and fast speeds
Wednesday	On skis 30 to 50 km This distance skiing should bring about "total" exhaustion. Stretching exercises
Thursday	Skiing 5 to 10 km at a quick pace Include a few sprints
Friday	Skiing slowly, preferably on the same course which will be used for the competition Rest
Saturday	Program similar to Friday

It should be indicated that the training should be related to the condition of the athlete and to the amount of competition in which he is involved. Normally he should not enter more than one race per week. The body requires this time to recuperate and to replenish its energy resources for the following competition.

Phase 5   April Post-Racing Period

The purpose of this training phase is to ensure that the athlete does not completely stop his training after competition. Although general relaxation is the theme of this phase, he should engage in some form of activity. Prolonged inactivity at this time could be most detrimental particularly when training is to be resumed. Participation in sports or in any form of physical activity should, therefore, be strongly encouraged. If snow is still available, this may be a good time to improve on some particular technique. Notwithstanding, this should be accomplished at an easy and relaxed pace. At this time, the athlete needs this relaxation phase if he is to reenter his forthcoming new training program with increased vigor and enthusiasm.

In completing this section, it should be emphasized that in planning for next year's program, the level of intensity of the new program should be increased. The athlete has developed a fitness potential during the past year which should now be improved. If the program, particularly in Phase 2, is not increased in intensity over that of the past year, then there is little hope that increases in organic capacity and performance will be developed.

DIET

If there is a group of athletes that attaches considerable interest to nutrition, it is certainly the cross-country skiers. This is readily understandable since training for cross-country is most demanding in caloric expenditure. Notwithstanding, there is little disagreement that a well-balanced diet of wholesome foods is as valid for the skier as for any other person. The cross-country skier, particularly during high intensity training, should consume sufficient food to meet the demands of his caloric output which can be as high as 6000 calories per day. In any case, the proportion of fat, including very little saturated fat, should not exceed 30 percent of the total diet. Carbohydrates can account for up to 50 to 55 percent of the total diet, while protein should constitute the remaining 15 percent. Such a diet contains all the nutrients needed for continued health and energy.[22,23,28]

Except for basic individual preferences, there is no scientific evidence to indicate that special food can provide enhanced performance. It should also be noted that no one particular diet is appropriate to all persons. Until the time when we can minutely match food intake with our own personal body chemistry requirements, a nutritionally sound diet is all that is necessary.

The athlete and coach who are fortunate enough to live in Canada should not have to worry about supplementing their diet with ergogenic aids. If a balanced diet of varied foods of animal and plant origins is enjoyed, all the required nutrients will be supplied.[13,23]

The one supplementary nutrient which has been shown to possibly offer improved training effects is wheat germ oil (WGO) which is known to contain vitamin E and octacosonol. WGO seems to be a daily dietary supplement taken by many cross-country skiers and is one that has outlasted most other athletic dietary supplements. Although Cureton[11] has favorably documented WGO as a desirable adjunct to the diet of the athlete, some exercise physiologists remain most skeptical.

The Diet Preceding Competition

Recent experiments have indicated that the initial glycogen in the skeletal muscles is a decisive factor in maintaining prolonged activity.[1,2] It was reported that glycogen depots could be increased by carbohydrate enriched diets, particularly if the glycogen stores were first depleted by heavy prolonged exercise.

The following diet sequence seems generally accepted by many international skiers and is presented for your consideration. If for instance, the competition is to be held on a Sunday, then the training sequence would be as previously discussed above and the diet plan would be as follows:

Monday	Diet to consist of proteins and fat
Tuesday	As above
Wednesday	Diet rich in carbohydrates, up to 75 percent of caloric intakes
Thursday	
Friday	Diet again rich in carbohydrates
Saturday	
Sunday	Breakfast at least three hours before the start of the competition. The amount should be left to the individual's preference.

There may be too much unfounded worry on what is a good precompetition meal. If the skier is going to burn some 3000 calories during his event, he should consume sufficient food to balance the loss. The athlete's past experience should be the main dictate of the constitution of his precompetition meal.

Laboratory Testing

Laboratory testing should be a standard and integral aspect of a serious cross-country training program. To intelligently design a program, it would seem logical to begin with a detailed analysis of the capabilities and potential of an athlete in light of the physical and psychological requirements of the sport. A profile of the athlete can then be outlined, scrutinized and compared with the profiles of world champions.[24]

For the laboratory data to prove meaningful, however, the athlete should be tested at regular intervals during his program. The most desirable times would be at the onset, midpoint and completion of the most intensive phase of the training. Such testing sessions could be utilized to pinpoint weaknesses, to modify the program of the skier and could well predict staleness and overtraining. The sessions should include those tests which will adequately measure the physiological and phychological characteristics of the cross-country skiers discussed earlier. Descriptions of tests and their application have been reviewed in various publications.[4,8,9,27]

Although the scientist can assist the coach in training specific characteristics required of the athlete, his main responsibility is in determining which particular characteristics require training and to what extent. If we are to develop a better understanding of the abilities of the cross-country skier and if we are to enhance his training programs, closer cooperation must be developed among the coach, the athlete and the scientist.

REFERENCES

1. Åstrand, P.-O.: Concluding remarks, proceedings of the international symposium on physical activity and cardiovascular health. *Can Med Assoc J*, 96:907, 1967.
2. Åstrand, P.-O. and K. Rodahl: *Textbook of Work Physiology.* Toronto, McGraw-Hill Book Company, 1970.
3. Bouchard, C., J. Brunelle and P. Godbout: Les qualités physiques et l'entraînement. Département d'Education Physique, Université Laval, Mai, 1969.
4. Bouchard, C., J. C. Mondor and P. Béliveau: Contrôle de l'état d'entraînement. *Rapport Technique 2*, Groupe Inter-Universitaire de Recherche sur l'Activité Physique, Janvier, 1972.
5. Brady, M.: *Nordic Touring and Cross-Country Skiing,* 2nd ed. Oslo, Dreyers Forlag, 1970.
6. Brouha, L.: Training. In *Science and Medicine of Exercise and Sports.* New York, Harper and Brothers Publishers, 1960.
7. Caldwell, J.: *The Cross-Country Ski Book.* Brattleboro, Stephen Greene Press, 1964.
8. Cureton, T. K.: New techniques of athletic training and conditioning. *J A Phys Ment Rehab,* 15:78, 1961.
9. ———: *Physical Fitness of Champion Athletes.* Urbana, University of Illinois Press, 1951.
10. ———: Principles of training and conditioning. *J Phys Educ,* 59: 1961.
11. ———: Wheat germ oil, the wonder fuel. *Scholastic Coach,* 24:37, 1955.
12. De Vries, H. A.: *Physiology of Exercise.* Dubuque, Wm C. Brown Company Publishers, 1968.
13. Durnin, J. V. G. A.: The influence of nutrition. *Can Med Assoc J*, 96:715, 1967.
14. Ekblom, B.: Effect of physical training on the oxygen transport system in man. *Acta Physiol Scand,* Suppl. 328, 1969.
15. Faulkner, J. A.: New perspectives in training for maximum performance. *JAMA,* 205:741, 1968.
16. Gollnick, P. D. and D. W. King: Effect of exercise and training of mitochondria of rat skeletal muscle. *Am J Physiol, 216*:1502, 1969.
17. Holloszy, J. O.: Effects of exercise on mitochondrial oxygen uptake and respiratory enzyme activity in skeletal muscle. *J Biol Chem,* 242:2278, 1967.
18. Holmgren, A.: Cardiorespiratory determinants of cardiovascular fitness. *Can Med Assoc J,* 96:697, 1967.
19. Jetté, M. J. and J. S. Thoden: A profile of the Canadian cross-country ski team. Proceedings of the Canadian Association of Sports Sciences, Quebec City, 1970, (to be published).
20. Kral, J. A.: The meaning of endurance and the kinds of training for endurance. Proceedings of International Congress of Sport Sciences, Tokyo 1964, Tokyo, The Japanese Union of Sport Sciences, 1966.
21. Margaria, R.: Anaerobic metabolism in muscle. *Can Med Assoc J,* 96:770, 1967.
22. Mayer, J.: *Overweight, Causes, Cost and Control.* Englewood Cliffs, Prentice-Hall Inc., 1968.

23. Mayer, J. and B. Bullen: Nutrition and athletic performance. In *Exercise and Fitness*. Chicago, The Athletic Institute, 1960.

24. Nett, T.: Qu'est-ce qu'un 'entraînement scientifique? *die Lehre der Leicht Athletik*, *30*(13):3, 1965.

25. Povarnitsine, A. P.: Particularités psychologiques des qualités de volonté du skieur de fond. *Revue Soviétique de la Théorie et Pratique de la Culture Physique*, 3:1–5, Mars, 1965.

26. Spence, J.: The energy cost of a five kilometer cross-country run. Unpublished paper, Department of Kinanthropology, University of Ottawa, April, 1970.

27. Thoden, J. S. and M. J. Jetté: Laboratory measurements applied to the development and modification of training programs. Proceedings of the Canadian Association of Sports Sciences, Quebec City, 1970, (to be published).

28. Van Itallie, T. B., L. Sinisterra and F. J. Stare: Nutrition and athletic performance. *Science and Medicine of Exercise and Sports*. New York, Harper and Brothers Publishers, 1960.

CHAPTER XV

SKI JUMPING*

R. B. WILBERG

BECAUSE OF the geographic, climatic, and monetary costs involved, there has been only a small amount of research performed on ski jumping. By and large the research has been descriptive, with major advances arising out of wind tunnel experiments, and the application of flight patterns to take-off platforms and/or landing hill curves. The end result of such experimentation has been to produce a relatively stereotyped body form while actually in the air, and to greatly extended jump lengths.[4] That is, given a specific velocity on the take-off, and assuming the ski jumper holds himself in the prescribed form at the prescribed angle throughout the various parts of his flight, his length of jump can virtually be predetermined.[5,6] Jump lengths are, therefore, under the most optimal conditions, a function of velocity. In essence, once an in-run slope and take-off have been built into a hill; the knoll, overbend to critical point, on the landing slope, followed by the out-run are also determined.[2] At the upper limit, the landing hill must be constructed such that the highest possible take-off velocity under optimal conditions will not produce a jump performance which exceeds the critical point. At the lower limit the knoll and upper sections of the landing hill should be constructed such that abortive and low velocity jumps do not result in excessive danger to the performer.[2,7]

Normally, a prospective ski jumping site is constructed in such a manner as to produce the longest possible jumps within the above limits. Unlike many other athletic events where "furthest" performance is measured in a two-space whose planes are horizontal to the earth's surface, the measure of jumping performance follows a profile whose planes are vertical to the earth's surface on one axis, and horizontal on the other. Consequently, measurement of distance is linear throughout the horizontal axis and curved through the vertical one.[2] Thus, total jump length must be considered through both an x and y component. Hill designs and construction, there-

* The author is indebted to Dr. R. C. Nelson, Director, Biomechanics Laboratory, The Pennsylvania State University, for his assistance in obtaining reference material. Readers desiring an in depth treatment of aerodynamic form throughout the jump profile should avail themselves to his reference sources.

fore, must be to a great degree mathematically defined as two approaching functions: one related to the ski jumpers velocity, aerodynamics, and gravity; the other related to a series of two curves which would fall away from the ski jumper in an accelerating then decelerating fashion.[6,7]

Although this set of constraints must appear somewhat vigorous, it is essential to the sort of ski jumping as is the fiber glass pole in pole vaulting. Improperly formed or mismatched approaches and landing hills are not only dangerous, they demand that the jumpers move away from the most appropriate aerodynamic posture. The end result is to jump lengths which are shorter than they should be, and less than perfect body forms at the outsets.[6,7]

During the last few years the method of assessing the goodness of a given ski jumping performance has come under considerable attack. Essentially, the competitor is given a maximum number of points for "form" prior to his initiation of the performance. As he proceeds down the in-run, makes his jump, and then lands, he is constantly being deducted points for errors made in form. The remaining points are then in a specific manner aggregated with his jump length to produce a total performance score which relates his performance to all others.[8]

As in most competitions where form is ajudicated by more than three judges simultaneously, the highest and lowest scores are removed. The

Figure XV–1. Finnish ski jumper moving from take-off position into full gliding position.

Figure XV–2. Same jumper approaching theoretically optimal glide posture for maximum distance and score.

ability of the judges to assess consistently in ski jumping, and indeed gymnastics or figure skating, has caused many arguments and a great deal of bitterness, particularly when different nationalities are involved. It is not surprising, therefore, that a new and highly objective method of scoring has been advanced.[2]

The basis of this objective method has its feet in three major considerations. First, there is a "best" aerodynamic posture to be held in the air, as was determined by the wind tunnel experiments. Second, major jumping hills are now in existence, which take into consideration the problem of the two approaching mathematical functions. And, thirdly, since distance jumped to velocity at take-off are highly related under optimal conditions, then movement away from those optimal conditions should produce shorter jumps. It is therefore possible to predict with considerable accuracy exactly how far a ski jumper should travel in the air, while maintaining the optimal posture, based upon his take-off velocity. The "objective" method as opposed to the subjective "traditional" method can compare jumps of different distances with consistency and accuracy by measuring the take-off velocity and the distance jumped.[2,6,7] For example, if two competitors have the same take-off velocities and one jumps further than the other, then his aerodynamic posture in the air approached the optimal form to a greater extent than did his opponent's. The performance tables which naturally result from the objective method are at this stage very crude and will surely undergo several modifications before they become the *only* measure of ski jumping excellence.

As intimated earlier, such an approach will lead to highly stereotyped performances as the competitors attempt to affect the optimal aerodynamic posture. If that proves to be true, then within a given jumping hill, on normal equipment, a definite but distinctly reachable limit will be imposed upon all competitors. Longer jumps can therefore only be accomplished by increasing the take-off velocity or changing the aerodynamics of the competitor and his equipment.

Normally a ski jumper will perform less than five "scored" jumps during a given day of competition. These do not require any unusual level of physical endurance or fitness below which the competitor's performance would suffer. In this manner it is considerably unlike long distance running and/or boxing, where cardiovascular endurance and strength are prime requisites.[1] In effect, gravity, proper waxing of the ski bottoms, and the condition of the in-run determine for the greater part the competitor's take-off velocity. The competitors' does not generate these—he is given it by the mechanics of the system. Providing he extends out of his croutch at the appropriate time near the lip of the jump, his ability to reach and hold the optimal posture in the air will determine the distance he travels and thereby his ultimate score.

The crucial points necessary to produce a "good" jump are therefore not particularly related to the aspects of exercise physiology normally considered.[3] The ability to anticipate the optimal take-off point, the ability to control the skis and body against the initial surge of air pressure, and the ability to maintain the optimum aerodynamic form throughout the jump are important. It would seem, therefore, that attainment of perfection in ski jumping performance would be gained more through the application of biomechanical principles than by any other subdiscipline.

REFERENCES

1. Hennon, J. S., and Tabakin, B. S.: Electrocardiographic telemetry in skiers, anticipatory and recovery heart rate during competition. *N Engl J Med*, 271:181–5, 1960.
2. Lang, Serge: "Le chronetrage recours a 1 electronique." *Larousse*, 1967, pp. 304–317.
3. Blatter, K., et al.: The role of adrenergic beta-receptors in emotional tachyeardia, radiometric studies on ski jumper. *Schweiz Z Sportmed*, 17:131–149, 1969.
4. Straumann, R.: Vom Skisprung zum Skiflug. In *Fortschritte der Vhrtechnik durch Forschung*. Stuttgart, Steinkopf in Komm, 1952.
5. ————: Vom Skisprung zum Skiflug. *Sport*, (Zurich), 1955.
6. ————: Skisprungstil, Flugbahnen, and Bewert—ungsfragen. *Sport* (Zurich), 1964.
7. ————: Die Wertung des Skisprunges. *Ski*, (Schweiz), 18:10:611–613, 1966.
8. ————: *Ski Jumping Instruction, A Manual*. Ottawa Canadian Ski Association, 1954.

CHAPTER XVI

BASKETBALL

A. D. YARR

PHILOSOPHY OF CONDITIONING

IN CONDITIONING any athlete or group of athletes there are several decisions that must be made by the coach as to the type of program undertaken. Will there be a slow build-up period gradually increasing the tempo
of activity until competitive speeds are reached? Will most of the training
be done at game speed gradually increasing the volume of work? How
much emphasis should there be on overload in the program? In basketball
specifically the variety, complexity, and difficulty of the skills suggests that
much of the training might well be done with the ball and in a basketball
setting. Wooden,[46] of UCLA, emphasizes this type of conditioning.

On the other hand weight training, circuit training, isometrics, cross
country running, hill and stair climbing, sprint training, calisthenics and
agility drills are rapidly taking their place in many programs of pre-season
and in-season conditioning to achieve what is considered optimum use of
the athlete's time. A certain amount of these types of programs may be
more efficient than basketball drills or play for conditioning.

Luitjins[31] has shown the advantages of specific programs for leg
strength if applied throughout the competitive season. There appears to
be a trend to heavier conditioning in the competitive season and this is
proving to be beneficial if properly controlled.

The skill of the players, the time available, and the facilities available
must all be given due consideration when designing your pre-season and
in-season conditioning program. If the desirable gym time is not available,
good use can be made of other facilities in reaching good condition.

Recent research has shown that explosive power, strength, endurance,
agility, speed, flexibility and choice reaction can all be improved to a
degree. If these factors are all well developed in your athletes the advantages are obvious if ball skills are equal or nearly equal to an opponent's.
Binns,[4] in his study of soccer players, showed that fitness level of teams
correlated with points gained by each in a competitive season. However, it
was subjectively determined that skill level was equal. In the late stages of

competition fatigue products in the muscles will have a detrimental effect on skill performance.[1] The challenge to every coach or trainer is to optimally condition his athletes within the available time and also to develop individual skills and team play.

To use your conditioning time efficiently it is probably wise to determine the percentage of time you can spend on conditioning and set specific goals or areas of emphasis during each period. A long-range programming may be advisable.

TABLE XVI-I

Month/Training	Conditioning	Skill Training
Oct.	70%	30%
Nov.	50%	50%
Dec.	40%	60%
Jan.–Feb.	30%	70%
Mar.	20%	80%

Table XVI-I is an oversimplification as many drills can satisfy a dual role; that is, develop skill and have a good training effect.

Table XVI–II. Weekly distribution, November 15–20. Adapted from Toyoda 43.

	Mon.	Tues.	Wed.	Thurs.	Fri.	Sat.
Speed Training	x	◎	x	◎	x	x
Agility Drills	△	O	△	O	△	x
Power Training	x	O	x	O	x	◎
Endurance	◎	x	◎	x	◎	x
Flexibility	△	△	△	△	△	△
Jumping Drills	O	x	O	x	O	x

KEY   ◎ Heavy
      O Moderate
      △ Light
      x None

PHYSICAL CHARACTERISTICS OF BASKETBALL PLAYERS

Extreme height often seems to be prerequisite of the exceptional basketball player. However, as obvious as this advantage might seem, small players with exceptional ball handling and shooting skill are continually playing an important role in the success of their teams. Smaller players

(5'4"–6'0") must be quick, well-conditioned and highly motivated but basketball is not exclusively a game for tall players. Weight is a factor of considerable importance in close-to-the-basket play. Gaining and holding position in a variety of situations, puts a premium on mass. However, basketball demands such a high degree of general condition that weight must be functional mass. The endomorph will find he is at a disadvantage in most aspects of the game. The mesomorph or well-conditioned and specifically trained ectomorph have far greater advantages.

Exceptional length of arms in a player is a great advantage in many key situations. Rebounding, shooting, ball handling and defense are all greatly aided by excessive limb length. Normal arm span approximates standing height, if the span exceeds this measure to a significant degree the athlete will have an advantage in many game situations. Most of the advantages pertaining to physical structure are obvious.

Stimulation of growth in skeletal structure in an adolescent is considered possible if activity is vigorous and diet and adaptation time are ideal. Controlled studies in this area are difficult; therefore few, if any, conclusive studies are available. Heredity is still the main determinant. There are presently commercial claims being made for systems that will significantly increase height. However the author was unable to find any scientific basis to these claims but future investigation may be indicated. Certainly basketball players with high aspirations would be eager to try any method that made claims of height increases. The responsible coach should investigate any such systems carefully, especially if drugs are involved. The use of anabolic steroids for weight gains in football players and weight men in track and field have proven to have serious side effects.[13] In addition a study by Fowler *et al.*[17] failed to substantiate most of the claims made for anabolic steriods.

A well-balanced diet that contains the ten essential amino acids and sufficient required vitamins with a vigorous training program are all that are needed for optimal growth. Work by Bicknell[9] shows that vitamin needs increase only in approximate proportion to metabolic activity. Therefore, special food supplements are rarely necessary if a proper menu is planned.

Women undergoing vigorous training programs, especially of an endurance nature, should take an iron supplement of some kind.

PHYSIOLOGICAL CHARACTERISTICS

The characteristics of explosive power, strength, endurance, agility, speed, flexibility and choice reaction time are all important to a basketball player. These factors should be considered when designing your pre-season and in-season conditioning programs. Research indicating the value of specific types of training, special programs and appropriate drills will now be related for these characteristics.

Explosive Power

There are five main areas in the problem of development of muscular power as outlined by Jarver: [25]

a. Application of force (Strength development).
b. Development of speed of movement.
c. Technique involved in providing the right force-velocity relationships.
d. Employment of the best lever system.
e. Coordination of the movement.

The last three of these are closely connected with the learning of skills. Jarver [25] goes on; in commenting on the great Russian high jumper, Brumel, that development of power for the execution of a particular skill cannot be attained by development of the components of power in isolation, but rather that the exercise must be closely related to the movements in the skill that is accompanied by repetitive practice of the skill itself.

A study by Barney and Bangerter [3] showed that significant increases in strength resulted in each of three different weight training programs. The traditional bulk program (three sets of 10 RM) and traditional power program (first set 10 RM; second set increase 5 to 10 pounds and complete as many repetitions as possible; in subsequent sets, continue to increase weight 5 to 10 pounds until the 1 RM is reached, then subject adds weight and attempts one more lift) showed strength gains significantly greater than the DeLorme and Watkins technique (first set of ten repetitions use ½ of 10 RM; second set of ten repetitions use ¾ of 10 RM; third set of ten repetitions, use 10 RM). Chui [11] showed that a weight training group showed significant improvement in both standing and running sargent jumps after a weight training program. Kusinity and Keeney [29] also showed significant increases in strength for an experimental group that weight trained for eight weeks. This program was done with adolescent boys. Berger,[7] using the bench press, showed that a group using three sets of six repetitions had higher means after nine weeks of training than a group that used three sets of ten reps but the mean differences were not significant. In a twelve-week program, Berger,[5] when testing all combinations of one, two and three sets with two, six and twelve reps, showed that three sets of six RM gave best results for improving strength over a twelve-week period. In a later study Berger [6] showed that the optimum number of repetitions for strength gain is between three and nine when one set three times per week is performed over a twelve-week period.

Jacobsen [24] tested the leg strength and vertical jumping ability of the South Dakota State College varsity and freshman basketball squads during an entire season. The teams did not weight train and a decrease in vertical jump during the season was found. Luitjins [31] showed that in-season weight training (¾ squats and heel raises) significantly increased explosive power during the season. In an Exer-genie® program of three sets of two exercises, with the same ranges of motion, a significant improvement was also shown. In fact the Exer-Genie program showed significant improvement in explosive power in just six weeks. The increases by the weight training group were not significant in this period. McCraw and Burnham [34] concluded from their study comparing isotonic, isometric and speed exercise programs that no single method is adequate in achieving maximum development of both strength and endurance. They also claim that muscle endurance can best be developed by repeated contractions of the muscle, performed as rapidly as possible against a reasonably heavy load.

In a well-controlled study by Boyd,[10] comparing a control group with a group using three pound ankle weights and a group using six pound ankle weights, found that all three groups increased vertical jumping significantly, beyond the .01 level of confidence. However, the groups using ankle weights showed no comparative advantage over the control group in a five-week program.

In a study to determine the contributive components in the vertical jump, Bangerter [2] showed significant gains for the groups that strengthened knee and/or hip extensors. Plantar flexor strengthening groups did not register significant jump gains.

It would appear from the studies above and trends in athletic conditioning that a weight training program is a worthwhile adjunct to conditioning for basketball. The program outlined here places an emphasis on knee and hip extensors especially during the in-season program where upper body work may have a deleterious effect on shooting and ball handling skills. It is also suggested that all training programs be combined with the playing of basketball. There should be a striving for a full range of motion in all exercises except the squat where a position of thighs parallel to the floor is recommended because of possible knee damage in a fuller squat. This danger is still a point of controversy with some but since the game patterns rarely call for a full squat this is an unnecessary action at best.

The pre-season program should be undertaken at least six weeks before the first game with no upper limit imposed. Athletes can benefit from a year-round program if allowed to adapt to each workout. If variability is included and measurable improvement is shown, athletes with ambition can maintain interest and enthusiasm for weight training in most if not all of the noncompetitive season.

This pre-season program consists of the three sets of six RM for each exercise unless otherwise noted. When three sets of six RM can be accomplished with some degree of ease, the load is increased by 5 to 10 pounds depending on the prime movers involved.

Pre-Season Program

1. Snatch (light to moderate weight for warm-up; 1 set, 10 repetitions)
2. ¾ squat
3. Heel raise
4. Leg press
5. Knee flexion (knee machine)
6. Knee extension (knee machine)
7. Inclined board sit-ups (knees bent; 10–30 reps)

The above program is basic; the following upper body and power exercises provide variability to the work out.

A	B	C (1 set only)
Curl	Reverse curl	Power curl (10)
Press	Bench press	Power press (10)
Upright rowing	Bent-over rowing	Power clean (10)
Bent Arm pullover	Lateral dumbell raise	Chinning (5–20)
		Alternate squat jumps (20)

End all weight workouts with two to five minutes of rope skipping. The ¾ squat and heel raise can be difficult and possibly dangerous to the lower back when very heavy weights are used. In advanced stages of the program the athlete can do one-legged squats and heel raises. The overload on the exercise leg is calculated by adding one-half the body weight to the weight of the dumbell used. Therefore, with a fifty pound dumbell a 200 pound athlete can get a one hundred and fifty pound overload on his exercising leg. In a two-legged exercise he would have to lift and support 300 pounds for the same overload.

The modified in-season program is primarily a leg and abdominal program. Depending upon the time available and overall stress on the athlete it is suggested that the athlete train two to three times per week after practice with one set of ten RM or up to three sets of six RM.

Basic Program

1. Snatch (warm-up)
2. ¾ squat
3. Heel raise
4. Leg press
5. Alternate squat jumps
6. Incline board sit-ups

Alternate Program

1. Snatch
2. ¾ squat
3. Heel raise
4. Knee flexion
5. Knee extension
6. Power clean
7. Frog hang

If upper body work is desired, chinning, parallel bar dips and medicine ball passing are good alternatives to weight training. Rebounding machines can fill a need here, if one is available.

Strength

To separate the factor of strength from explosive power is difficult. However, power is related to the rate of doing work (producing force). We may therefore think of power as the result of two factors: (1) strength to produce the force and (2) speed to increase the rate at which the force can be applied.[13] Increasing strength, in addition, to being a factor in power has its own value in basketball. The grip on the ball in rebounding, holding a desirable position once gained, overcoming the contact of a foul in shooting and ball handling, these and other situations put a premium on strength.

Berger and Blashki[8] found that dynamic strength was more highly related to motor activity than was static strength. Jones[27] suggests that not all individuals possess the same physiological inclination or propensity for isometric training. He shows wide variability in individuals trained in a like manner. It is felt that isometric strength training has a place in the program but mainly as an adjunct to weight training and direct practice because of the specificity of strength as it relates to dynamic basketball skills. A specific weakness may be found in an individual and an isometric exercise may be indicated as the best way to strengthen this weakness.

The following program of ballet exercises for athletes is a marriage between art and science. Over a great number of years ballet has developed a series of exercises that promotes efficient human movement. In many ways the explosive but controlled jumps in ballet are similar to the jumps to shoot, to rebound or to catch a high pass in basketball. Little evidence is available to objectively evaluate the worth of these exercises. However, they have isometric components and subjectively have been judged worthwhile after four years of use.

Ballet Exercises For Athletes[19]

Other isometric exercises can be designed for any specific strength need. If a sticking point is found in any weight training exercise, duplicating this position with an isometric exercise can overcome this weakness. Isometric positions can be created to duplicate almost any part of a skill where strength improvement is deemed important. It is felt that isometrics is best suited to solve these special problems as opposed to making it a part of the general conditioning program.

Hettinger and Muller[13] published their work on isometric training in

1953. Their figures of one daily six second isometric contraction with two thirds of an individual's maximal contraction has held up as an efficient training load. However, five to ten repetitions at maximal contraction for five seconds shows greater strength gains.[36]

Endurance

There is a close relationship between strength and local or muscle endurance.[13] To develop this endurance overload training is especially important as demonstrated by Hellebrandt and Houtz.[20]

In basketball we are primarily interested in circulo-respiratory endurance as gross body activity is of prime importance and this taxes respiration, circulation, heat dissipation and the nervous system. When work begins, there are three available sources of energy: (1) high energy phosphates (alactacid O_2 debt), (2) glycogen used without O_2 (lactacid O_2 debt), (3) glycogen used with O_2.[13] The first two anaerobic sources cause an oxygen debt when used. The third is an aerobic source.

Both O_2 debt mechanisms have finite limits that can be improved with training.[12,37] This training must be of short duration and high intensity. Margaria *et al.*[33] reported that at least a 25 second recovery was needed after a high intensity work bout to improve the alactacid debt involvement. The efficiency of these mechanisms is obviously important in an explosive sport that also sometimes demands sustained action, such as basketball. With a work time of up to two minutes there is a 50:50 ratio and with longer work time the aerobic power becomes gradually more dominant.[1]

The aerobic power of the athlete is important as much of the activity in basketball can be carried out aerobically if the athlete is well conditioned in this factor.

A figure of 55 ml/kg or more is a desirable aerobic power. Training can increase maximal oxygen uptake 10 to 20 percent[1] so athletes endowed with high aerobic power have advantages in basketball, which demands high endurance in top level competition. The training program should have elements to develop both aerobic and anaerobic factors efficiently while considering the specificity of basketball action.

Intermittent exercise is much more efficient than continuous exercise as shown by Astrand[1] in studies of different work bouts followed by equal rest, compared with continuous work. This is because of the rapid repayment of the debt during early recovery that prevents extreme lactic acid build-up. Astrand[1] found three minutes' work followed by three minutes' rest places the maximal load on the oxygen-transporting organs. If heavy resistance work is needed, work periods should be shorter (one minute or less). Maximal oxygen uptake can be attained in short duration work of high intensity providing the rest periods are equal to or less than the work period.[1] Finally, light exercise between work bouts seems advisable as the elimination of lactic acid is faster than at complete rest.[18]

The ability to endure continuous activity at a fairly intense level includes a psychological component. Continuous activity such as cross-country running may have a place in the program for this reason and, in addition, will have a training effect on aerobic power. Many athletes perform better if there is variability in their training, and cross-country running can add another facet to the program. For efficiency this should be a minor part of the program.

From the above information regarding work and rest periods to optimally and efficiently condition the athlete, guidelines can be set. These are guidelines only but have been arrived at by surveying the literature on these components of endurance training.

Component	Work	Intensity	Rest
1. Alactacid O_2 debt	5–15 sec	High	30 + sec
2. Lactacid O_2 debt	15 sec–1 min	High	4–5 min
3. Aerobic	3 min	Moderate	3 min
	30 sec–1 min	High-moderate	30 sec–1 min

One and two above will train aerobic power as well, especially if a high number of repetitions are performed. There is an overlap in training effects in many of these programs. Programs with a shorter rest time than work time are also possible but it is felt that efficient training allows for reasonable recovery during the exercise period. To reach a point of exhaustion or collapse is not desirable or necessary. Game conditions may demand extended effort with little rest but a planned progressive program that allows the athlete adaptation time can prepare him for these rigorous demands.

Many basketball activities or similar skills can be performed in an interval pattern that will lend itself to the above guidelines of endurance training. It is highly recommended that skills and drills, such as those that follow, make up the majority of your training program as a high degree of motor specificity is involved in basketball.[21]

1. Repeat jumps—touching rim or backboard (A set of 20 takes 12–15 secs).
2. Eagle jumps—splitting legs wide and touching toes with fingers.
3. Jump and tuck—jump high and tuck knees to chest.
4. One leg hops (can be done straight up and down, forward, backwards, or over a pattern of direction changing).
5. Partner resisted jumps—helper stands behind jumper with hands on his hips; jumper springs from half squat with partner resisting, partner lets go at peak so as not to force the jumper into a hard landing.
6. Continuous tipping—ball against backboard or wall (use left hand, right hand and alternate hands).

7. Skipping rope.
8. Defensive shuffle—assume a defensive stance and move as directed by a leader, by voice, by signal, or by following the leader.
9. Squat thrusts.
10. Stair running or hopping.
11. Hill running.
12. Mazes or obstacle courses with or without the ball.
13. One on one full court.
14. Two on two full court.
15. Line drills—follow the lines of the court with predetermined moves at certain points. (e.g. backward running, defensive shuffle, pivots, fake left go right, etc.)
16. Stutter steps—lift arm and lower feet as quickly as possible, barely clearing floor.
17. Backward and forward runs—run forward to the foul line, run backward back to the baseline, then forward to the center line and backward to the foul line, forward to the other foul line and backward to the center line and forward to the far baseline, pivot and sprint to the start.

Many of these drills have components of power, agility and skill training. This is a bonus. If the correct work and rest periods are chosen the athlete can be well trained in all three factors of cardiorespiratory endurance.

A model will be developed using drill seventeen to show how it can be adapted to train in various ways. A. Alactacid debt training. With groups of three have one runner run forward and backward until the far end line is reached; the athlete waits there. Runner two starts when runner one stops. Runner three begins when runner two stops. When runner three completes his turn, runner one starts the same procedure going the other way. A work time of about 17 seconds results with approximately a 35-second rest. This can be run as a competitive relay to keep effort high. Progression is attained by increasing the number of repetitions. B. Lactacid debt training. Five runners are put in a group each runs a double trip which will take 50 to 60 seconds. If runner one's teammates run singly then approximately a four-minute rest results. C. Aerobic power. Runners in pairs are asked to do a number of continuous repetitions that is known to take about three minutes. While partner one is resting partner two is running. D. Aerobic power. Runners in pairs again but each runs one complete effort (approximately 25 seconds) while partner rests. Alternate. E. Aerobic power. Early in the season groups of three can be run with one working a full turn and two resting. This gives a 25-second run and a 50-second rest.

To see that your athletes are sufficiently stressed and also adapting to the training, pulse counts can be used for training evaluation. Immediately on cessation of exercise the heart rate should approximate 180 if a good work load is given, however, the recovery should be to below 120 in two and one-half to three minutes after exercise or the work bout is too strenuous for the athlete at that time. Again these are *guidelines.* The 180 maximal heart rate is a general figure with values over 200 noted.[1]

Most of the drills can be adapted to the different kinds of training, however, the strenuous jumping drills should probably not be attempted in doses of more than one minute. Skipping, of course, can be done for more extended periods. The three-minute work and three-minute rest workout may be unwieldy for many basketball situations. Astrand[1] shows that two minutes' work with two minutes' rest is almost as efficient for developing aerobic power.

Agility

A study by Hilsendager *et al.*[22] shows that agility is best developed by agility exercises. They had groups working on strength and speed and combined programs but none improved agility more than agility exercises. The group participating in agility exercises demonstrated statistically significant superiority over one or more of the other groups on four of the seven agility tests.

This study would indicate that specific agility drills are important if this factor of condition is considered important. Lateral motion with great demands on choice reaction time and agile movements have a high priority in basketball especially in playing man-to-man defense. The drills that follow, place an emphasis on agility in specific basketball situations. It is important to deemphasize endurance or extended effort because if improved agility is your goal the other factors will take away from this primary target. You are unlikely to improve direction changing without stressing this factor. It is suggested that bursts of effort of ten seconds or less be your work time with rests of ten to forty seconds.

Drills

1. Deny the ball drills. Several situations can be created where your defensive player prevents the offensive player from receiving the ball with a coach or a third man as a passer.

This is a superior drill as the offensive player does not have a ball to protect or to slow him down. There is maximum stress on the agility and choice reaction of the defensive player and a game situation may be practiced. A time limit may be used on this drill.

2. One-on-one full court. (Can be done with or without a ball with the defensive man using his hands or hands behind his back.) Again agility is stressed as the offensive player has great freedom. However, competitive conditions are approached.

3. Two-on-two full court. This drill introduces new actions and new choices but puts a high premium on agility because of the relative freedom of the offense. The offense may initially be limited; no dribbling, no crossing or by restricting the distance ahead of the ball the other player may go; however, these limitations can be removed as condition and skill improve.

4. Defensive shuffle. The drill places the team in a group in a defensive stance. They can move and react as they follow a leader or react to a leader's signal. Forward, backward, lateral and jumping actions can be used in a variety of sequences. Bursts of five to ten seconds with equal to double rest time should be the pattern if agility is the main objective. Extended periods of action are possible but this will put the emphasis on aerobic power and it is doubtful if significant agility improvement will occur.

5. Agility mazes. A wide variety of agility mazes can be created using chairs or football dummies to outline the course. These mazes can be run with or without the ball and should have a variety of moves related closely to basketball. Pivots, reverse turns, changes of pace and fakes with change of direction are examples of suitable maneuvers.

6. Line drills. The lines on the court can be used to describe a course along which the players perform moves as in the agility mazes plus backward running, defensive shuffling, and jumping of various sorts. This drill is usually done without a ball.

7. Right and left hook shots underneath. This drill is excellent for big men as it develops the hook shot and also stresses changing direction and jumping off the right and left leg for height with control. Emphasis should be placed on working in a minimum area and catching the ball as soon as it leaves the net. Sets of from 6 to 20 shots should be attempted.

8. Stops and starts. Stops and starts can be executed with or without the ball on the coach's visual signal, whistle or verbal command. Attention should be spent to action and rest time because if the team is driven to exhaustion without recovery time, improved agility is not likely to result.

The remaining drills are less specific to basketball but can provide a change of pace and do relate somewhat to basketball action.

9. Footwork squares. Several patterns can be marked on the floor with adhesive tape or chalk. The players hop on one or two feet, forward,

sideways or backward or change legs. Distances between the spots should be realistic but challenging. Quickness and control are always stressed. Two Examples:

(1)   (2)

In example one, hopping with one or two legs can be done quickly around the square. Half or full twists can be employed on each jump. This pattern is so simple that it may not be necessary to mark it on the floor. In example two, the pattern can be hopped forward and backward with a change of direction made at each dot. It can also be stepped through alternating feet. Of course, other patterns can be devised.

10. Run around a dummy. A large football bell dummy is used and the player runs a quick tight circle around the dummy three times and reverses and goes three times the other way. Tight figure eights can also be run around two dummies.

11. Bench exercises. Benches can be used in a variety of ways with a player jumping on and off, over, forward, backwards, sideward and with twists. These exercises can also be used for developing jumping endurance.

12. Tire hopping. Old car tires can be put to good use. Again hopping, stepping, and turning in the air can be combined in numerous ways with one or several tires.

Speed

Top running speed is generally accepted to depend upon the variables of stride, length and stride frequency.[14] However, in basketball where the distance from baseline to baseline is at a maximum, 94 feet, and in that it takes approximately six seconds to reach top speed,[15] top speed is probably not an important consideration. The ability to accelerate is, of course, very important in a sport of stops and starts and many changes of direction.

The strength and power exercises discussed earlier are important in development of maximum acceleration. In addition drills that specifically emphasize maximal acceleration are especially important. As in speed training[13] to maximize results it is important to perform each effort after nearly complete recovery from the previous effort. Maximal acceleration is not possible if fatigue products have accumulated in the muscles. For this reason acceleration or speed runs should be done early in the practice with generous intervals of rest. An example might be five to ten seconds of work followed by thirty to sixty seconds of rest. As Dintiman[13] states, windsprints at the end of the practice, with uncontrolled rest periods, are of very questionable value.

Following are a few drills that are suitable for speed development. Many of the agility drills given earlier can improve acceleration and speed.

1. Forward and backward sprint. This is an all-out sprint from baseline to baseline with the return trip run backwards.
2. Court length hopping. One leg hopping from baseline to baseline returning on the other foot.
3. Shuffle to midcourt. The player shuffles sideways to mid-court and returns while facing the same direction without crossing the legs.

Quick change of direction and acceleration are stressed. It is very important to have adequate recovery periods between bursts.

Hand speed is an important factor in many basketball skills. Whitley and Smith[44] showed that with two strength training programs, isometric-isotonic and dynamic-overload, there were significant increases in speed of arm movement; however, the difference in speed gain between the two programs is nonsignificant. In complex basketball skills where hand speed is specific and where learning is probably more important than power—rarely is there any resistance—practicing the skill, emphasizing hand quickness is recommended until more closely related research is available.

Flexibility

Flexibility is usually developed for two reasons; to prevent injuries, and to positively effect relevant skills. Little definitive work is available to show that in fact increased flexibility, over what is normal for the individual, actually achieves these two goals in basketball. It is reasonable to believe that to maintain flexibility is desirable and advisable. In a later section, on prevention of injuries, some specific exercises will be discussed.

Where it is deemed necessary to develop or maintain flexibility three different methods are possible. These three methods will be described here briefly and evaluated as to their apparent uses.

"Ballistic stretching" is done in many common calisthenic movements. These exercises usually involve bouncing or bobbing movements and are caused by one muscle group putting a body segment in motion until it is arrested by the antagonistic group. Thus the antagonistic group is stretched.

In "static stretching" the origin and insertion of the muscle are held in positions that give the muscle its maximum length. This technique is similar to many yoga exercises.

In comparing these two methods de Vries [13] found that both methods resulted in significant gains in static flexibility; there was no significant difference between methods. de Vries claims three advantages for static stretching: (1) There is less danger of exceeding the extensibility limits of the tissues involved; (2) Energy requirements are lower; (3) Although ballistic stretching is apt to cause muscular soreness static stretching will not; in fact the latter relieves sorness.

The third method is Proprioceptive Neuromuscular Facililation (PNF) which involves a maximum contraction of the agonist (muscles to be stretched) followed immediately by a concentric contraction of the antagonists. [23] Holt *et al.* [23] studied a modified version of PNF employing a simpler, unidimensional approach and refer to it as 1A–CA (isometric contraction of the agonist 1A, followed by a concentric contraction of the antagonist, CA).

This technique has distinct advantages for increasing range of motion and may be desirable especially if a specific muscle group is tight. However, a partner is needed and this can be a disadvantage in efficiency. One of the coach's main responsibilities is to find a balance between all the things that an athlete might do to improve his performance so that the most efficient use of practice time available results.

The author feels that flexibility exercises that assist in the prevention of injuries common to basketball are worth the time and effort. However, extra flexibility is of questionable importance in many joint actions for basketball. It is up to the individual coach to decide where special flexibility exercises might be advisable for the individual athlete and then select the method that best meets the need. A total program of stretching exercises is probably unnecessary. Some specific exercises on injury prevention appear in that section.

PSYCHOLOGICAL CHARACTERISTICS

Motivation

It is important for the coach or trainer to be sensitive to the needs of his athletes. Especially when strenuous conditioning programs are undertaken it is important that the coach be aware of what drives the participant. If the athlete is highly motivated, demanding conditioning can reinforme the basic motivation. An athlete will not likely give up easily what he has paid a high price to obtain. However, proper progression is important as stress that cannot be adapted to will eventually break down rather than build up. It is important psychologically that the athlete can see that a workload that previously was very demanding can now be handled with ease. Therefore a conditioning program must be presented in cycles so that the new levels reached are apparent to the athlete.

The athlete with aspirations for success can usually be sold on the importance of superior conditioning. It is obvious that if two teams have approximately equal ability and skill, the best-conditioned team will have an advantage in the late stages of a game. The importance of this factor toward realization of potential should never be underestimated.

When a team appears to have won because of superior conditioning this point should be emphasized and it will often lead to a greater pride in condition and a greater effort in future conditioning drills. A real "snowball" effect can occur here and your team may start looking for the physical breakdown of your opponent and thus develop a positive outlook toward their own performance.

If the coach feels that goals are important to the motivation of an athlete then the goals of the conditioning program should be clearly defined. This is often neglected because methods of objective evaluation are not always available. It is worthwhile to make the effort to evaluate progress, and to design programs where improvement is readily apparent to the participants.

There is an innate difficulty in sustaining human effort, therefore, it is important to reinforce or reward exceptional effort in this area.

A schedule of rewards can be used to reinforce achievement of predetermined conditioning goals. In addition, a surprise award can be an effective positive reinforcement.[39] Skinner[41] emphasizes the importance of positive reinforcement for best results.

Rushall and Pettinger[38] discussed program boards in their study on reinforcers in swimming. Apparently, the process of checking each workout unit as it is completed is sufficient reinforcement to maintain a high level of performance. It was demonstrated as being as effective as the coach-controlled situation. This idea can be adapted to an individualized conditioning program for basketball. The evaluation of the team may reveal different conditioning needs; some players may be lacking in leg power, others in endurance, still others in agility. Conditioning can be more efficient if each athlete has a program designed to strengthen his weaknesses and motivation to perform well is kept high. A variety of programs can be completed in the same time period with only one coach with the use of a program board.

If the team establishes its conditioning goals, a board with desirable behaviors can be listed and the team encouraged to reinforce these behaviors and discourage undesirable behaviors. Some conditioning drills are adaptable to small group competitive situations where peer encouragement and positive reinforcement is easily achieved. These group drills can establish the intervals between work bursts that were discussed earlier along with the desirable reinforcement of teammates' vocal support.

Stress

Stress is an important consideration when overloading athletes physiologically and psychologically. Selye[40] defines stress as a temporarily induced physiological or psychological imbalance, caused by an event that is considered threatening. Selye[40] describes a "General Adaptation Syndrome." In this theory a stressor can be anything which forces an adaptation; these include fatigue, thirst, pain as well as frustration and threat. This implies that the coach must be aware of the total stress that the athlete is under and must reduce outside undesirable stresses as much as possible if they can be controlled in any way by him. In addition, the coach must be ready to reduce the training load on an individual basis if a particular athlete is unable to adapt to the total stress he is undergoing.

To be continually aware of the total stress of an athlete is of vital importance. This is a complex task but knowing the athlete and being able to communicate with him on an informal basis can allow the coach to evaluate the total stress and therefore to individually adjust programs.

Anxiety levels must be carefully considered and it is important to bring each athlete into competition at the right level. Johnson[26] demonstrates that anxiety levels are raised to a much greater degree in an individual rather than a team event. Malmo and Davis[32] found that too much anxiety was found to produce pointless, inflexible, and rigid motor performance. Anxiety can certainly be reduced if the athletes feel they are in excellent physical condition. In fact they may look forward to the late stages of a demanding game confidently, feeling that their superior condition will play a vital part in a successful effort. Kaiman[28] showed that activity itself can reduce anxiety levels but this study was done with an aged population and low activity levels so that more research is needed to draw conclusions for athletes in hard training.

Finally, it must be realized that each athlete has an optimal level of anxiety for performance and, therefore, the coach must look at all factors and each participant individually to arrive at the best possible accumulative level. Obviously much work must be done in this area as psychological preparation for competition is a major contributor to final results.

SOCIOLOGICAL CHARACTERISTICS

Team Attitude

There is very little research to show how team attitudes are affected by conditioning programs. However, it is the writer's hypothesis, based on empirical evidence, that a team which undergoes a demanding conditioning program as a cooperative unit establishes a kinship and closeness that can be of benefit in competitive and stressful situations.

A cooperative attitude should be the emphasis during the hard training period; use this period to draw the team together as opposed to an emphasis on competitive activity which may have the opposite effect. It may help if the team is involved in setting their own conditioning goals. It is important to realize that team selection, which often occurs concurrently with heavy conditioning, is highly competitive and, therefore, is probably very stressful to the athletes.

Decision Making

It was suggested in the last section that the team might be involved in setting their goals. It is felt that motivation can be stronger if the team is asked to make inputs in this way. Different groups are going to use the opportunity in different ways but until given the opportunity it is difficult to predict the reaction.

In many instances self-discipline is important in achieving the best conditioning because, for most teams, diet, rest and off-court activity cannot be controlled by the coach. For educational and practical reasons it is worthwhile to get the athlete involved in the decisions pertaining to training. This may lead to dedication, motivation and discipline of a higher order than if autocratic control over the many conditioning factors is attempted.

PREVENTION OF INJURIES

Lower Leg

The coach, often unknowingly, through a very vigorous training program develops imbalances that create potential physical problems for the athlete. The nature of the anatomy and kinesiology of the lower leg and ankle predisposes this area to problems that can be largely avoided through a proper preventive exercise program. This area rarely sees permanent disabling injuries, however, chronic conditions and loss of activity time are often the result of lower leg and ankle injuries.

There is naturally an imbalance in favor of the plantar flexors and invertors of the foot over the dorsi flexors and evertors as described by Steindler.[42] The strong action in running and jumping is, of course, plantar flexion and inversion. When special progressive resistance exercises for plantar flexion are introduced this natural imbalance is even further exaggerated. The integrity of the joints depends in the first line upon ligaments and only secondarily upon the muscular apparatus. However, as

McQueen [35] states, the "functional" integrity of most joints depends upon the condition of the surrounding muscles.

Through the use of the stretch reflex and protective reflex strong dorsi-flexors and evertors can help protect the ankle against an injury and certainly reduce the severity should a sprain occur.

"Shin-splints" is a controversial term when discussed by medical doctors and physical educators. It is a general term for pain in the anterior lower leg. Various theories have been put forward to explain its etiology, but all are based on the anatomical peculiarity of the tibialis anterior in that it lies between two bones, a fibrous septum and a well-developed fascial layer. One view is that pain is due to ischemia—the more likely explanation is that symptoms are due to intramuscular tension [45] or muscle spasm. A tear that involves the anterior tibiofisular ligament as well as the interosseous membrane is considered by some athletic trainers to cause the condition referred to as "shin-splints" to a greater or lesser degree. [16]

From the author's observations of this condition it is felt that individuals with imbalance between dorsi and plantar flexors and/or individuals who have put on a fair amount of weight between seasons are those most susceptible to this syndrome. A preventive exercise to be discussed later, that has worked for us even in severe cases, tends to support the view that muscle imbalance and a shortened Achilles tendon predispose this condition. An unyielding floor surface will certainly aggravate the problem.

As indicated in the preamble the muscles to be strengthened to prevent ankle injuries are the dorsi-flexors and evertors. The peroneus longus and brevis are the chief stabilizers when the foot is plantar flexed; however, in dorsi-flexion the extensor digitorum longus is the chief muscle concerned with eversion along with the peroneus tertius if one is present. [16] A strength building program must be progressive to be effective. It is difficult to design a weight training exercise to develop the muscles involved so that partner resisted exercises are recommended. Exact measurement of progression is therefore impossible, however, if the partner is constant some measure of subjective progression can be attained.

Exercises: The athlete sits with knee bent with his foot in the neutral position; the partner grasps the leg with one hand and places the other on the outer border of the foot to resist dorsi-flexion and eversion. The athlete attempts to overcome the resistance of the partner and moves through the inner range of this action. Four to six seconds is a suitable duration. The athlete then starts with foot plantar flexed and attempts to evert his foot against the resistance of his partner. Then exercise one is repeated. These three exercises are then done with the leg straight at the knee; thus making a series of six exercises for each ankle. It is desirable to do these exercises daily but three times per week will have benefits.

Shin splints have been prevented with a wall lean exercise that stretched the achilles tendon and isometrically contracts the muscles of the anterior aspect of the lower leg. The athlete places both feet about one foot apart at right angles to a wall while facing the wall. Place both palms about shoulder height against the wall and slowly lower the body to the wall and hold this position from 10 to 30 seconds. Each day the feet can be placed progressively further from the wall. There may be slight stretch pain while leaning but there should be no pain a few moments after standing erect again.

A second exercise recommended by de Vries [13] relieves the pain of this syndrome if it is caused by muscle spasm. The athlete kneels on the floor with feet plantar flexed and sits back toward or on his heels. This position is held for ten seconds and then the stretch is released for a few seconds and then repeated twice more.

Low Back

Another area where aggravating injuries are common is the low back area. Again there is controversy as to cause, prevention, and cure. A simple exercise program appears to eliminate this problem but in cases of chronic problems a physician should be consulted. The following two exercises are presented as prevention and not cure. For some conditions the second is contraindicated and the coach should stop this exercise if any aggravation of an injury occurs. The first exercise is a twisting sit-up done from a lying flat position to a touch of elbow to opposite knee. The leg is raised and knee is bent during the action. A set of 20 to 30 is done daily. The second exercise is back hyperextension done slowly from a front lying position with hands at the side and feet kept on the ground. This exercise is repeated ten times very slowly with a slight pause in the hyperextended position.

The conditioning programs presented earlier should help prevent most injuries if proper and carefully supervised progressions are used. The lower leg and lower back seem to need special attention.

Blisters

Blisters are a common problem in early season conditioning if not given special consideration. As always prevention is better than cure. Two pairs of clean socks and properly fitted shoes are an important first step. If a "hot spot" develops caution your athletes to stop activity. Time off here will save time later. Going barefoot around the house at night will dry skin and thus aid in blister prevention. Treatment of blisters should be by a trainer or physician.

TESTS FOR SELECTION OF ATHLETES

There are several basketball skill tests that can give some objective measure of your players' ability. None should be used to replace subjective appraisal but tests can be a useful adjunct for selection.

The modified Lehston [30] is given here as the five items correlate .968 with the earlier eight item battery. If a test is desired these five items can provide useful data.

1. Baskets per minute. The first shot is attempted from the foul line and each subsequent shot is taken from the semi-circle of the key area or further.
2. Dodging dribble. The player weaves around four chairs dribbling a basketball and returns to the start. Chairs ten feet apart.
3. Forty foot dash.
4. Vertical jump.
5. Wall bounce. Bounce a basketball into a target two feet across and four feet high which starts three feet off the floor, for ten seconds. The player stands behind a restraining line six feet from the wall.

Standard scores are not necessary as for any group a rank ordering on each test and a sum of these ranks will give a relative skill rating which is useful in selection. Naturally a closer analysis of the scores will give some idea as to the players' strengths and weaknesses.

REFERENCES

1. Åstrand, P. O., and Rodahl, K.: *Textbook of Work Physiology*. New York, McGraw-Hill, 1970.
2. Bangerter, Blauer L.: Contributive components in the vertical jump. *Res Q*, 39:432–436, 1968.
3. Barney, V. S., and Bangerter, B. L.: Comparison of three programs of progressive resistance exercise. *Res Q*, 32:138–146, 1961.
4. Binns, Richard: An assessment of physical fitness in soccer players and a possible correlation between fitness and team performance. *N Z J H.P.E.R.*, 1:22–27, 1968.
5. Berger, Richard: Effect of varied weight training programs on strength. *Res Q*, 33:168–181, 1962.
6. ———: Optimum repetitions for the development of strength. *Res Q*, 33:334–338, 1962.
7. ———: Comparative effects of three weight training programs: *Res Q*, 34:396–398, 1963.
8. Berger, Richard A., and Blashke, Leon A.: Comparison of relationships between motor ability and static and dynamic strength. *Res Q*, 38:144–146, 1967.

9. Bicknell, F. and Prescott, F.: *The Vitamins in Medicine.* New York, Grune and Stratton, 1953.
10. Boyd, Laurence P.: A comparative study of the effects of ankle weights on vertical jumping ability. M.S. Thesis, Springfield College, Springfield, 1969.
11. Chui, Edward: The effect of systematic weight training on athletic power. *Res Q, 21:*188–194, 1950.
12. Cunningham, D. A. and Faulkner, J. A.: The effects of training on aerobic and anaerobic metabolism during a short exhaustive run. *Med Sci Sports, 1:*51–60, 1969.
13. deVries, Herbert A.: *Physiology of Exercise in Physical Education and Athletics.* Dubuque, Wm. C. Brown Co., 1966.
14. Dintiman, George B.: *Sprinting Speed.* Springfield, Ill., Thomas, 1971.
15. Doherty, J. Kenneth: *Modern Track and Field.* Englewood Cliffs, Prentice-Hall, 1963.
16. Dolan, Joseph P. and Holladay, Lloyd J.: *Treatment and Prevention of Athletic Injuries.* Danville, Ill., Interstate, 1967.
17. Fowler, W. H. Jr., Gardner, G. H. and Egstrom, G. H.: Effect of an anabolic steroid on physical performance of young men. *J Appl Physiol, 20:*1038–40, 1965.
18. Gisolfi, D., Robinson, S., Turrell E. S.: Effects of aerobic work performed during recovery from exhausting work. *J Appl Physiol, 21:*1767–1770, 1966.
19. Hardie, Andrew: *Ballet Exercises for Athletes.* London, Amateur Athletic Assoc., 1900.
20. Hellebrandt, F. A. and Hantz, S. J.: Mechanisms of muscle training in man. *Phus Ther, 36:*371–383, 1956.
21. Henry, F. M.: Specificity vs. generality in learning motor skills. *Proc College Phus Educ Assoc, 59:*126–28, 1958.
22. Hilsendager, D. R., Straw, M. H. and Ackerman, K. J.: Comparison of speed, strength, and agility exercises in the development of agility. *Res Q, 40:*71–75, 1969.
23. Holt, Laurence E., Travis, Thomas M., and Okita, Ted: Comparative study of three stretching techniques. *Percept Mot Skills, 31:*611–616, 1970.
24. Jacobsen, Donald D.: The effects of a basketball season on leg strength and explosive power as shown on a select group of players. M.S. Thesis. South Dakota State College, 1962.
25. Jarver, Jess: Training procedures for development of muscular power. *Track Technique, 11:*333–334, 1963.
26. Johnson, Warren: Study of emotion revealed in two types of athletic sports contests. *Res Q, 20:*72–79, 1949.
27. Jones, Robert E.: A neurological interpretation of isometric exercise. *Res Q, 39:*1126–1127, 1968.
28. Kaiman, Bernard et al.: Therapeutic effectiveness of minimal activity in an aged population. *Psych Rep, 19:*439–443, 1966.
29. Kusinitz, Ivan and Keeney, Clifford E.: Effects of progressive weight training on health and physical fitness of adolescent boys. *Res Q, 29:*294–301, 1958.
30. Lehston, N. G.: A measure of basketball skills in high school boys. *Phys Educ, 5:*103–109, 1947.
31. Luitjins, Larry L.: Leg strength and vertical jump of basketball players as affected by two select exercise programs conducted throughout the competitive season. M.S. Thesis, South Dakota State University, Brookings, 1969.

32. Malmo, R. B. and Davis, J. F.: Anxiety and behavioral arousal. *Psych Rev, 64:*276–287, 1957.

33. Margaria, R., Oliva, R. D., diPrampei, P. E. and Cerretelli, P.: Energy utilization in intermittent exercise of supramaximal intensity. *J Appl Physiol, 26:*752–756, 1969.

34. McCraw, Lynn W. and Burnham, Stan: Resistive exercises in the development of muscular strength and endurance. *Res Q, 37:*79–87, 1966.

35. McQueen, I. J.: *Physiotherapy, 42:*83, 1956.

36. Muller, E. A. and Rohmert, W.: Die geschivindigkeit der musklekraft zunahme bei isometrischen training. *Int Z Angew Physiol, 19:*403–19, 1963.

37. Pyke, Frank: Effects of training on the alactacid anaerobic energy release mechanism in men of different ages. Unpublished Doctoral Dissertation, Indiana, 1970.

38. Rushall, B. S. and Pettinger, John: An evaluation of various reinforcers used as motivators in swimming. *Res Q, 40:*540–545, 1969.

39. ————: Behavior Control in Swimming. Address to Australian Sports Medicine Federation, Camperdown, New South Wales, March, 1971.

40. Selye, Hans: *The Stress of Life.* New York, McGraw-Hill, 1956.

41. Skinner, B. F.: *The Technology of Teaching.* New York, Appleton-Century-Crofts, 1968.

42. Steindler, Arthur: *Kinesiology of the Human Body.* Springfield, Ill., Thomas, 1955.

43. Toyoda, Hiroshi: *Training Theory for Volleyball in Japan.* Scarborough, C.V.A. Publications, 1971.

44. Whitley, Jim D. and Smith, Leon E.: Influence of three different training programs on strength and speed of limb movement. *Res Q, 37:*132–142, 1966.

45. Williams, J. G. P.: *Sports Medicine.* London, Arnold, 1962.

46. Wooden, John: *Practical Modern Basketball.* New York, Ronald Press, 1966.

CHAPTER XVII

ICE HOCKEY

GASTON MARCOTTE, RAY HERMISTON

THE NATURE OF HOCKEY

HOCKEY IS ONE of the most complex team sports to learn because of the very nature of the game. Unlike other sports the players have to contend with two artificial extensions of their body, namely, a pair of skates, and a stick. The apprenticeship in hockey is extremely long. In order to master the fundamental techniques one must first master the thin blades of the tube skate which create, at the outset, a tremendous problem in both strength and balance. Secondly, the wooden stick demands the development of a high degree of sensory perception for satisfactory puck control. In addition, the hockey player must learn to keep his head up and hence view the puck only by development of his peripheral vision. To these two limiting factors one must add great speeds over the icy surface, steel goalposts, sharp skate blades, a frozen puck travelling at times over 100 miles per hour, wooden boards and sticks, as well as the awesome but legitimate body contact. Therefore, hockey has to be classified as one of the world's most demanding, dangerous and exciting team sports.

Hockey is equally demanding on the cardiorespiratory system because of the numerous bursts of speed, its exciting pace constantly at near-maximum workload, and its back-to-back games as shown in the National Hockey League's 78-game schedule. In the last ten years, the ever-increasing popularity of hockey has been matched by a similar ever-increasing speed of movement in the game. This increased speed of the game is due primarily to rule changes, better equipment and coaching techniques that have cut the time spent on the ice by the players to approximately one-half that of previous decades. Even though the faster pace, longer seasons, and warmer arenas, have constantly increased the stress on the players' adaptive physiology, scientifically based training programs are practically non-existent in professional ranks in North America. On the other hand Russia, Czechoslovakia and Sweden have steadily been moving towards more scientifically oriented hockey programs for their national teams playing in the Amateur World Hockey Championship. The unexpected results of the first Canada-Russia Serie clearly demonstrated the importance of conditionning in the game of hockey. It is hoped that the hard lesson that the Russians have taught professional hockey will encourage the development of more scientifically sound training programs adapted to all age groups.

PHYSICAL CHARACTERISTICS

Data on the weight and fatfolds of college, semi-professional, and National Hockey League hockey players have been collected by Hermiston and Marcotte.[6] The data on junior hockey players has been collected by Seliger[9] in Czechoslovakia. In the more advanced level of competition, the hockey player as shown in Table XVII–I is heavier and presumably

TABLE XVII–I
PHYSICAL CHARACTERISTICS OF HOCKEY PLAYERS
ACCORDING TO LEVEL OF COMPETITION

Level	Team		Weight (Lbs)		% Fat		
			$\bar{X}$	SD	$\bar{X}$	SD	n
JUNIOR 16.5 yrs	CZECHS	a	143	(12.7)	12.9		15
UNIVERSITY	MICH. STATE	b	170.0	(17.0)	12.3	(8.4)	17
	MICHIGAN		170.9	(17.7)	11.4	(2.5)	18
SEMI-PRO	MUSKEGON	b	179.8	(12.6)	11.8	(3.5)	16
	TOLEDO		177.8	(12.7)	12.6	(3.1)	14
	TORONTO	b	186.3	(11.7)	12.1	(4.8)	19
PROFESSIONAL	NEW YORK		188.8	(12.4)	12.7	(4.6)	18
	BOSTON		184.1	(13.0)	12.7	(3.9)	17

a Calculated from Seliger.[9]
b Unpublished data of R. Hermiston and G. Marcotte collected in March 1966.[6]

taller. Mean adipose tissue, however, appears to remain constant at about 12 percent. When compared with top athletes in other sports who average around 8 percent body fat, it would appear that hockey players rarely play at peak condition. National Hockey League players are selectively bigger, but they maintain the same percentage of adipose tissue, as those players of lower levels. Strength, power, agility, speed, endurance, and the capacity to give and take hard body checks are the prerequisites to the game of hockey. This, by and large, automatically eliminates the fat individual from all positions except goaltending where an appreciable amount of excess fat has been found when examining National Hockey League goaltenders.[6] It is the contention of the authors that there appears to be a minimum level of fat that is best suited for the hockey player. This fat tissue appears to absorb the many contacts one's body has with the boards, the ice, opponents' sticks, and the puck. Perhaps this is the basic reason why the skinny individual (< 5% adipose tissue) has little or no place in professional hockey. The ideal hockey player appears to be a man who would be approximately six feet tall, weighing 190 pounds, extremely muscular with a very thin layer of fat in the neighbourhood of 7 to 10 percent, highly aggressive, agile, possessing the speed of a world champion sprinter and the endurance of a marathon runner. Howe, Béliveau, Mahovalich, Esposito combine some of the most important characteristics of great hockey players. Fortunately, the small player still has a place in hockey if he is strong and aggressive and if he is capable of compensating for his lack of height and weight by a high degree of speed, agility, and technical skill. Dave Keon, Henri Richard, Marcel Dionne and Richard Martin are examples of this breed of hockey player.

PHYSIOLOGICAL CHARACTERISTICS

Despite the overwhelming interest generated by hockey, few attempts have been made to measure the physiologic response of individuals ice skating. Consequently, energy expenditure and physical work capacity have not been quantified in ice skating as they have been in running, swimming and cycling. Until 1969, no ice skating test had been reported with reproducibility data for either the measurement of maximum oxygen uptake or maximum work capacity. As a result, it has been impossible to evaluate different training methods in ice hockey or to assess the relative importance of height, type of skate, length of stride, equipment, and temperature on the energy expenditure and the physical capacity of skaters. Most of the data available is sparse and unpublished.

Based on the data of Watson,[12] Faulkner,[3] Ferguson, Marcotte and Montpetit,[4] Hermiston,[5] Thoden and Jette [10] the mean capacity of college hockey players is approximately 55 ml/kg/min. The hockey players from Canada's National Team averaged 55 ml/kg/min in 1968. In 1966 the Swedish National Hockey Team averaged 56 ml/kg/min. The data on six [5] professional hockey players indicates a mean capacity of 51.0 ml/kg/min. These data are presented in Table XVII–II. Nevertheless, the maximum oxygen uptake of world class cross-country skiers, long distance runners, speed skaters, and orienteering and cycling teams have all shown superior oxygen uptakes well in excess of 70 ml/kg. Saltin and Åstrand [8] have reported maximum O_2 intakes of 83 ml/kg/min for the male members of the Swedish national cross-country ski team. The low values for professional hockey players may be partly accounted by the fact that they were measured during the summer prior to the training camp. Nevertheless, the low maximum O_2 uptake values for hockey players would indicate a relative weakness in our training programs to develop adequately the aerobic capacity of the players. Selinger [9] reports data on cost of playing hockey. When compared to maximum oxygen uptake data there is an indication that the average expenditure during a hockey game is about 66 percent of the aerobic capacity of a particular individual. This can be compared to the 75 percent for marathon runners, 88 percent for speed skating, and 82 percent for cross-country skiers. It may be that the optimal level for playing ice hockey does not demand a higher aerobic capacity or perhaps that the present training methods do not emphasize improvement of the oxygen transport system.

The average hockey player skates approximately two and one-half miles per game. According to the speeds at which hockey players are

TABLE XVII–II
AEROBIC CAPACITY OF HOCKEY PLAYERS

		Team	V_{O_2} (Liter/Min)	V_{O_2} (ML/KG)	n
Watson	12	U. Alberta	4.12 (0.29)	54.3 (14.9)	10
Faulkner	3	U. Michigan	4.05	55.1	6
Ferguson, Marcotte, Montpetit	4	U. Montréal	4.08 (0.44)	55.3 (5.8)	17
Hermiston	5	U. Windsor	4.10 (0.62)	53.2 (6.1)	9
Thoden Jette	10	U. Ottawa	4.19	54.5 (7.8)	15
Coyne	2	Canadian National	4.19	53.4 (5.9)	34
Agnevik	1	Swedish National	4.45	56.0	
Thoden Jette	11	N.H.L.		51.2	4
Metivier	7	N.H.L.		50.8	2

capable of travelling, the maximum upper limit for a 20 minute period could be approximately three miles. Furthermore, it has been estimated that N.H.L. players move at top speed only 20 to 25 percent of the time spent on the ice. This is basically the reason why the Russians believed they could successfully challenge the professionals. They had trained their players to work at full speed 65 to 75 percent of the time on the ice. The Canada–Russia Serie seemed to have proven the validity of this assumption.

Because of the very intense bursts of activity in hockey, probably the most important physiological component is the anaerobic capacity of the individual. Consequently, coaches should train their players to endure high levels of lactic acid accumulation in order to have the players work at full capacity 75 percent of the time on the ice. Since endurance and speed are both necessary to meet the specific demands of hockey, conditioning programs should train the anaerobic as well as the aerobic capacities of the hockey player.

Basic principles to be respected and implemented in building conditioning programs for the entire spectrum of hockey skills and techniques are as follows:

1. Technical improvement in a skill at any level and particularly at peak performance demands a high level of general physical condition. Any type of exercise that improves components of speed, strength, agility, power, endurance, and balance is without question, worthwhile.

2. The conditioning program should take into account the environmental conditions of arenas, as well as the duration, the frequency, and the intensity required of the players. Since activities in actual games require violent exertion from one to three minutes, the athlete is limited by the amount of oxygen debt that can be contracted and the concentration of lactic acid that can be tolerated. Players should then exercise at maximum speeds from two to three minutes with a five- to six-minute rest period. The coach must utilize the rest periods for the development of basic techniques that require very little movement, for example, shooting.

3. Because of the specificity of training the coach should choose movements that will be utilized in competition and have the players exercise in full equipment on the ice if at all possible.

4. Since strength is a limiting factor in endurance, weight training should always be included in a well-balanced program. The weight training program must have a speed base instead of the weight base.

5. Adipose tissue or percent body fat is also a limiting factor. A well-balanced diet should be prepared for individual players according to the individual's tastes as well as needs. Since the nature of hockey is one of intense exercise, the coach should be aware of the advantages of high carbohydrate diets for the pregame meal. The sooner the hockey coach gets away from the pregame "steak" and high protein diet meal, the more likely he is to make the meal meaningful in the energy expenditures of his athletes during a particular game.

6. Speed is one of the fundamental characteristics of hockey. All movement should be performed at close to maximum speed. Granted learning the techniques might be done at a slower pace but the techniques must be practiced at near maximum speed as soon as possible.

7. Since skill may influence speed, and endurance may influence speed as well as skill every player and coach should appreciate the importance of constantly improving the fundamental techniques of hockey within the context of simulated reality.

8. A motivated player will accept the discomfort of pain at maximum

effort and still work diligently at exercises. Therefore the coach should constantly strive to prepare lively and interesting practices with particular attention paid to motivation and competition within the practice.

9. At the first of the season the coach should begin slowly but as the players' condition improves the coach should likewise increase the frequency, the intensity, and the duration of the practices. During any particular practice the coach should begin slowly, working up to near maximum pace for a major portion of the practice and then driving the hockey players into complete anaerobic debt at the end of the practice.

10. Year-round training is necessary in order to reach the highest possible peaks of aerobic and anaerobic power in the winter. A one-year cycle must have three basic categories of training periods:

   a. pre-season training;
   b. competitive season;
   c. post-season training.

Gone are the days of the seasonal player for the athlete striving for peak performance.

Pre-season training

The pre-season should be defined as that period of time extending from approximately three months before the regular season until the first regular game. There are several principles that must be followed in this period.

1. The training program must be progressive and reach a peak just prior to the start of the season. It is of utmost importance that the athlete build towards this peak and not reach it much prior to the season of play.

2. The early portions of this pre-season training program should be based on the development of maximum strength. The middle section to bring the athlete to his maximum oxygen uptake and the latter stages to his maximum debt tolerance.

3. The development of skill, agility, and technique on ice must be left until the latter stages of the pre-season program but should be worked on prior to the team practices in training camp.

4. The training camp session must be utilized to bring the team play into focus and act as a sounding board for the maintenance of condition and strength.

Competitive season

By and large the hockey team will play enough games and have enough practices to maintain the pre-season physical condition of the players. It should not be used to raise their condition except prior to playoffs. Over the period of a six-month season the maximum oxygen uptake will increase several ml/kg and the coach must therefore increase the intensity of his in-season conditioning program to take advantage of this physiologic phenomenon.

1. One of the best methods of assessing the condition of the players during the season would be mile sprints.
2. The coach must be aware of the fatigue involved in a 60-game season and he should use his practices for team play, individual technique improvement but not as conditioning sessions, if the pre-season scheme has been followed. Only in the latter stages must the coach reevaluate the condition of his players. Coaches should be aware of the detrimental effect of a two week lay-off period over the Christmas Holidays. Players tend to over-eat while they exercise and sleep very little. A coach should be able to assess the player's condition when he leaves so as to be able to bring him back to his former level as quickly as possible.

Post-season training

The post-season session should begin with at least two weeks of rest from any major activity. It is detrimental to the general body condition to extend this period but the athlete should be advised to run, play games such as handball, squash and paddleball in this period to maintain his oxygen uptake above 55 ml/kg.

Each player should know his time on a mile run when he is at approximately this oxygen uptake level and he would therefore be required to maintain this level.

1. Basic weight training would be used in this period to build muscle bulk for players who are underweight.
2. The maintenance of adiposity levels is a prerequisite for the pre-season training period and the athlete must be aware of this type of weight gain problem.

CONCLUSION

The lack of data on the physical and physiological characteristics of hockey players at different age levels and the absence of a test capable of measuring the maximum oxygen uptake or maximum work capacity of hockey players has made it impossible to evaluate different training programs in ice hockey. Until such a test is available hockey coaches will have to develop training programs that respect the basic principles of physiology and the basic requirements of ice hockey.

REFERENCES

1. Agenvik, G.: Unpublished data. Fysiologiska Institutionem of the Central Gymnastic Institute of Stockholm. 1966.
2. Coyne, L.: Unpublished data. University of Calgary. 1968.
3. Faulkner, J. A.: Unpublished data. University of Michigan. 1966.
4. Ferguson, R. J., Marcotte, G. and Montpetit, R.: A maximal oxygen uptake test during ice skating. *Med Sci Sports,* 1:207–211, 1969.
5. Hermiston, R.: Unpublished data. University of Windsor.
6. Hermiston, Ray and Marcotte, Gaston: Unpublished data collected in March 1966, Ann Arbor, Michigan.
7. Métivier, G.: Unpublished data. University of Ottawa.
8. Saltin, B. and Åstrand, P. O.: Maximal oxygen uptake in athletes. *J Appl Physiol,* 23:353, 1967.
9. Selinger, V.: Energy metabolism in selected physical exercises. *Int Z Physiol,* 25:104–120, 1968.
10. Thoden, J. S., Jetté, M.: Laboratory measurements applied to the development and modification of training programs. In Taylor, A. W. (Ed.): *Training—Scientific Basis and Application.* Springfield, Thomas, 1972, pp. 103–114.
11. Thoden, J. S., Jetté, M.: Unpublished data, University of Ottawa.
12. Watson, R. C.: The respiratory effects of ice hockey upon treadmill performance. Unpublished Master's Thesis, University of Alberta, 1964.

CHAPTER XVIII

VOLLEYBALL

LORNE SAWULA

THE GAME we play today, called volleyball, was originally known as "Minonette." Minonette contained the skills and rules borrowed from tennis, handball, and baseball. Devised by William C. Morgan in 1895, this game was played by businessmen for exercise. The Y.M.C.A. was the catalyst for the spreading of the game which spread throughout the United States and neighboring countries. It was introduced into Europe during the First World War where its popularity grew. Today, over eighty countries play competitive volleyball, with some twenty-five recognizing the game as a major sport. Today the Communist countries led by U.S.S.R. are dominating competitive volleyball.

The forming of the International Volleyball Federation (F.I.V.B.) in 1946 and the First World Championships in 1949 were a great boost to the growth of the sport. Volleyball's greatest advance came in 1964 when volleyball was included for the first time in the Olympic Games held in Tokyo, Japan. Volleyball has progressed from a slow, helter-skelter, bat-the-ball-over-the-net-at-any-cost game to a smooth, deliberate, accurate, fast and exciting game.

In Canada, volleyball has been slow in developing, since it was introduced into Canada around the turn of the 20th century. Canada initiated a Canadian championship in 1953, with the Eastern teams, mainly Hamilton and Toronto, dominating the championships. Canada started real international competition in 1959 during the Pan-American Games. In the 1967 Pan-American Games in Winnipeg, the volleyball matches outdrew basketball and excited even the sportscasters. In 1969 Canada participated in its first international competition outside of the Pan-American Games when the National Teams travelled to Mexico City for the North Central American and Caribbean Zone Championships where both men and women finished fourth. The future holds exciting possibilities for Canada, as for the first time, in 1976, Canada will be able to enter a team in the Olympic Games to be held in Montreal.

RESEARCH

Research in the volleyball area is very limited. Various studies have taken place from time to time but little has been done on the psychological or physiological factors influencing the player. The Japanese lead the way in this general area with their scientific training methods.[15] Studies by Jan Prsala,* a Czechoslovakian, have attempted to analyze the motion of certain volleyball skills using film photography.

Recently, Dr. R. MacNab and Don Irwin have used the University of Alberta Golden Bear Volleyball team in the Maximal Oxygen Uptake Study. Blood samples for lactic acid build-up were also taken during the testing which occurred before the season started (October), before Christmas break (early December), returning from Christmas break (one month lay-off), and at the end of the season (March). The final results are in the process of being written up.†

Another test in Canada is that designed by Mike Farawani, Canada's National Men's Coach. This test was used to examine national team candidates and has been in use since 1971. Included in the test are: (a) run test —90 metres; (b) total body reaction time; (c) right hand movement time; (d) left hand movement time; (e) running vertical jump; (f) diving movement time; (g) leg extension strength; and (h) arm extension strength.‡

Professor Saul Ross at the University of Ottawa is in the middle of conducting two pilot projects in volleyball. These are an analysis of eye-hand coordination in the spike and an analysis of eye-hand coordination in the two-hand overhead pass. The purpose of this research was to determine, in a pilot study, if it is possible for a highly-skilled athlete to take his eyes away from the ball before hand contact, and still complete the skill successfully. This study will give additional depth into the possibility of teaching a spiker or setter to look at the opposition's weakness before he sets or spikes the ball.

Other research has mainly been done in the area of skill testing. A list of these may be found at the end of this chapter.

---

* Dr. Jan Prsala is a native of Czechoslovakia. His approach to his teaching of skills is based on detailed analysis of the mechanics of the overhand and underhand contacts. He is currently at Dalhousie University, Halifax

† For more information, contact Dr. R. MacNab, Faculty of Physical Education, University of Alberta, Edmonton, Alberta.

‡ For more information, write: M. Farawani, c/o Canadian Volleyball Assoc.

THE FUNDAMENTALS

A The Set

Before a spike can be completed, the ball must be put in a correct position for the spiker to hit it. Until this basic technique is completed, there can be little offense of a uniform nature.

The basic type of set is a high pass to the outside corners of the net. This set usually originates from the middle front position. Basically, sets can be of two types:

a) the overhead or front set   b) the spill or back set

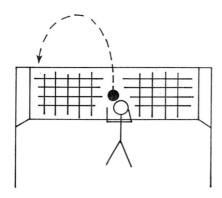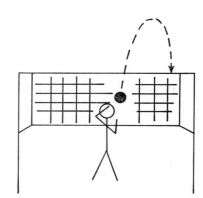

The front or overhead set moves forward from the direction that the setter is facing. The spill or back set, is set with the back facing the direction of the set. Basically, both sets should be high sets (15–20′ above the net).

Technique in both sets is similar for the lower body action. In both, the feet play an important role. During the front set the toes of the feet should point the direction that the ball is going to take.

This is also the same in the back set, except it is the heels that lead the way.

The basic foot stance should feel comfortable to the setter. Basically the feet should be shoulder width apart, either even or with one foot slightly ahead of the other. Whichever stance is used, the setter must be able to plant both feet simultaneously on the floor before contact is made with the ball. This will help to absorb some of the force of the falling ball. The weight should be slightly forward and mainly on the "balls" of the feet. Legs should be bent (i.e. to absorb the ball upon contact) when the ball is about to be contacted by the hands. Upon contact in returning or setting the ball, the legs uncoil and extend, even to the point of having the toes leave the ground.

The upper body is coordinated with the legs. The hands should be in a "2–4" position. This means the thumbs should be about 4 inches apart and the forefingers about 2 inches apart, thus forming a diamond shape with the fingers. This will cause the elbows to stay outside in a comfortable position.

Contact should be made on all fingers with the upper-half of the fingers.

The ball should be contacted on the front of the forehead. The diamond shape of the hands can be used as a guide to bring the ball to the forehead. As the ball begins to fall, the hands should be immediately brought up to the forehead (a ready position). Upon contact, the arms should absorb the ball by dropping the wrists back and slightly lowering the arms. This is done in conjunction with the legs' coiling action. This extended contact enables the setter to get better control of the ball. As the 100° angle is reached with the legs, the body begins to uncoil and extend. The ball is moved forward from the forehead with the extension of the legs, arms, and wrists. Follow-through is important. Without the use of the legs and arms, a long set can prove quite troublesome. The back, seat, and legs should be nearly straight upon follow-through with the arms slightly forward.

The preceding has been mainly for the front set but much of the same applies to the spill or back set. The key in the back set is fourfold:

a. use legs;
b. arch back and watch the ball;
c. follow through;
d. contact the ball on the back part of the head rather than on the front part.

The back set may be used as an element of surprise but it should be as efficient as the front set. It should be stressed here that both play a basic part in the beginning of an attack.

Basic types of set can be incorporated into the attack system. A set can be low, high, fast, slow, on the outside corner, or in the middle of the net. A setter should be able to put the set anywhere for any given situation. The shoot and the quick set are two basic types of sets that could be used to change the speed in your offensive attack. A shoot set is one where the ball travels one to three feet above the height of the net to the outside corner. The set can be slow or fast. If it is fast the set should be expected to pass through a spot above the net where the spiker can reach it. If it is slow it should have a higher arc and drop on the spot from which the spiker is to attack from.

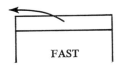

FAST

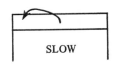

SLOW

Both types of shoots serve this purpose. The latter is easier to use and offers some measure of error whereas the fast shoot needs delicate timing by both spiker and setter. The other "quick attack" set is the quick set. It is usually set about one foot above the net and right above the setter's forehead.

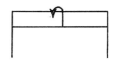

Both the shoot and quick set require the spiker to be in the air upon hitting the ball. More will be discussed about hitting the shoot and quick sets under spiking.

Now the question that comes up is, "How do I tell my players what type of set to hit?" A basic numbering system will serve this purpose. The purpose of an elementary numbering system is that the setter and spiker can coordinate on the type of set as well as the spot where the set should land. A basic number system is based off the center player when he is in the middle of the court by the net. Six numbers are applied to six different types of sets.

1. One foot above the middle of the net
2. Two feet above the middle of the net
3. slow shoot—half-way between setter and sideline—3 feet high
4. higher set—6 to 8 feet—half-way between setter and sideline

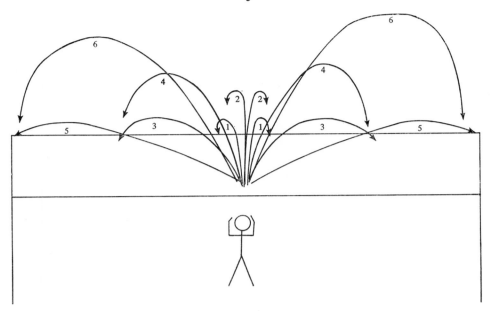

5. shoot set—fast to outside—2 feet high
6. high set—20 feet—to outside

This type of numbering system applies for the front half of the net in front of the setter and as well to the back half of the court behind the setter.

Variations can be made to this system to allow for a more varied attack. For example, the #1 set or #2 set could take place anywhere along the net, not necessarily at the center of it.

Drills: Overhead Pass

   1. For beginners check:
      a. hand position—"2–4", elbows out
      b. stance—comfortable, legs shoulder width apart
   2. Place ball in setter's hands. Apply pressure to ball by placing your hand on the ball. This will cause the setter to bend slightly as if the ball's impact were being absorbed. As legs bend down to 100°, then the setter should slowly uncoil, pushing the ball up against a slight resistance by your hand. Make sure a full extension occurs with hands and arms and legs. Then slowly apply pressure to start the movement over again.
   3. Two players lie down on stomach facing each other about 2 feet apart. Place a ball on the ground between them. One should extend his arms and wrists, imitating the release of the ball, while the other should contract his arms, hands, and wrists back, imitating the reception of the ball. Repeat slowly.

4. Same drill but move 3 to 6 feet apart. Work on technique.
5. One ball to a person. Bend over from the waist so back is parallel to the ground. Hold ball in both hands in correct hand position and correct foot position. Allow to fall to the ground. As the ball comes up, absorb it by bending the wrists and arms back. Slowly allow the ball to drop again, but this time concentrate on the follow-through, so the wrists will extend fully. Try to get smooth wrist and arm motion.
6. Change the speed of the ball while standing still.
7. Add movement to the ball.
8. Review technique by asking players what to do.
9. Two players, one ball—Stand about 6 to 10 feet apart. One throws a high ball about 15 to 20 feet in the air with a two-handed, underhand throw. The other player concentrates on technique and tries to volley the ball back to the other player who catches the ball and then repeats the throw. The thrower should not attempt to make the setter move. Repeat 10 times and change.
10. After players become more confident, introduce running. As player A runs into center of court, the ball is thrown high into the air by the thrower. Player A concentrates on placing both feet on the ground simultaneously with the toes pointing in the direction of

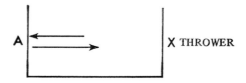

the ball. He volleys the ball to the thrower and then backs out backwards to the side line. Then he repeats the forward motion. Meanwhile, the thrower has caught the ball and again prepares to throw the ball high into the air.
11. Same drill but in diagonal direction; concentrate on facing partner —2 to a ball.

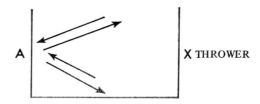

12. Volley back and forth with commands getting more difficult as the players become better setters.
    a. high passes

b. low passes
c. long high pass—get further apart
d. start 10 feet apart, get closer and closer until 1 foot apart, then move apart
e. two hits each, low pass to yourself—high to partner
f. two hits each, high pass to self, low to partner
g. three hits—high to self, ¼ turn, low to self, high to partner
h. these types of drills can be interspersed with bump, spills, etc. or combination of all kinds of sequences

Spill Drills:

1. Repeat drill #1 and #2—concentrate on 4 main points of spilling.
2. One to a ball—volley the ball high in the air, let it bounce, walk under it and spill it high. Turn and repeat after ball drops. Concentrate on pushing up.
3. Three players, one ball

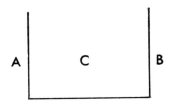

player in middle faces A who throws ball high in air. Player C tries to spill the ball to player B. Player B catches the ball and waits for C to turn around and face him. Then he repeats the sequence.
4. After some mastery of overhead setting, the players can progress. Do the same drill as #3, except player A and B should volley the ball high to player C who is continually spilling. Always try to do drills 3 and 4 close to net.

More advanced drills combining overhead set and back set:

1. 4 players, 1 ball

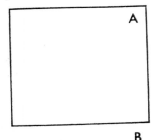

Player A has ball. Player B has to volley the ball back to A four consecutive times with the overhead set. Player A places the ball high in different parts of the court. After fourth return A volleys to C who in return volleys to B who has switched with A. Drill is continuous. Repeat 3 times each.

2. Repeat drill #1 with the back set.
3. Four players, one ball

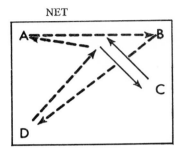

NET

Sequence. A passes high to B who passes high to D. D passes high to the middle of the net in the attack zone. Player C running in sets the ball to A. After setting to A, player C drops back to base line. Player A passes to B and repeat.

4. Same drill as #3 except player C spills ball to B. Player B then set to A who passes it back to B who sets D and starts the sequence all over again.
5. Repeat drill 3 with C staying stationary; D passes to C who sets A.

In all drills above, rotate players frequently.

B The Bump

This is perhaps the most important play on offense. It is the foundation of your attack. Without an adequate bump you will be unable to get good sets. Without good sets you will be unable to spike. Thus, you will find yourself without an offense, a terrible experience.

The bump is used on nearly all receptions of the serve. The key in the bump-pass is concentration. The following are important points to concentrate on in learning the bump-pass:

1. Foot position
   —find a comfortable position.
   —most players will find a staggered stance the most beneficial.
   —either the left foot or the right foot should be forward, with the legs about shoulder width apart. This will allow a player better range to either side up and back.
2. Hand position
   —hand should be in one of two positions.
   a. form right hand into ball and then close left hand loosely around so thumbs are up.
   b. right hand open, place left hand open on top of palm of right hand. Close down the thumbs together locking left hand on right hand.
3. Reception of ball
   —concentrate on ball coming into forearms. Lock the ball into your forearms.

4. Contact with ball
   —the ball should be picked up on the inside forearm or fleshy part of the arms, in the area from the wrists to elbows. Ball should be in line with the midline of the body.
4. Contact with ball (con't)
   —elbows should be straight and nearly parallel with the ground depending on the trajectory of the ball.
   —upon contact partially open the hands by breaking the wrists down and shrugging the shoulders.
   —lift up and toward the ball with the legs.
5. Follow-through
   —make sure arms do not swing up above shoulder level.
   —lift with legs keeping back nearly straight.

Drills:

Learning Technique
1. Check foot and hand position.
2. One player hold ball and follow the path of a simulated ball as it drops onto the forearms of partner. Apply a little pressure as partner goes through technique of receiving ball then follow through.
3. Step back—3 to 6 feet

O throws the ball high in air (10′) to partner who tries to bump the ball back to you.

4. Step back further.

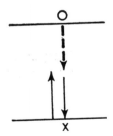

5. Separate about court width apart. One player stands still and throws ball into center area of court as partner approaches. Partner concentrates on foot position and bumps ball back. After follow-through, he runs back to the edge of the court and starts over. Repeat 10 to 15 times each.

At this point the players should have learned the technique which will enable you to move on. The player should then learn how to bump a ball that comes to either side. The technique will remain the same if you have the player remember to play the ball on the midline of the body. If the ball is to the right, the player should move his right leg out and swing his body out and behind the ball. At its furthest reach, the right leg should pivot slightly to a 45° angle (leave space). The left leg will shuffle in to allow for a solid base of support. Again technique is as before. However, the approach to the ball should be at 45° if possible, thus allowing the person bumping to face the spot where the ball is to go.

Drills:

1. X steps to right to bump ball to thrower. Then steps back to middle position, then to left. In each case, the thrower should wait until the person bumping the ball is in position.

2. Same drill as before but speed it up.

3. Both players are about 10 feet apart—bump back and forth.

4. Increase distance.
5. Add commands i.e.
   a. two hits each, low to yourself, high to your partner
   b. two hits each, high to yourself, low to your partner
   c. two hits each, high to yourself, ¼ turn bump to partner
   d. two hits each, ½ turn bump to partner
   e. three hits each, etc.
   f. bump to partner, sit down and get up before the ball comes back (high bumps)
   Use your imagination.

6. Apart 20 feet—have partner serve softly into your awaiting arms. Try to concentrate on form, bump ball back to partner who catches the ball.

7. Same drill but O₂ should move forward and backward. Server should wait until partner is coming forward.

8. a. Coach throws ball over net to player who is moving forward, tries to bump ball to X_1.

b. Coach serves ball over net, players try to bump ball into air near center of court.

9. Combination drills (see combination drills).

The key again is concentration. Lock the ball into your arms. Always be moving forward, if possible, and keep the ball in the midline of the body.

C Blocking

Blocking is not only a defense but also an offense, depending upon its use. It should play an important part in the development of team strategy. Without adequate blocking, a defense cannot begin to operate, for the block plays a very important role in the defense you are trying to set up.

Generally, blocking can be divided into two parts, upper body and lower body actions. In the lower body, the most important action is the footwork. Blocking footwork, like spiking footwork, requires the player to be prepared at all times. The set by the opposition may be high or low, slow or fast, inside or outside, far back or close, or some combination of these. The blocker has only a limited time to react to the opposing spiker's movements. For this reason, the blocker should use a 120° power angle, not a 90° angle as in a spike. The blocker has to be quick and ready to uncoil at any instant. Also, since the play is taking place at the net and the rules allow the touching of the ball over the net (if your opponent is going to send the ball towards your side), the blocker must be close to the net at take-off. Before the take-off the blocker may be up to 6 feet away from the net until the ball direction is determined. Because the blocker jumps close to the net, his jump must be in a vertical axis, not in a horizontal one. A horizontal jump will carry the blocker into the net or over the line. The blocker, especially the center blocker, must be able to move either to his right or left quickly. To do so fast, the blocker uses a sliding motion, keeping the shoulders parallel to the net. His legs never cross behind but only slide together as in a shuffle step. In movement to the right, the right leg always moves first.

The upper body plays an important role as well. The hands and arms are probably the most important. Being situated close to the net, the blocker has to react quickly. The hands should be in a ready position,

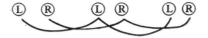

about chest height, and the eyes are on your opposing spikers. Concentration should be kept on the ball until the direction is determined, then resume concentration on the approaching spiker. The spiker's motion will help you follow the ball but so will your own eyes. Since you are already situated close to the net, you should be ready for this approach whether it is fast or slow, straight or diagonal. As the blocker, you must time your jump as if you were the spiker coming in to hit the ball. The arms are quickly thrown back, sometimes not in a full extension, but as far back as time allows. As the arms swing forward, they are brought up close to the chest, so as not to touch the net. Ideally, arms and hands are raised to the top of the net, still not at full extension. As the spiker makes his arm motion, the blocker *who has his eyes open,* watches the motion of the arm and hand. Then, after a partial hang, the hands are stretched up and reached over the net as far as possible. Sometimes, it will be necessary to stretch the hands diagonally instead of straight forward. The hands are spread wide apart, as are the fingers, to get as much surface area covered as possible. Upon contact with the ball, a downward motion results from the elbows to the wrists. The ball is then pushed down into your opponent's court. As the blocker comes down, he should be ready to play any ball that comes down in front of him and get hung up on the net. Never, I repeat, never reach for a ball that falls behind you. Another player should be there to pick it up.

In volleyball, the block most often occurring is a two-man block either on the right or left corner of your side. There are many things the blockers have to be aware of. First, who should initiate or set the block. Most teams use the outside man to set the blocking range. It also can be done with the middle man setting the block. For basic discussion purposes, I will use the outside man setting the block. The outside blocker either on the right or left should first judge the type of set, then the approach of the spiker. As the ball drops, the outside blocker (assuming block is on your left hand side) should attempt to have his right hand on the ball and the left turned into court. The center man, after watching the direction of the set, should move sideways in a side shuffle step to the outside blocker. Concentration on the planting of the outside foot is important as it will add stability to the blocker. As the center blocker jumps into the air, he should try to concentrate on leading with his left hand, thus preventing the ball from going between the block. The right hand should follow and then both hands of the center blocker would be placed straight on, so as to cut off the angle hit from the spiker. The hands of the two blockers would look like this:

The key in the block is to put the hands over the net. If the hands are not placed over the net, the ball will probably roll down the hands and down the net on your side. A blocker's job is done when a solid wall is formed causing the spiker to go around or over the top. When this wall is accomplished, then the rest of the defense can be completed.

A center block is sometimes important. If a team is using a multiple offense against you then you have to be prepared to block man-on-man. This means you will pair up with the man opposite you after they have completed their switches. For now I will assume that there will be no crossing of players because this adds more difficulty in setting up the block. The center blocker is in a very difficult position. He must be center conscious as well as moving to his right and left. If the set is high enough, a triple block can be formed. This would mean the center blocker would take the ball straight on. The left blocker would move to his right and place his right hand along the wall formed by the center blocker. His left hand would again turn in to keep the ball in bounds. The right blocker would do the same thing. His left hand would form the wall and his right hand would be turned in. The block would look like this:

A two-man block in the center is likely all you usually will have time to set up for. If this occurs, the center blocker should try to set the block, especially if the set is not exactly in the middle. Again, both blockers should have their outside hand turned in to keep the ball in bounds.

If an attack is quick enough, then only a one-man block will be formed. This is when watching the hand and arm action of the approaching spiker will pay off. If you have a vulnerable middle area on your defense, then you should try to block straight on, thus doing your job and causing the spiker to hit around you. However, if the ball is close to the net, you may be willing to take a chance and go after the ball, that is, to reach as far as possible over the net to attack the ball.

Since volleyball is becoming a very quick game with quick attacks, the volleyball player must be very mobile. If there is mobility in your team, then the outside blockers can be stationed in about 3 to 6 feet from the sidelines. This would give added depth to blocking in the middle but would require more coordination on a block in the corner.

A final suggestion would be to make sure the blockers watch the approaching spiker. Certain hits can be given away by the spiker's approach or his arm, hand and shoulder action. As a blocker, you should be able to read the spiker "if he is off-balance or out of control far from the net," then a block need not be put up. More times than not, a blocker who does not watch the spiker gets caught in a wipe-out situation. Try to watch for this as it will enable you to become a better blocker.

I have concentrated on the attack block. Another type of block is used, but usually in special instances. This is the "save" block. This block is usually used by a blocker when the ball is further from the net and the spiker is hitting with power or if the blocker is too small to get his hands adequately over the net. The basic principles are the same for all aspects of this block except for the hands. Instead of reaching over the net, the hands are placed on the net and bent back so as to let the ball roll off upon contact. This usually will result in a ball coming high off the block. As I said, this type of block is only useful for certain people and certain instances. To sum up, the following general points can be followed:

1. Hands in a ready position—chest high.
2. Concentration first on setter and ball, then on spiker.
3. Hands stop at net then move over the net.
4. Hands are spread wide.
5. Footwork—shuffle step and planting of outside foot.

The following drills can be used for improving the basic techniques of blocking:
Drills: Foot & Hand Coordination—Beginning Techniques

1. Slide and jump reaching hands over the net and breaking wrists downwards—3 times at net.

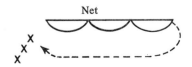

2. Pair up, slide and jump, clap hands on top of net.

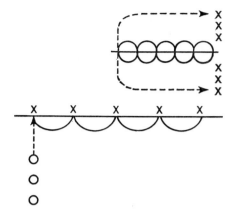

3. Each player holds a ball at top of net. Player 1 jumps up and tries to touch ball by breaking wrists down. DO NOT TOUCH NET. After first touch, slide over and touch next player and so on. Go down and come back.

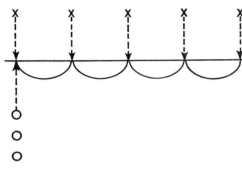

4. X number of players stand back from net. Each in turn throws ball underhand so as the blocker gets to the net, the ball is there. The blocker tries to stuff the ball down by breaking wrists. Slide over to next man to meet throw. Down and back.

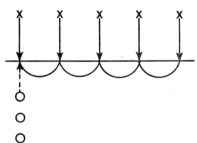

5. X number of players approach blocker and attempt to throw ball through block or spike it through. Blocker slides down the line and then back.

(Drills 1–5 can be done on a net that is lower than 8 feet, about 6′6″.)

6. Middle Block—endurance and shuffle technique.
At the coach's command, player jumps up and attempts to block ball. After a block that falls in court, the players shuffle to the sideline and step out of court to go around the post. On their way back they must shuffle into position and concentrate on planting their feet and leading with inside hands.

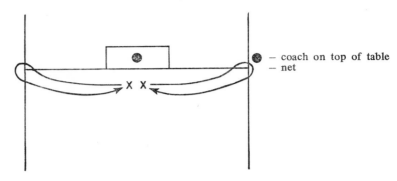

7. Coach concentrates on blocks—X_2 must slide over and lead with right hand. X_1 must set block and turn right hand in to prevent wipe-off. The coach looks for the hands and concentrates on wipe-offs and angle spikes. Players try to block the ball. When ball is blocked, one player drops deep to catch a second ball which is thrown deep by the coach. He then tries to set the ball to his teammate who then, in turn, sets him for an offensive play—each pair must have two good blocks and two good hits before they are finished. The next two then come in.

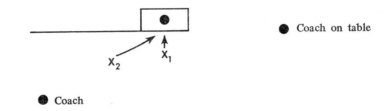

8. Coach throws ball over blocker's head. Blockers must attempt to watch spiker and move accordingly.

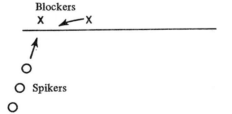

9. Thrower throws ball on net. It is up to the blockers to try to stuff the ball down on their partner's court. Play a game with a point for your partner each time the ball falls on your court.

10. Follow Ball Technique

Coach on table—blockers jump, he moves the ball to either side. Players must watch ball and react accordingly with their hands.

11. Setting of Block and Middle Shuffle

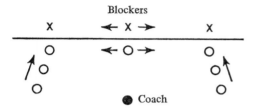

Coach throws ball to middle setter who sets or spills the ball. Blockers must react.

12. Multiple Block Reaction Offense

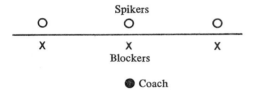

Coach tells plays on far side where to move. Blockers react to motion of spikers. One-on-one situation.

13. Coach adds a multiple offense. Blockers must be aware of center hit.

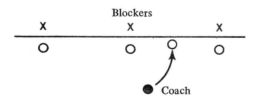

Practice blocking man-on-man. Coach throws ball to backcourt setter who runs the offense.

(For drills 6–13 a large ball bag is usefull to keep the action going. Also players not involved in drill should be used in retrieving balls.)

These are only a few of the drills that can be used. Your imagination can be your guidebook. Make sure the drills serve the purpose you intend them to. You can only work at the highest level of your team's ability. The numbers used in each drill are variable and can be changed depending if you want the drill to be technique or endurance or a combination of both. Practice is the key. The key to having a more than adequate defense is blocking. If your blockers do a good job, then you have the makings of a strong defense.

D The Spike

This is perhaps the most satisfying play in volleyball from the player's standpoint. The feeling of just having hit a hard spike cannot compare with any other play in volleyball except perhaps a defensive dig.

Basically, the purpose of a spike is to drive the ball into your opponent's court with some force so as to score a point or side-out. The extreme mental concentration and physical prowess can be seen when the skill has been analyzed and broken down into its parts.

A. *Approach*

The approach has its best results in a two foot, two step take-off. This means that two steps are taken prior to take-off with both feet.

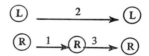

As both feet are used in the take-off, a rocking motion should be attempted with the feet. This is a heel-toe action. As the two steps are taken and as both feet come together, the heels slam into the floor slightly ahead of the toes, causing a braking action which throws the body forward onto its toes. This results in a rocking action of the body —heel to toe. The purpose of the rocking motion is to transfer horizontal momentum into a vertical direction.

Probably the most effective approach is from the 10-foot line with the shoulders parallel to the net and about 1 foot inside the court. This is the straight approach.

The straight approach will allow you to watch the ball and then be able to move forward, backward, or sideways very effectively.

Another approach is the diagonal approach, again starting from 10 feet back but this time the approach is from out of court into the court. This type of approach allows for a much better angle hit but is difficult for balls that are to be hit down the line or set out in the extreme corner.

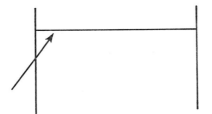

These two approaches are basic. Later more involved footwork can be learned, but it is best to start with the above.

B. *Take-Off*

The take-off should be aided by the motion of the arms being swung back at the point of take-off. The legs should be bent at approximately 90° before jumping.

BEFORE TAKEOFF   AFTER TAKEOFF
(arms swing back)   (arms swing forward)

As the spiker springs up, the hands are thrown upward to aid the body in attaining additional height. The jump should be straight up and down with *no* horizontal motion. All the motion is needed to attain a higher vertical jump. As the hands and arms swing through and up, they should be brought up close to the body so as not to hit the net.

C. *Contact With Ball.*

As the hands swing up and the body rises, attention should be given to: (i) concentration on getting the ball (for a right-handed hitter) on the right shoulder about 1 foot away and in front; (ii) point with the left hand to the ball. This acts as a rifle sight as if you are arming the ball for the right hand to contact with; (iii) bend the arm at the elbow and try to pick a flower out of your ear. Concentrate on keeping the elbow tight in front of the shoulder. As you swing through for power, the elbow will naturally go out; (iv) body—before contact

—ideally a leg hang should be attempted

—after contact

—bent forward at the waist;

(v) as you contact the ball, follow through and swing down with right hand, concentrate on snapping the wrist. The motion is comparable to hitting the ball through a hole and then diving through after it. However, this is done in one motion and causes you to get on top of the ball.

D. *After Contacting Ball.*

The follow-through should bring you down facing the net with the hands out in front, ready to pick up a blocked ball. *Never* reach behind your head or back to play a ball. That is someone else's job.

Drills:

1. Walk through a two-foot heel-toe take-off.
2. Add the hands—thrown back on take-off.
3. Slowly walk through motion, throw hands up and jump slightly.
4. Pick a line on the floor, make your take-off from the line and look to see that you land on the line.
5. Move to net—practice full approach.
6. Get tennis balls—use full approach. Try to throw tennis balls over the net and land close to net. Do not touch the net or go over the line.
7. Stand near wall, about 5 feet away. Practice soft hits so they bounce on floor then to the wall and then back to you. Repeat and try to keep the ball moving. Gradually increase force and distance. A one-walled handball can be played (2 or 4's). Pick out a certain area; ball must be hit with spiking motion.

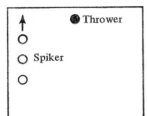

8. Lower nets—at least 1 foot lower than normal. Have one person throwing from center. Throw ball high, 15′ with two hands (underhand throw—concentrate on body), about 2′ away from the net. Four or five people take turns and approach to try and hit the ball lightly.

9. Again with low nets try setting the ball.

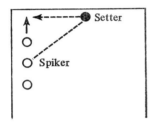

Spiker throws the ball to the setter who sets a high ball into the corner. Spiker hits and retrieves the ball.

10. Gradually raise the net to the proper height once the proper technique is achieved. Remember, technique is all-important.

Once the basic spike is achieved, much more can be begun. The wipe-off, round house, cut, delay, change-up, and tip can be added to the repertoire of the spiker. In the beginning, a basic rule can be followed. "Never hit the same type of spike twice and never in the same spot twice in a row." Again this is just basic. For more details consult books by Val Keller, A. E. Scates, or B. Bratton.

Combination Drills:

As you progress in your practices you will try to add combination drills to your basic drills. Again, your imagination is the answer. For example:
1) interchange types of sets, bumps, etc.
2) add blockers to the spikers. Fifth touch by the blockers means two more blockers come in.
3) Japanese drill—3 men covering whole court

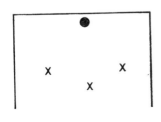

—1 man at net
—3 back men try to get the ball back to the man at the net without making him move
—man at net attempts to make the other 3 men work to get ball back to him. He can do anything.
—change after 1 minute

4) Net drills

Coach spikes ball to first spiker. He tries to bump ball to setter who sets it to the spiker who just bumped the ball. End off with a smash.

Again, your imagination is the key. However, remember to set the drills for a purpose and do not try to do too much at once or be above the playing ability of your team.

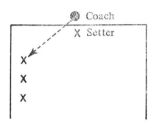

E Defensive Position

Basically defensive positioning can be thought of as follows:

1. Be low to the ground—"knees ahead of toes; hands ahead of knees."
2. Weight on the inside part of large toe and body weight forward. The feet should be a little wider than shoulder width, with one foot ahead of the other.
3. Never be standing still.
4. Watch spiker and his motion—try to anticipate. Is he off balance when he is hitting, will a long ball result—he has just hit 3 in a row, perhaps a tip? etc.
5. Hands should be close together ready to clasp together to dig up the ball.
6. Do your job thoroughly, do not try to do your partner's job. Remember, it's a team game you're playing, if everyone does the job then everything will turn out all right. It is never "a good play by the other side" but a "bad defensive play."
7. A good defense will win more games than a good offense. All teams concentrate on offensive power. Perhaps because it is the spectacular. But all you have to do is return one of the so-called spectacular hits to gain the psychological advantage.

There are two basic defensive patterns:

1. Middle Man Up
   Responsibilities:
   X_1—set block and turn the spike into court (turn right hand in)
   X_2—form the wall, hands are straight protecting the middle area
   X_3—covers angle spikes and wipeoffs the block towards his area

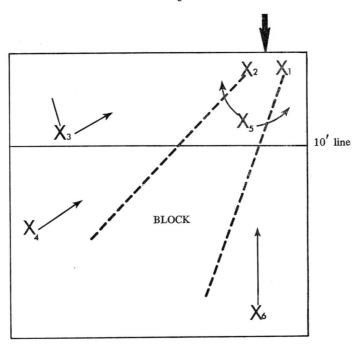

X₄—direct spikes that come around block and ball coming partially off the block

X₅—covers for short attacks (tips) left and right

X₆—line spikes and balls towards his area that come off spikes

Strength: covers short behind blocker

Weakness: only two men to cover back court—leaves deep middle and deep corners open

2. Middle Man Back

$\left.\begin{matrix} X_1 \\ X_2 \end{matrix}\right\rangle$ same as before

X₃ — angle spikes and short tips to left and block and middle

X₄ — drives and partially touched balls

X₅ — covers balls to deep middle never leaving the base line by more than 3 feet

X₆ — line concentration and tips ahead and left

Strength: covers deep middle and line—3 men in back court

Weakness: leaves middle area open—have to depend on X₃ and X₆ to cover

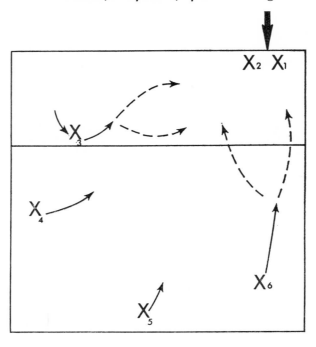

F Service Reception

Basically, the two basic defenses lead to the two basic types of serve receptions.

Inverted V (or middle man up)—I have assumed a 4–2 offensive set (4 spikers and 2 setters).

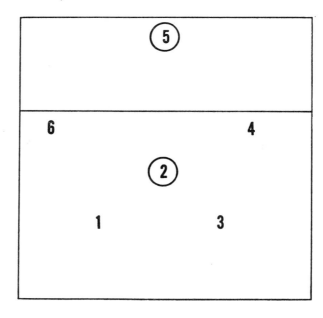

Responsibilities:

1. deep left, behind 6 and deep right behind 2, as well as straight ahead.
2. short middle area, not deep back (1 & 3's responsibility)
3. deep right and behind 2 as well as straight ahead
4. concentrates on attack—lines up with server and deep corner of his court—(about 8 to 10′ from side line)
5. setter in offense, never receives first ball
6. concentrates on attack, 1 foot from side line

Strength: covers middle area well
Weakness: leaves deep corners and middle back open
Half-Moon Service Reception (or middle man back)—Again, I have assumed a 4–2 offensive set.

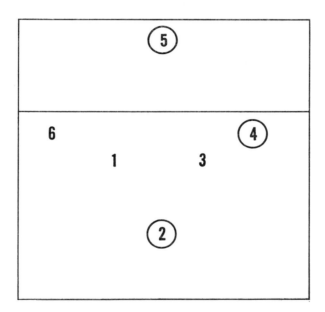

Responsibilities:

1. 6, 5, and 4 have the same responsibilities as before
2. 3, 2, and 1 are now concerned with forward movement

Strength: in back for deep service
Weakness: middle area

As you can see, a basic defense can lead to one of the basic service receptions in a 4–2 offensive set. The type of service reception you will use will depend upon the type of service to be expected. Do not be afraid to change during a game to confuse your opponent. The most important fundamental is: "ALWAYS HAVE AN OPEN LANE BETWEEN YOU AND THE SERVER, NEVER BE BEHIND ANOTHER PLAYER."

G Offense

Again, a basic system is the one already mentioned, the 4–2 set. This gives you maximum offensive power. The purpose of having the spikers on the sidelines is to force the middle defensive man to commit himself. By forcing him to come over to the sidelines to block it may lead to an error being committed. In the 4–2 set you have 4 spikers and 2 setters. To start the game, your most powerful and consistent hitter should start in the left-back or front-left position depending on whether you have the serve or not. The setters should be adjacent to each other. Your second strongest spiker should be on the diagonal from the strongest spiker.

4th Strong Spiker	Setter	2nd Strong Spiker
Strong Spiker	Setter	3rd Strong Spiker

Team should rotate forward one position if they have the serve.

If you do not have the serve, a basic switch has to occur sometimes. This occurs when the setter is in a corner position. The setter should switch to the middle and the spiker to the side line. The rules are simple. When a setter is in a corner position in the front court:

a. the setter should move to the corner net and then after service move to the middle;

b. spikers should always be as far apart as possible.

So when you are in any of these positions when receiving the service: you can follow this plan.

$$\frac{1\ 6\ ⑤}{②3\ 4}\ ;\ \frac{②\ 1\ 6}{3\ 4\ ⑤}\ ;\ \frac{4\ 3\ ②}{⑤\ 6\ 1}\ ;\ \frac{⑤\ 4\ 3}{6\ 1\ ②}$$

Adopt the floor position you are in to the type of service reception you are using, then follow the above rules.

When in the front left or right corner the setter (in this case #2) always moves up to the net and right next to the side-line.

#1 moves as far away from 6 as he is able and still be to the right of 2.

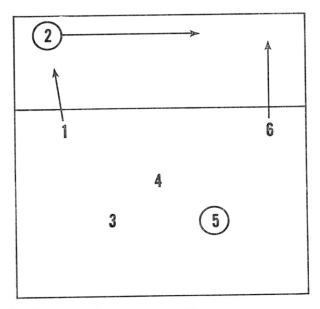

#6 takes his normal service reception.

#3, 4 and 5 are in their normal receiving positions.

When ball is served two slides over to the middle position to set the ball. One, who is already in the attack position, moves into the attack area. Six already is in the attack zone.

You can now see how a basic defense and service reception blends itself into an 4–2 offensive set. Now to give added defensive strength you must add defensive coverage for a ball spiked from your side. What happens if the ball is blocked? What do you do now? A middle man up defense leads perfectly to the coverage.

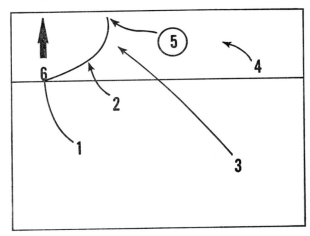

6—attacks to hit the ball

5—after set moves down low to the ground

4—moves in and closer to net

3—moves into space between 5 and 2 about 6′ from spiker

2—moves in directly behind spiker

1—moves in along the side line

What results is a half-moon coverage. You say the back court is not covered? You are right, but we have to take this chance and depend upon the speed of your players to get back in time for any deep ball that is blocked. The main purpose of this coverage is to defend against a ball following back on your side. But, another reason, very important also, is to have your team moving all the time. You can tell a player, "If you're not moving, you are out of position." A player should never be caught standing still, upright or in the same spot. Stress this and half your battles are over. The same type of coverage can be used with a deep middle defense, but involves more movement.

The basic 4–2 offensive set will eventually lead you into a multiple offense. A multiple offense is one where you have three spikers in the front court at all times. You say three spikers but what about our setter? Right, but if he can hit, even slightly, you have a 3-player attack system if you bring a setter from the back court. For additional detail on this, see Val Keller [7] or Scates. [13]

Organizing a Tournament *

The organizing of a tournament is the key to the improvement of volleyball in your area. The more adequately prepared you are in the hosting of your tournament will mean how well the tournament runs and how your work is appreciated. Little recognition is usually the reward for a well-organized tournament but a badly organized tournament will lend itself to much recognition, usually of the wrong type. For Junior High and Senior High School tournaments, the following is important in organizing a tournament. Some of the little hints given will mean the difference between an adequately run tournament and a good tournament.

1. At least one month prior to the tournament, send out entry forms to the teams involved. Make sure you have the sanction of your athletic body. Entry forms should include: space for name of team (women's or men's section), name of coach, manager and players, numbers for players, return mailing address, date of tournament, and time involved, place where it is to be held, entry fee (entry fee is usually to cover cost of referees and awards), and entry deadline (usually about

---

* For a detailed tournament manual write to the Canadian Volleyball Association.

one week prior to the event). Also contact officials who are to umpire and referee at that tournament and other awards.

2. Day of entry deadline
   a. Count the number of teams, both male and female. Decide upon the type of draw (usually round-robin is the best).
      Guideline: (1) Count the number of courts available.
      (2) Look at the time available and allow for at least two 15-point games (two 11-point games can be used if there is not enough time available) against each time during the preliminary round-robin.
      (3) Allow for 2 games to 15 points
         —Junior High—30 minutes
         —Senior High—45 minutes
      (4) If semifinals and finals are needed, they should be involved in the best 2 of 3 series.
      (5) Allow for best 2 of 3 series
         —Junior High—45 minutes
         —Senior High—60 minutes
   b. Make sure you indicate the method of determining the placing for the semifinals and finals and how you will break the ties.
   c. Schedule should include:
      (i) Names of teams competing and their division.
      (ii) Type of tournament—indicate preliminary rounds and final rounds.
      (iii) Method of breaking ties.
      (iv) Team vs. team, court number and time of playing.
      (v) Requirements (ex. bring your own balls, etc., which teams line at certain times, etc.)
   d. Food available, places for eating, map and directions to gymnasium, practice areas, etc.
   e. Emphasis on starting time. Teams should be dressed 30 minutes prior to that time.
   f. Send all this information to the teams and coaches involved so they get it a few days before they play.
3. Before Tournament (1 week or so)
   a. Check equipment, nets, benches needed, what equipment has to be removed, etc.
   b. Get score sheets ready, as well as score cards for players and public to see.
   c. Have spare parts for nets, etc. and have tools handy.
   d. Make sure gymnasium will be opened at least one hour before tournament is scheduled to start.

e. Check into changing rooms for teams, etc.
f. Draw up master tournament sheets to record wins, losses, and placings of the various teams, also one for semifinals and finals.
g. Check for first-aid and injury help.
h. Make direction signs, etc.
i. If you are using your own officials, linesmen, scorer, umpire, and referees, you should have a rule clarification session.

4. Night Before Tournament
   a. Set up equipment—a group of people will greatly reduce the hours to be put in.
   b. Put up signs showing directions to lockers (male and female), gymnasium, food, etc.
   c. Set up chairs and tables for scorers.
   d. If there are guide wires on the floor, make sure they stand out, so players do not run into them.
   e. Mark the courts with their numbers and post up draw.

5. Day of Tournament
   a. Have someone welcoming the teams, give directions, etc.
   b. Have spare schedules ready.
   c. Show officials to change room.
   d. Have a tournament whip (preferably someone who is not involved with coaching or playing) run the tournament. He posts scores, makes decisions, etc.

6. After Tournament
   a. Send letter thanking teams for coming. Include the results of all games and final standings.
   b. Send results to your High School representative for volleyball as well as to the Provincial Volleyball Association involved, press, TV, etc.
   c. Send out a questionnaire asking how the tournament could be improved.

Officiating

In Canada, volleyball officials are governed by the policies set forth by the Canadian Volleyball Association. The National Officials Chairman is the spokesman for the Canadian Volleyball Association. This chairman works in close cooperation with Regional Officials' Chairmen in each region of the Association.

In order to become an official, an individual proceeds as follows:

a. Studies and learns the rules and their interpretation.
b. Game practical experience.
c. Attends an official clinic sponsored by the Regional Association.

d. Submits to written and practical examinations composed by the Regional Officials' Chairman.

If successful, the official is rated as a Provincial Referee. The second level is qualification of an official as a Regional Referee, which includes the following:

a. Being active as a Provincial Referee for one full season.
b. Attending an advanced officials' clinic.
c. Written and practical examination for a Regional Referee's certificate.

The third state of qualification is as a National Referee, which requires:

a. Being active as a Regional Referee for at least one full season.
b. Recommendation of the Regional Officials Chairman for upgrading.
c. Attend a National Clinic or Seminar.
d. Submit to a written and practical examination at a major competition.

The official, if successful, will be rated as a National Referee of the Canadian Volleyball Association. To maintain this status, the official must remain active and submit for reexamination at regular intervals.

The fourth and highest qualification for a referee is the international rating.

Hand Signals

The proper procedure for indicating a signal is:

a. Blow whistle to stop play.
b. Give proper signal for infraction occurred.
c. Hold signal for a few seconds.
d. Indicate clearly point or side-out.
e. Hold the signal for a few seconds.

Point
Raise index finger and arm on the side of the team which scores the point.

Side-out
Stretch out arm horizontally to the side which is to serve

Double Fault
Raise arms from elbow and hold up the thumbs.

Double Hit
Hold up two fingers to the side of the offending player's team, then point to player who made the error.

Four Hits
Hold up four fingers to the side of the offending team.

Lifted Ball
Raise one or both hands with palms upwards, then point to player who made the error.

Hand Over Net
Stretch hand over the net from the side of the offending team and point to the offending player.

Contacting Net
Touch the net and point to the offending player.

Crossing Center or Attack Line
Point to foot on the offending side and point to player.

Out of Position
Move hand back and forth in a sweeping motion on the side of the offending team.

Time-out
Form a 'T' with the hands on the side requesting a time-out.

Substitution
Move hands in circular motion and point to team requesting the substitution.

End of Match
Cross arms at chest.

Held Ball
Raise arms from elbow, hold hands up, palms facing each other, move hands slowly closer together.

Training and Conditioning

Training and conditioning should be related to the length of season you have, the type of schedule you play, and the amount of practice time available. Early in the season, endurance conditioning should be the most important factor while at the end of the season, technique and team execution should occupy most of the practice time. See the Japanese handbook [15] or Scates [13] for a more detailed approach.

Probably the most important aspect that can be improved in volleyball is the player's jump. Without a jump, a player is lost, for in 3 positions the player can be involved in some type of jumping either offensively or defensively. The following criteria should be involved in a training program.

a. "Overload Principle." In order to develop either new muscle strength or endurance, one must either increase the load placed on an exercising muscle or increase the rate and duration of work.

b. "When to Train." There is no easy way to increasing your jump. Researchers have shown that the best results are obtained from a daily schedule. However, a three-times-per-week training schedule will bring about increases at a slow rate.

c. "What is Strength." Some have defined strength as the force that a muscle group can exert against a resistance in one maximal effort. However, others have defined the power of a muscle as the time rate of application of muscle force. In other words, power is not so much brute strength as it is how fast the efforts can be applied. A portion of the weight training schedule should contain power work. Overload in power training is when the desired action can be performed at a minimum 75 percent normal speed or to jump 75 percent of normal vertical jump.

d. "Type of Game." Volleyball is a sport which requires great muscular conditioning but not a great O_2 transportation system. As a result, weight training of high repetitions and increased rate should be included in the program, as well as exercises designed for strength.*

The following is a weight program designed by this author and used with the University of Alberta Golden Bear Volleyball team for the past two years.† Accurate records should be kept of the progress from month to month, especially on the weights.

GOLDEN BEAR VOLLEYBALL TRAINING PROGRAM

The following is a basic workout schedule for jump training. This program will only bring results if it is followed for at least *four months* and is done *consistently*. The player should try to have at least three training sessions spaced out during the week. For example: First week   M.W.F.

Second week   T.Th.S.

etc.

At least one item from A, B, C, D, and E should be attempted at each practice session. As you work up (after a month or so) start to add more items from each category. Category F, the mile run, should only be started near the end of the four-month period (i.e. around July or August). For the

---

* See for more detailed discussion: Conly, G.: Weight lifting—different approach. *The Spiker*, 87:3–4, 1971.

† This program is based on one done by John C. Lowell, U.S. Olympic Manager.

mile run, time yourself at least once a week at the end of your training session. Vary the repetition of the categories.

First day   A B C D E
Second day   A C D E B
Third day   A D E B C
Fourth day   A E B C D
Fifth day   A B C D E
etc.

When doing squats, make sure you have warmed up enough. At first, use only a ½ squat, eventually try to increase it. However, do not attempt full squats if your knees are bothering you.

Categories C, E, and F can be done alone if you are not able to get weights. The best place to work out would be at the University. Keep a constant record of your weights and repetitions.

A. *Warm-up*
   1. —do some running (slow—2 minutes)
      —various exercises to loosen muscles
      —do some jumps (10) gradually increasing the height
      —pick a light weight (40–50% of your body weight) and do various lifts with it
   2. —play a game of basketball, squash, handball, etc.; however, still pick a light weight and do various lifts with it
   3. —warm up as previous (1) but take light weight (50% of your body weight) and do 50 squats (start at ¼ squat and eventually work your way down to a full squat); this is only a warm-up

B. *Power*
   1. —full squats with heavy weight on shoulders
      —3 sets of 10 repetitions
      —start at body weight and increase; 350 to 400 lbs are not unusual
      —try to work with a partner for safety
   2. —jump with weight on shoulders (use a towel for padding)
      —use no more than 50 percent of body weight (start with 25%)
      —do two sets of 15 repetitions
      —increase weights as you become stronger and eventually increase the repetitions
   3. —use same weights as 1 but put toes on a 2″ board—raise toes and then lower gradually
      —three sets of 10 repetitions

C. *Skill*
   1. Standing jump for distance—10 times for maximum distance 2-foot take-off.

2. Jump daily 50 to 100 times—in sets of 10 jumps, 30 second rest

—concentrate on jumping from a near full squat position

—alternate each week—use a two-foot approach and take off one week, then a standing jump the next.

D. *Universal Weight Machine*

Leg Push

—start out with a weight near 1½ times your own

—10 × 3 repetitions on lower pedal

—5 × 3 repetitions on higher pedal

—gradually increase the weights

E. *Endurance*

1. Interval Jumping

—jump two minutes, rest one, repeat 3 to 5 times

—increase jumping time as your stamina increases

—alternate the types of jumps used each week

2. Use Stadium Steps

—two foot-jumps up the steps to the top and then back to the bottom (concentrate on squat for each jump)

—repeat but with hands tucked to the chest

—then left foot—to top and back

—then right foot—to top and back

—repeat the whole sequence at least three times before resting

—do about three repetitions and gradually increase

F. *Mile Run*

—in late July, August, or September

Upper Body

Isometrics

1. Elbow Extension

—stand in doorway

—place palms on both sides at shoulder level

—6 seconds—repeat 8 to 10 times

2. Shoulder-Arm Adduction

—stand in doorway

—hands at side

—press, back of hand against door

—try to raise up

—6 seconds—repeat 8 to 10 times

3. Chest

—stand in doorway facing side of wall

—place one hand on each side of wall
—try to squeeze hands together
—6 seconds—repeat 8 to 10 times

Weight Training

1. Bent arm pull-over
   —lie on floor
   —bring weight over head to face—use elbows only
   —light weight—three reps of 10 times
2. Straight arm pull-over
   —same as above
3. Bent-arm rowing—Outward grasp
   —feet apart, back bent to 90°
   —bend over grasp bar, at widest angle, bring up to chest
   —medium weight—three reps of 10 times
4. Bent-arm rowing—Inward grasp
   —same as above except hands together in middle
   —three reps of 10 times
5. Curls
   —stand upright, weight on hands, curl the weight up to the chest, keeping back straight
   —light to medium weight—three reps of 10 times
6. Tie a 5 foot piece of strong string to a 10 lb weight. At the other end, tie to a small board (piece of hockey stick 18" long), stick the arms out in front at eye level (straight at elbows), roll the string up and then roll it down—do not let it fall, control it all the way—repeat five times.
7. If there are pullies on the wall, use light weight and repeat many times. Try spiking with a diving action—try sitting and standing.

CONCLUSION

What I have shown was only a very elementary start towards volleyball. Much can yet be learned. Probably the best way to learn more about volleyball is to contact the Canadian Volleyball Association (333 River Road, Vanier City, Ottawa KIL 8B9) for information on possible clinics to be held in your area. These clinics are usually held during the months of September to March.

Presently, Canadian Volleyball Association has an appointed Provincial Coaching examining board for each region in Canada. They will be responsible for certifying the first three levels of volleyball coaching, namely club, regional, and provincial. The National and International ratings will be examined by the National Technical Committee which is a board set up by the Canadian Volleyball Association. The successful applicant will obtain a coaching passport which must be renewed every three years. In addition, a complete coaching resume of the individual will be kept in Ottawa.

REFERENCES

There are two main volleyball periodicals available:

The Spiker—the official news bulletin of the Canadian Volleyball Association (cost $3.00/year).

Mailing Address: 333 River Road, Vanier City, Ottawa

International Volleyball Review—volleyball around the world (cost $2.50/year).

Mailing Address: Editor, H. E. Wilson

                      Box 554

                      Encino, California

                      91316, U.S.A.

1. Bratton, R. D.: *Power Volleyball for Player, Teacher and Coach.* Scarborough, Canadian Volleyball Association, 1968.
2. Cherebetiu, G.: *Volleyball Techniques.* Hollywood, Creative Sports Books, 1969.
3. Cohen, H.: *Power Volleyball Drills.* Hollywood, Creative Sports Books, 1967.
4. Egstrom, G. H. and Schaafsma, F.: *Volleyball.* Dubuque, W. C. Brown Co., 1966.
5. Emery, C. R.: *Modern Volleyball.* New York, The Macmillan Co., 1958.
6. Heck, A. and Schaafsma, F.: *Volleyball: For Coaches and Teachers.* Dubuque, W. C. Brown Co., 1971.
7. Keller, V.: *Point, Game and Match.* Hollywood, Creative Sports Books, 1968.
8. McGowan, C. M. (Ed.): *It's Power Volleyball.* Los Angeles, United States Volleyball Association, 1968.
9. Odeneal, W. T. and Wilson, H. E.: *Beginning Volleyball.* Belmont, Wadsworth Publishing Company, Inc., 1962.
10. Peck, W.: *Volleyball.* London, Collier-Macmillan Ltd., 1970.
11. Prsala, J.: *Fundamental Volleyball Contacts.* Scarborough, Canadian Volleyball Association, 1971.
12. Scates, A. E. and Ward, J.: *Volleyball.* Boston, Allyn and Bacon, Inc., 1969.
13. Scates, A. E.: *Winning Volleyball.* Boston, Allyn and Bacon, Inc., 1972.
14. Thigpen, J.: *Power Volleyball for Girls and Women.* Dubuque, W. C. Brown Company, 1967.
15. Toyoda, H.: *Training Theory for Volleyball in Japan.* Scarborough, Canadian Volleyball Association Publication, 1971.
16. Welch, J.: *How to Play and Teach Volleyball.* New York, Association Press, 1962.

Additional Readings

Enoka, R. M.: The effect of different lengths of run-up on the height to which a spiker in volleyball can reach. *N Z J Health Phys Educ Recreation,* 4(3):5–15, 1971.

McCloy, C. H.: How fast does the volleyball travel. *Int Volleyball Rev,* 8:26:14, 1948.
  —a mean velocity of 91 feet/second (62 mph) and a maximum velocity of 162 feet/second (110 mph)

Mohr, D. R. and Haverstick, M. J.: Relationship between height, jumping ability, and agility to volleyball skill. *Res Q, 27*(1):74–78, 1956.

—a significant relationship was found to exist between jumping and volleying, between agility and volleying, and between height and volleying at a three-foot distance.

Lamp, N. A.: Volleyball skills of junior high school students as a function of physical size and maturity. *Res Q, 25*:189–200, 1954.

—positive correlations were found between volleyball playing ability (of boys and girls) and the factors age, height, weight, and strength. Also a decided relationship between pubescent status and volleyball performance for both boys and girls. Pubescents and post-pubescents made higher scores at each age level than did pre-pubescents.

Nelson, R. C.: Follow-up investigation of the velocity of the volleyball spike. *Res Q, 35*(1):80–84, 1964.

—Nelson used 8 spikers from the best teams in the U.S. Standard cinematographic procedures were used to determine the velocity of the spiked ball. The maximum velocity observed was 99.3 feet/second (67.7 mph) and the highest mean was 91.2 feet/second (62.2 mph).

Shick, J.: Effects of mental practice on selected volleyball skills for college women. *Res Q, 41*(1):88–94, 1970.

—conclusion was that there was no significant results for volleying skill but two studies yielded significant results for serving skill.

Singer, R. N.: A sequential skill learning and retention effects in volleyball. *Res Q, 39*(1):185, 1968.

—four physical education volleyball classes were taught four distinct volleyball skills in varied sequential order (serve, dig, set-up, and spike). He concluded that the order in which volleyball skills are taught had little bearing on their learning or retention.

Other research includes:

Brady, G. F.: Preliminary investigations of volleyball playing ability. *Res Q, 16*(1):14–17, 1945.

Butler, W. M.: Comparison of two methods of measuring the degree of skill in the underarm volleyball serve. *Res Q, 32*(2):261–262, 1961.

Chrastek, J.: Damage to the locomotor system in championship volleyball. *Acta Chir Orthop Traumatol Cech, 35*:76–85, 1968.

Clifton, M. A.: Single hit volley test for women's volleyball. *Res Q, 33*(2):208–211, 1962.

Cunningham, P. and Garrison, J.: High wall volley test for women's volleyball. *Res Q, 39*(3):486–490, 1968.

Franks, B. D. and Moore, G. C.: Effects of calesthenics and volleyball on the A.A.H.P.E.R. fitness test and volleyball skill. *Res Q, 40*(2):288–292, 1970.

Fulton, R. E.: Relationship between teammate status and measures of skill in volleyball. *Res Q, 21*:274–276, 1950.

Kronquist, R. A. and Brumbach, W. B.: A modification of the Brady Volleyball Skill Test for high school boys. *Res Q, 39*(1):116–120, 1966.

Liba, M. R. and Stauff, M. R.: A test for the volleyball pass. *Res Q, 34*(1):560–563, 1963.

Nelson, D. O.: Studies of transfer of learning in gross motor skills. *Res Q, 28*(4):364–373, 1957.

CHAPTER XIX

COMPETITIVE SWIMMING

ROBERT EYNON and JAMES THODEN

FAULKNER, Cureton,[16,17,31-33] Carlisle, Karpovich,[44-46,8] and Counsilman[11] have all made very significant contributions to the study of competitive performance in the water. Faulkner's[31] detailed presentation outlines the physical, physiological and psychological data pertinent to competitive swimming. A vast majority of the material pertains to descriptive data on competitive swimmers, the effect of water immersion on selected physiological variables, kinesiological research in aquatics, and the effect of swimming training on fitness and performance variables. Counsilman's[11] outstanding contribution is an exception in that he does present both stroke mechanic analyses and training techniques which have been derived from an empirical base. This chapter will attempt the collation of information from these and other coaching and researching authors as well as from our personal research and experience. It is hoped that the result will provide an informative and practical base from which the novice and experienced coach alike can expand the benefits of their existing programs.

As stated by Faulkner,[31] successful competitive swimming depends upon the interaction of a number of factors. These include: a highly motivated, well-trained, skilled athlete; a good program providing adequate facilities, coaching and competition; and societal and parental support. It might also be added that there is an undeniable advantage in having the opportunity to choose one's parents for their optimum physical, physiological and psychological characteristics. It is in the recognition of the impossibility of the last requirement that the others become so important. While coaches maintain a constant vigil for that "ideal" swimmer, it must be accepted that the chances of ever finding such an individual are very minimal. Therefore, the satisfying experience of fielding a successful team each year must be provided for by getting the most out of every available athlete and in performing such modifications in swimming style and the selection of event as will give the best results. This is the art of coaching and the technique of training.

The focus of this chapter will be on the presentation of training techniques for competitive swimming. Areas to be discussed include cardio-

269

respiratory, strength and flexibility training, and warm-up. Since successful utilization of aerobic and anaerobic energy resources depend upon the ability to swim an optimum pace, this will be discussed in conjunction with cardiorespiratory training. Moreover, since the ultimate success of any competitive training program depends to a large degree upon the development and implementation of a multiseasonal training plan, concepts relative to this area will be presented. It should also be recognized that the motivational level of the athlete and the incentives provided have a large bearing upon the success of both athlete and coach. This area and that of nutrition will not be discussed in any detail as both topics would appear to require the more extensive treatment offered by other chapters in this book.

Relatively little research pertinent to either the immediate or chronic effects of selected training programs for swimming has been published. Consequently, principles drawn from the scientific training literature of other sports will be applied to competitive swimming. Track coaches such as Wilt [67] are an obvious source for this type of information. However, it should be noted that swimmers train in a medium which, in addition to requiring less energy expenditure for body support and more energy to overcome the resistance to forward movement, is also more favorable to heat loss. Thus, considerations of temperature control and performance techniques demand a certain degree of modification when applying information from other activity areas. Nevertheless, extensive use can be made of semirelated training-oriented research and this will be taken advantage of here. In addition, an attempt will be made to indicate the present practices of successful swimming coaches.

CARDIORESPIRATORY TRAINING

Energy Sources

As for all activities from getting up in the morning to running a 3:50 sec plus mile, swimming is simply a controlled release of energy which has been derived from our solar system, captured by vegetation and ingested by the performer in one form or another. It is the choice of musculature which will release the energy, the sequence in which the musculature is used, and the rate at which the energy is released as well as the unique environment and body position which make competitive swimming different from other activities. Thus, the trained swimmer must possess adequacy in the amount of energy that his muscle can release (or its strength); in controlling the sequence of muscular contractions (or skill); and in the rate at which the muscle can be provided with its energy source. It is this latter characteristic toward which a large portion of most training programs is directed and to which the following discussion applies.

A certain amount of energy is stored in the muscle in a form called adenosine triphosphate or ATP and creatine phosphate or CP which is instantly compatible with the requirements of contraction. The amount of energy which is available from this source is approximately equivalent to seven or eight seconds of contraction at the maximum possible rate. Therefore, while this energy is available to provide for an instantaneous change in activity levels (such as making the transition from the starting position to swimming the first length), it will be necessary to continually supplement it in order to continue performance. The supplementation is accomplished by one or both of two methods which are popularly known as aerobic and anaerobic metabolism.

The term "aerobic metabolism" is used to describe the process by which energy is released when oxygen, supplied by the cardiorespiratory system, is consumed in oxidizing carbohydrate and fat stores. The entire process is multidimensional with a dependency on the integrity of the respiratory system, the cardiovascular system and blood tissue, the muscle mass involved, the entire process of intermediary metabolism, and the central nervous and endocrine control systems. While these systems, collectively referred to as the oxygen transport system, can supplement the ATP and CP form of energy for an almost indefinite period of time, the maximum amount per unit of time or rate of energy release that they can provide is only about 25 percent of the rate at which ATP and CP can be used. This fact is especially significant when one calculates the forces required in swimming (from Karpovich's [44] formula $f = kv^2$ where: f is force in kg; k is a constant of 3.17 for the average size male swimmer in the prone position; and v is velocity in m/sec). For example, forces are 7.13 kg/m in swimming at 1.50 m/sec (or a 16:39.0 sec 1500 m event, 11.35 kg/m in swimming at 1.89 m/sec (or a 53.0 sec 100 m event) and 14.95 kg/m in swimming at 2.17 m/sec (or an 11.5 sec. 25 m event). This means that there is a slightly more than 100 percent increase in the force requirement from the 1500-metre speed to the 25-metre speed.

Moreover, the resistive characteristic of water changes with the velocity of force application to affect swimming efficiency and the net result is that a good 25 metre speed requires about 400 percent that rate of energy expenditure as used for a good 1500 metre. Therefore, a swimmer can take advantage of the fast rate of energy release from the 7 to 8 second supply of ATP and CP in producing a high speed over 25 metres. But he must cut the rate of energy release to one-quarter by reducing his speed to the 1500-metre level if he expects to maintain his performance for a 16 to 17 minute period.

It might logically be hoped by the coach that the total amount and rate of supply of energy from both ATP-CP and aerobic sources could be changed with training. The degree of potential increase in ATP and CP stores is still somewhat open to question. But it is probably safe to say that, at least under presently known approaches to training, changes will be minimal if they appear at all. However, the rate of energy release is partially a function of muscle mass and strength and it is well known that training will produce greater strength and allow a man to move the same weight at a faster velocity. It is also well known that significant changes can be produced in one's aerobic capacity. This occurs partially through increases in the heart muscle capacity, in the number of vessels supplying muscle, in the oxygen transport mechanism of cells, and although less well known, perhaps also in the biochemical mechanisms of the muscle cell.

However, the preceding discussion does not explain the performance of the swimmer who can maintain speeds ranging from 1.89 m/sec for a 53.0 sec 100 m down to 1.55 m/sec for an 8:35.0 800 m. The 100-metre speed requires about 60 percent more force and a rate of energy expenditure greater than the 1500-metre speed. Allowing for the energy derived from aerobic and ATP-CP sources, the 100-metre swimmer must depend on some other mechanism which will supply energy at about twice the rate of the aerobic system. This source is known as anaerobic metabolism and is, along with the ATP and CP, responsible for oxygen debt.

Anaerobic metabolism is most simply explained as a mechanism in which the body uses a material which substitutes for oxygen in the process leading up to aerobic metabolism. The result is the anaerobic or "without oxygen" release of a certain amount of energy and, although inefficient, the rate of release is about twice that of the aerobic system. The major shortcoming of anaerobic metabolism is that the body cannot get rid of the leftovers or meabolites by the same processes as are used for the carbon dioxide and water products of aerobic metabolism. Instead, the irritating metabolites of anaerobic metabolism (lactic acid) are, for the most part, retained until oxygen is used to break them down in the manner of aerobic metabolism. Thus, in creating these metabolites and in using up the available ATP and CP supply, the body becomes a debtor for oxygen, some of which it may pay back during exercise if the intensity of work is low enough but most of which it will save until the exercise is terminated.

Theoretically, the body might continue to produce energy in this way until it has exhausted the carbohydrate fuel source which anaerobic metabolism uses exclusively. However, the resulting metabolites, in addition to providing a beneficial stimulus for increasing aerobic metabolism, also lead to significant changes in the bodies internal environment; changes which will eventually lead to exercise termination by the Central Nervous System far in advance of exhausting fuel supplies. The point of environmental change at which termination occurs is largely a function of the individual's attitude toward the pain of effort and this leads to a variation of from 40 sec to 60 sec among swimmers in the total time duration of maximum anaerobic performance.

As with the ATP-CP and aerobic mechanisms, the coach would hope to change anaerobic capacity with training. This might be done in one or both of two ways: by increasing tolerance to exercise stress and by improving the biochemical processes involved. It is probably the former which, in combination with overcoming the slight anemia and tearing of connective tissue to result in muscle soreness that accompany the start of training, is solely responsible for the large improvements in the early season. When Counsilman [12] is heard to refer to the necessity of shoving swimmers through the stages of "hurt, pain, and agony" in training, he is probably referring to the process of increasing pain tolerances as well as to providing the greatest stimulus for cardiovascular improvement. As for the improvement of the biochemistry of anaerobic systems, there are some data which identify training benefits but the picture is not as yet clear. Suffice it to say that a concentration of training on the anaerobic mechanism as a whole will realize striking improvements.

To recapitulate, a swimmer can reach and maintain great speed for up to 25 metres but no further as he will simply run out of the high rate energy supply. He is able to cover up to 100 metres at a reduced speed but will then reach his limits of withstanding exercise stress. The 1500-meter distance can be covered only when speed is reduced to levels compatible with the aerobic system. Moreover, at least the aerobic and anaerobic mechanisms can both be significantly improved.

In practice, the swimmer learns to derive his energy proportionately from each of the three sources. Consequently, the speed for each distance between 100 metres and 1500 metres is steadily decreased so as to deplete the oxygen debt related sources at a reduced rate which will theoretically leave them exhausted at the finish line. Each event then will depend on the total energy from all sources but has a specific dependency on a single source. An approximation of these dependencies is presented in Table XIX–I for the time spans encountered in competitive swimming.

It might also be mentioned that, although not well documented at this time, it is currently being suggested that the maximum benefits of training are produced by well-controlled programs during the growing or pre-pubertal and pubertal years. It is well to note a caution, however, that the lack of evidence on this point makes it impossible to identify the intensity of stimulus or training required to produce such increased benefits and the actual amount of change that can be realized. Moreover, it is not known whether too great an intensity will retard development or even be injurious. All that can be said is that a strong intensity of training will be

necessary for improvement but the coach must be well aware of the significance of indicators such as weight loss, irritability or an extremely slow
rate of physical maturation in his swimmers.

The preceding implies specific training programs for competitive swimmers preparing for specific events. Specificity in training for swimming has
been either suggested or alluded to by Huesner,[38] Counsilman,[11] and
Daland.[18] However, a vast majority of swimming coaches, including some
very successful ones, appear to disregard this concept and it is hard to
argue with success, especially when it is known that aerobic endurance
does play a role in sprinting and anaerobic capacity in long events. In

TABLE XIX–I

AEROBIC AND ANAEROBIC ENERGY
SOURCES FOR DIFFERENT SWIMMING
EVENTS *

Distance (yd or m)	Approximate Duration	% Energy Source	
		Aerobic	Anaerobic
50	25 sec	12	88
100	01 min	25	75
200	2–2.5 min	40	60
400	4–5.0 min	50	50
1500	16–18 min	85	15

* Applicable portions taken from Mathews and
Fox.[49]

addition, the problem of deciding upon specificity in training is com-
pounded by competitors performing in more than one event.

Some justification for maintaining a balance between the training of
anaerobic and aerobic systems can be found in the interaction of the two
during exercise. In essence, anaerobic metabolism can be considered a
"second choice" source of energy. The body would prefer to maintain the
status quo of its internal environment by providing energy aerobically and
thus avoiding the disruptive effects of anaerobic metabolites. Unfortunately,
the aerobic system is a relatively slow starter and needs time to adjust to
increased levels of exercise; up to five or ten minutes depending on the
levels of exercise intensity. Consequently, in exercise that the aerobic system can handle entirely, ATP and CP provide the energy to get exercise
started and the rapidly accommodating anaerobic pathways keep things
going until the aerobic system can catch up. In fact, it is the anaerobic
metabolites which provide part of the stimulus to increase aerobic function
and it seems that the aerobic mechanism will never reach its maximum
levels of performance unless there are anaerobic metabolites present or, at
the very least, anaerobic type activities being performed.

It is well known that the body systems will not improve unless overloaded. Further maximum improvement will not result unless near maximum overload is applied. It follows then that the aerobic system needs

anaerobic activities in training to attain maximum improvement. The trick is to do this without suffering the long recovery periods that accompany continuing anaerobic performance. This will be explained in the section on interval training but for now, suffice it to say that carrying the specificity of aerobic training too far will actually suppress its improvement. However, the available data support the position that much more efficient training programs could be developed if the concept of specificity were more closely adhered to than at present. This topic is a logical choice for applied research programs designed to show how much concentration should be applied to specificity in order to gain maximum benefits.

Aerobic Training

Previously reported energy source data (oxygen uptakes of 55 ml/kg/min for highly trained college swimmers reported by Magel and Faulkner [48] and similar oxygen uptakes presented by Cunningham and Eynon [14] for a sample of provincial age-group finalists) indicate that relatively high aerobic capacity is required for success in swimming. But these and unreported values of 60 to 70 ml/kg measured in the author's laboratories on Dominion calibre swimmers are below those reported on distance runners, speed skaters and cross-country skiers.

Data reported by Astrand and Rodahl [3] and Faulkner [32,33] show that relatively little increase in aerobic capacity occurs in mature, trained, endurance athletes who continue to train for four to eight years. The obvious implications are: that the subjects had reached their maximal capacity prior to the initial measurements; that their training programs were not correct or severe enough; or that, if current suggestions prove correct, the subjects were beyond the age of attaining maximal improvements. Examination of their training programs and their continued improvement would appear to make the first observation more logical. This probably does not hold true for younger, less experienced competitors. However, these data, coupled with that reported in typical and relatively long training studies such as that by Robinson and Harmon [56] which showed oxygen uptake increases of less than 20 percent, indicate the extreme importance of both natural capacity and the coach's selection techniques.

Another explanation can be pointed out for the lower capacities and slower improvement rates of mature or maturing competitive swimmers. As has been pointed out by Faulkner [32,33] and Astrand and Rodahl,[3] swimmers do not usually reach the same levels of aerobic performance in the water as they do on land. It must be concluded then that the smaller upper body muscle mass used in swimming as compared to that used in running, the weight supported condition of swimming, the restricted breathing habit of swimmers due to style and water pressures resisting thoracic expansion and exhalation, and the more yielding characteristic of water in resisting force all combine to reduce the intensity of swimming as a training stimulus. This does not mean to deemphasize the recognition of the stress that a swimmer experiences but merely suggests that a less maximal stimulus is placed on the aerobic mechanism in swimming training. Experiments on supplementing swimming programs with heavier types of exercise in much the same way as weights are used to increase strength are currently under way in our laboratories.

The development of training programs designed to overload the aerobic capacity involves the subtle manipulation of a number of variables including continuous versus intermittent work, intensity and frequency of work, length of work period, and length of rest period. These will be discussed briefly and example programs will be outlined in Table XIX–III.

Continuous Versus Intermittent Work

The vast majority of swimming training since the early 1950's has been based on some form of intermittent work. The rationale for this approach is based on the necessity of providing high intensity loads which require anaerobic metabolism in order to maximally stimulate maximum improvement of the aerobic mechanism as well as performance speed and stress tolerance. The intermittent approach allows for this without carrying the swimmer into anaerobic exhaustion or high levels of oxygen debt. The extreme and most effective application is one which uses maximum speed for eight to ten seconds followed by an equivalent rest period and may be effectively used in the 25 metre pool. The swimmer is thus able to repeat the high speed performance more often for a greater total number of yards in a training session than if he had worked continuously. Consequently, a greater stimulus is provided for functional improvement and the requirement of specificity is satisfied both with regard to swimming skill and aerobic improvement.

Comparisons of continuous and interval training by Stuart,[63] Turkington,[65] Mellerowicz *et al.*[51] and Roskamm[57] did not indicate that interval training is a more effective training method when the total work done using the two methods was kept constant. It is, however, necessary to remain cognizant of the fact, that interval training, as demonstrated by Christensen *et al.*,[13] is basically an aerobic training system and, in allowing more total work at higher intensities, results in a greater training stimulus, greater physiological adaptation, and improved performance.

Amount and Frequency of Work

The amount and frequency of work necessary for success in competitive swimming is as yet unknown. Although Montrella[52] reported success with as few as 6,000 yd per day, the general practice in competitive swimming is to use much greater yardage. Counsilman [12] has recently stated that swimmers, training less than 12,000 yd per day in the summer are recreational, not competitive swimmers. This too is a fertile area for practical research on the benefits of making programs more efficient with the proper use of specificity in stimulating energy systems and skill improvement.

Table XIX–II outlines some typical training programs of competitive swimmers. Counsilman [12] has reported an attempt to train for aerobic endurance through relatively low intensity work. But an examination of his presentation [11] of typical workouts for a number of extremely successful swimmers who were working under a variety of coaches indicates that most training is carried out at an intensity of 80 to 90 percent based upon best competitive and training performances. It is immediately apparent that these regimes are well beyond those found in typical training experiments such as those of Shephard,[60] Jackson et al.,[40] Sidney et al.[61] and Hill

TABLE XIX–II

TRAINING PROGRAMS OF SELECTED
GROUPS OF SWIMMERS

Group	Selected Reference	Freq/Week	Yd/Day 1000	Intensity %
International	Counsilman (1968) Daland (1971)	12–14	12–18	80–90
Canadian	Eynon (1971)	06–12	04–08	80–90
College Ontario Age-Group	Eynon (1971)	05–12	1.5–08	70–80

et al.[36] These authors all report significant improvement with frequencies of two to five sessions per week, durations of 15 minutes per session, work intensities eliciting heart rates of only 135 beats per minute and programs six weeks in length. The initial capacities of subjects for these studies were obviously below those of the competitive swimmer and a comparison is impossible! One can only surmise that the possibility of an aerobic training effect in younger swimmers is high, while with older swimmers, in view of the data presented by Faulkner [32,33] and Astrand and Rodahl,[3] the mechanism for improvement is other than aerobic.

Duration of Work Period

I. Astrand *et al.*[2] and Magel and Faulkner [48] have reported increases in maximum oxygen uptakes with work periods ranging from three minutes to approximately 30 seconds. In the former study rest periods were equal to work periods and in the latter rest periods were approximately one half of the work periods and, in both programs, the work rates were often very intense. The training of aerobic capacity can thus apparently be done with a relatively wide range of work durations. However, Roskamm's [57] training data indicated that relatively longer work periods resulted in a greater improvement of maximum performance than did shorter work periods. This would appear to mean that a more efficient use of time is accomplished with relatively longer work periods, providing the athlete trains at a sufficiently high intensity. As such an approach promotes higher oxygen debt, one is tempted to conclude that the results relatively greater improvement in anaerobic capacities and an accompanying higher metabolite stimulus on aerobic performance.

Intensity

Typical intensity studies, such as those of Karvonen *et al.*,[43] Bouchard *et al.*,[5] Shephard [59] and Horvath,[37] all reported training effects from moderate work loads eliciting heart rates in the range of 130 to 160 beats per minute. Sharkey and Holleman [58] showed greater training effects with heart rates of 180 beats per minute. Shephard [60] supported this result when he demonstrated that intensity was the most crucial variable in his training regime as did Karlsson *et al.*[42] when they showed that a work load of 80 to 90 percent of maximum work overloaded the oxygen uptake mechanisms. Swimming coaches have based training programs upon this concept for some time i.e. training time = best time − 10%. Data such as that of Faulkner and Stager,[30] Eynon *et al.*[29] and Stockholm[62] indicate that many typical training drills achieve heart rates of 170 to 180 beats per minute and apparently are capable of overloading the aerobic mechanisms.

Rest Period

Relatively little has been published relative to the length of the rest period but Yakolev *et al.*,[68] in using very short training distances, demonstrated that short rest periods caused a greater training effect. As work intensity and duration increase, the rest period will necessarily increase but there is no evidence to indicate how much of an increase is optimum.

Rest periods may be determined by allowing the swimmer's pulse rate to return to a predetermined level, by using a standard rest period, or by employing a start interval in which rest time is a function of work time. The latter is most common in competitive swimming, especially where training sessions involve many swimmers in the pool at the same time. Counsilman [11] outlines drills commonly used in which swimmers perform with work to rest ratios of four or five to one as standard rest times arrived at through a consideration of the individual's performance and current condition. This is probably the best approach if one has the pool space and timing devices which can be seen by all swimmers. It does, however, require a close monitoring of day-to-day and week-to-week performance through the use of swimming times and the preferable addition of physiological indices such as post-exercise heart rate.

Monitoring Progress

Whether the program is directed toward the specific improvement of aerobic mechanisms as described above or of anaerobic mechanisms as described in the following section, the most efficient use of time will be ensured only through a constant monitoring of the swimmers' progress. The most obvious approach to use in this task is the recording of performance times. However, the simple use of a weekly "time-trial" or the restricted use of only time data is entirely too gross and far outmoded by modern techniques. The following discussion may, on first reading, seem to introduce a great deal of work into the program and, in fact, this is true. But, when weighed against the loss of coaching and performer man-hours and the possible loss of disgruntled swimmers, it is really a small price to pay.

To begin with, the performance time, either in practice or in competition, is probably the most important information available. Counsilman, Carlisle and others all base their training sessions on distance times that are chosen to illicit a particular degree of fatigue or to be compatible with a particular pace. If they are so basic to the program, then they are worth recording, not only from day to day but from repeat to repeat. A great deal of information can be gained from repeat times which are plotted side by side and, if it is the swimmer himself who is doing the plotting, his own interest can be heightened. Even his willing acceptance of this task will give the coach some information and the swimmer who feels himself above remembering and recording such data in his own "day" book probably deserves a second evaluation with regard to his value to the team.

The really tangible information from recorded times is interpreted in light of the program specificity. If aerobic continuous or interval training is being used and the lap times go steadily slower throughout the training session, then the intensity may be too high or, in the case of interval work, the rest period may be too short. The intensity and rest times can be adjusted gradually until the pace can just be maintained or drops off only slightly and this keeps the training stimulus just at the optimum level. Monitoring the postexerecise heart rate to keep it between 165 to 180 beats per minute will assist the proper selection of performance and rest times. Comparison of these records from day to day provides a good basis for assessing the progress of training and the recovery between training sessions. This information is added to by similarly recording the heart rate just before rising in the morning, just after the training warm-up, and just following the training session. If taken at the same relative time each day, there should be a good constancy over long periods and perhaps a drop in the morning rate. A rise over time, perhaps accompanied by weight loss, might indicate over-training, detraining, poor nutritional habits, the onset of disease or, at the very least, some emotional problem. A similar recording of body weight should show a relative constancy or appropriate change if weight loss or gain is desirable and planned for. Undesirable changes might indicate the necessity of a short rest from training or, at the very least, some diversionary program. If a rest period is begun, a continued monitoring of pulse rates and weight help to determine when training should be resumed by reestablishing themselves to former patterns.

Should a record of performance times and pulse rates be erratic, the swimmer may be either loafing or have a poor pacing sense. The former situation may require the coach's personal timing and pulse counting in order to be found and the remedies for both situations are obvious.

When improvement as indicated by any or all measures seems to have plateaued there are a number of possibilities to consider. It may be that the swimmer has reached his biological limits but this conclusion should be avoided until all other possibilities are exhausted, especially in athletes below 20 to 25 years of age. Perhaps pubertal growth periods are interfering and there is little else to do but wait these out while maintaining performance levels without hurting the current status. However, the likelihood of this answer is also slim as growth generally produces increased performance. It must also be accepted that growth will eventually stop and improvement will have to be gained in other ways. Assessing this latter point is complicated by the fact that puberty may end anywhere from the age of 16 years to the early twenties in different individuals. This does not mean, however, that growth in the capacity of tissue will be stopped at the same time. Probably the most common answer is related to the program itself. The most important variable in any program is intensity and, in a plateau, the likelihood is that increased stimulus levels are required. It may also be that it is the method of applying intensity which is at fault and, as this is a fairly individual thing from swimmer to swimmer, each performer must collaborate with the coach in using the aforementioned principles in experiments with the program.

An additional approach which is available to some teams is provided for in the application of laboratory monitoring programs. Specific measurement and prediction techniques for the constituents of the aerobic mechanism are well described by Åstrand and Rodahl [3] and are practiced in the more complicated forms by many laboratories throughout the country. The simplified approaches can be used by virtually anyone who can find $300.00 to $500.00 for the equipment or, in the simplest versions, with little more than a stop watch. The use of such measurements on a monthly or quarterly basis is virtually the same as for the data of the day book and serves to verify or point out errors in the daily recording program. Åstrand and Rodahl [3] even gives some existing data for various sports and this can provide a basis for gross comparisons to international athletes.

It should not be necessary to add that, whether the laboratory system or only the record keeping is used, all athletes should be medically examined annually at the least and preferably semiannually. In addition, the physician should be made aware of the nature of the swimmer's activity in order that his assessment can be the most beneficial.

In summary, it might be said that, in view of the fierce competition at the national and international levels, program efficiency is an absolute necessity. The only real way to assure this and promote the most rapid improvement in swimmers is to institute a precise monitoring system. Even at the very least, it will assist the coach in selecting the events according to the capacities of his swimmers and, ideally, maximize the benefits for all concerned.

Anaerobic Training

A number of investigations have been conducted in which increases in oxygen debts and lactate concentrations were demonstrated following training programs, i.e. Robinson and Harmon,[56] Knehr *et al.*,[47] Karlsson *et al.*,[42] Ekblom *et al.*[27] and Cunningham and Faulkner.[15] Notwithstanding these data, the specific training of anaerobic processes is not as well understood as the aerobic processes, especially with regard to the intensities, duration of exercise and rest periods which will bring about optimum improvement.

The relatively high values for lactate shown by Astrand's *et al.*[2] experiments with intense work of three minutes' duration, and by Yakolev et al.,[68] with very short and intense work periods indicate that the anaerobic energy release pathway can be stressed, and presumably trained, with a wide variety of intense drills. Consequently, the drill which most closely resembles the desired performance can be chosen in order to satisfy specificity in both swimming style and energy resource.

As with aerobic training, the control variables in anaerobic work as distance, speed, rest time and number of repeats. However, their use has quite a different end point: producing exhaustion in a controlled way. This result might be obtained simply by continuous swimming at a 400-meter or 800-meter pace but, while sometimes beneficial for swimmers of these events, it will do little for the 100-meter and 200-meter competitor other than give some opportunity for stroke correction in the early season. A more sensible approach would be to swim 100-meter or 200-meter repeats at the event speed while using rest times short of those required for complete recovery. The repeat speed and distance should be sufficient to give postexercise heart rates from 190 to 210 or more beats per minute in the trained athlete and rest times should not give recovery rates much below 130 to 135 beats per minute. One thus expects a decrease in performance times. An improvement in performance drop-off indicates the necessity of increasing intensities. However, this approach is quite severe and it may be necessary to increase rest times for more complete recovery if any semblance of performance specificity is to be maintained. The once popular acceleration drills accomplished the same sort of thing but have lost favor because of their lack of specificity with regard to performance style and pace. Table XIX–III gives some indication of the nature of aerobically and anaerobically oriented intervals.

TABLE XIX–III
TYPICAL SWIMMING TRAINING SKILLS

Purpose	Approximate Work Duration	Inten-sity	No.	Approximate Rest	Example
Aerobic	20 minutes	80%	01	—	Continuous mile
Aerobic	4.5–5.0 minute	80%	05	1.0–1.5 minute	5 × 400 yd starting every 6 minutes
Anaerobic	2.0–2.5 minute	90%	06	2.5–3.0 minute	6 × 200 yd starting every 5 minutes
Pace	Race time	100%	01	30 seconds	All-out 150 m rest 30 sec sprint 50 m B.T. 3 days before world record: (2:24.4) 150—1:48.4 50— 34.5 2:22.9
Speed Aerobic	10 seconds to 2 minutes	100%	01– 10	25–30 sec 50–02 min 100–06 min	8 × 25 start every 45 sec 6 × 50 start every 2.5 min 4 × 100 start every 7.0 min 1 × 200

The major significance for being aware of one's pace is explained in two ways: through comparison of energy cost at different speeds; and through an examination of the way the system responds to exercise. It should be apparent from the earlier discussions of the forces required at different velocities that the extra energy expended by swimming ten percent faster than a pace speed will be far greater than that which will be saved by swimming ten percent slower than the same pace. In addition, the cost of accelerating is much greater than the saving in decceleration. Therefore, if one wishes to gain the most efficient use of available energy and to just exhaust ATP-CP and the anaerobic system at the finish line, a maintained or controlled variation of pace is essential.

It might be assumed that one needs only to break a race and the desired time into a series of parts in order to design a pacing program. However, the simplicity of this approach is contraindicated by certain factors, not the least of which is the difficulty of being within tenths of a second in maintaining the same pace throughout an entire 400 m or 1500 m race. Only a minor error in pace would be necessary in the optimally planned pace (exhaustion at the finish line) in order to upset the desired result.

It is well known that the time taken to increase the performance of the aerobic mechanism is an indirect function of intensity. Thus, it may be an advantage to start aerobically dependent events relatively fast, slowing down somewhat in the middle portion of the race in order to allow the well accelerated aerobic system to assume a higher proportion of the load, and then finish fast. This pattern is common in middle distance running but probably has less potential in swimming because of the extreme cost in producing acceleration. However, the speed of the start can offset this disadvantage somewhat and, while it is being investigated with runners (Ferguson [34]), the possibility of patterning the pace in the same way probably deserves some attention in swimming as well.

It is also probably relevant to mention that, as swimming is somewhat of a psychological game, an unvarying pace might make a swimmer too easy to race against. The point to remember here is that all swimmers will differ slightly in personality and the same approach will probably not be universally applicable.

The creation of "broken" or "simulated swims" also provides a fertile area for both aerobic interval training and for "speed" or "sprint" training. In the aerobic approach, a slightly accelerated pace can be used in the early season over the shorter distances with progression toward the optimum pace and shorter rest periods. Where specificity is to be directed at extending the distance of higher speed, the first portions of the total distance can stress anaerobic limits while the last portion is kept shorter to promote total exhaustion while speed is still high. If this approach is used without promoting complete exhaustion, it becomes an extremely good rehersal activity and "peaking" device. Table XIX–III shows a successful example of the latter system which was used by Elaine Tanner prior to her world record performance in 1967.

Speed Training

The development of speed is essentially a year-round process for sprinters and, except as is necessary to conform to the demands of pace, is of lesser importance to distance swimmers. However, it becomes relatively more important to everyone as the peak competitive season approaches and the emphasis on it becomes proportionately greater in relation to the specific events of the competitor.

The process as outlined in Table XIX–III is essentially one of demanding the peak rate of energy expenditures in each repeat of performance so that the specific conditioning and techniques of sprinting can be promoted. If peak performance is required each time, the rest periods must be appropriately increased and the expectation of total daily yardage reduced. The system is thus a promotor of aerobic endurance as well as speed at least in the short yardage versions. Therefore, use of speed training can justifiably be intensified somewhat in the early season if the problems of boredom and exhaustion can be avoided. Use of performance time records, pulse counting and weight records become extremely helpful for this purpose. At the repeat yardage increases, the stimulation of anaerobic systems becomes proportionately greater. The rest times must thus increase and the percentage of maximum effort should be related to the specific pacing speed rather than to the rate of energy expenditure.

A Season Training Plan

Carlisle,[8] Counsilman,[11] and Daland[18] all advocate a season training plan. The basic concept as outlined in Figure XIX–I normally has the competitive season broken into three phases: early, championships and taper. It is, at present, impossible to specify the exact features of training during the different phases of the year because they will vary with the event, swimmer skill and conditioning, and the facility. However, in general, an examination of typical training schedules shows that most of them have some aerobic and anaerobic training at all times and the degree of emhapsis tends to shift towards anaerobic training as the season progresses. Pace and sprint training receive their greatest emphasis towards the latter part of the year. Aerobic training benefits are not realized rapidly and essentially demand year-round effort. The increased tolerance effect of anaerobic training is produced more quickly but only at the expense of extreme exhaustion. Therefore, in an effort to assure the best potential for physiological performance, even if it has not yet reached optimum levels, total yardage should be reduced somewhat before relatively important competitions and to a minimum before major events.

Strength Training

A number of studies have been conducted investigating the effect of an increase in strength upon swimming performance. Campbell[6] showed that there was a significant relationship between arm and shoulder strength and speed in swimming while Davis[19-21] drew similar conclusions from two studies involving 17 and 30 male swimmers on 12 and 9-week weight training programs. Wilk[66] in a better designed study also found a significant relationship between strength and swimming performance while Nunnery[54] employed circuit training instead of weight training and found that the experimental group improved their swimming time more than the controls.

More sophisticated studies have been attempted by Edington[26] who compared different rates of exercise and Jensen[41] who compared the effect of four different strength programs upon swimming performance. Neither

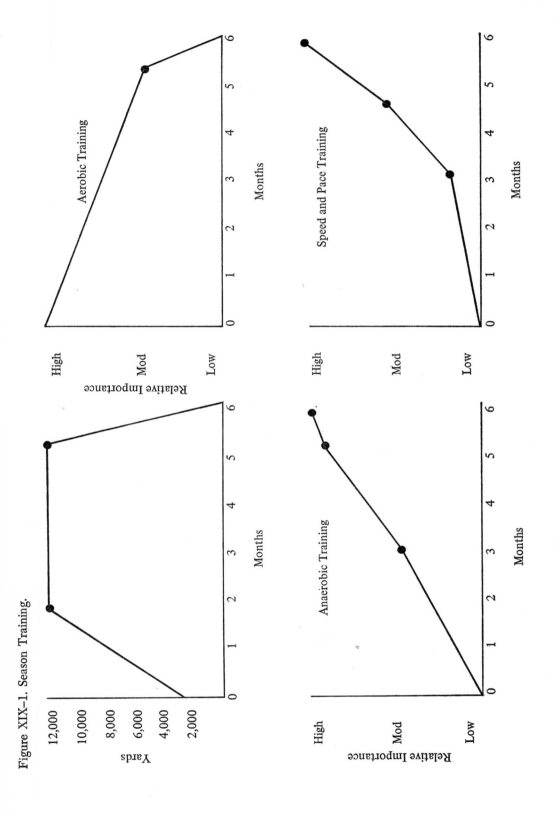

Figure XIX–1. Season Training.

of these latter two studies found any significant effects on swimming performance.

In view of the relatively low force requirements in swimming as calculated earlier, it would seem that endurance rather than maximum force potential is most desirable. In addition, the requirements of specificity and the limitations of training time in already heavy schedules would seem to demand that only the applicable musculature and range of motion be trained. Unfortunately, published eletromyographical data on competitive swimmers are limited to that of Ikai *et al.*[39] and the major method available for determining the muscle groups involved in swimming is still the traditional kinesiological approach. As indicated by Counsilman[11,12] the major muscle groups in swimming are the arm depressors, the arm rotators, the elbow extensors, the wrist flexors and the hip, knee and ankle extensors.

Strength training programs have been presented by a variety of authors including Counsilman.[11] In view of the fact that a majority of coaches face problems of limited budgets, limited time and relatively large squads, imaginative isotonic, isometric and isokinetic strength programs have been developed. These have involved partner exercises, self-constructed equipment and relatively expensive commercial equipment. The common factor of course is resistance.

The available strength training data support isotonic programs based upon Berger's[4] work i.e., three sets of four to eight repetitions with a frequency of three times per week and isometric programs based upon the work of Hettinger[35] Although some of the concepts advanced in this classic work have been modified by more recent work, it still forms the basis of most isometric programs. Very limited research by Thistle *et al.*[64] suggests that isokinetic exercises might be the most efficient of all strength training programs. This might prove to be a fertile field of research in both strength training and swimming performance specifically.

Current practices among swimming coaches as indicated by Dawson[22] and more recently Counsilman[11] include a wide variety of strength exercises, repetitions, sets and frequencies. A number presented by the former author do not appear to be based upon available data.

FLEXIBILITY

Ankle and shoulder flexibility is generally considered to be advantageous for competitive swimming performance, although modification of stroke technique has permitted competitors with very poor flexibility to achieve high standards of competitive excellence. Cureton's[16] data indicated that swimmers from a variety of Olympic teams exhibited greater flexibility than normals while Pickens[55] indicated that swimmers tended to be generally more flexible than other athletes. More recent data such as that of Dickinson [25] point out the need for studies involving more specific measures and the relationship of these to specific strokes.

Flexibility may be improved by a variety of techniques but according to De Vries,[24] static stretching is the preferred method. Recommended stretching techniques for competitive swimmers include both individual and partner drills. These are outlined by Colwin [9] and, in the interest of time, should probably be limited to the applicable motions and coordinated with strength training.

WARM-UP

Theoretical considerations regarding the advantages of warm-up center around an increased metabolic rate and a more rapid exchange of oxygen between the blood and tissues. Asmussen and Böje [1] demonstrated increased performances in very short (12–14 sec) events and, in relatively longer (5 min) ones, with warm-ups ranging from 5 to 50 minutes. The majority of improvement occurred after 5 to 15 minutes of warm-up and, according to Astrand and Rodahl,[3] the beneficial effects of warm-up persist for 15 minutes.

The effect of warm-up on swimming performance has been examined by Muido,[53] Carlisle [7] and De Vries.[23] Improvements attributable to warm-up are in the range of 1.5 to 5.0 percent.

Available data would suggest a warm-up of approximately 30 minutes with the first half consisting of relatively intense work. The lower lactate levels reported during interval training compared to continuous work by Astrand *et al.*[2] suggest that interval work would be considerably more beneficial as a warm-up than continuous work. An obvious added advantage is a final opportunity to rehearse race pace. Since lack of warm-up pools prohibit both adequate warm-up and warm-up within 15 minutes of an event except at every major competition, it would appear logical for competitive swimmers to take advantage of hot showers prior to competition. The warm-up effects of these approaches have been demonstrated by Asmussen and Böje [1] and Carlisle.[7]

SUMMARY

Competitive swimming is a sport in which the major orientation is towards training and one in which most coaches are very systematic in preparing their athletes for competition. The major weaknesses appear to be too great a reliance on overloading the aerobic mechanisms too late in the year through continuous rather than with short, high speed intervals; and the insufficient attention paid to the concept of specificity. In addition, because of the very low working efficiencies such as reported by Karpovich and Millman [46] more emphasis might be placed on investigating and promoting skill development. The latter is particularly true with younger swimmers.

REFERENCES

1. Asmussen, E. and Böje, O.: Body temperature and capacity for work. *Acta Physiol Scand, 10*:1–22, 1945.
2. Åstrand, I., Åstrand, P. O., Christensen, E. H., and Hedman, R.: Intermittent muscular work. *Acta Physiol Scand, 48*:448–453, 1960.
3. Åstrand, P. O. and Rodahl, K.: *Textbook of work physiology.* New York, McGraw-Hill, 1970.
4. Berger, R.: Effect of varied weight training programs on strength. *Res Q, 33*:168–181, 1962.
5. Bouchard, C., Hollman, W., and Herkenrath, G.: Effects of a minimum program of physical exercise on physical working capacity of group of adults. Paper read at C.A.H.P.E.R. Conference, Fredricton, N.B., 1965.
6. Campbell, C.: A study of the relationship of arm and shoulder strength and endurance in freestyle swimming. Unpublished master's thesis, State Univ. of Iowa, Ames, Iowa, 1948.
7. Carlisle, F.: Effect of preliminary passive warming-up on swimming performance. *Res Q, 27*:143–151, 1956.
8. ———: *Forbes Carlile on Swimming.* London, Pelham Books, 1963.
9. Colwin, C.: Dry-land exercises. In Dawson, B. (Ed.): *A Swimmer's Book of Dry-Land Exercises.* Ann Arbor, Swim Central, 1963.
10. ———: *Cecil Colwin on Swimming.* London, Pelham Books, 1968.
11. Counsilman, J.: *The Science of Swimming.* Englewood, Prentice Hall, Inc., 1968.
12. ———: Training international swimmers. Clinic presented at Toronto, Ont., 1971.
13. Christensen, E. H., Hedman, R., and Saltin, B.: Intermittent and continuous running (a further contribution to the physiology of intermittent work). *Acta Physiol Scand, 50*:269–286, 1960.
14. Cunnigham, D. A. ad Eyon, R. B.: Maximum oxygen uptakes of selected Ontario age-group finalists. Unpublished research, Univ. West. Ont., London, Ont. 1971
15. Cunningham, D. A. and Faulkner, J. A.: The effect of training on aerobic and anaerobic metabolism during short exhaustive run. *Med Sci Sports, 1*:65–69. 1969.
16. Cureton, T. K.: Mechanics and kinesiology of swimming. *Res Q, 1*:87–121, 1930.
17. ———: *Physical Fitness of Champion Athletes.* Urbana, Univ. of Ill. Press, 1951.
18. Daland, P.: Planning the season. Papar presented at 1971 National U.S.A. Swimming Coaches Clinic, Aneheim, Cal., 1971.
19. Davis, J.: The effect of weight training in swimming the crawl stroke. Unpublished master's thesis, State Univ. of Iowa, Ames, Iowa, 1951.
20. ———: Effects of training and conditioning for middle distance swimming upon measures of cardiovascular condition, general physical fitness, gross strength, motor fitness and strength of involved muscle groups. Unpublished doctoral dissertation in physical education. Univ. of Oregon, Eugene, Oregon, 1953.
21. ———: The effect of weight training on speed in swimming. *Phys Educ, 12*:28–29. 1955.

22. Dawson, Buck: *A Swimmer's Book of Dry-Land Exercises.* Ann Arbor, Swim Central, 1963.
23. De Vries, H. A.: Effects of various warm-up procedures on 100-yard times of competitive swimmers. *Res Q, 30*:11–20. 1959.
24. ———: Evaluation of static stretching procedures for improvement of flexibility. *Res Q, 33*:222–229. 1962.
25. Dickinson, R. V.: The specificity of flexibility, *Res Q, 39*:792–794. 1968.
26. Edington, D.: Relative effectiveness of two resistive exercises for the arms in relation to speed in swimming the crawl stroke. Unpublished master's thesis in physical education, Florida State Univ., Gainesville, Florida, 1960.
27. Ekblom, B., Astrand, P. O., Saltin, B., Stenberg, J. and Wallstrom, B.: Effect of training on circulatory response to exercise. *J Appl Physiol, 24*:518–528. 1968.
28. Eynon, R. B.: Training programs of selected Canadian swimmers. Unpublished research, Univ. West. Ont., London, Ont. 1971.
29. Eynon, R. B., Yuhasz, M. S. and Hauch, P. P.: Heart rates elicited during selected interval training drills. Unpublished research, Univ. West. Ont., London, Ont., 1971.
30. Faulkner, J. A. and Stager, G.: The heart rate as a measure of endurance, efficiency, and performance in swimming. Unpublished research, Univ. of Mich., Ann Arbor, Mich., 1962.
31. Faulkner, J. A.: *What Research Tells the Coach About Swimming.* Washington, N.E.A. Publications, 1967.
32. ———: Physiology of swimming and diving. In Falls, H. B. (Ed.): *Exercise Physiology.* New York, Academic Press, 1968, pp. 415–446.
33. ———: New perspectives in training for maximum performance. *JAMA, 205*:741–746. 1968.
34. Fergusson, R., 1970, Personal Communication.
35. Hettinger, T.: *Physiology of Strength.* Springfield, Thomas, 1961.
36. Hill, J. S., Wearring, G. A., and Eynon, R. B.: Effect of frequency of exercise on adult fitness. Paper read at joint meeting of C.A.S.S. and A.C.S.M. Toronto, Ont., 1971.
37. Horvath, S. M.: The physiological stimuli to training in a normal climate. *Can Med Assoc J, 96*:697–702. 1967.
38. Huesner, W. W.: Specificity of interval training. Unpublished paper, Mich. State Univ., East Lansing, Mich., 1963.
39. Ikai, M., Ishii, K. and Miyashita, M.: An electromyographical study of swimming. Data from laboratory for physiologic research in physical education. School of Education, Univ. of Tokyo, Tokyo, Japan, 1966.
40. Jackson, J. H., Sharkey, B. J., and Johnston, L. P.: Cardiorespiratory adaptations to training at specified frequencies. *Res Q, 39*:295–300, 1968.
41. Jenson, C.: A study of the relative effect of five different training methods on swimming. Unpublished doctoral dissertation, Indiana Univ., Bloomington, Ind., 1963.
42. Karlsson, J., Astrand, P. O., and Ekblom, B.: Training of the oxygen transport system in man. *J Appl Physiol, 22*:1061–1065. 1967.
43. Karvonen, M. J., Kentala, E., and Mustala, O.: The effect of training on the heart. *Ann Med Exp Biol Fenn, 35*:307–315. 1957.
44. Karpovich, P. V.: Water resistance in swimming. *Res Q, 4*:21–28. 1933.
45. ———: Respiration in swimming and diving. *Res Q, 10*:3–14. 1939.
46. Karpovich, P. V. and Millman, N.: Energy expenditure in swimming. *Am J Physiol, 142*:140–144. 1944.

47. Knehr, C. A., Dill, D. B. and Neufeld, W.: Training and its effect on man at rest and at work. *Am J Physiol, 136*:148–156. 1942.
48. Magel, J. R. and Faulkner, J. A.: Maximum oxygen uptake of college swimmers. *J Appl Physiol, 22*:929–933. 1967.
49. Mathews, D. K. and Fox, E. L. *The Physiological Basis of Physical Education and Athletics.* Philadelphia, W. B. Saunders, 1971.
50. Maidorn, K. and Mellerowicz, H.: Comparative studies on increase in efficiency by interval training using a different time interval. *Int Z Angew Physiol 19*:27–34. 1961.
51. Mellerowicz, H., Meller, W., and Mueller, J.: Comparative research on increased work by interval training. *Int Z Angew Physiol, 18*:376–385. 1961.
52. Montrella, J.: The lakewood program. Paper presented at 1971 National U.S.A. Swimming Coaches Clinic, Aneheim, Cal., 1971.
53. Muido, L.: The influence of body temperature on performance in swimming. *Acta Physiol Scand, 12*:102–109. 1946.
54. Nunnery, D.: Relation of circuit training to swimming. *Res Q, 31*:188–198. 1960.
55. Pickins, W. L.: A study of flexibility in swimmers. Unpublished master's thesis, Univ. of Oregon, Eugene, Oregon, 1950.
56. Robinson, S. and Harmon, P.: The effects of training and of gelatin upon certain factors which limit muscular work. *Am J Physiol, 133*:161–169. 1941.
57. Roskamm, H.: Optimum patterns of exercise for healthy adults. *Can Med Assoc J, 96*:895–898. 1967.
58. Sharkey, B. J. and Holleman, J. P.: Cardiorespiratory adaptations to training at specified intensities. *Res Q, 38*:698–703. 1967.
59. Shephard, R. J.: Initial fitness and personality as determinants of the response to a training regime. *Ergonomics, 9*:3–16. 1966.
60. ———: Intensity, duration and frequency of exercise as determinants of the response to a training regime. *Int Z Angew Physiol, 26*:272–278. 1968.
61. Sidney, K. H., Eynon, R. B., and Cunningham, D. A.: The effect of frequency of exercise upon physical work performance and selected variables representative of cardiorespiratory fitness. Paper read at C.A.S.S. Quebec, Que., 1970.
62. Stockholm, A.: The effects of swimming interval training. *Swimming Technique, 6*:8–10, 1969.
63. Stuart, D. G.: The effects of speed and pace training on certain physiological measures. Unpublished master's thesis, Mich. State Univ. East Lansing, Mich., 1956.
64. Thistle, H., Hislop, H., Moffroid, M. and Lowman, E.: Isokinetic contraction: a new concept of resistive exercise. *Arch Phys Med Rehab, 48*:279–282. 1967.
65. Turkington, H. D.: A comparative study of an interval and a traditional method of training for competitive swimming. Unpublished master's thesis, Washington State Univ., Pullman, Wash., 1958.
66. Wilk, E.: A study to determine the relationship between an increase in strength of the muscles involved in crawl stroke swimming and speed in swimming the crawl stroke for a distance of forty yards. Unpublished master's thesis, Springfield, Coll., Springfield, Mass., 1956.
67. Wilt, F.: Training for competitive running. In Falls, H. B. (Ed.): *Exercise Physiology.* New York, Academic Press, pp. 395–414, 1968.
68. Yakolev, N. N., Kaledin, S. V., Krasnova, A. F., Leshkovich, L. G., Popova, N. K., Regozkiw, V. A., Chagovets, N. R., and Kostygova, L. A.: The physiological chemistry of adaptation to muscular exercise and the length of rest intervals between execution in the course of training. *Sechenov Physiol J,* U.S.S.R., 47:752–757. 1961.

CHAPTER XX

COMPETITIVE DIVING

Ross Hetherington

COMPETITIVE DIVING involves a near vertical jump from either a spring-board or platform, a variety of acrobatic movements during the flight through the air, and an alignment of the body for entry into the water. The entire performance from the time the diver begins his approach until he surfaces after the entry is less than ten seconds. Between practice dives there is always a rest period of a moment or two or more, and between dives in competition there is often a waiting period of about 30 minutes. Therefore, cardiovascular fitness is not an essential requirement for the diver, but each phase of the dive requires a high degree of proper muscular conditioning if the diver is to excel.

Muscular conditioning programs for the diver aim at developing those muscles which will assist the diver to obtain the highest jump on the take-off; to acquire the necessary flexibility and strength to gather the body into tuck, pike, or twisting positions as rapidly and as compactly as possible; and to acquire the strength and flexibility to align the body properly and maintain this alignment during the entry into the water.

A question which arises immediately when one considers strength and flexibility programs, is if these are general or specific qualities. In other words, are some divers naturally strong or flexible, and are there certain exercises which will develop traits of general strength or general flexibility? Some of the best research in physical education has been directed toward finding the solution to this question. Traditionally many have thought in terms of people possessing either good or poor general coordination, or being either generally strong or weak, or as possessing either a generally flexible or inflexible musculature. However, research investigations have repeatedly indicated that there is a high degree of specificity between different types of physical performance, which led Franklin Henry [11] to propose a theory of neuromotor specificity and to state that ". . . it is largely a matter of chance whether an individual who is highly coordinated in one type of performance will be well or poorly coordinated in another."

The implications that this research has to the diver is that his conditioning programs should be directed toward specific objectives. He should not try to make himself strong, but try to strengthen those muscles which are actually required to perform a dive successfully. The same is true for flexibility. Toe touching exercises are not going to develop total body flexibility. One diving book author suggested that stunts such as the forward roll help develop general coordination. There is no evidence to support such a statement, and in fact there is evidence which contradicts it. The diver, then, must isolate the specific actions required for diving, and prepare his body as best as he is able to perform these actions.

The first portion of this chapter discusses findings from research investigations which have applicability for conditioning for diving. The second portion includes a list of exercises which tries to encorporate the conclusions from research and apply them to specific movements utilized in diving.

FINDINGS FROM RESEARCH

Development of Jumping Ability

Numerous research investigations have monitored the value of training programs in the development of jumping ability. Bangerter [1] in his review of the literature found that gains in jumping ability had been reported up to as much as 3.2 inches in a period of 12 weeks or less. However, most of the studies reported less improvement than this, and some have shown only one to two inches. Two investigations which trained only the plantar flexor muscle found no significant increases. Bangerter found in his experiment that both knee and hip extensor strength increases were associated with an increased ability to jump, but increases in plantar flexor strength were not associated with an increased ability to jump.

Berger [3] compared four types of training programs for their effect on jumping ability. One group did knee bends with 10-RM (maximum weight which could be lifted for 10 repetitions), another did jumping squats with 50 to 60 percent of the 10-RM, another trained statically, and another practiced ten vertical jumps at each training period. The training was held three times per week for seven weeks. The 10-RM group had a mean improvement of 0.89 inches, and the jumping squats group with 50 to 60 percent of the 10-RM improved 1.10 inches. The statically trained group and the group which practiced vertical jumping did not make significant improvements in jumping ability. The author concluded that dynamic overload training is more beneficial for increasing vertical jump ability than static overload training.

A partial explanation for the limited increase in jumping ability resulting from isometric and weight training can be found from the principles of physics involved. Newton's second law states that force is equal to mass times acceleration ($F = ma$). Acceleration is defined as being equal to velocity divided by time (a = v/t) when the initial velocity is zero and mass is defined as being equal to the weight divided by the acceleration due to gravity which is about 32 ft/sec.[2] Therefore, since:

and

and

$$F = ma$$
$$F = m \, v/t$$
$$Ft = V \text{ or } V = \frac{Ft}{M}$$

Now the height jumped is determined by the velocity with which the body is thrust into mid-air ($V^2 = 2 \, aD$). If the diver's weight does not change, the height is determined by the product of the force and the time over which this force acts. Increasing the ability to exert force does not necessarily mean that the product of force and time will increase. Smith [19] has found that the time factor evidently is very important since the correlations between the force/mass ratio and ability to jump was only 0.168. This low correlation could be either because muscular force as measured on a dynamometer is not the same type of muscular force as used in jumping, or because some performers are more skillful at delivering the force they can exert over a longer period of time than others.

The definitions above also make it clear that large improvements in jumping ability would not be automatic even if the diver were able to fully utilize an increased ability to exert force. To illustrate, a diver who weighed 160 pounds (mass = 160/32 = 5) and could exert 500 pounds on a dynamometer before training and 525 pounds after training would have a force ratio of 100 before training and increase to only 105 after training. This would not cause a substantial increase in upward velocity. It is also true, however, that the ability to exert a large amount of force is of advantage to the diver, and if two divers had equal skill, and equal mass, the one who could exert the greatest force would gain the greatest height off the springboard or platform. Heavy resistance type exercises for the development of the jumping muscles are beneficial, and it would seem that a serious diver would spend some time in exercises designated for this purpose. The diver should not expect to add a foot or more to his take-off, but may add an inch or two of height which would make the difference between being able to complete a 3½ sommersault and not being able to do so.

Little research has been conducted on the relationship between the diver's strength and his ability to gain height from a springboard. Experimentation of this type is very difficult to control, because the skill factor is so important in obtaining maximum efficiency from the springboard. However, the principles of physics discussed above apply equally as well in this case, and it could well be that since the time involved in the take-off is longer than it is from the platform, the diver may have more opportunity to bring his ability to exert force into action. Taking the same examples as above, assume the springboard diver weighing 160 pounds averages a force of 500 pounds downward for 0.16 seconds giving him a take-off velocity of 16 ft/sec and a height jumped of 4 feet. If he is able to exert an average force of 25 pounds more, that is 525 pounds for the 0.16 seconds, his take-off velocity becomes 16.8 ft/sec and the height jumped is 4.41 feet or an increase of about 5 inches. Again, the reader is warned that this is only a fictitious example and it is virtually certain that a diver would not be able to utilize 100 percent of his increased ability to exert force throughout the entire phase of the take-off. The example does illustrate, though, that increases in ability to exert force should theoretically be more beneficial for a springboard diver, than for one who must jump from a solid surface.

Proper arm action can also assist the diver in gaining height on either the hurdle, or the take-off. Lifting the arms causes the body to exert more force downwards, resulting in greater reaction from the springboard or platform. Most divers prefer to keep their arms straight for appearance sake, and if they do so, the muscles which lift the arms work at a very poor mechanical advantage, and consequently must be very strong. An observer might first be inclined to recommend strengthening exercises for the elbow extensor muscles for someone who cannot keep his arms straight, but the arms tend to bend because this decreases the angular inertia, and not because of insufficient strength of the elbow extensors.

To conclude the discussion on strength training relative to vertical jumping, the following points can be made.

1. The most successful training programs for developing jumping ability are those most closely resembling the actual activity. Dynamic training appears to be superior to static, and the type of dynamic training which seems best is practicing jumping while carrying heavy weights.[3]

2. The hip extensors seem to be intimately involved in the vertical jump, so training should be directed towards the development of these muscles as well as the knee extensor muscles.[1]

3. Divers who become overweight cannot expect to jump as high because of the subsequent decrease in their force/mass ratio.

4. The time over which the force acts in jumping is crucial, so the diver must recognize that there is an important skill element in jumping. Large increases in jumping ability are not automatically associated with an improvement in the ability to exert force.

5. Since the muscles which lift the arms work at a poor mechanical advantage when the arms are held straight, these muscles must be very strong if maximum assistance is to be derived from the arms while hurdling or jumping.

Development of Flexibility

As mentioned earlier, flexibility is a highly specific quality, and there is no one test which could be used to ascertain an individual's general flexibility. People who possess high or low flexibility in one joint do not necessarily possess high or low flexibility at another joint of the body. Hupperich and Sigerseth [13] reported no evidence of "general flexibility" after intercorrelating the results of 12 flexibility measures on 300 girls from the ages of 6 to 18. Almost all of the intercorrelations were below 0.3, and no girl was significantly above average in all 12 measures, and none was significantly below. Harris [10] found similar results in 1969 in a factor analytic study of 42 individual joint measures and 13 composite measures. Harris [10] and Dickinson [7] have also found that flexibility is not even general to the same joint in that there is little correlation between flexion flexibility and extension flexibility of the same joint.

There is little controversy over the question of whether flexibility can be improved or not. Divers, gymnasts, dancers, etc. know from practical experience that the range of movement of joints can be increased substantially by practicing appropriate exercises. Experiments on the development of flexibility have verified that flexibility can be developed, and that significant changes in range of joint motion can often be accomplished in a very short period of time. Fieldman [8] found that in a toe-touch test his subjects increased 1.04 inches simply by trying the toe-touch once. Then after doing preliminary exercises improved 2.33", 3.09" and 3.64" respectively on three tests placed one week apart and on the last test five weeks after the first with no preliminary exercises touched 1.39" lower than on the first test. Therefore, preliminary loosening greatly improved performance, and five practice days placed one week apart each improved performance by 1.39 inches. DeVries [5] found that both Yoga type static stretching and ballistic stretching for seven practice periods over a period of 3½ weeks significantly increased range of joint motion, although there was no significant difference between types of training. DeVries advocates a static, even type of training for developing flexibility since the results are about equal, and the likelihood of causing sore muscles is much less than when bobbing or jerking types of movements are utilized. DeVries [6] also suggests that static stretching is theoretically better since a forceful, sustained stretch of a muscle activates the inverse myotatic reflex which causes relaxation.

Some critics of weight training have charged that weight training causes "muscle-boundness" and a resulting loss of flexibility. Counsilman [4] made selected flexibility measures on 18 competitive weight lifters and found that squat-type weight training exercises actually improved the flexibility of the knee. Therefore, research investigations do not substantiate the accusation that weight training will decrease flexibility. Kinesiologically there is no logical reason why strength development should decrease flexibility, as long as muscular development is done uniformly. However, if one group of muscles are exercised over only a limited range of motion, and the antagonistic muscles are not exercised, it is quite possible that the range of motion of that joint will decrease. Therefore, although it is not correct to state that weight training will reduce flexibility, it is still possible that it can do so if not done intelligently.

In concluding this section on development of flexibility the following points seem apparent:

1. Individuals as a rule do not tend to fall into general categories of flexible or nonflexible. Therefore, it is quite possible for divers who have good flexibility at the knees to be stiff in the shoulders, or vice versa. Obviously, then, the flexibility exercises that the diver practices should be precisely those movements in which flexibility is required in diving.

2. Divers who do not possess adequate flexibility in some joints need not become discouraged, or decide that they do not have the proper physique to be good divers. Since flexibility can be developed, the diver should simply set himself to work at developing the required range of movements in those joints where it is not adequate.

3. Strength development exercises do not automatically decrease flexibility, and if done properly can actually increase flexibility. The diver should be careful not to over develop a muscle group out of proportion to its antagonists, and also practice the resistance exercises in such a way that the joint being exercised is fully straightened with each repetition.

Development of Strength

Some diving coaches are reluctant to prescribe strength development exercises for divers, because they fear that the diver will develop large, grotesque looking muscles which will detract from his or her entries as well as appearance while diving. Their apprehensions are justified to a degree when one considers that the stereotype of the weight lifter's physique is far different from the stereotype of the typical diver's physique. However, the comparison is not valid because strength development exercises do not make a person heavier. A person's body weight is controlled by the balance between the amount of physical activity and the calories of food consumed. Some people, of course, may consume more food than others without gaining weight because of differences in metabolic rate and other physiological processes. However, within one individual, gains in weight are due to an excessive intake of food and drink, as compared to the amount of energy consumed due to physical exertion. It is true that some growth will occur in exercised muscles, but this exercise will not alone cause an increase in total body weight. Evidence that people who practice strength training do not necessarily become large can be seen from some competitive weight lifters. At the Olympic Games the bantam weight class is for men 56 kilograms (123.2 lbs) or less. These men do not look grotesque, and in fact both they and the lightweights (67.5 kilograms or 148.5 lbs) often have physiques which would look excellent in diving trunks. No attempt is made here to criticize anyone for overemphasizing the need for a pleasing appearance. The appearance of the diver is equally as important as the performance of the take-off, acrobatics, and entries. The point which is being made is that strength training need not make the diver larger, or look grotesque. In some instances the diver's appearance may even be improved by improving muscle tone.

In recent years controversy has arisen regarding the relative merits of isometric and isotonic methods of strength development. Isometric methods can be practiced much more quickly than weight training, and little or no apparatus is required, so it is not surprising that they would be very popular if they produced comparable results to weight training. In a recent comprehensive review of research on strength development [12] the following points were concluded:

1. Research has not shown that isometric exercises are clearly more beneficial than isotonic exercises, or that isotonic exercises are clearly more beneficial than isometric exercises.

2. Training two or three times per week appears to be as beneficial in the development of strength as does training five times per week.

3. Although some earlier studies have reported gains in strength of as high as five percent per week, one and one-half to two percent is a more realistic figure.

4. Young boys do not gain in strength as quickly as high school and college-aged boys.

Several investigators have found that the degree to which strength may be utilized is dependent upon how it was acquired. Berger [2] found that a group who trained isometrically performed better on an isometric test, and that a group who trained isotonically performed better on an isotonic test. Berger [3] also found that dynamic training was superior to isometric training in the development of jumping ability. Gardner [9] and Logan [15] found that improvements in strength were specific to the angle at which the training was administered, although others [12,18] have found this not to be true. Laycoe and Marteniuk [14] found that correlations between isometric strength and eccentric strength of the knee extensor muscles was virtually zero both before and after isotonic training. Rasch and Morehouse [17] concluded after studying the effects of dynamic exercises that when striving for muscle strength for a particular activity, the best training is that activity itself. The diver, it appears, would be well advised to practice strength training by performing movements, or holding positions which resemble as closely as possible those which are employed while diving.

PROPOSED EXERCISES

Flexibility Exercises

SHOULDER FLEXIBILITY. In order for the diver to achieve proper alignment for entries he should be able to place his arms overhead and to hold them tight against the sides of the head. When the diver is standing in this position, he should also be able to have his arms pointing directly upward. If he cannot do this, or has to arch his back in order to do so, he does not possess the required flexibility.

Some good divers possess an extreme amount of shoulder flexibility, and are able to point their arms not only straight up but backward at an angle of 20 to 30 degrees. These divers have to be somewhat careful on entries so as not to have the arms behind the head, particularly on forward rotating dives. However, this extra flexibility can be of advantage on backward rotating dives in which the diver has insufficient rotation. By arching the back, and utilizing this flexibility they can sometimes change this poorly executed dive into a satisfactory entry, where the diver with poor flexibility would have had to settle for an entry short of perpendicular. All divers with less than this amount of flexibility should regularly practice shoulder loosening exercises.

A good exercise is hanging with the hands together on a horizontal pole. Another is to stand facing a table, bend over at the waist and lay the palms of the hands on the table with the hands as nearly to each other as possible. Have an assistant push down with a steady pressure at the back of the neck.

TRUNK FLEXION. Divers who wish to do any dives well in the pike position must have the ability to bend forward from the hips. If the diver cannot sit on the floor with the legs held straight and touch his forehead easily on his knees without his knees raising, he does not possess the required flexibility. The diver may develop this flexibility by sitting with the legs straight and pulling with his hands from behind the knees. He may also grab the feet and pull the upper body downwards toward the legs. Some divers prefer to have someone push down on the back of the shoulders. If this technique is used, caution should be used, with only a steady pressure being applied with no bouncing. If the diver experiences pain from any of these exercises, he should consult his physician before continuing with them.

If the diver can assume a deep pike position, he will have no difficulty in bringing his knees close to his chest in a tuck position. The hamstring muscles at the back of the legs, restrict forward bending with the legs straight, but do not do so when the knees are bent. Therefore, the exercises described above are beneficial for both the tuck and pike positions.

HIP EXTENSION. If sufficient flexibility is not possessed in the hip extension muscles the diver when standing, or aligning his body for the entry will have an arch in his back. This is because the iliopsoas muscles attach to the lower back (lumbar vertebrae) and the top of the legs. If these muscles are too short, the lower back is pulled forward, causing a postural defect known as lordosis. To check to see if he has lordosis, the diver may stand with his back to a flat wall, and try to flatten his lower back against the wall. If there remains more than about an inch of space at the lower back it is too much.

To stretch the iliopsoas muscle, a hyperextension of the hip joint is required, but the diver should attempt to do this exercise while holding the lower spine as straight as possible. He may lie on his back on a table with the edge at his gluteal muscles and then lower the legs from a position above the table as low as possible, remembering to hold the lower back straight. Again, extra pressure may be added to this exercise by having someone push downward on the front of the knees, or by holding a small weight with the feet. This muscle may be stretched in other ways such as by arching the back so that the hands and feet are on the floor with the hips and stomach high in the air. This exercise is not recommended for the diver, because this position is not conducive to good diving form.

KNEES. A diver must keep his knees absolutely straight on all dives except tuck dives while in the air, and for all entries. Most divers have the ability to straighten their legs, so special exercises for this purpose are not required. In rare cases, a diver cannot quite form a straight line at the knee, but if lack of flexibility is the problem, this will also be cured by practicing the exercises described above under trunk flexion. Some divers have the ability to hyperextend their knees. An extreme degree of hyperextension is not desirable so these divers should refrain from exercises which stretch the hamstring muscles, and may benefit from extra practice at strengthening the hamstring muscles.

ANKLE. For appearance sake, the diver must be able to plantar flex his ankle joints so that a straight line is formed with his foot and lower leg. Most beginners do not have this great of a range of movement, but may acquire it. The best exercise for developing this degree of plantar flexion is to kneel on a mat or towel with the legs together and ankles plantar flexed. The diver can then sit back and put his weight on his heels, and as flexibility improves, raise his knees higher and higher off the mat or towel.

TOES. There are actually a series of joints in the foot which may be stretched. About two inches before the toes begin there is a joint where the metatarsal bones join to the other bones of the foot. Then of course, there is the joint between the toes and the metatarsals, and the toes have two joints each except the great toe which has only one.

The exercise described above for the ankle will assist in stretching these joints, and the diver may apply pressure on the top of one or both feet while he is standing or sitting, and some divers are even able to walk on the tops of the feet with the toes curled under. The diver may manipulate these joints with his hands, also, by bending one foot and then the other backwards as far as possible. Divers who possess nice looking ankles and feet practice these exercises regularly while waiting between practice dives, or at home while reading or watching television.

Strength Exercises

A diver needs strength in order to accomplish three things. Firstly, he requires a very dynamic type of strength which will allow him to gain height on both the hurdle and take-off. Secondly, while in mid-air he requires a dynamic strength also to bend his body briskly from a straight position to a tuck or pike position, and then to unbend again to the straight position. Thirdly, a static or isometric type of strength is required to hold the body rigid as it enters the water. Exercises for each of these types of exercises are described below.

Exercises for Hurdling and Jumping. The research described earlier has indicated that the closer the exercises resemble the actual performance, the better will be their opportunity of success in actually improving the performance. Obviously some divers will need exercises of this type more than others, but since few divers suffer from being able to hurdle or take-off too high, practically all divers could benefit from these exercises.

Probably the best exercise to develop height on the hurdle is to hold weights in the hands and hop on the foot used to hurdle with. If stairs are available, the diver can also hop upstairs on one foot, and then start increasing the amount of weight he can carry while doing this exercise.

For improving the take-off from either the spring board or platform, the same exercises that were described for the hurdle are beneficial, except done off both feet, and with increased weight. Use of heavy weights is also recommended for developing the jumping muscles. A barbell placed on the shoulders and loaded with heavy weights can be used for both half-squat exercises and heel raises. It is not necessary to practice the squat exercises with the knees bending more than 90 degrees, because the diver never does so while performing. This will avoid the possibility of pulling the muscles and ligaments around the knee joint. Also, for safety purposes, the diver should take caution to keep his back straight to avoid pulling back muscles, or putting undue strain on the intervertebral discs. It is recommended that reasonably small weights be used at first, and then add them slowly from day to day or week to week. The diver, whether male or female, should be able to build up to do both half-squat and heel raise exercises with twice their body weight on their shoulders, and some will find that they are capable of considerably more than this. The half-squat exercise will develop the extensor muscles of the knee joint, and the extensor muscles of the hip joint, both of which are actively involved in jumping. The heel raise exercise will develop the plantar flexor muscles of the ankle joint, which are the calf muscles. Many schools and universities are now purchasing elaborate weight training machines. These machines usually have a station at which the participant is seated to practice knee extension exercises. These are safer, in that heavy weights do not have to be held on the shoulders. Their disadvantage is that they provide limited exercises for the hip extensor muscles, which are believed to play an important role in jumping.

To develop the muscles which lift the arms, the diver can practice the exact movements that he uses in hurdling and taking off, but while holding weights in the hands. Care should be taken to make the movements identical to those used while actually performing. For example, if the thumbs are pointed inwards toward each other while the arms are lifting in the actual hurdle or take-off, the weights should also be lifted with the thumbs pointing inward. The muscle action is quite different when the arm is rotated and the arms are lifted with the palms facing inwards. The weights used for these exercises need not be too heavy, since the resistance is held so far from the shoulder joint compared to the attachment of the muscles.

Most divers try to delay their arms at a position to the side and slightly above shoulder height while they are descending from their hurdle. This requires strength in the deltoid muscles primarily, and strength for holding this position may be developed by holding dumbbells in a static position at the same level as is desired in the hurdle.

EXERCISES FOR ACROBATIC MOVEMENTS WHILE IN MID-AIR. While in mid-air, the diver sometimes holds his body straight, and therefore utilizes the same muscles as those discussed below for entries. The other alterations in body position are to assume a tuck or pike, and then straighten. The arms are moved in a variety of ways in mid-air, but this author believes that if sufficient flexibility is developed, no more strength is required for these movements than any normal person would possess. Therefore, the only exercises discussed here are those required for tucking and piking, and for straightening from the tuck or pike.

The ease with which a diver may tuck or pike in mid-air is very dependent upon his flexibility. To perform a compact back-dive (pike) for example, the diver requires both strong hip flexor muscles, and flexible hamstring and back extensor muscles to allow him to do so. The less flexibility possessed, the more strength that will be required to obtain this position.

To develop the muscles used in piking, the diver may lie on his back and practice coming to the back dive (pike) position. An alternative is to hang from a horizontal bar and bring the feet to the hands. The tuck position may be practiced likewise. Lay on the back and pull the knees to the chest, and also bringing the heels to the buttocks. To open from the pike position, the hip extensor muscles are involved. To exercise these, lay chest down on a table with the edge of the table at the pelvis. While holding on to the table with the hands, raise the legs to a horizontal position. After this becomes relatively easy either add weights or have an assistant offer passive resistance. An alternative is to lay with only the legs on the table, with the legs held down. Flex at the hips until the forehead is near the floor, and then lift the head, shoulders and upper body to the horizontal position. If this becomes too easy hold some weight behind the neck. These exercises will also assist in coming out of the tuck, and of course the exercises described for developing the jump will assist both of these movements also.

EXERCISES FOR DEVELOPING THOSE MUSCLES WHICH HOLD THE BODY STRAIGHT ON ENTRIES. To achieve and maintain proper alignment on entries requires a combination of several things. If the diver has not rotated sufficiently, or has rotated too far he will have to make whatever improvisations possible in order to get in the water. Considerable skill is also required to align the body correctly, so it is not slightly arched or piked, and the head and arms are placed properly. The third thing, required is to hold the body rigid, and maintain this alignment as the body enters the water. Few divers realize the strength which is required for proper entries, and how the appearance of the finish of the dive would be improved with more strength.

Fortunately, many of the muscles used to maintain body alignment are the same ones as are used for jumping and for closing and opening from the pike position. Therefore, the above exercises will help to a degree, but specific exercises should also be practiced. An excellent exercise is the arm-stand. This is very useful to practice, since all men and some women must employ this skill in platform diving. Once balance is attained, the diver may practice bringing his body from a slight arch or slight pike back to a straight position. The diver can also practice tightening his whole body, including his calves, thighs, buttocks, stomach, and triceps to hold the body straight. The diver should learn that it is not enough to simply have the body straight, but it must be locked straight by having the hip flexors and hip extensors isometrically pulling against each other. The legs are not simply straight, but locked straight by vigorous isometric contraction of the quadriceps muscles on the front of the thigh, the plantar flexor muscles on the back of the lower leg, and even the toe flexor muscles. If the diver is capable of holding his balance well, he can hold these isometric contractions for approximately six seconds and then relax, and practice about three of these contractions per workout. These contractions should be as vigorous as possible.

The diver may also practice these isometric contractions to hold body alignment while hanging from a horizontal bar. These are not quite as good because the body is inverted, and also the arms do not have to be held straight.

Some divers feel that elbow extension strength is extremely important to prevent the arms from buckling when platform diving. This author is of the opinion that great strength is not required here, if the elbows are in fact straight when contact with the water is made, and if the arms are properly placed so they contact the water pointed in the proper direction. If the diver can hold himself well in an armstand, additional strength should not be required. In practice, also most divers lift themselves from the pool, and in doing so are actually continuing practicing weight training for the elbow extensors.

DIVING PRACTICE. As with most sports, one of the best ways to condition the body for diving is to practice diving. Only then is the diver practicing precisely what he must do in competition and his body is given the best opportunity to adapt appropriately. Also, when divers attend competitions they are required to stand in line for long periods for practice sessions, and the continual climbing from the pool, climbing ladders, diving, and towelling the body can be fatiguing both mentally and physically. The diver must prepare himself for this regime as well as for the actual diving and can do this best by simply putting in sufficient hours at the practice pool. The diver must carefully analyze his practice schedule to ensure that his strength and flexibility exercises are not taking too much time away from actual diving practice.

Traditionalists might argue that since the above things are true, the diver would be best advised to practice diving only, and let the body adapt itself as best it can. The difficulty with this approach is that there are going to be some individuals who lack either sufficient strength or flexibility to dive at a high calibre, and the natural development of the deficiency can be extremely slow unless specific attention is paid to it. Rather than recognize a slight deficiency which could be rectified, the traditionalist might easily be inclined to label such people as possessing low ability. These people may have just as much ability, but simply need to develop some aspect of their strength or flexibility.

TRAMPOLINE AND PORT-A-PIT. This chapter is not concerned with learning, but conditioning. However, both the trampoline and port-a-pit besides being useful to practice skills, are also useful in developing jumping and hurdling height, simply because the exercise may be practiced much more often in the same period of time than off the diving board, and the skill is virtually identical.

RUNNING OR SWIMMING. Divers who have problems with excess weight can remedy their problems either by reducing the number of calories of food that they eat, or by increasing the amount of exercise they do. For the diver, running or swimming are usually the simplest exercises to choose, although cycling and cross-country skiing are other sports which could be used for this purpose.

For the diver who is not overweight, these exercises are not apt to improve his performance. However, all divers and coaches should consider the fact that diving is one of the few sports which does virtually nothing to develop the cardiorespiratory system of the body. Therefore, these people, if they are interested in the health of their bodies both during their time as competitors and later, would be well advised to become involved in exercises which will cause positive development of the cardiorespiratory systems of the body.

REFERENCES

1. Bangerter, Blauer L.: Contributive components in the vertical jump. *Res Q,* 39:432–436, 1968.
2. Berger, Richard A.: Comparison of static and dynamic strength increase. *Res Q,* 33:329–333, 1962.
3. ———: Effects of dynamic and static training on vertical jumping ability. *Res Q,* 34:419–424, 1963.
4. Counsilman, James E.: Does weight training belong in the program? *J Health Phys Educ Recreation,* 26:17–22, 1955.
5. DeVries, Herbert A.: Evaluation of static stretching procedures on vertical jumping ability. *Res Q,* 34:419–424, 1963.
6. ———: Flexibility, an overlooked but vital factor in sports conditioning. *International Symposium on the Art & Science of Coaching,* Toronto, Canada, October 1–5, 1971, pp. 209–222.
7. Dickinson, R. V.: The specificity of flexibility. *Res Q,* 39:792–794, 1968.
8. Fieldman, Harold: Effects of selected extensibility exercises on the flexibility of the hip joint. *Res Q,* 37:326–331, 1966.
9. Gardner, Gerald W.: Specificity of strength changes of the exercised and non-exercised limb following isometric training. *Res Q,* 34:98–101, 1963.
10. Harris, Margaret L.: A factor analytic study of flexibility. *Res Q,* 40:62–70, 1969.
11. Henry, Franklin M.: Coordination and motor learning, *Proc College Phys Educ Assoc,* 59:68–75, 1956.
12. Hetherington, M. Ross: Trainability and generality/specificity ratios of the ability of grade five boys to develop torque. Microcarded Ph.D. Thesis, University of Alberta, 1971.
13. Hupperich, Florence L., and Peter O. Sigerseth: The specificity of flexibility in girls. *Res Q,* 21:25–27, 1950.
14. Laycoe, Robert and Ronald G. Marteniuk: Learning and tension as factors in static strength gains produced by static and eccentric training. *Res Q,* 42:299–306, 1971.
15. Logan, Gene A.: Differential applications of resistance and resulting strength measured at varying degrees of knee extension. Unpublished Doctoral Dissertation, University of Southern California, 1960.

16. Meyers, Earl J.: Effect of selected exercise variables on ligament stability and flexibility of the knee. *Res Q, 42:*411–422, 1971.
17. Rasch, P. J., and L. E. Morehouse: Effects of static and dynamic exercise on muscular strength and hypertrophy. *J Appl Physiol, 11:*29, 1957.
18. Richardson, John R.: The effect of brief isometric and isotonic exercise programmes on the development of strength and muscular endurance. Microcarded M.S. Thesis University of Alberta, 1963.
19. Smith, Leon E.: Relationship between explosive leg strength and performance in the vertical jump. *Res Q, 32:*405–408, 1961.

CHAPTER XXI

RUGBY

G. Reid and D. Sturrock

ALL SPORTS REQUIRE of each player a certain degree of physical fitness. Contact sports, in particular, demand a considerable amount of physical conditioning to enable the player to participate effectively and with a reduced risk of being injured.

Rugby is a strenuous and very exhausting game in which every player should maintain a very high level of physical fitness. Physiologically, the player requires an efficient cardiovascular system to enable him to perform in vigorous physical activity for an eighty minute period with only a five minute interval between halves. Anatomically, the player must be strong and well conditioned to prevent himself from injury. Tackling has a major role in Rugby and body contact is therefore frequent. The incidence of injury is definitely reduced when a player had conditioned his body by performing flexibility exercises and strength training (weights) prior to the commencement of the season. This can be attested by the very low level of player injury in a well conditioned physically-fit team. Apart from physiological and anatomical conditioning, the player must be prepared or conditioned psychologically. The confidence of each player must be improved and maintained at an optimum level. If it is not, an indecisive or timid player exposes himself to possible injury by not putting force into a tackle, or by not applying adequate resistance in tight play.

Man possesses within each of these parameters of condition (anatomical, physiological, and psychological) the ability to adapt to stress as applied through a training program. He can adapt to the stress of a progressive training program to a level which is usually far beyond his expectations and, normally, beyond the level attained by individuals undergoing the most vigorous training programs used in team sports today.

Specificity of training has become a well-accepted term within all sports, including Rugby. The training program for Rugby should be specific to the demands made by the game upon the individual player. Progressive training programs which imply "overload training" are also universally accepted means of improving performance in sport. Should not, then, the training for Rugby be the playing of Rugby? Ideally, this would be so if it was not for the psychological implications (loss of motivation, boredom, etc.) which can arise, and the fact that as it is a contact game, the risk of injury may be increased and the overload principle may not always be met in this form of practice. To produce a training program which is specific to the demands of Rugby, one needs, through analysis of the game, to simply separate the various aspects or phases within the game and train the players using these by means of overload training techniques.

Basically, Rugby is a running game which involves body contact in the form of tackling, pulling, and pushing opponents; and the passing, catching, and kicking of a ball. Although it is a team game, each player must become proficient at performing the many individual fundamental skills to enable the fifteen members on a team to combine their talents into a cohesive, effective unit. Individual skill practices should be plentiful in the training of Rugby players; however, these skills should always be practiced in groups to enable the structuring of team play and unity.

Pre-Season Training

Ideally, each player should commence the competitive season in splendid physical condition. Throughout the off-season and particularly during the two or three months prior to the commencement of the competitive season, all Rugby players should participate in a training program. The program need not be formally structured but should include an hour's exercise daily. If a player enjoys tennis, squash, badminton, or similar games, he should become involved in the playing of the games. Cross-country running, hiking, cross-country skiing, snow shoeing, and the like are excellent activities for improving or maintaining one's level of physical fitness. During the last month of pre-season training such traditional methods as Fartlek and Interval Training should be encouraged.

In-Season Training

The players should be at a high level of physical fitness at the commencement of the competitive season. The training and practice during this period should be aimed at maintaining and even improving the level of fitness of the players, teaching and improving individual skills, developing tactics, and establishing the team into a cohesive unit.

New players, regardless of age, should be taught activities that they can do, and enjoy doing. The activity should be simple and the players should achieve success. For example, it is better to teach beginners a simple passing game, since Rugby is a running and passing game, than it is to teach them how to scrummage. In addition to being enjoyable, this approach encourages some useful habits, such as looking for a receiver, catching, passing, and positioning. By using small groups, each player has a chance to participate and further maximize his enjoyment. This type of activity readily becomes competitive and the teacher or coach can quickly evaluate abilities and regroup if necessary. Other features of the game can be introduced subsequently.

Experienced players should never neglect the practising of the fundamental skills necessary for good Rugby. The following drills should be useful for practice sessions for players of all calibre; they are related to the game situation and their inclusion in a practice ensures both enjoyment and the type of pressure encountered when having to perform the skill in a match.

1. *Passing and Handling*

(a) Free Passing

Within a defined area, many groups of three run and pass in any direction, giving passes to players in their own group only. Players must avoid contact with all other players. Competition can be introduced by counting the number of completed passes within a time limit (15, 20, or 30 seconds).

(b) Three-on-Three

One group of three runs and passes in any direction within a defined area. The other group can only intercept the ball. No contact is allowed. Each group counts the number of consecutive passes made without error or interception within a time limit (15, 20, or 30 seconds).

(c) Six-on-Six

Same as 1(b) only introduce, separately, no forward passing or contact. Emphasis should be on each player working when not in possession of the ball, in order to provide an opportunity for the ball to be passed laterally or backwards. Group sizes can be altered (6-on-5, 5-on-4).

(d) Speed Pass (Fig. XXI–1)

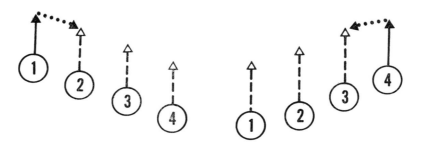

A   B

Figure XXI–1. Speed Pass.

Groups of 2, 3, 4, or 5 should run a specified distance, passing the ball with accuracy (no forward passes). Emphasis should be on acceleration on receiving a pass and passing as soon as possible after receiving the ball. Pressure can be increased by varying the distance and the time.

(e) Backing-up (Fig. XXI–2)

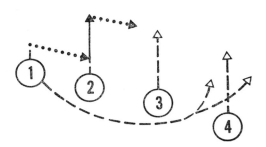

Figure XXII–2. Backing Up.

Groups of 3 to 6. Pass, then run behind the line in support and come into the line at another point. No special formation is kept and the ball is passed to both the left and right as players beckon. Competition can be added by counting the number of passes, or the number of players who handle the ball, in a given distance.

(f) Coming-around

Groups of 3 to 6. Pass, then move to the far end of the line, as shown in Figure XXI–2.

2. Scrummaging

(a) One-on-One

Players lean forward, place head under partner's chest and grasp partner's jersey for stability. Players try to push each other backwards. Emphasis is placed on correct position of the back legs.

(b) Three-on-Three

The front row of the scrum practices pushing against opposition. Ball may be used to practice hooking and timing of push.

(c) Five-on-Five

Same as 2(b) with the inclusion of the second-row forwards.

(d) Eight-on-Eight

Scrummaging practice with the full scrum. Emphasis should be placed on a "snap" forward push with the legs, pulling in with both arms, pushing down with hips, head up position, and correct foot positioning.

3. Line-out

(a) Throw-Catch-Feed   Groups of 3 (Fig. XXI–3)

Thrower (T) throws ball high so catcher (C) must jump for the ball.

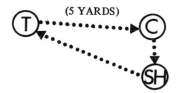

Figure XXII–3. Throw, Catch, Feed.

Scrum-half (SH) passes the ball back to the thrower after the "feed." Rotate positions after ten receptions by the catcher.
(b) Group of 6 (Fig. XXI–4)

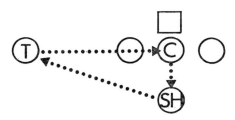

Figure XXII–4. Throw, Catch, Feed.

Add two players to 3(a) to bind on the catcher and a third player to act as a resistor. The resistor may jump for the ball or try to take the ball from the catcher after the ball has been caught. Rotate positions.
(c) Increase number until full line-out is being practised. (Fig. XXI–5).

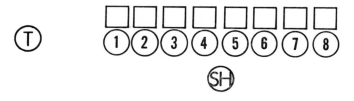

Figure XXII–5. Line-Out.

Use calls to indicate where the thrower should throw the ball i.e. number 3,5, or 8. Practice both open-side and short-side sweeps, rucking and mauling, and the quick catch-feed play.

4. *Mauling*

(a) Run, Turn and Pass Behind. (Fig. XXI–6).
In groups of five to eight and in a five-yard width, the first player runs several steps, turns and passes to a closely trailing player, before returning to the end of the line. Repeat back and forth varying the distance covered by the group.

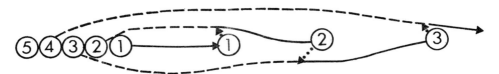

Figure XXII–6. Run, Turn, and Pass.

(b) Run, Stop, Give.

Same as 4(a) but give the ball instead of passing.

(c) Run, Down, Pick-up.

The first player runs a few steps and puts the ball on the ground. The next player picks up the ball, runs a few steps, and puts the ball down. Repeat. Competition is intensified by taking two steps only.

(d) Run, Fall, Pick-up.

The first player runs with the ball and falls to the ground. The next player picks up the ball, runs a few steps and falls to the ground. Repeat.

(e) Run, Fall, Pick-up, Give

The first player runs and falls to the ground. The next player picks up the ball, turns and gives it to the third player who runs and falls to the ground. Repeat. Add variety by using either one-half turn or no turn when giving the ball, and by imposing a two stride maximum.

(f) Run, Hit, Give. (Fig. XXI–7).

Figure XXII–7. Run, Hit, and Give.

The first player is tackled by (or runs into) #2, handing off from his hip to #3 who takes the ball and is tackled by #4, as he hands off to #2 who is tackled by #5 as he hands off to #4. Repeat.

(g) Throw-up

One player runs forward, throws the ball in the air behind him and becomes a resistor. Another player catches the ball and is hit by the resistor. The others bind quickly on the player with the ball. The last man takes the ball, sprints forward and throws the ball in the air behind him and becomes the resistor. Repeat.

(h) Eight-on-Eight

A ball is thrown in the air or on the ground by the coach, to a player on either side (no indication given) (Fig. XXI–8a). The team with possession practices rucking or mauling and maintaining control. The opposition attempts to gain possession of the ball while avoiding being drawn off-side. (Fig. XXI–8b). Repeat.

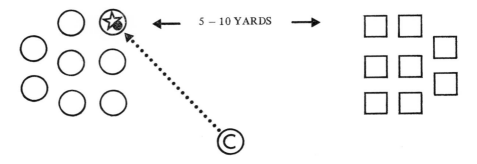

Figure XXII–8(a) Eight-on-Eight.

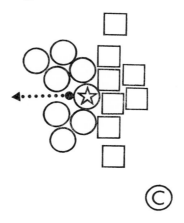

Figure XXII–8(b). Eight-on-Eight.

5. *Rucking*

(a) The ball is thrown or kicked to a spot.

A group of four players run to the ball and ruck. The emphasis is on stepping over (going beyond) the ball, getting low, binding and pushing with the shoulders.

(b) Same as 5(a) but provide one or more resistors for others to push.

(c) Same as 5(a) but have two groups compete with each other for the favoured positions.

(d) The ball is thrown or kicked to a spot.

The first player falls on the ball while the others go beyond the man and the ball and ruck. Provide resistors for competition. Expand to eight players in the group. Repeat many times in succession.

Organization of Practice Sessions

The most important principle in the organization of practice sessions is preparation. A definite plan of the points to be taught and the time to be spent on each is essential if progress is to be made. The practice itself must be progressive, demanding, and interesting. Since a very high level of physical fitness is needed by all Rugby players, it is recommended that a variety of activities be offered to improve or maintain it, and to provide enjoyment. Unless players enjoy a game, they cannot play it well, and unless they play it well they will not improve.

Match conditions should be simulated whenever possible by structuring useful drills related to the game. Encourage the players to make quick, instinctive decisions and to react quickly. Mini-groups of three to eight should be used in most drills. Beginners should be thoroughly saturated in the fun of handling the ball before being introduced to other facets of the game. Throughout, players will profit best if made to perform under pressure in the form of speed and opposition, and an open and attractive brand of Rugby will emerge.

Coaches must ensure that practice sessions are planned and conducted for the benefit of the players' enjoyment, for Rugby is essentially a players' game.

REFERENCES

1. Allen, Fred and McLean, Terry: *Fred Allen on Rugby*. London. Cassell and Company Limited, 1970.
2. Craven, D. H.: *The Seven Pillars of Rugby*. Johannesburg, South African Rugby Board, 1965.
3. Higham, E. S. and Higham, W. J.: *High-Speed Rugby*. London, Heinemann Limited, 1960.
4. Hudson, D. C. N. and Dyer, P. S.: *Your Book of Rugger*. London, Faber and Faber Limited, 1968.
5. Reid, J. Gavin: *Rugby. The Players' Game*. Dubuque, Iowa, William C. Brown Company Publishers, 1971.
6. Rugby Football Union: *A Guide for Coaches*. Twickenham, Rugby Football Union, 1966.
7. Rutherford, Don: *Rugby for Coach and Player*. London, Arthur Barker Limited, 1971.
8. Van Heerdon, Izak: *Tactical and Attacking Rugby*. Auckland, N. Z., A. H. and A. W. Reed Publications, 1963.
9. Venables, Cedric: *Coaching for Rugby Football*. London, Museum Press Limited, 1962.
10. Williams, Gerwyn: *Modern Rugby—A Comprehensive Guide for Players and Coach*. London, Stanley Paul Limited, 1948.
11. ———: *Tackle Rugger This Way*. London, Stanley Paul, 1968.
12. ———: *Rugby: Skills, Training and Tactics*. London, Stanley Paul Limited, 1962.

CHAPTER XXII

SPEEDSKATING

GORDON R. CUMMING

FOR PRECISE ADVICE to coaches, we need to know the exact requirements of a sport in terms of measurable parameters—oxygen transport system, muscular strength, body build and composition—we should know the most efficient way of training to attain these goals and we should then evaluate our training programs to see if these goals are being attained with specific test measurements. We then need to know the specific motor skills, strategic goals and psychologic factors required for the sport, and the optimal way to train for these.

Fitness Requirements of Different Types of Skating

There are three types of speedskating. In Olympic style skating, only two skaters traverse the 400-meter track at a time—they use different paths and the race is as much against time as a race with one athlete against another. Distances vary from 500 to 3,000 meters for women, and 500 to 10,000 meters for men. The serious skaters prefer this competition as being the best test of skating speed. The physical demands in the distance events in this type of skating are large.

In outdoor mass start skating, the event is a race with all contestants on the starting line. Tremendous skill and experience may be required to properly manoeuver in a pack. In a long race, the skaters more often than not skate the majority of the race at a relatively slow speed, and then break for the line with 200 to 600 meters remaining in the race. Skaters use their opponents to break wind, but may be required by the referee to take turns doing this. Because of the slower speed, less endurance fitness is required for this type of skating compared to Olympic style. If a skater thinks he is superior in endurance fitness, he may strike out on his own rather than take his chances breaking out of the pack near the end. However, because of the importance of the wind resistance factor, superior fitness may not be enough, and this strategy often fails.

Indoor skating is a completely different sport; it is usually performed in a hockey arena, the track is about 100 meters, and races vary from

314

100 meter to 2,000 meter distance. Skill and manoevering, turning, a quick start, and experience, are of more importance than fitness; skaters thirty to fifty years of age can compete successfully indoors because of the importance of skill and strategy factors.

Oxygen Requirements of Skating

Skating at slow speeds (4 to 8 M/sec), O_2 uptake is linearly related to skating speed. Approximate values of O_2 uptake at various speeds are listed in Table XXII–I and are taken from Figure 16–5 of Astrand and Rodahl.[3] After 8 M/sec, O_2 uptake increases out of proportion to speed because of reduced efficiency of all-out efforts, and the importance of wind resistance which increases in proportion to speed in the second power. The only data available on skating at top speeds were collected by Ekblom *et al.*,[8] and are summarized by Astrand and Rodahl[3] and in Table XXII–I. The Douglas bag method may have interfered a little with skating technique and increased the oxygen requirements. There was considerable scatter but no data was available for speeds of over 10 M/sec. Ice conditions, wind, clothing, weight of the skater, are additional factors. Overcoming wind resistance may account for at least 70 percent of the energy needed, and

TABLE XXII–I
OXYGEN REQUIREMENT—SPEEDSKATING

Speed *M/sec*	*500 M* *time—secs*	*Oxygen requirement* *L/min*
4.0	125	2.0
8.3	60	3.4
9.1	55	4.0
10.0	50	5.0
11.1	45	6.2 ?
12.5	40	8.0 ?

ice friction only 30 percent. Hence, skating speed may be more dependent on total power available (i.e. litres of oxygen per minute) rather than power in relation to weight ($\dot{V}_{02}$ in ml/kg/min). In this respect, skating may resemble swimming more than running, and excess weight is not likely nearly as much a handicap to the skater as to the runner.

It is evident that skating at speeds of over 10 M/sec (and one of the main features of distance skating is that speeds very close to sprinting speed must be maintained for the long distances) requires an oxygen uptake of about 5.0 L/min. Olympic style speedskating is thus one of the sports, along with distance running, cross-country skiing, and road cycling, demanding a highly developed oxygen transport system. In most speedskating meets, an overall champion is selected who must compete at all distances from 500 meters to 3,000 meters for women, and 500 meters to

TABLE XXII–II

ESTIMATED ENERGY PARTITION—
SPEEDSKATING

Event	Duration	Percent Aerobic	Percent Anaerobic
200 M	20 sec	15	85
500 M	40 sec	30	70
1,000 M	90 sec	40	60
1,500 M	125 sec	50	50
3,000 M	4.5 min	70	30
10,000 M	16.0 min	90	10

10,000 metres for men. The scoring system requires the sprinter to perform well in the long races as well as the shorter ones to become champion.

Possibly because of the difficulties of skating all-out wearing the measuring apparatus, the $\dot{V}_{02}$ max during skating is on the average only 87 percent of $\dot{V}_{02}$ max of the same subject running on the treadmill.[3] This is similar to the difference in V_{02} max between cycling and running, or running level vs running up an incline, or swimming vs running. In speedskating, the oxygen requirements of competing in the different distances have not been worked out. If we assume that the energy demands in any all-out racing contest are similar, data available for treadmill running can be transferred to skating events of similar duration. Table XXII–III shows that aerobic sources contribute only about 15 percent of the energy required in the 200-meter sprint, but this increases to 90 percent for the 10,000-meter event. The successful sprinter may not need a $\dot{V}_{02}$ max of over 50 ml/kg/min.

Lack of a Marked Fall in Speed With Added Distance in Speedskating

Table XXII–III shows that men skate 10,000 metres at 86 percent of the World record speed for the 500-metre sprint. Women skate the 3,000-metre event at 90 percent of the speed of World record for the 500-metre sprint. Contrast this to the runner who loses 40 percent of his speed going from 100 metres to 10,000 metres, or the swimmer who loses 30 percent of his speed going from 100 metres to 1500 metres. Speedskating coaches cannot make top distance skaters from those who do not have World class sprint speeds.

Training of Speedskaters

There is no scientific information available to indicate that one method of training is better than another. Some top skaters bicycle only; some run through the woods in a crouched position with weights on their waist and legs; some lift weights, others do not. Sprinters may concentrate on sprints

TABLE XXII–III

1971 OLYMPIC STYLE SPEEDSKATING RECORDS AND PERCENT OF SPRINT SPEED REQUIRED

| | MEN | | | WOMEN | |
Distance	World Record Time	% of Sprint Speed	Distance	World Record Time	% of Sprint Speed
500 M	38.4	100	500 M	42.8	100
1,500 M	1:58.7	97	1,000 M	1:27.7	98
5,000 M	7:12.0	89	1,500 M	2:15.8	95
10,000 M	14:55.9	86	3,000 M	4:46.5	90

and weight training; skaters participating in all distances need to develop a high degree of endurance. Training for speedskating is made difficult because of the short competitive season and lack of adequate ice facilities, although many areas of Europe (especially the Netherlands), and Japan, are developing 400-metre artificial ice surfaces and provide ice at least six months of the year. Some parts of Canada have outdoor natural ice tracks for only three to eight weeks, and Canada does not have an Olympic size artificial ice track.

Training programs for skaters are just as intense and varied as for any sport (Table XXII–IV). Conditioning training of all types is utilized, but specific on-ice training is the most important. For some the skating technique is easily acquired, while others never acquire an adequate technique, and the best conditioning in the World is no substitute for lack of skating skills.

As ice time is limited by its availability and climatic factors, some off-

TABLE XXII–IV

TYPES OF TRAINING USED BY SKATERS

Long distance running	Run 6 plus miles/day, get down to 7 min per mile, and/or cycle 30 miles/day 20 mph
Intermediate distance running	Run 800 M, 12 repeats, 4 min rest, get down to 3 min each, and/or cycle 3 miles, 25 mph, 12 repeats
Interval training	Run 200 M, 32–36 sec, recovery to heart rate 120, increase up to 20 repeats
Tempo training	Run 200 M, 28–30 sec ⎫ 4 min recovery Run 400 M, 60–65 sec ⎭
Weight training	Endurance, light weight 100 reps Tempo, heavier weights, rapid sequence 40 reps Thigh, back, lower leg
Skating simulations	Floor in front of mirror, "skate" jumps Skate board—sliding
Stretching and callisthenics	
Ice training	2–6 hrs daily—the most important
Cycling and bicycle ergometer training	There seems to be some carry-over between the muscle action of cycling and skating.

ice training should continue through the competitive season. As skating may not utilize maximum oxygen uptake capability, this aspect of fitness can decline during the skating season unless a few hours a week are given to running or cycling. In my experience, young skaters participating in vigorous pre-season training programs have consistently shown a decline in their $\dot{V}_{02}$ max during the skating season if they did not maintain some dry training. Skaters who start the skating season without the benefit of intense preseason training generally improve in $\dot{V}_{02}$ max during the skating season, but do not reach the same levels as those taking part in off-ice programs.

Maximum Oxygen Uptake of World Class Skaters

$\dot{V}_{02}$ max values have been reported for Swedish speedskaters noted for their performances in the long distance event (10,000 M).[3] The very high values for some of these skaters from Sweden (Table XXII–V) is a little overwhelming, but this seems to be a characteristic of many of the athletes from this country and may account for their excellent showings in endurance competitions.

In contrast is the $\dot{V}_{02}$ max value reported for Terry McDermott, the American who took home an Olympic Gold Medal in 1964, a Bronze in 1968, in the 500-metre event. The $\dot{V}_{02}$ max of this top athlete was only 44.2 ml/kg indicating that at least for this sprint event a high $\dot{V}_{02}$ max value was not essential.

The $\dot{V}_{02}$ max values of Canada's skaters competing in the 1968 Olympic Games are given in Table XXII–VI; these athletes performed best in distances of 500 to 1500 metres so that perhaps their V_{02} levels were adequate for the distances they competed at.

The Swedish national female skaters (n = 5)[12] had a mean $\dot{V}_{02}$ max of 3.1 L/min or 54 ml/kg/min, only a little higher than Canada's top female skaters. This compares to the peak values of up to 74 ml/kg/min found in a Russian cross-country skier (cited by Saltin and Astrand).[12]

The greatest problem with $\dot{V}_{02}$ max values is to estimate the importance of the oxygen transport system in the event of the athlete. Most top level serious athletes carry out general conditioning training that will improve

TABLE XXII–V

$\dot{V}_{02}$ MAX SWEDISH 10,000-METER SKATERS

	L/min	*ml/kg/min*
O.S.	5.77	79.0
J.N.	5.70	79.2
J.H.	5.39	71.9
C.	5.39	64.9
I.N.	5.20	76.5

the peak power of their oxygen transport system, but if an athlete's $\dot{V}_{02}$ max value is relatively low and does not come up easily with training, it is difficult to know how much time should be devoted to an endurance type of training at the expense of specific training. There are definite problems in comparing $\dot{V}_{02}$ max values in athletes tested in different laboratories.

The testing methods may be different—i.e. type of bicycle, bicycle vs treadmill; the oxygen uptake may be measured directly or predicted,[2] and in the direct measurement there are many possible technical errors that can lead to inaccuracies. All too often the top athlete is persuaded to come to the laboratory for a one- to two-hour test, it is often difficult to retest the same subject to see that peak values or consistent values are obtained (i.e. of 133 athletes tested by Saltin and Astrand[12], only six had two tests).

TABLE XXII–VI

CANADA OLYMPIC TEAM 1968

$\dot{V}_{02}$ max—ml/kg/min *

WOMEN		MEN	
D.M.	54.6	P.W.	61.9
W.T.	52.0	P.L.	62.8
C.B.	50.9	B.B.	69.1
		B.H.	61.3

* Douglas bag method—bicycle ergometer

There is still a wide discrepancy between $\dot{V}_{02}$ max values measured in different top athletes competing successfully in the same event,[7] some of these differences may be methodological, but, in many instances, either a high capacity of the aerobic system is not required, or technique and strategy so predominate the event that moderate differences in aerobic power are unimportant. In young girl skaters, thirteen to fifteen years of age, we have found no correlation between skating times in 1000 metres and $\dot{V}_{02}$ max (speeds average 25% slower than World record).

Radio Telemetry of ECG

The electronic advances of the 1950's provided the means to monitor the heart rates of athletes under competitive conditions.[10] The initial hopes that this would provide useful information has not been fulfilled. In all athletes, there is a variable anticipatory increase in heart rate, and any all-out activity is associated with a rise in heart rate to near maximal levels in within thirty to forty seconds. Table XXII–VII shows the mean heart rates of twelve skaters skating in timed 500-metre sprints. These skaters were well known to the investigator, the sprints were done at the start of a training session, the subjects had prior experience with ECG's and physiologic testing. There was still a large anticipatory increase in heart

TABLE XXII–VII

RADIO TELEMETRY OF SPEEDSKATERS ECG
Ages 12–17—500 M timed training

	Mean	*Range*
In clubhouse	133	118–156
Waiting by start	139	106–169
On the line	152	142–185
5 sec	160	158–188
10 sec	180	168–193
15 sec	183	172–190
30 sec	196	184–199
Near finish	194	185–200
Immediately after	194	183–203
10 sec recovery	184	175–193
20 sec recovery	174	170–178

rate, and values up to 140 beats/min were noted on the starting line in this practice event of no importance to the subjects. The mean rate reached 95 percent of maximal within 30 seconds. It would be of interest to know the heart rates of World class distance skaters in the course of a 10,000-meter race, but this information is unlikely to be of great practical value.

Cold Exposure

In Canada some meets and many training sessions are conducted at −10 to −30°C. Add the skater's speed of 40 km/hr, a wind speed of the same, and wind chill factors are extreme. Frostbite of the face is preventible with a woollen face covering. As skates need to be tight fitting, it is often not possible to use extra footwear, and cold feet often limit the duration of training sessions. Frostbite is a real threat. Skaters complain of a burning sensation in the throat, trachea and chest after breathing large volumes of very dry cold air, and may have a dry cough for two or three days after a meet held in the extreme cold. However, pulmonary function tests obtained immediately after competing in severe cold, showed no decline from control values. There have been no permanent sequelae from competition in the severe cold.[5]

Warm-up presents some problems to the skaters. If one believes in the value of warm-up,[1] and the recommendation[3] that an athlete warm-up for about fifteen minutes before his event stopping only two to five minutes before the event, the skater would cool down rapidly in the severe cold. Warm-up clothes should be kept on until the skater is on the starting line.

The effect of cold on the working leg muscles may theoretically be beneficial. Cold is reported to increase the endurance time for a sustained muscular contraction.[4] Muscular pain may be reduced by cold, and muscular cramps should be theoretically reduced by cold.[9]

The duration of exposure to the cold in any one race is short for the skater. The skater is active and produces excess heat, physical fitness is usually well above average, and no disturbances of temperature regulation are likely to occur. The main problem is pulmonary. Available experiments suggest that cold air is warmed close to body temperature by the time it reaches the trachea, and certainly the alveoli. However, data is not available for athletes breathing 100 or more L/min through their mouth. The drying effect of cold air with low moisture content seems to cause symptoms. Actual freezing of airways and lungs is a distinct possibility, but further investigation is required. The response time of available temperature sensing devices is not adequate to measure temperature accurately, and volunteers to allow such sensing devices to be placed in the trachea and bronchi are difficult to recruit.

Lung Function

There may be no relationship between lung function and performance.[6] Once growth is completed, training programs may not alter lung volumes. Lung volumes of skaters are larger than normal subjects (Table XXII–

TABLE XXII–VIII

PULMONARY FUNCTION—MEAN VALUES
9 Males United States Olympic Team 1968 [13]

	Percent of Predicted Based on Normal Population
Vital capacity	110%
Functional residual capacity	126%
Residual volume	112%
Total lung capacity	113%
Forced expiratory volume 1.0 sec	112%
Forced mid-expiratory flow rate	5.41 liters/second
Diffusion—ml/min/torr	
Rest	35.2
Exercise	52.7

VIII), but no different than those of other athletic groups.[11] There was little difference between the nine skaters who were named to the United States Olympic team in 1968, and the nine unsuccessful candidates when the values were normalized for body size, suggesting that superior lung function did not account for the differences in skating success. The superior values in athletes compared to nonathletes are possibly due to genetic factors, strong muscles of respiration, and greater airway diameters, and are not a requirement for top performance in the sport.

Fatigue in the Skater

In an all-out effort in 1500 meters, the skater is generally most fatigued in the leg and back muscles, and still has some reserve of "wind." This is because of the demand placed on these particular localized muscle groups. In skating, some muscles are constantly in a state of contraction, lacate build-up and fatigue occur in these muscles. The good skater likely learns to relax these muscles alternately between strokes although we have no scientific data (i.e. electromyographic) evidence of this. At a given $\dot{V}_{O_2}$, lactate levels are higher for skating than for running,[3] further evidence of the sustained muscular contractions needed for skating and the resultant ischemia.

For women the longest race is just over five minutes, and for men under fifteen minutes when performed at near World record speed. We have perhaps placed too much emphasis on maximum oxygen uptake which is relatively simple to measure as criteria of fitness for skaters, and insufficient stress on strength and endurance in the muscles required for skating. These factors are more difficult to assess.

Problems for Investigation in Speedskating

1. Does excess weight penalize the skater, and how much?
2. Starting and skating technique—for speed, for efficiency, correlation of simultaneous metabolic, electromyographic, force plate measurements and computerized time-motion studies.
3. Degree of "endurance fitness" needed for sprinters and middle distance skaters.
4. Weight training—any value—what type?
5. Dry training techniques—optimal.
6. Optimum teaching methods of skating skills.

Speedskating is no different than any other sport. The best advice remains, "Do what last year's champion did—only a little harder." A great deal still depends on natural skating ability and speed. Most of the training should be on the ice. Technique is so critical that where possible special coaching aids, such as videotape, should be used. Skating skills can substitute for fitness, but not vice versa.

REFERENCES

1. Asmussen, E. and Böje, O.: Body temperature and capacity for work. *Acta Physiol Scand, 10:1,* 1945.
2. Astrand, I.: Aerobic work capacity in men and women with special reference to age. *Acta Physiol Scand, 49,* Suppl: 169, 1960.
3. Astrand, P. O. and Rodahl, K.: *Textbook of Work Physiology.* New York, McGraw-Hill, 1970, pp. 524, 1948.
4. Clarke, R. S. J., Hellon, R. F. and Lind, A. R.: The duration of sustained contractions of the human forearm at different muscle temperatures. *J Physiol, 143:*454–473, 1958.
5. Cumming, G. R.:—Unpublished data.

6. ———: Correlation of athletic performance with pulmonary function in 13 to 17-year-old boys and girls. *Med Sci Sports 1*(3):140–143, 1969.

7. Di Prampero, P., Lumas, F. P. and Sassi, G.: Maximal muscular power, aerobic and anaerobic in 116 athletes performing at the XIXth Olympic Games in Mexico. *Ergonomics, 13*:665–674, 1970.

8. Ekblom, B., Hermansen, L. and Saltin, B.: Hastighet så kning på Skridsko, *Idrottsfysiologi,* Rapport nr 5 Framtiden, Stockholm, 1967.

9. Eldred, E. et al.: Effect of cooling on mammalian muscle spindles. *Exp Neurol,* 2:144–157, 1960.

10. Goodwin, A. B. and Cumming, G. R.: Radio telemetry of the electrocardiogram, fitness tests, and oxygen uptake of water polo players. *Can Med Assoc J,* 95:402–406, 1966.

11. Maksud, M. G., Hamilton, L. H., Coutts, K. D. and Wiley, R. L.: Pulmonary function measurements of Olympic speed skaters from the U.S. *Med Sci Sports,* 3:66–71, 1971.

12. Saltin, B. and Åstrand, P. O.: Maximal oxygen uptake in athletes. *J Appl Physiol,* 22:353–358, 1967.

AUTHOR INDEX

324

SUBJECT INDEX

DATE DUE

MAR 1 7 1977		
NOV 5 1979		
GAYLORD		PRINTED IN U.S.A.